D0644181

Politics in ENGLAND

We live under a system of tacit understandings. But the understandings are not always understood.

—Sidney Low, The Governance of England

The Little, Brown Series in Comparative Politics

Under the Editorship of

GABRIEL A. ALMOND

JAMES S. COLEMAN

LUCIAN W. PYE

A COUNTRY STUDY

Politics in ENGLAND

AN INTERPRETATION

Second Edition

Richard Rose

University of Strathclyde (Glasgow)

Boston Toronto

LITTLE, BROWN AND COMPANY

323.441
R72
Cop 1

TO MY FATHER

COPYRIGHT © 1964, 1974, BY LITTLE, BROWN AND COMPANY (INC.)

ALL RIGHTS RESERVED. NO PART OF THIS BOOK MAY BE REPRODUCED IN ANY FORM OR BY ANY ELECTRONIC OR MECHANICAL MEANS INCLUDING INFORMATION STORAGE AND RETRIEVAL SYSTEMS WITHOUT PERMISSION IN WRITING FROM THE PUBLISHER, EXCEPT BY A REVIEWER WHO MAY QUOTE BRIEF PASSAGES IN A REVIEW.

LIBRARY OF CONGRESS CATALOG CARD NUMBER: 73-20921

FIRST PRINTING

Published simultaneously in Canada
by Little, Brown & Company (Canada) Limited

PRINTED IN THE UNITED STATES OF AMERICA

Foreword

The Country Studies of the Little, Brown Series in Comparative Politics are now going into second editions. The conceptual innovations initiated in the series have been widely accepted in the literature of comparative politics. Revisions of the volumes and new contributions to the Country Studies reflect our pedagogic experience and the significant innovations that have occurred since the series began. The new editions give greater stress to policy-making processes, the performance of political systems, and developmental patterns and prospects.

The first edition of Richard Rose's *Politics in England* appeared just ten years ago. It had a substantial impact on the study of British politics, bringing to the fore such themes as political socialization and culture, political communication, and participation. The second edition with its stress on the performance of the British political system is likely to have a similarly significant impact. Its central theme is the responsiveness and performance of British politics and government, tracing the effects of historical, economic, cultural, and political factors on party goal-setting, public policy-making, and the allocation of public resources. It offers sober and illuminative perspectives on Britain's internal prospects and international role.

Gabriel A. Almond
James S. Coleman
Lucian W. Pye

Acknowledgments

This book sums up my experience in two decades of studying politics while moving back and forth between England and America. To an American with an English wife and binational children, the experience has been personally congenial as well as professionally stimulating.

In this second edition of a book initially published a decade ago, every page has been rewritten and every chapter completely rethought. In addition to describing individual political behavior, this edition especially emphasizes the behavior of government in handling major problems of public policy. The great expansion of research into British politics has made it possible to expand the size of this study too. Reviewers can debate whether English politics, the study of politics, or the author has changed most in the interval. Readers are invited to approach this text as the author has done: as a new product.

The debts acquired in writing a book as wide-ranging as this are many. The suggestion that started it all came from Gabriel Almond. In writing successive drafts and in thinking about politics generally, I have specially benefited from the views and criticisms of James Douglas and W. J. M. Mackenzie and others who belong to the diaspora from Dover Street. As this edition was being prepared, the following kindly commented in detail on parts of the manuscript: Jay Blumler, James Curran, Arthur Green, Martin Harrison, Hugh Heclo,

George W. Jones, Maurice Kogan, Eric Nordlinger, Sheldon Rothblatt, Colin Seymour-Ure, and Jeremy Tunstall.

Many organizations and individuals within organizations have responded promptly and courteously to requests for information or materials for statistical analysis. Footnote citations give credit to the sources of published materials and provide guidance for further reading. Unpublished machine-readable survey data has been kindly made available by the Gallup Poll, Louis Harris Research, National Opinion Polls, Opinion Research Centre, Dr. Ted Tapper and, through the Inter-University Consortium for Political Research, D. E. Butler, and Donald Stokes. The facilities of the Survey Research Centre of the University of Strathclyde have been invaluable in processing survey data; Peter Willetts has provided helpful and imaginative programming assistance. Mrs. R. West has promptly and accurately typed and retyped manuscript from an unusual amalgam of typewritten and handwritten sheets.

None of the individuals or organizations mentioned by name necessarily endorses any particular point in this study. They share responsibility for merits, not demerits.

Richard Rose

Contents

Figures and Tables

FIGURES

TABLES

Politics in

ENGLAND

Only connect . . .
—E. M. Forster, Howards End

The United Kingdom
(New Standard Statistical Regions, 1973)
SCOTLAND
ATLANTIC
OCEAN
Edinburgh
Glasgow
NORTH SEA
NORTHERN
Belfast
IRELAND
Tyne R.
NORTH
ENGLAND
YORKSHIRE
AND
HUMBERSIDE
Leeds
Irish Sea
REPUBLIC
OF
IRELAND
Dublin
Liverpool
Manchester
Mersey
Sheffield
NORTH WEST
EAST
MIDLANDS
WEST
MIDLANDS
Birmingham
EAST ANGLIA
WALES
Severn R.
SOUTH
EAST
Thames R.
Greater London Council
Cardiff
Bristol
0
100
Scale of miles
SOUTH WEST
English Channel
FRANCE
Sanderson

Introduction

*The Americans of 1787 thought they were copying the English Constitution, but they were contriving a contrast to it.**

Understanding England is important for the study of comparative politics, because England is a deviant case. Violence and revolution are common features of twentieth-century domestic politics in the largest nations of Europe: France, Germany, Italy, Russia, Poland, and Spain. Violence is also intermittently a feature of American political life. For the past three centuries Englishmen have settled domestic political differences without resort to force. From an aristocratic basis Englishmen have developed institutions of representative government that are admired and imitated on many continents. Just as Alexis de Tocqueville traveled to America in 1831 to seek the secrets of democracy, so today one might journey to England to seek the secrets of stable, representative government.

Modern societies with stable, representative governments are rare. Many of those nations which have long combined both characteristics owe much to the direct influence of England. The relationship between the United States and England is particularly close because America, besides being the first colony to revolt successfully against the Crown, was the first major English colony to be planted in the New World. As Bernard Bailyn, the author of *The Origins of American Politics* notes: "The pattern of political activity in

* The epigraphs in this book are taken from Walter Bagehot's classic, *The English Constitution* (1867).

the colonies was part of a more comprehensive British pattern and cannot be understood in isolation from that larger system."[1] In spite of many quarrels and great changes – both in England and America – a special relationship has persisted since.

The international significance of British political institutions is indicated by the widespread adoption of parliamentary forms in many countries. Parliaments can be found in India and Canada as well as in England, although the majority of the 72 members of the Inter-Parliamentary Union conduct politics in very un-British ways. The disciplined two-party system of Britain is admired not only in countries that have such a system but also in countries that lack it. The character of the British civil service has served as the model for many developing nations, and its impress has been strengthened by the example set by British administrators in colonial days. Yet nations such as Pakistan have demonstrated that it is possible to imitate the form of British administration without capturing its spirit and degree of efficiency. Events in Northern Ireland – that strange fruit hanging from the Union Jack – have shown time and time again that political institutions that work well within an English context are not necessarily fit for export to other parts of the United Kingdom.[2]

To understand politics in England today, one must understand England's past as well as its present. Unlike the United States, England began to develop modern institutions in a feudal society. Many problems now familiar in developing nations have analogues in earlier stages of English history. In the eighteenth century, governments were not chosen by popular election but by intrigues and by the liberal use of corruption within the political elite. Kinship and local ties counted for more than abstract principles. At the beginning of the nineteenth century, the civil service for which the country is famed had not yet developed. The administration of government was shaped by particularistic traditions. Countries such as France and Germany have shown how industrialization can occur simultaneously with great political upheavals. England

1 (New York: Vintage, 1970) p. ix.

2 See *The Future of Northern Ireland: A Paper for Discussion* (London: Her Majesty's Stationery Office – henceforth abbreviated HMSO – 1972).

is distinctive in that it became industrialized without political revolution and counterrevolution.

The development of modern institutions of representative government in the nineteenth century was not the end of political change, nor an end to political problems. Like India, Egypt, or Mexico, England is a society in transition. In the late nineteenth century and again today, the Irish problem has proven resistant to resolution by parliamentary debate; both government and rebels have resorted to trial by force. After World War I, successive British governments were sorely tested by economic depression and by the threat of a second world war. Since 1945, successive British governments have been challenged by recurring economic difficulties. The country's early industrialization and freedom from wholesale destruction by war has, ironically, led it to be outstripped in international economic competition by its former enemies, Germany and Japan. When America faced the unusual experience of runs on the dollar and devaluation in 1971 and 1973, Englishmen could claim that in this respect England was ahead of America. England devalued the pound in 1949 and 1967, and has experienced foreign exchange crises far more frequently than America.

The distinctive character of politics in England is most readily illustrated by comparison with other countries. The use of generic social science concepts makes it possible to compare political institutions and processes, even when their names differ from country to country. To confront abstractions with the realities of politics in England can be illuminating whether the confrontation confirms or refutes assumptions and hypotheses of social scientists. Potentially, there are many lands that may be compared with England. The old Dominions of Canada, Australia, and New Zealand, along with the United States, constitute a universe of "Mother Country" and former colonies.[3] The Republic of Ireland and the Republic of South Africa were once dominions too, but both left the Commonwealth. Comparisons between England and Afro-Asian members of the Commonwealth that succeeded the British Empire emphasize differences rather than similarities.

[3] See Louis Hartz, *The Founding of New Societies* (New York: Harcourt, Brace & World, 1964).

Englishmen disagree about how comparable or incomparable they are, *vis à vis* the peoples of France, Germany, Italy, and other founder members of the European Economic Community. Englishmen usually see no point in comparing themselves with non-English citizens of the United Kingdom; the relative smallness of the populations of Wales, Scotland, and Northern Ireland is not, however, a valid theoretical objection to comparative studies within the United Kingdom.

Comparison can show contrasts as well as similarities. A comparison of nominally similar institutions of parliamentary government in England and in African societies, whether in white or black hands, emphasizes the effects that differences between societies can have upon political institutions. Where differences are found, one may ask why two sometimes similar political systems vary in a particular respect and what the consequences are. What accounts for the persistence of a monarchy in England when most democratic governments are republics? Does having the Queen make government different in any significant respect? Where similarities exist between nations, one must seek explanations in terms of conditions common to both countries. Explanations specific to single nations are unsuited to more general phenomena. For example, the development of welfare policies in England cannot be explained solely by reference to English history. A European perspective shows that compulsory education, pensions, and unemployment insurance are common features of modern industrial societies. Comparison need not imply global judgments about the superiority of one society to another. The author has lived too long on each side of the Atlantic to believe this is practicable. As any traveler can verify, the grass *is* greener on the moister, cooler, and British side of the Atlantic. But the machinery for gardening is more advanced in America. Comparison must always involve careful specification of the topic: different (or better) in what respect?

The primary object of this book is deceptively simple in appearance: to describe how politics in England works today. Description must precede explanation. Because politics resembles ballet more than it does a still life picture, any description must emphasize movement and the relationship among the parts of the ensemble. The question then arises:

Which parts does one describe? An uncritical empiricist might use words or numbers to describe everything from Westminster Abbey to the weather, in the Micawberish hope that something politically significant might turn up. In deciding what aspects of society to analyze, one finds it helpful to think of society as a series of analytically separate systems: the political system, like the economic system, is one of these.[4] Government is at the center of the political system because it alone claims the right and the power to compel citizens to obey its decisions. The political system embraces individuals, groups, and institutions who seek to influence how government works. It is an open empirical question whether or to what extent bankers, trade unionists, Old Etonians, or pop musicians are part of politics in England today.

The second object of this book is to analyze the chief influences upon politics in England. Studying relations of cause and effect makes one move from a static description of people and institutions to a dynamic view of political processes. Often an institution will be both the subject and object of influence. For example, Cabinet ministers expect ordinary citizens to obey their laws, yet they also expect to respond to the political demands of ordinary citizens. To confirm or reject explanations, evidence is adduced from a variety of historical, institutional, and statistical sources. Where the train of thought leads beyond available evidence, the author has drawn upon research findings from other lands, theoretical works, and his own insights to suggest tentative conclusions.

A third object of this book is to ask: What impact does government have upon life in England today? Politicians repeatedly proclaim their desire to make government policies improve social conditions. It does not follow from this aspiration that the consequences are always what is intended. For example, in 1938 Neville Chamberlain went to Munich to seek peace by negotiating with Hitler; a year later, war followed. In 1966, Harold Wilson drastically cut government plans for economic growth to maintain the value of the

[4] The logical weakness and limitations of system as a concept are succinctly stated by S. E. Finer in "Almond's Concept of 'The Political System,'" *Government and Opposition* V:1 (1969). See also W. J. M. Mackenzie, *Politics and Social Science* (Harmondsworth: Penguin, 1967).

pound; a year later, devaluation followed. Because of the sparse literature on the subject and the complex relationship between intentions, causes, and effects, the discussion of the impact of policy is exploratory. Understanding may be enhanced by raising questions as well as by answering them.

This study has as its fourth object a consideration of how politics in England is changing. The political phenomena studied here are not immutable but variable; therefore, one must always allow for the possibility of political change. Because continuities from the medieval past remain evident in England, from the figure of the Queen to forms of local government taxation, one must also allow for the persistence of established ideas and institutions. In contemporary terms, the most important question about the political past is: How much has persisted into the present? Academics differ about the definition of "modern" England; a professor of history might even date modern England from 1485. Consideration of the dynamic features of politics is specially suitable in the second edition of a book initially written a decade ago. Deciding whether to alter or retain earlier statements forces the author to consider the extent to which a decade has made major differences in English politics.

In any study of this breadth, organizing information is a basic problem. If facts could be left to speak for themselves, then the national budget, the census, an almanac, and the election returns might suffice as a guide to politics. If political leaders could be left to speak for themselves, memoirs and biographies would suffice. But this cannot be done. Facts have meaning only as they are related to conceptions of politics. The choice of concepts is not an easy one. The boundaries between different parts of society are not so clear as the boundaries between the academic disciplines that study them. Englishmen cannot be divided into citizens, consumers, and churchgoers as certainly as professors can be divided into political scientists, economists, and theologians. In England there is always the danger of embracing the aristocratic fallacy that general conditions of society do not influence individuals in particular situations.[5] One must look beyond the activities of

[5] See "Why the Americans show more aptitude and taste for general

the monarch, the prime minister of the day, and the few who assemble in Parliament. In expanding the scope of study, there is a danger of transforming the study of politics into the study of economics, sociology, or clinical psychology. This, emphatically, is not the intention of this book.

In writing this study, the author has drawn upon concepts common to many contemporary social scientists. The writings of Gabriel Almond provided the analytic framework of the first edition of this study. The changes in that framework [6] and the changes in this book reflect the evolution of ideas about the basic concepts of politics. The author's own approach to the study of comparative politics is presented in *People in Politics: Observations across the Atlantic*.[7] The present book tests to what extent a whole repertoire of theoretical writings improves our understanding of the very particular political system of England.

Because of a common language, Americans have easy access to the literature of English politics; English people less readily read tomes from across the Atlantic. The experience in nineteenth-century England of great social and political change stimulated writings that carefully and discerningly examined political fundamentals. Walter Bagehot's *The English Constitution,* published in 1867, is outstanding among these works. The bulk of writing about English politics since World War II has concentrated upon describing the formal institutions of government.[8] Studies end without generalization; description is valued as a thing in itself. Many students of politics have argued against the possibility or desirability of generalizing about the premises of political action. For example, R. B. Mc-

---

ideas than their forefathers, the English," Chapter 3, first book, Vol. II, Alexis de Tocqueville, *Democracy in America.*

[6] See Gabriel Almond, "Introduction" to Almond and J. S. Coleman, *The Politics of the Developing Areas* (Princeton: Princeton University Press, 1960); Gabriel Almond and G. Bingham Powell, Jr., *Comparative Politics: A Developmental Approach* (Boston: Little, Brown, 1966), and Gabriel Almond, *Political Development* (Boston: Little, Brown, 1970).

[7] (New York: Basic Books, 1970). See also Richard Rose, editor, *Lessons from America* (London: Macmillan, 1974).

[8] See John Palmer, *Government and Parliament in Britain: A Bibliography* (London: Hansard Society for Parliamentary Government, 2nd edition, 1964).

Callum, the founder of the Nuffield College series of election studies, objected to sample surveys of voters on the ground that the ballot is "the great Eleusinian mystery of the democratic state." Politicians, too, have repeatedly objected to attempts to understand what lay behind their myths.[9]

The 1960s saw the emergence of a broader and more questioning approach to the study of politics in England. One stimulus was political: the recognition that England was no longer a world power. In reaction, Englishmen began to look for seemingly superior political systems to emulate. Negotiations for entry to the European Common Market encouraged some Englishmen to discover many hitherto unseen political virtues in the peoples of France and Germany. On the other hand, opponents of the Market have emphasized the superiority of English institutions against their continental equivalents. American models became temporarily popular when a youthful John F. Kennedy and an aging Harold Macmillan were the leaders of the two nations. The subsequent difficulties of American domestic and foreign policy have reduced the attraction of looking west for light. Simultaneously English academic awareness of American social science efforts have grown greatly. In the 1970s, a decreasing number of professors of politics would seriously repeat Sydney Smith's gibe of 1820: Who reads an American book?

In such a situation, it is sensible and desirable to seek the best in both old and new traditions of scholarship. Like the work of the Victorians, this study is broad in scope; it treats politics as a part of society, and not as a world apart. Yet it also accepts the great changes that have occurred in the methods of political study since Bagehot's time. As the subtitle indicates, *Politics in England* is no more and no less than an interpretation. It achieves comprehensiveness by the use of judgments that are tentative and at times subjective. This book not only attempts to sum up what is known about the theory and practice of politics in England today. It also explores what may be learned by further study tomorrow.

[9] See Iain Macleod, "The Private World of Political Science," *The Times,* (London) October 30, 1969; R. B. McCallum, "The Study of Psephology," *Parliamentary Affairs* VIII:4 (1955) p. 509, and Michael Oakeshott, *Political Education* (Cambridge: Bowes and Bowes, 1951).

CHAPTER I

England's Place in the World

Are they (the English) not above all nations divided from the rest of the world, insular both in situation and in mind, both for good and for evil?

THE ISLAND POSITION of England is its most significant geographical feature: Insularity is one of its most striking cultural characteristics. London is physically closer to France than it is to the geographical center of England, but the English Channel has for centuries fixed a narrow but deep gulf between England and the continent of Europe. Although there is no other continent to which the island could conceivably be assigned, Englishmen do not consider themselves Europeans. Even when Europe was the center of world affairs, England held aloof from commitments on the Continent and intervened only when action was required to maintain a balance of power. Today the country's military dependence upon America is as meaningful politically as its geographical propinquity to France, Belgium, and the Netherlands. Entry into the European Common Market does not reflect English identification with things European, but has occurred in spite of perceived differences between Englishmen and Europeans. Close links in all but a geographical sense with Commonwealth countries further reduce the significance of physical geography. Politically Englishmen may claim to be equally close to or distant from Europe, America, and nations of a global Commonwealth.

Establishing England's place in the world is a complex task. First, one must decide with what other group of nations it is most appropriately linked. The answer to this question can depend upon whether one is using a political, economic, geographic, or cultural frame of reference. Second, one must determine how England relates to the non-English parts of the United Kingdom. Behind the facade of unitary political institutions are political and social complexities, for English people, notwithstanding their insularity, do not inhabit an island of their own: They must share the island of Great Britain with the Scots and the Welsh.

INSULARITY AND INVOLVEMENT

England is set apart from most nations in the world by its population and its wealth of resources. In population it is the world's eleventh largest country and the most urban of industrial nations. Economically, it ranks sixth in the size of its gross national product. When gross national product is related to population, Englishmen are among the richest 10 per cent of the world's population. England ranks second to America in the production of scientific articles, and fourth in the consumption of energy. Because England's population is much smaller than that of America or of the Soviet Union and because it does not anticipate a major war, it ranks lower in military manpower. England's political significance is indicated by the fact that it ranks second only to America in the number of diplomats sent to and received from other countries (Table I.1).

On conventional measures of national strength, England more than holds its own. Its large population and established industrial resources assure international eminence, setting England apart from three other groups of nations. One cluster consists of countries such as Sweden and Canada, which have a higher per-capita income but less aggregate productivity because their population is but a fraction of England's. A second cluster comprises countries with a greater population than that of England, but which are much less developed economically. The category includes three former territories of the old British Empire — India, Pakistan, and Nigeria — as well as

TABLE I.1 *National Resources of Large Industrial Societies*

	United Kingdom	*USA*	*France*	*West Germany*	*Italy*	*USSR*	*Japan*
Population (in millions)	55	205	50	60	54	242	103
Urbanization (% population in cities over 100,000)	72	50	34	51	24	25	42
Diplomats exchanged	2708	4200	1863	1449	1218	2077	1132
Gross national product, 1970 (billions of US $)	121	991	147	186	92	434	196
Energy Consumption (millions of metric tons)	282	1790	144	250	92	833	175
Military manpower (thousands of men)	424	3000	550	450	390	3150	250
Scientific capacity (authorship index)	10.2	41.7	5.5	6.9	2.0	8.2	4.2

Sources: C. L. Taylor and M. C. Hudson, *World Handbook of Political and Social Indicators* (New Haven: Yale, 2nd edition, 1972), and *Basic Statistics of the Community* (Luxembourg: E.E.C., 1971).

China, Indonesia, and Brazil. The great majority of the more than 130 countries in the world lack both size and wealth. The median member of the United Nations has about one-tenth the population of England and a median gross national product one-seventy-fifth that of the United Kingdom. Whatever the problems of Englishmen, they are those that befall the wealthy few rather than the many poor.

For centuries, England's insular position has been an additional national resource, saving it from a heritage of invasion that has cost European countries so much in this and in past centuries. Only Japan can claim similar isolation. The last successful foreign invasion of England was the Norman conquest of 1066; in France, it was the German invasion of 1940. In both world wars of this century, England was free from land occupation, while the continent of Europe was a battlefield. Unlike Germany, France, Italy, and Japan, England has not had to build new political institutions in the aftermath of the havoc of war.

Insularity is not to be confused with isolation. As an island with a long seafaring tradition, the country has been, in the words of Sir Eyre Crowe, "a neighbour of every country accessible by sea." By acts of policy and by the adventurous initiatives of public officials and private traders, England came to administer an empire that at one time included nearly one-fifth of the population and land area of the world. The British Empire drew together territories as scattered and various as India, Nigeria, Cyprus, and Samoa, as well as the old Dominions of Canada, Australia, New Zealand, and South Africa. The success of empire builders left Britain at the end of World War II with political commitments on every continent.

The end of empire began with the grant of independence to India and Pakistan in 1947. Political, economic, and military considerations argued for similar action elsewhere. Labour and Conservative governments differed in tempo and even more in mood. But both parties accepted that there was little that England could do at a distance of thousands of miles to enforce its authority against colonial peoples articulately demanding independence. The violence and upheavals that have occurred subsequently in many ex-British territories have reinforced judgments about the difficulties of governing Afro-Asian nations. Empire has been replaced by a free association of more than two dozen sovereign states, the Commonwealth. The independent status of its chief members is shown by the absence of the word "British" from the title of the Commonwealth. It is also evidenced by the wish of a number of Afro-Asian nations, beginning with India, to replace loyalty to the Crown with the status of a republic. The old Dominions of Canada and Australia have shown their independence by such symbolic measures as abandoning the use of "God Save the Queen" as their national anthem. The only colonies remaining from days of the Empire are a miscellany of islands such as the Falklands and Saint Helena, and small land enclaves such as Gibraltar and Hong Kong. Today, a variety of Commonwealth institutions assist economic and cultural exchange among members, but meetings of Commonwealth countries emphasize the political and social conflicts among its very heterogeneous membership.[1]

Since World War II, England has also abandoned the assumption that its military forces could play a major role in many strategic areas of the world. A century ago, the Royal Navy claimed to rule the waves everywhere. The emergence of America, the Soviet Union, Japan, and China as major military forces in world politics has so dispersed and expanded the arena of international politics that England can no longer hope to maintain significant power east of the Suez Canal. Concurrently, the development of airpower, nuclear weapons, and guided missiles has greatly reduced the strategic importance of England's insular situation. But these relatively recent changes in weapons technology have not canceled the great benefits of centuries of impregnability.

Britain remains one of the five permanent members of the United Nations Security Council; like France, its influence is of a different and lesser kind than that of the three superpowers: America, the U.S.S.R., and China. The story of postwar

[1] Cf. H. Victor Wiseman, *Britain and the Commonwealth* (New York: Barnes & Noble, 1965); and A. P. Thornton, *The Imperial Idea and its Enemies* (London: Macmillan, 1959).

British foreign policy is a story of ever-contracting commitments, forced by the rising cost – in money and manpower terms – of efforts to keep up with the superpowers. The atomic capability that Britain developed in the 1950s is no longer adequate to deter, given the weapons technology of the 1970s. The burden of rearmament accepted by a Labour government following the outbreak of the Korean War in 1950 was scaled down as impracticable by its Conservative successor. In 1956, Britain and France sought to use force to regain control of the Suez Canal, then regarded as an essential strategic interest. The two European powers together were unable to stand up to the combined opposition of America and the Soviet Union, and the Suez Canal remained in Egyptian hands.[2] In 1965, the Labour government showed an inability (or unwillingness) to use force against the Southern Rhodesian regime of Ian Smith, which unilaterally declared independence in defiance of London's sovereignty. Its defiance has been maintained by 200,000 white settlers in a land of four million Africans. The continuous scaling down of military commitments has left the country a military force only in Europe. After killings commenced in Northern Ireland in 1969, London found that it had to withdraw troops from its NATO forces in Germany for use within the United Kingdom, so limited are its strategic reserves.[3]

The decline in England's world role has been followed by a decline in its special relationship with America. After the end of World War II, England and America worked closely together to secure the economic and military reconstruction of Europe. Ideas were outlined in Winston Churchill's Iron Curtain speech at Fulton, Missouri, in 1946. The Marshall Plan, launched in 1947, provided economic assistance. The creation of the North Atlantic Treaty Organization (NATO) in 1949 was the climax of a series of American responses to British

[2] See, e.g., Leon Epstein, *British Politics in the Suez Crisis* (London: Pall Mall, 1964).

[3] For American views of Britain's power, see Kenneth Waltz, *Foreign Policy and Democratic Politics* (Boston: Little, Brown, 1967); R. N. Rosecrance, *Defense of the Realm* (New York: Columbia University Press, 1968); and William P. Snyder, *The Politics of British Defence Policy 1945–1962* (Columbus: Ohio State, 1964).

requests for military commitment in Europe, beginning with America's replacement of British forces in Greece and Turkey in 1946. The Korean war and the Vietnam war turned American attention toward Asian affairs. The Soviet-American détente has reduced the significance of Europe, including Britain, to America. Anglo-American differences have been great in the Suez war, in the supply of weapons by America to Britain, and in devaluation crises. Good will is insufficient to insure agreement when a mutuality of political interest is lacking between two countries.[4]

In economic affairs England must always be involved internationally. Much of the nation's food and raw materials for heavy industry are imported. England must export to live. In addition to exporting industrial and manufactured products, money is also earned by "invisible" exports, such as banking and insurance, from the City of London; it is, like Wall Street, one of the world's great financial centers. The countries from which England imports food and raw materials are not identical to those that are its main customers for its exports; hence, import and export trade vary independently of each other. During much of the postwar period, England has benefited from a trend down in the relative price of major imports. Deficits in the balance of payments between imports and exports have recurringly caused financial crises in postwar Britain.

Because of its dependence upon exporting manufactured goods and commercial services to pay for imports of food and raw materials, England is always affected by changes in the international economy.[5] It entered the postwar period with a historic advantage of accumulated wealth and resources, and with substantial debts – including interest on a multi-billion dollar loan from America in 1946. Economic difficulties since then have not arisen from problems of mass poverty or of industrialization but rather from the difficulties of maintaining

[4] See Richard E. Neustadt, *Alliance Politics* (New York: Columbia University Press, 1970). Cf. Bruce Russett, *Community and Contention* (New Haven: Yale, 1963).

[5] For problems of British economic policy, see successive editions of Samuel Brittan, *Steering the Economy* (Harmondsworth: Penguin, 1971).

national income relative to national demands for expenditure in a world where traditional markets for exports have declined. For instance, Indians no longer need to import cotton cloth from Britain, now that they have built mills to spin their own raw materials. Competition has increased from other industrial nations, such as resurgent Germany and Japan. The postwar difficulties of Britain's aircraft and computer industries illustrate problems of developing technologically advanced industries. The country's automobile industry remains an important exporter, but a large portion of the industry has become part of the multinational production of American companies: Ford, General Motors, and Chrysler.

The use of the pound sterling as a major currency in world trade, banking, and international speculation in money has further intensified England's sensitivity to world economic trends. The international role of sterling is a legacy from the days of the Empire; the City of London remains among the largest finance and banking centers in Europe. With the gradual removal in the 1950s of wartime restrictions on the movement of money in and out of England, the value of the pound has been subject to short-term and long-term pressures. The long-term pressures arise from difficulties in exporting British goods. Devaluing the pound, which occurred in 1949 and again in 1967, makes exports relatively cheaper in world markets and makes imports relatively more costly. This is an incentive to manufacturers and traders to find domestic substitutes for imports. Short-term pressures arise from the speed with which investors can withdraw money from London, selling sterling short if they fear devaluation. Ironically, the more short-term funds that the government attracts to London by high interest rates, the greater the losses that can result from a sudden run on the pound. If this run were not stopped in a matter of days, then the nationally owned Bank of England, like any privately owned bank, would be bankrupt, that is, unable to offer creditors foreign currency in exchange for sterling. In an effort to reduce these pressures, in 1972 the Treasury decided to "float" the pound. It no longer has a fixed exchange rate as it did formerly ($4.20, then $2.80, then $2.40). Instead, its value depends upon supply and demand. It can float below $2.40 or above it. The lower it floats, the more speculators may buy the cheap sterling in hopes that it will rise in value. The Bank of England as well as private investors can speculate, in efforts to maintain the value of the pound by market pressures.

The decline of England's world role – diplomatically and economically – has occasioned limited popular interest or controversy. English people have always been divided about the advantages of a world role. The actions of diplomatists and empire builders were consistently criticized by the so-called Little Englanders; like American isolationists, they argued that the country would be better off with fewer international commitments. The scaling down of England's world power has been masked by the retention of many symbols of great power status. Critics have charged that foreign and economic policies have been more concerned with status symbols than substance. For example, after Britain sought American aid to maintain an independent British nuclear deterrent in 1962, following the cancellation of the American Bluestreak missile, an American official commented that independent nuclear weapons had become "the most expensive status symbols since colonies."[6] In 1971, Roy Jenkins, a former Labour finance minister, called for the floating of the pound, arguing that the fixed exchange rate made the pound "a national status symbol, and not an instrument of economic management."[7]

Economic and diplomatic considerations have combined to make England look to Europe. British governments were initially chary of association with the European Coal and Steel Community, founded in 1951, and the European Economic Community (the Common Market), founded in 1957. They did not see compelling economic advantages arising from association with their six European neighbors, and disliked the restrictions upon ties with extra-European nations. In the 1950s, the per-capita growth rate of the Common Market countries was higher than that of Britain, but Britain had a higher standard of per-capita wealth, because of its earlier industrial

[6] Richard E. Neustadt, *Alliance Politics,* p. 112. See also, Kenneth Waltz, *Foreign Policy and Democratic Politics,* pp. 152 ff.

[7] *Labour Party Conference Report* (London: Labour Party, 1971), p. 229.

achievements. The continued economic growth of the Common Market countries in the 1960s and the slow rate of growth within Britain has altered economic relationships. From 1960 to 1970, the annual rate of growth in Britain was 2.9 per cent, substantially lower than that of any of the countries of the Community. Every Common Market country but Italy has achieved a higher per-capita gross national product than Britain.

In 1961 the Conservative government of Harold Macmillan began to negotiate terms for British entry into the Common Market. These efforts were vetoed by General de Gaulle in 1963. The Labour government of Harold Wilson reactivated the application for membership in 1966. Success finally came to the Conservative government of Edward Heath. Britain entered the Common Market on January 1, 1973. Independently of these negotiations, England and its European neighbors have come closer together in many activities, ranging from "Eurovision" song contests and European Football Cup competitions to trade and politics. The speed of air travel now means that a businessman commuting from London to Paris, Brussels, or Frankfurt spends longer getting to and from the airports than in flying from London to the continental cities.

Proponents of entry to the Common Market have stressed the benefits presumed to accrue to the British economy by entry and the decline that would occur in default of joining. Critics point out that of Britain's total exports in 1970, the Commonwealth took 21 per cent, almost as much as the 22 per cent taken by Common Market countries; both areas are more important than America, the customer for 12 per cent of British exports. Opponents of entry, as well as many advocates, have concentrated their evaluation upon economic terms; little desire is shown for political integration in a federalist United Europe.[8]

Entry into the Common Market represents an important shift in emphasis but not an abandonment of England's other attachments. The world role of the English language – even

[8] See Uwe Kitzinger, *Diplomacy and Persuasion* (London: Thames & Hudson); and Robert J. Lieber, *British Politics and European Unity* (Berkeley: University of California Press, 1970).

TABLE I.2 *Elite Attitudes toward International Links, 1963–1971 (in percentages)*

Grouping	*Proportion saying 'very valuable'* 1963	1971	*Change*
Commonwealth	69	34	-35
NATO	63	58	-5
USA special relationship	53	30	-23
United Nations	44	31	-13
Common Market	42	62	+20
EFTA (European Free Trade Area)	22	23	+1

Source: British *Who's Who* sample, reported in *The Times*, London, October 1, 1971.

if spoken with an American accent – encourages the maintenance of historic extra-European ties both within the Commonwealth and with America. Britain is third among all nations in the number of international organizations to which it belongs, ninety six. It also has the most dispersed range of countries purchasing its exports of all nations in the world.[9]

Within England, there is no agreement about the priority of ties with different groups of nations: the old white dominions, the sterling-area countries of the multiracial Commonwealth; the United States; the founder nations of the Common Market; and the smaller nations of Northern Europe, with which Britain was once associated in a short-lived European Free Trade Area. Attitudes are unstable as well as varied. A sample of prominent Englishmen listed in the British *Who's Who* showed that in 1963 more than half of those questioned found the country's links with the Commonwealth, NATO and America very valuable (Table I.2). But by 1971, when the same questions were again asked, only one-third thought Commonwealth or American ties important. The Common Market is now most often considered valuable. England's

[9] For detailed rankings, see Charles L. Taylor and Michael C. Hudson, *World Handbook of Political and Social Indicators* (New Haven: Yale, 2nd edition, 1972).

uncertain position allows British diplomats, between defense, sterling, and diplomatic crises, to speak of the country's unique role as a broker between very different groups of nations. At moments of crisis, there echoes the comment of the American diplomat Dean Acheson: "Great Britain has lost an empire and has not yet found a role." [10]

ONE CROWN AND MANY NATIONS

The English Crown is the oldest and best known in the world, yet there is no such thing as an English state. In international law as in the title of the Queen, the state is the United Kingdom of Great Britain and Northern Ireland. The island of Great Britain, the principal part of the United Kingdom, is divided into three parts: England, Scotland, and Wales. England, in size smaller than Alabama or Wisconsin, constitutes 55 per cent of the land area of Great Britain. The other part of the United Kingdom, Northern Ireland, consists of six counties of Ulster that have preferred to remain under the Crown rather than to join an independent Irish Republic ruled from Dublin. Insofar as territorial contiguity is politically significant, one might expect a state to occupy an island to itself or a pair of neighboring islands. Irish nationalists have always argued that geography implies the existence of two island states, Ireland and Britain; unionists have argued for a United Kingdom of the two islands. The international boundary of the United Kingdom today cuts across the northeast of Ireland, the one arrangement that is not implicit in insular geography.

As in other European countries, the boundaries of the United Kingdom result from centuries of diplomatic negotiations, battles won and lost, and the accidents of dynastic succession. Wales was joined to England by dynastic inheritance, formalized by legislation in 1536. Scotland was similarly joined in stages from 1603 to 1707. England has been sending troops to Ireland intermittently from 1169 to the present, in an effort to maintain some sovereignty in at least part of the

[10] See "Britain's Independent Role About Played Out," *The Times*, December 6, 1962. (This and all successive citations of *The Times* refer to the London newspaper.)

island. While the descent of the Crown may be traced back to Alfred the Great in the ninth century, the current boundaries of the state date only from the Anglo-Irish treaty of 1921.

The peoples of the United Kingdom demonstrate their distinctiveness in many different ways. In Scotland the established Church is Presbyterian, whereas the Church of England is episcopal; the Queen, by a political compromise that long antedated the ecumenical movement, is officially a Presbyterian in Scotland and an Episcopalian in England. Scotland also maintains a separate and distinctive legal system, showing the influence of the Roman law tradition as well as the English. Its educational system also differs from England. The universities of Scotland provided the model for American liberal arts colleges. Scottish differences from England have been maintained, notwithstanding the concentration of Scotland's population in the industrialized Lowlands around Glasgow and Edinburgh and the reduction of the Highlands' dwellers to 5 per cent of Scotland's population.[11]

The most distinctive feature of Welsh society is language. The proportion of Welsh people speaking Welsh has declined from 53 per cent in 1891 to 27 per cent. Many with Welsh ties, like Charles, the Prince of Wales, show a little knowledge of Welsh in tribute to the very different cultural values implied by the gulf between the English and Welsh languages. In religion Welsh people are overwhelmingly Protestant but not Episcopalian. Welshmen campaigned for generations against the established episcopal Church of Wales; it was finally disestablished in 1920. Within Wales differences between the more populous and English-speaking industrial South and the Welsh-speaking rural North and West create substantial internal contrasts.[12]

Northern Ireland is the most un-English part of the United Kingdom, by the common agreement of both English and

[11] See H. J. Hanham, *Scottish Nationalism* (London: Faber, 1969); and James G. Kellas, *Modern Scotland* (London: Pall Mall, 1968).

[12] See K. O. Morgan, *Wales in British Politics, 1868–1922* (Cardiff: University of Wales Press, 1963); and Kevin R. Cox, "Geography, Social Contexts and Voting Behavior in Wales, 1861–1951," in Erik Allardt and Stein Rokkan, editors, *Mass Politics* (New York: Free Press, 1970).

Ulster people. Formally, Northern Ireland is a secular state, but in practice differences between Protestants and Catholics dominate its politics.[13] Protestant loyalty to the Crown rests upon the English monarch's historic status, according to the Bill of Rights of 1689, as "the glorious instrument of delivering this kingdome from Popery and arbitrary power." Protestants constitute two-thirds of the population of Ulster. They have held power locally since the establishment of a separate and nominally subordinate Northern Ireland Parliament at Belfast in 1921, following the secession of Southern Ireland from the United Kingdom. Most Catholics have refused to support this regime, holding that national identity justifies Ulster's merger in a 32-county Republic of Ireland, with its capitol in Dublin. Such a merger would result in a society in which Catholics outnumbered Protestants approximately three to one. Protestants reject such a merger. To challenge the Protestant majority's monopoly of power, Ulster Catholics began civil rights demonstrations in 1968. These were met with counterdemonstrations by Protestants. The resulting violence escalated to civil war proportions, with the British Army seeking to hold a middle ground between sectarian guerilla forces of the Catholic-based Irish Republican Army, illegal in the Republic, and the Protestant-based Ulster Volunteer Force.

In political and sociological terms, the United Kingdom is a multinational state.[14] The great majority of Welsh people think of themselves as Welsh, and Scottish people think of themselves as Scots. In Northern Ireland, there is no agreement about national identity; more than two-thirds see themselves as Irish or Ulstermen. Except in Northern Ireland, these distinctive identities can be harmonized with a British identification. Literally speaking, to be "British" is to identify with a part rather than the whole of the United Kingdom. Differ-

[13] For a detailed analysis, see Richard Rose, *Governing without Consensus: an Irish Perspective* (Boston: Beacon Press, 1971); and Richard Rose, "Ulster Politics: a Select Bibliography of Political Discord," *Political Studies,* XX:2 (1972).

[14] See Richard Rose, *Governing without Consensus,* Ch. 2, "The United Kingdom as a Multi-National Regime."

TABLE I.3 *The Division of the Vote in the United Kingdom, 1970 (in percentages)*

Party	*England*	*Scotland*	*Wales*	*Northern Ireland*	*United Kingdom*
Conservative	48.3	38.0	27.7	54.2	46.4
Labour	43.4	44.5	51.6	12.6	43.1
Total Conservative and Labour	91.7	82.5	79.3	66.8	89.5
Nationalist	–	11.4	11.5	24.5	2.3
Liberal	7.9	5.5	1.5	6.8	7.5
Others	0.4	0.6	2.4	7.2	0.7
Population (in millions)	46.2	5.2	2.7	1.5	55.6

ences in national outlooks lead to different profiles of party support in the four nations of the United Kingdom, for parties have "national" as well as class images. Conservatives have been consistently stronger than Labour in England and Northern Ireland, and Labour runs well ahead in Wales and Scotland. Support for nationalist parties, urging more-or-less separatist policies, is variable but noteworthy (Table I.3). Only England can claim electoral competition restricted to two parties.

Confusion often arises about the political structure of the United Kingdom, because there is no federal form of government, as occurs in such multinational states as Canada or Belgium. Yet the absence of a federal form of government does not make the United Kingdom a simple unitary state. Special institutional arrangements exist for governing each of its non-English parts.[15] These institutions – and the geographical segregation that makes such institutions possible–permit Scots, Welsh, and Ulstermen to maintain many customs without Anglicization. Northern Ireland has experienced the most

[15] See James G. Kellas, *The Scottish Political System* (Cambridge: University Press, 1973); articles on Wales by E. Rowlands and by P. J. Randall in *Public Administration* L (Autumn, 1972); and R. J. Lawrence, *The Government of Northern Ireland* (Oxford: Clarendon Press, 1965).

extreme form of devolution, a Parliament of its own at Stormont from 1921 until it was suspended by London in 1972, and a British Cabinet minister, William Whitelaw, placed in temporary charge of its affairs. Events since have only underscored the independence of Ulster politics from London's control. In Scotland the Scottish Office, with administrative headquarters in Edinburgh, provides a separate administration for health, education, agriculture, housing, and economic development. Administrative devolution in Wales led to the creation of a Welsh Secretary of State in 1964, with ambitions for his status and power to match that of his Scottish counterpart. Differences in administration are not infrequently matched by differences in legislation. The extreme is reached in laws regulating drinking in public houses; they differ for each of the four nations of the United Kingdom.

The existence of separate national groups within the United Kingdom creates difficulties in terminology. For example, Northern Ireland is normally included in reports of election results, but excluded in sample surveys of voting. Statistics on "British" education or "British" crime usually refer to England and Wales only. Because of differences in laws and institutions within Great Britain, Scotland reports many social statistics separately. These inconsistencies must inevitably be reflected in some tables in this book.

Politics in England is the subject of this book, because England dominates the United Kingdom in so many ways. Its people constitute five-sixths of the population (Table I.3). The remainder is divided unequally among three noncontiguous nations. The largest, Scotland, is but one-ninth the size of England — though it is more populous than three member states of the European Community, Denmark, Ireland, and Luxembourg. On occasions of conflict, non-English people are expected to adapt to English ways. The term "British" reflects this asymmetry. When an Englishman calls something British, the chances are he thinks of things English. Scots, Welshmen, and Ulstermen have a pluralistic frame of reference. What is central to England will never be overlooked by any British government. Politicians who wish to advance in Parliament must accept English norms if they wish to prosper. It is thus correct to speak of British government in conjunction with English society.

The significance of national differences within the United Kingdom is further underscored by examining the regions of England, most of which have more people than have Wales or Northern Ireland. The absence of a politically meaningful sense of regional identity is shown by the government's lack of any single, standard definition of region used for all purposes. There are no regional assemblies or regional elections, nor are regional offices of central government perceived as centers of political power.[16] Cities, rather than regions, constitute the second level of English government. Regions tend to be so large and dispersed that there is limited opportunity for people to meet together, as do people who live in a city. Some of the differences between regions reflect differences in class composition. Southern regions, including London, tend to have a larger proportion of middle-class residents; northern regions, such as Lancashire and Yorkshire, tend to have more working-class residents. Consequently, the Conservatives have won a majority of parliamentary seats in southern England at every election but two since 1900, and Labour has won a majority of seats in northern England at every election since 1945. Differences among English regions are of less consequence politically than differences between Scotland or Wales and England.[17]

Within England, London occupies a preeminent place. With 7.4 million people, Greater London is seven times larger than Birmingham, the second largest city in England. Only four other English cities have more than half a million people: Liverpool, Manchester, Sheffield, and Leeds. New York City is as large as London, but it does not similarly dominate American cities. New York contains less than one twenty-fifth of the population of America, but London contains one-sixth the population of England. Unlike Washington, Bonn, Ottawa, and many other capitals, London is simultaneously the center

[16] See J. A. Cross, "The Regional Decentralization of British Government Departments," *Public Administration,* XLVIII (Winter 1970).

[17] See David Butler and Donald Stokes, *Political Change in Britain* (London: Macmillan, 1969), pp. 135–143.

of government, finance, the mass media, and the arts. Leaders in many sections of English life can thus easily meet each other. Nearly three-quarters of the people meriting biographies in the British *Who's Who* live within a sixty-five-mile radius of the capital.[18] Most of the society's leaders are thus geographically segregated from the two-thirds of the English people living in what are symbolically called the provinces.

The preeminence of London has increased in the past century, with the political decline of an aristocracy based upon landed interests in the countryside and the decline of the economic autonomy of the great nineteenth-century industrial cities. Social distance is intensified by the fact that more than half the Members of Parliament today have not been residents of their constituency before election. Among civil servants, a similar pattern is apparent. Successful administrators expect to rise within London offices and not to be posted to a regional office outside London. Moreover, a disproportionate number attended secondary school and university in the vicinity of London. Their only experience of England north of Oxford and Cambridge may be confined to short business trips or holidays in the most rural and atypical parts of the United Kingdom.[19] The concentration of attention upon London is aptly symbolized by the two slots in the mail boxes of the capital city; they are labeled "London" and "All Other Places."

BLACK BRITONS?

For centuries small but noteworthy numbers of people have come as immigrants to England, including the present Royal Family. The Queen is immediately descended from the heirs of the Princess Sophia of Hanover. George I came from this German princely state to assume the English throne in 1714, succeeding the Scottish-bred Stuarts. German connections were maintained by Queen Victoria's marriage to Albert, Prince of Saxe-Coburg and Gotha, and by the marriages of their off-

[18] Mark Abrams, quoted in Lord Windlesham, *Communication and Political Power* (London: Cape, 1966), p. 234.

[19] See Edwin Hammond, *An Analysis of Regional Economic and Social Statistics* (Durham: Rowntree Research Unit, 1968), Table 2.7.3.

spring. Until the outbreak of anti-German sentiment in World War I, the surname of the Royal Family was Saxe-Coburg-Gotha. George V by Royal Proclamation changed his name to Windsor in 1917. Larger numbers of less noble immigrants have always come to London; as a great port and trading center, it has been accessible to all of Europe. The chief influx of immigration in the first half of this century consisted of Jews from Eastern Europe before World War I, and refugees from Nazi Germany in the 1930s.[20] By the standards of America, Canada, or Australia, immigration has always been numerically small.

In the late 1950s immigrants began to arrive in England from the West Indies, Pakistan, India, and other parts of the Commonwealth. Between 1955 and 1970, the net inflow fluctuated between 16,000 and 110,000 annually. The great majority of the immigrants were attracted to England by the certainty of a job, whether as a doctor, a factory worker, or a hospital orderly. Because these migrants had few local attachments, they went to the English cities where jobs were plentiful and wages highest. Those who disliked England and returned home were more than offset by those who liked it and sent for their relatives to join them, in some instances creating permanent nonwhite populations in various English cities. By 1971 the estimated nonwhite population of the United Kingdom had risen from the 74,000 (0.2 per cent) of twenty years previously to 1,500,000 (2.3 per cent).

The immigrants had little in common upon arrival. British West Indians came as native English speakers, albeit some spoke with a calypso accent. The bulk of the early migrants were skilled manual workers. Immigrants from the Indian subcontinent – whether from India or Pakistan – came with alien cultures. While some were bilingual graduates of schools and universities, the majority were uneducated, unskilled, and often ill at ease in speaking English. Muslims and Sikhs follow religious practices that have made them especially distinctive. In several cities Sikhs have had to fight political cam-

[20] See, e.g., Paul Foot, *Immigration and Race in British Politics* (Harmondsworth: Penguin, 1965), and Bernard Gainer, *The Alien Invasion* (London: Heinemann, 1973).

paigns to become bus conductors, because the municipally owned bus companies said they would not be employed unless they wore caps rather than their ritual turbans.[21] The small number of African immigrants have been distinctive from other immigrants, as well as divided among themselves by tribe and citizenship. These cultural differences and the differences in skin color have made it difficult to establish an American-style "black" political movement. Instead, there is a heterogeneous assortment of "nonwhite" groups. The nonwhite population is also disadvantaged by the fact that, unlike America's blacks, it comprises recent arrivals in the society.

Initially, the government took no official note of the flow of immigrants; unofficially, it welcomed the addition they provided to the labor force. Conservative and Labour leaders did not believe that the absence of racial tension in England was caused by the absence of a nonwhite population. They assumed that Englishmen were intrinsically incapable of racial animosity. The 1960s proved the optimistic assumption wrong. In 1962 the government for the first time restricted the entry to Britain of Commonwealth citizens. At the 1964 general election, a surprise victory by a racialist parliamentary candidate at Smethwick shattered the illusion that race could be kept out of politics. By 1970, Enoch Powell could become prominent as the proponent of a "white England" policy.[22]

Public opinion from the first has opposed the level of colored immigration that was acceptable to Conservative and Labour governments. In 1958 two-thirds of the English public endorsed stricter controls upon immigration; by 1968 95 per cent of Englishmen wished to see stricter controls on immigration.[23] Attitudes toward immigrants already resident in England are complex. Surveys usually find only a small minority who believe that nonwhite people are innately inferior to white people. A survey in two communities with high levels of

[21] See David Beetham, *Transport and Turbans* (London: Oxford University Press, 1970).

[22] See Bill Smithies and Peter Fiddick, *Enoch Powell on Immigration* (London: Sphere, 1969).

[23] See Richard Longaker, "The Race Relations Act of 1965," *Race*, XI:2 (1969), p. 145.

immigration found that more than half the whites thought it a good thing for people of different races to mix together, and three-quarters of the nonwhite immigrants endorsed mixing. About half the colored respondents thought they were discriminated against at work; fewer than one-quarter thought the police or the schools discriminated against them. The majority of Indian and Pakistani immigrants, who said they came to Britain for economic reasons, expressed satisfaction with their experiences. But half the West Indians, whose motives for migrating were less definite, said that if they had known what Britain would be like, they would have stayed at home.[24]

Once Conservative and Labour governments began passing race-relations laws, two points of principle have become prominent. The first is that immigration to England should be limited, to prevent a potential sudden influx of hundreds of thousands of Indians or Pakistanis. Since 1962, the quota of new immigrants has been successively revised downwards. In 1971 restrictions were introduced which were expected to have the effect of a color bar, limiting free entry to patrials – persons who could claim British-born family relationships. Ironically, the continued entrance of dependents of immigrant families already in Britain has resulted in a greater net immigration to England in the eight years after the introduction of controls than in the previous eight years.[25] Moreover, the arrival in England from Uganda in 1972 of expelled Indians holding British passports, a relic of the Empire, has also breached racial restrictions upon immigration. The second point of principle is encouragement of integration. In 1965 an act was passed to prevent discrimination in public accommodations, such as hotels and pubs; in 1968 it was extended to housing and employment. Community Relations Commissions

[24] See National Opinion Polls, *Political Bulletin* No. 98 (May, 1971). For other surveys, see W. W. Daniel, *Racial Discrimination in England* (Harmondsworth: Penguin, 1968); and E. J. B. Rose and associates, *Colour and Citizenship* (London: Oxford University Press, 1969) Ch. 28.

[25] See E. J. B. Rose and associates, *Colour and Citizenship,* p. 69; "Immigrants up 400,000 in four years," *The Times,* June 4, 1971; and David Kohler, "Commonwealth Coloured Immigrants and the 1971 Census," *New Community,* II:1 1972).

have been established at central and local government levels, and financial assistance has been given areas of high colored immigration. The policies are often modeled upon American legislation, except that provisions for the judicial enforcement of rights are weaker than those in America.[26]

The number of colored immigrants to England is small, absolutely and relatively, when compared with the number of nonwhite people in America or the number of foreign workers in Germany. English politicians have reacted on the assumption that even a little could be "too much." A few, like Enoch Powell, have asserted a positive and racist nationalism. Most politicians have concluded that the transition from a monoracial to a multiracial society is so difficult that the slower the pace and the fewer people involved the less the burden of change. The future will show whether colored immigrants and their children born in England are granted the status of black Britons or assigned an inferior role as British blacks.

Both past and present circumstances give English people a strong and unreflective sense of their place in the world. The existence of a national government for nearly a millenium has developed a sturdy sense of national identity. This stands in marked contrast to the experience of Germans and Italians, who established their own nation-states only in the nineteenth century. Imperial experience has further underlined differences between England and other lands. The English ideal was not to encourage the natives to adopt their rulers' ways, as was often done by France and, latterly, America. Instead, Englishmen accept differences in ways of life as inevitable, justifying different political powers for colonized and colonizers. The end of the Empire and the movement to England of citizens from nonwhite Commonwealth lands has only sharpened this English sense of difference. The exclusive

[26] See Nicholas Deakin, "On Some Perils of Imitation," in Richard Rose, editor, *Lessons from America;* and, more generally, Ira Katznelson, *Black Men, White Cities: Race, Politics and Migration in the United States, 1900–30, and Britain 1948–68* (London: Oxford University Press, 1973).

nature of Englishness is best suggested by the common use of the word "race" to differentiate persons of other nationalities without regard to color.[27]

When Englishmen decide to emigrate, and many have done so in past generations, they do not look to their European neighbors for a new home, nor do they look to their former colony, America. Surveys consistently show that Englishmen prefer to settle in Australia, New Zealand, Canada, or Southern Africa.[28] In spite of their geographical remoteness, these places appeal because they are perceived as closest to what Englishmen know at home. It is an open question whether working with continental peoples in the European Common Market will encourage Englishmen to develop a European identity, or simply reaffirm a sense of England's national distinctiveness.

27 The point comes out most clearly in English discussions of Anglo-Irish relations. See Nicholas Mansergh, *The Irish Question 1840–1921* (London: Allen & Unwin, 1965); and L. P. Curtis Jr., *Anglo-Saxons and Celts* (Bridgeport, Connecticut: Conference on British Studies, 1968).

28 See "Two in Five Want to Quit Britain, says Gallup," *Sunday Telegraph* (London), March 21, 1971.

CHAPTER II

The Constraints of History

It was natural — perhaps inevitable — that such an undergrowth of irrelevant ideas should gather round the British Constitution. Language is the tradition of nations; each generation describes what it sees, but it uses words transmitted from the past. When a great entity like the British Constitution has continued in connected outward sameness, but hidden inner change for many ages, every generation inherits a series of inapt words — of maxims once true, but of which the truth is ceasing or has ceased.

HISTORY IS MORE than a record of past events; the residues of history constitute what we familiarly regard as the present. Nowhere is this more true than in the politics of England, where the heir to an ancient Crown pilots jet airplanes and a medievally styled Chancellor of the Exchequer tries to pilot the pound through the deep waters of the international economy. Clement Attlee aptly summarized the interpenetration of influence from *different* periods of the past in a tribute to Winston Churchill:

> There was a layer of seventeenth century, a layer of eighteenth century, a layer of nineteenth century and possibly even a layer of twentieth century. You were never sure which layer would be uppermost.[1]

[1] *The Guardian* (Manchester), April 21, 1963.

England is outstanding among the world's nations because of the continuity of its governing institutions. Unlike France, Germany, and Russia, England has never had a revolution that overthrew governing institutions in favor of a new order. Unlike America, England has never had governors able to contemplate a land where the future was unconstrained by a feudal past. Nearly every feature of the constitution incorporates forms from the far distant past and assumptions grounded on the less distant past. Even something as modern as an election is governed in part by procedures dating back to the seventeenth century. In apportioning electors into constituencies, the Boundary Commissioners are not only expected to attend to current population figures but also to respect "communities that are integral, human entities which have both a history and a very lively sense of corporate feeling." [2]

The idea of continuity is often invoked to mask great changes in English life. Nowhere is this more true than in what Bagehot described as the "undergrowth of irrelevant ideas" gathered around the institutions of government. For example, Parliament was once a supporter of royal authority; then it was a restraint upon it, deposing monarchs; latterly it has been a body making laws and unmaking Cabinets. Today it is a forum in which the actions of the Cabinet can be discussed but not determined. Paradoxically, the persistence of an institution for centuries usually indicates that it has been adapted, often more than once, to meet great changes in the country's circumstances.

To understand politics in England, it is necessary to understand the origins of institutions, as well as their current rationale. A deductive approach to the analysis of government, inferring an explanation of institutions and processes from their contemporary consequences, cannot produce an accurate explanation of the political system. Englishmen, unlike their counterparts in many other countries, have never had to sit down under pressure of military defeat or domestic revolution

[2] Chuter Ede, quoted in Vincent Starzinger, "The British Pattern of Apportionment," *Virginia Quarterly Review,* XLI:3 (1965), p. 328.

to deduce a constitution from first principles. Instead, government in England has developed inductively and organically: Old institutions have been adapted to undertake new tasks, and new institutions have been grafted onto old. One cannot appraise British government by asking what "needs" the society has and how men have chosen to meet them. Nor can one lapse into the comforting tautology that whatever form of government history produces must be the best form of government for the society. One must ask a different question: To what extent is British government today a product of the past?

Every country is constrained by its history, for past actions limit the alternatives among which present governors can choose. Present choices, in turn, have consequences that constrain the future. Past events can also be important when they have no heritage. For example, the seventeenth-century settlement of the English Civil War has left no legacy of conflict about authority like that enduring in France since the Revolution of 1789. In the eighteenth century English slave traders exported slaves to the New World and not to their homeland, thus avoiding a legacy of racial problems like that of America. Past events have not left England free of all problems. The Anglo-Irish Treaty of 1921 gave de facto independence to two-thirds of the population of Ireland but left a persisting and virulent challenge to political authority in Ulster. A long and continuous political history is neither good nor bad of itself; failures as well as successes can endure through time.

THE CONTRIBUTION OF OLD ENGLAND

In ten pages or less, there is no point in seeking to recapitulate the ten centuries of English history that preceded the rise of modern representative government. One can only establish themes important today, as well as important in the past. The most important generalization is that the legitimacy that characterizes government today (see Chapter IV) existed before England faced the challenges of the industrial revolution at home and political revolution in America, France, and, potentially, England itself. This sequence of events made the "load" of government far less than that in countries where crises have accumulated through time.[3]

The Crown established a central political authority in late medieval times. The authority of the Crown was not the despotic will of an individual monarch, but rather the resultant of a "push and pull" of influence between the monarch and his servants, Parliament, and local landowners with substantial collective influence. The maintenance of nationwide authority depended upon the cooperation of the monarch and territorial magnates to advance their mutual self-interest. The rights and obligations expressed in feudalism constrained both monarch and subjects.

The supremacy of secular power over spiritual power was unambiguously determined in the sixteenth century, when Henry VIII broke with the Roman Catholic Church. In its place he established the Church of England, with bishops subject to national rather than papal authority. Henry's successors were strong enough to sustain this policy in a series of wars with Spain and France. Equally important, the government was strong enough to carry out the mass conversion of Great Britain to Protestantism. In England, religious allegiance and national allegiance reinforced each other. The great religious enemy – Roman Catholicism – lay outside.[4] This identity of loyalties was not achieved in Ireland; since the Reformation, Protestants and Catholics have fought each other because religious differences dictated conflicting political loyalties.

Central institutions of government, reinforced by the sanctions of religion, confirmed a sense of common national identity among Englishmen. When the invention of printing in the fifteenth century made possible the diffusion of books in a wide variety of tongues, Englishmen had adopted a standard

[3] See Sidney Verba, "Sequences and Development," in Leonard Binder *et al., Crises and Sequences in Political Development* (Princeton: Princeton University Press, 1971).

[4] In Scotland and Wales and, to a lesser extent, in England, differences between the Established Church and nonconformist churches caused difficulties up to the first part of the twentieth century.

speech. The literary language of Shakespeare and Milton was supplemented by dialect variants, but there was no significant group speaking an older language, as occurred in Ireland and in Wales.

The resolution of the civil war of the 1640s was, characteristically, a compromise involving both continuity and change. The conflict between Parliament and Crown led to the beheading of Charles I and rule by Oliver Cromwell as Lord Protector. This was followed by the restoration of the monarchy. But the powers of the restored monarchy were not what they had been. The importance of Parliament was made clear when James II was deposed in the "Glorious" Revolution of 1688. The Bill of Rights of the following year was a further attempt to confine the powers of the Crown. The legacy in the generations that followed was not a series of revolutions and counterrevolutions. Instead, it was what J. H. Plumb has called *The Growth of Political Stability*, "the acceptance by society of its political institutions, and of those classes of men or officials who control them."[5]

The constitution prevailing in England when industrialization began was a "mixed" constitution. Authority was divided between Crown and Parliament in a way that was consciously intended to provide checks and balances against dominance by either. The Crown had to live with Parliament, just as an American president today must learn to live with Congress. The coincidence of a series of weak kings and an independent Parliament led to the rise of politicians skilled in the art of managing both monarch and independent-minded Members of Parliament. Robert Walpole established the office of Prime Minister in the early eighteenth century as a broker between King and Parliament. The result was limited but not ineffectual government. The government was strong enough to carry out enclosure laws that canceled traditional peasant rights to communal land, vesting large tracts of land in individual proprietors. But it did not establish a rigid mercantilist code of

[5] J. H. Plumb, *The Growth of Political Stability* (London: Macmillan, 1967), p. xvi.

economic practices that would have been an obstacle to subsequent economic development.[6]

Political power was in the hands of the few. The right to vote depended upon a variety of qualifications, of which property was the most important. Status was primarily determined by birth, although a wealthy self-made man could compensate for lowly birth by purchasing a peerage and having his son educated as a gentleman. Virtue consisted in acting consistently with the expectations of one's station in life. Each man made a contribution and each drew benefits from society, but these were in no sense equal. The outlook is well summed up in the funeral monument at Christ Church to an eighteenth-century Oxford servant "who, by an exemplary life and behaviour, and an honest attention to the duties of his station, deserved and obtained the approbation and esteem of the whole society." This philosophy could not withstand the great upheaval of industrialization.

Industrialization became a pervasive feature of English life far earlier than anywhere else in the world. By the early eighteenth century England had already developed the commercial skills and resources important for transforming an agricultural and handicraft economy into an industrial one. Judged by present criteria of "socioeconomic" modernization, England became a modern society more than half a century before America, Germany, or France.[7] By 1821 the proportion of the population engaged in manufacturing, mining, and industry was greater than that in agriculture and other primary industries. By 1851 half the population lived in cities, and many rural areas had coal mines and cotton or woolen mills. The invention of the railroad gave England internal communications matching its maritime transport. Ideas were in-

[6] See Robert T. Holt and John E. Turner, *The Political Basis of Economic Development* (Princeton: Van Nostrand, 1966); on legislative forms, S. A. Walkland, *The Legislative Process in Great Britain* (London: Allen & Unwin, 1968), Ch. 1.

[7] For a detailed discussion of criteria, evidence, and sources, see Richard Rose, "England: a Traditionally Modern Political Culture" in Lucian Pye and Sidney Verba, editors, *Political Culture and Political Development* (Princeton: Princeton University Press, 1965).

creasingly diffused on a nationwide basis. The consumption of printing paper began to rise in the 1780s, and virtually complete literacy was achieved by the late nineteenth century. Literacy did not threaten national identity, except in Celtic parts of Wales and Ireland, because English was the language of industry and commerce as well as of the church and government. On almost any indicator, England had become the world's first modern industrial society by the middle of the nineteenth century. The repeal of the Corn Laws in 1846, signifying the shift from an agrarian society producing its own food to an industrial one paying for imported food by exports, is a useful landmark date for the change.

Industrialization challenged the institutions of the Old Constitution. They were designed for a rural society, in which traditional face-to-face ties between individuals were important, and expectations of action by central government few.[8] Because the institutions of government were centuries old, their procedures were sometimes literally medieval; for example, until 1834 the Treasury kept accounts in Roman numerals and Latin prose. In the late eighteenth century reformers began to complain that a "Gothic" constitution could no longer meet the problems of modern society.[9] The pressure of change was most evident in population. Between 1801 and 1851, England grew from nearly 9 to 18 million people; its population nearly doubled again by 1900. The concentration of people in cities transformed the countryside, especially in Lancashire, Yorkshire, and the Midlands. Parish authorities had neither the power nor ability to govern rapidly growing industrial centers. Two decades of war with France posed an ideological as well as a military threat. Concurrently with the march of Napoleon's armies, France was spreading novel political and social ideas derived from the Enlightenment.

In the face of such problems radicals, stimulated by the ra-

[8] For a description of the parochial nature of preindustrial English life, see Peter Laslett, *The World We Have Lost* (London: Methuen, 1965).

[9] See S. E. Finer, "Patronage and the Public Service," *Public Administration,* XXX (1952), pp. 329–60.

tionalistic philosophy of Jeremy Bentham, lobbied for specific measures of reform, and for reform of the institutions of government. Police, public health, and poor law measures were adopted to cope with the problems resulting from the changes in the environment resulting from industrialization. The enactment of measures to regulate society required the establishment of new teams of administrators. The experience and arguments of the most zealous administrators provided evidence of need for more legislation and more administrative machinery. The dynamic for growth was thus instilled within government, as well as articulated by popular demands. The great growth in government led gradually to the elimination of the old corps of administrators, many of whom owed their jobs to patronage. The Northcote-Trevelyan report on the civil service in 1853 was a major move forward in the development of a modern civil service. It took decades to fulfill its intentions. By the last quarter of the nineteenth century, England had established a constitutional bureaucracy capable of organizing everything from the economical saving of candle ends to the prototype laws of the modern welfare state.[10]

It is impossible to say when England achieved a "modern" system of government, because political scientists do not have criteria for appraising political modernization as clear as those used in assessing economic or social systems. The separation of government administration from the personal affairs of the king might be regarded as the first step in modernization; this occurred in late medieval England. Recognition was given to the status of a Loyal Opposition by the end of the eighteenth century. There was nothing resembling modern political parties with nationwide popular organization until after late nineteenth-century election reforms had created a mass electorate. Dating modernization from Victorian times avoids false precision, for Queen Victoria reigned from 1837 to 1901. Even though one cannot date the creation of a new style of

10 See e.g., Henry Parris, *Constitutional Bureaucracy* (London: Allen & Unwin, 1969); Oliver MacDonagh, *A Pattern of Government Growth* (London: MacGibbon & Kee, 1961); and Gillian Sutherland, editor, *Studies in the Growth of Nineteenth-Century Government* (London: Routledge, 1972).

government, it is possible to date the demise of the old ways of governing. In 1841, the Earl of Aberdeen noted that the job of Foreign Secretary, which he had also held in 1830, "has increased beyond measure since I was here before, and I know not how it is to be overcome." [11]

The final contribution of the governors of Old England was to adapt gracefully to political change. The adaptability of the defenders of the traditional order was first tested by Catholic Emancipation in 1829. A major argument against removing civil disabilities from Catholics was that it would justify any reform by legislation. The Duke of Wellington, the Prime Minister of the day, argued for reforms "because I considered them necessary for the safety of the country; and for no other reason." [12] Similarly, Earl Grey, the Prime Minister at the time of the 1832 Reform Act, the first of a series of measures leading to universal suffrage, endorsed the Reform Act because "unless the privileged sections of the community were prepared to adapt and to 'improve,' waves of dangerous and uncontrollable innovation would completely drown the existing social order." In consequence, as G. Kitson Clark notes:

> After 1848 the classes which had flourished and monopolized power under the old regime showed no intention to retreat from a world in which they should have been anachronisms. In fact, after 1848 their position was stronger than it had been before, for they had abandoned what was indefensible in their position and retained what was material for their power.[13]

THE CONTRIBUTION OF MODERN ENGLAND

The creation of a modern industrial society in mid-nineteenth-century England transformed government but did not make the problems of governing disappear. Politicians in the time of Sir Robert Peel, William Gladstone, and Benjamin

[11] Henry Parris, *Constitutional Bureaucracy,* p. 108.

[12] Quoted from Allan Silver, "Social and Ideological Bases of British Elite Reactions to Domestic Crisis in 1829–1832," *Politics and Society,* I:2 (1971), p. 190.

[13] *The Making of Victorian England* (London: Methuen, 1962), p. 43.

Disraeli were as uncertain about the future as their counterparts are today.

The first problem to face politicians was how to relate the new industrial masses to government. The Reform Act of 1832 was not a move to increase popular influence, but rather to rationalize the selection of voters. Under the Old Constitution, the qualifications for the franchise varied greatly from constituency to constituency. The 1832 Act simply created uniform franchise requirements; it gave the vote to about 7 per cent of the adult population of England. The country was no more governed by "the people," in the twentieth-century sense of the term, than it was governed by the monarch of the day. At that time the people fit to govern were defined as those several hundred thousand men with sufficient leisure, intelligence, and wealth to allow them to form an independent judgment upon public affairs. They stood in contrast to the other nine-tenths of the population, "the mob" unfit to rule.[14]

The governors of mid-Victorian England saw themselves as an oligarchy, justly and wisely ruling the country in trust for the multitude. In Bagehot's classic formulation: "Certain persons are by common consent agreed to be wiser than others, and their opinion is, by consent, to rank for much more than its numerical value. We may in these happy nations weigh votes as well as count them." [15] Conservatives thought that the best governors were often those literally born to rule, hereditary aristocrats with seats in the House of Lords. Of eleven Prime Ministers in the period 1832 to 1885, seven were peers. The bulk of Cabinet ministers were connected with noble families until the election of the middle-class Liberal government of 1906. The Whigs justified government by moderate men of high rank and property, "who in bad times keep alive the sacred flame of freedom, and when the people are roused, stand between the Constitution and revolution, and go with the people, but not to extremities." In the blunt language of

[14] See Cecil S. Emden, *The People and the Constitution* (Oxford: Clarendon Press, 1933), Appendix I.

[15] Walter Bagehot, *The English Constitution* (London: World's Classics edition, 1955), p. 141.

the radical Richard Cobden, the Whigs were "buffers placed between the people and the privileged classes, to deaden the shock when they are brought into collision." [16] A third theory, advanced by educational reformers was that the best governors were those with the best education. Until well into the twentieth century, however, English higher education was the preserve of a minority whose parents could afford fees for secondary and university education. The best graduates were expected to be Oxford or Cambridge men with gentlemanly manners, demonstrating achievement in such nonvocational subjects as Latin and Greek. Lord Macaulay put the point succinctly in the mid-nineteenth-century debate on civil service reform: "If, instead of learning Greek, we learned the Cherokee, the man who understood the Cherokee best, who made the most correct and melodious Cherokee verses, who comprehended most accurately the effect of the Cherokee particles, would generally be a superior man to him who was destitute of those accomplishments." [17] Radicals such as the Chartists spoke for government by a Parliament elected by universal suffrage, with members drawn from many walks of life. They also expected the executive to respond to parliamentary pressures, as in centuries past it had responded to pressures from the Crown.

In the course of three generations of reform, the oligarchs accepted that ever-increasing groups of the populace were citizens with rights to participate in government. The first set of reforms allowed full political rights to persons who were not adherents of the Church of England. Catholics were allowed to sit in Parliament in 1829, Jews in 1866, and self-described atheists in 1886. Adherents of minority religions were allowed to vote only if they also met property qualifications for the franchise.

The right to vote was gradually extended to larger propor-

[16] See Norman Gash, *Reaction and Reconstruction in English Politics 1832–1852* (Oxford: Clarendon Press, 1965), p. 162; and W. L. Guttsman, *The British Political Elite*, pp. 38, 78 ff.

[17] *The Life and Letters of Lord Macaulay, Vol. II* (London: Longmans, 1923), pp. 585 ff.

tions of the population by Reform Acts in 1867 and 1884. The latter gave the right to vote to the majority of adult English males. Property qualifications for voters were not abolished until 1918; women were first enfranchised at this time. Vestiges of older electoral practices remained until 1949, providing extra votes for owners of business properties and university graduates. The ballot was made secret in 1872, and corruption was successfully legislated against in 1883. Salaries were first paid to Members of Parliament in 1911. It was not until 1918 that the bulk of the demands made by the Chartists in 1837 were met.[18]

The grant of the franchise could only allow Englishmen to influence government if they had a meaningful choice between representatives competing for their vote. Even in the late nineteenth century, many MPs were considered the natural spokesman for their communities, by virtue of birth, status, or wealth, and were returned without an electoral contest. In 1900, for example, 243 of the 670 persons elected to the House of Commons were returned unopposed. The "nationalization" of political participation required the creation of nationwide political party competition. But until the last quarter of the nineteenth century, "general elections were not general." [19] Candidates often stood without clear identification with national party labels, and there was no nationwide party organization to give or withhold endorsement. After the 1867 Reform Act, Liberals and Conservatives, the two largest groups in the House of Commons, began to organize their supporters in the constituencies. Thus, before any working-class political party was formed, both major parties had already integrated manual workers into parties that rejected political divisions along class lines. Joseph Chamberlain took the lead in mobilizing popular support for the Liberals in local constituency associations. In 1886 he defected to the Conservative Party with a group of Liberal Unionists, because the Liberal

[18] One demand — the annual election of Parliament — has never been achieved.

[19] H. J. Hanham, *Elections and Party Management* (London: Longmans, 1959), p. 191.

government endorsed Home Rule for Ireland. The first manual worker to sit in Cabinet, John Burns, was a member of the Liberal Government of 1906.

The growth of working-class political institutions in the late nineteenth century broadened representation in the political process. Trade unions and nonprofit cooperative and friendly societies organized to make collective provision for individual needs. Their philosophy of mutual aid was in contrast to that of laissez-faire economists. It also contrasted with the Marxist ideology of class conflict, prominent among continental Socialist parties. The early leaders of the British labor movement were strongly committed to conventional social beliefs; they were not seeking to transform society by revolution but rather to transform it by the gradual amelioration of social evils.[20] In the epigrammatic phrase of Morgan Phillips, the labor movement drew more inspiration from Methodism than it did from Marx, notwithstanding the fact that Karl Marx's major works were written in London, stimulated by England's industrial revolution. The leaders of the labor movement believed that they could achieve significant gains by working through the existing institutions of government. The characteristic labor view was succinctly put in an 1896 pamphlet of the Fabian Society:

> Since England now possesses an elaborate democratic state machinery, graduated from the Parish Council or Vestry up to the central Parliament, and elected under a franchise which enables the working class to vote to overwhelm all others, the opposition which exists in the Continental monarchies between the state and the people does not hamper English Socialists. . . . The difficulty in England is not to secure more political power for the people, but to persuade them to make any sensible use of the power they already have.[21]

[20] For a contrast between the German SPD and the British Labour Party, see Egon Wertheimer, "Portrait of the Labour Party," reprinted in Richard Rose, editor, *Studies in British Politics* (London: Macmillan, 1969).

[21] Fabian Tract No. 70, 1896, quoted in H. J. Hanham, editor, *The Nineteenth Century Constitution* (Cambridge: University Press, 1969), pp. 22 ff. More generally, see Richard Rose, "Class and Party Divisions: Britain as a Test Case", *Sociology,* II:1 (1968).

The Labour Party was founded in 1900 to secure the election of working-class MPs. Its founders considered it necessary, because of a failure of local Liberal associations to accommodate trade union demands when nominating candidates. Trade unions were stimulated to support the party by court decisions that jeopardized their legal rights to organize.

The supremacy of a popularly elected government was not fully established until the resolution of a dispute between the hereditary House of Lords and the elected House of Commons in 1911. For generations the Lords had been dominated by Conservatives. The Liberal government, elected by a large majority in December, 1905, sought to pass a series of reform measures affecting the budget and Home Rule for Ireland. The Lords opposed the measures and, as their assent was necessary for a bill to become a law, their veto was absolute. The Liberal government sought a renewal of its electoral mandate in January, 1910. It secured a plurality but not a majority of seats in the Commons; it depended upon the votes of Irish Nationalists for a majority. This deadlock intensified the dispute between the elected government and the Lords. A second election was held in December, 1910, to test popular opinion again; the result was virtually identical with the January poll. Confronted with this constitutional deadlock, the King was prevailed upon to promise to create sufficient Liberal peers to give the Liberals a majority in the Lords, if the Lords would not assent to the government's legislation. The Lords bowed before this threat to dilute their hereditary status, and the Liberal government's Parliament Act of 1911 converted the veto power of the Lords into a power to delay nonfinancial bills for a period of two years.

The second great problem confronting the governors of the newly modernized society was whether or not government should play a positively interventionist role in social affairs. While philosophers differed among themselves about the correctness and flexibility of the principles of laissez faire, successive governments began to regulate such things as public health, on an ad hoc basis. Positive action to improve society was undertaken in such measures as the 1870 Education Act, which made schooling compulsory. The growth of modern

British government is most easily indicated by the vast expansion of government expenditure, both in absolute terms and relative to the nation's gross national product (Table II.1). In 1850, when England reached the status of a modern industrial society, government expenditure was 11 per cent of the gross national product. Government spending had risen by three and one-half times since 1790, measured in terms of money spent at constant prices. But it had fallen 1 per cent in proportion to the gross national product, because of the great increase in national wealth resulting from industrialization. In the period from 1850 up to the outbreak of World War I, government expenditure increased by four times in real terms. But the proportion of the national product taken rose by only 1 per cent compared with that of 1850, because of continued growth in the economy. Government spending rose more than four times (as measured in constant prices) in the last half of the nineteenth century; increased spending was primarily financed by economic growth.

All fields of government activity have grown with industrialization. The cost of administration has grown least, increasing by "only" thirty-seven times in real terms since 1790, and by four times since 1890; the number of government employees has grown much more slowly than public expenditure. Spending on social services has increased by 382 times since 1790 and by more than 30 times since 1890 (Table II.2). Prior to industrialization, the basic government services of defense, administration, and payment of the national debt consumed 82 per cent of all public expenditure. This percentage did not begin to decline until the second half of the nineteenth century; in 1890 these minimum services accounted for 65 per cent of public spending. In this century spending on social services, economic affairs, transportation, and housing has risen greatly in absolute terms; the total share of public expenditure has increased less dramatically, rising from 52 per cent in 1910 to 63 per cent in 1961.

The growth in government expenditure has been matched by a great growth in the number and size of institutions required to administer government. New boards and commissions were established promptly, starting in 1832; the responsi-

TABLE II.1 *Economic Growth and the Growth of Public Expenditures, 1790–1961*

		Gross national product			*Total government expenditure*			
Year	*Population (in millions)*	*At current prices (in millions of £)*	*At constant prices (index)*	*Per head of population at constant prices (index)*	*At current prices (in millions of £)*	*At constant prices (index)*	*Per head of population at constant prices (index)*	*Government expenditure as proportion of G.N.P. (in percentages)*
1790	14.8	186	100	100	23	100	100	12
1800	16.1	308	111	102	67	197	180	22
1810	18.4	407	128	103	94	238	191	23
1820	20.9	403	169	120	70	239	169	17
1830	24.0	438	221	137	65	266	164	15
1840	26.5	598	291	162	64	250	140	11
1850	27.3	562	356	193	64	330	179	11
1860	28.8	778	431	221	87	393	202	11
1870	31.2	988	530	251	92	402	191	9
1880	34.6	1,132	679	290	112	542	232	10
1890	37.5	1,468	1,015	401	123	687	272	8
1900	41.2	1,840	1,235	443	265	1,441	519	14
1910	45.0	2,143	1,383	455	258	1,349	444	12
1920	43.7	6,070	1,455	493	1,592	3,096	1,048	26
1926	45.2	4,303	1,409	461	1,107	2,938	960	26
1932	46.3	3,973	1,498	479	1,138	3,477	1,113	29
1938	47.5	5,294	1,900	592	1,587	4,619	1,444	30
1946	49.2	8,778	1,888	568	4,530	7,900	2,379	52
1951	50.2	12,926	2,265	667	5,217	7,410	2,185	40
1956	51.2	18,373	2,569	743	6,688	7,579	2,194	36
1961	52.8	23,701	2,871	805	8,955	8,792	2,468	38

Source: Jindrich Veverka, "The Growth of Government Expenditure in the United Kingdom since 1790," *Scottish Journal of Political Economy*, X:2 (1963), p. 114. Reprinted by permission.

TABLE II.2 *The Growth of Government Expenditure by Function, 1790–1961*

Year	Administration		Debt		Defense		Social services		Economic & environment	
	Millions of £[a]	Total %[b]	Millions of £	Total %	Millions of £	Total %	Millions of £	Total %	Millions of £	Total %
1790	34	17	7	39	5	26	2	9	1	9
1840	7	16	20	42	11	23	4	9	4	9
1890	28	22	19	15	36	28	24	20	19	15
1910	35	14	18	7	66	27	80	32	49	20
1932	44	7	158	25	62	10	287	45	88	14
1951	88	6	144	11	343	25	584	43	203	15
1961	111	7	164	10	322	20	764	47	256	16

Source: Jindrich Veverka, "The Growth of Government Expenditure in the United Kingdom since 1790," *Scottish Journal of Political Economy*, X:2 (1963), p. 119. Reprinted by permission.

[a]Expenditure at constant 1900 prices.

[b]Of total public expenditure.

bilities of many were subsequently transferred to new government departments, some founded in the quarter century before World War II and others thereafter. The names and sizes of the departments in which central government organizes its business have been far more changeable than their numbers. In 1832 there were twelve government ministries. The number has but doubled since. Of twenty-one government departments that existed in 1900, fourteen have remained in being and seven have been abolished or altered out of all recognition. Fifty-three different government departments have been created, some for short periods of time, as in wartime, and others persisting.[22] The number of public employees has increased from 554,000 in 1891 to 6,043,000 in 1967. Local government, including education, has been the largest employer of public officials. Nationalized industries are the second largest employer. The central government is third. Central government employees exceed the number of those in nationalized industries only if members of the armed forces and post office staff are counted with other central government employees.[23] The House of Commons has changed least in size. Between 1832 and 1918 the number of MPs fluctuated between 652 and 670, including about one hundred from Ireland. In 1970 the Commons had 630, including 12 from Northern Ireland. The number of hours that the Commons sits has risen, but much less than other indicators of government activity.[24]

World War I, appropriately called the Great War in Britain, forced political changes.[25] England's claim to be the world's dominant power could not survive four years of bloody trench warfare. The loss of nearly a million British lives and

[22] See D. E. Butler and J. Freeman, *British Political Facts, 1900–1968* (London: Macmillan, 1969) pp. 49 ff; and F. M. G. Willson, "Ministries and Boards: Some Aspects of Administrative Development since 1832," *Public Administration,* XXXIII:1 (1955).

[23] See Moses Abramovitz and Vera Eliasberg, *The Growth of Public Employment in Great Britain* (Princeton: Princeton University Press, 1957).

[24] Calculated from D. E. Butler and J. Freeman, *British Political Facts, 1900–1968,* pp. 124–25.

[25] For a review of various theories of the impact of both world wars and a detailed bibliography, see Alan S. Milward, *The Economic Effects of the World Wars on Britain* (London: Macmillan, 1970).

the territorial upheavals that followed World War I overshadowed the guerilla war that preceded the secession of most of Ireland from the United Kingdom in 1921. The Liberal Party split and destroyed itself as a major electoral force in the political maneuverings that led to the emergence of David Lloyd George as coalition Prime Minister in 1916. The contribution of women to the war effort was recognized by the granting of women's rights. The participation of Labour Party leaders in the coalition government secured no comparable recognition for Labour. The Labour Party turned to the left during the final months of the war, formally adopting a Socialist program in 1918. Because of the Liberal split, Labour gained the opportunity to become the second party in the land.

Since the end of World War I in 1918, successive British governments have faced a third great problem: maintaining the country's economic well-being in competition with newly industrialized nations, while simultaneously meeting popular demands for more welfare services. Government expenditure rose three and one-half times in real terms between 1910 and 1938. This was an increase from 12 to 30 per cent of a gross national product that itself had increased by half. World War II saw another major shift upward in the level of public expenditure. The increase in relation to the gross national product understates the real rise of 90 per cent in expenditure between 1938 and 1961. Economic growth financed one part and taxes financed another part of the greater activity of British government.

The aftermath of World War I was years of economic slump. The nation's gross national product per capita grew by only 5 per cent in real terms between 1910 and 1932. Unemployment fluctuated between 9 and 20 per cent from 1922 to 1930, and reached a high of 22 per cent in 1932. The economy began to improve in the late 1930s, but very high levels of regional unemployment remained in Northern England, Scotland, and Wales.[26] Governments sought unsuccessfully to cope

[26] For a compendium of interwar social statistics, see G. D. H. and M. I. Cole, *The Condition of Britain* (London: Gollancz, 1937). On economic conditions see Robert J. Skidelsky, *Politicians and the Slump* (Harmondsworth: Penguin, 1970).

with economic hardship. By contrast to America, where Franklin Roosevelt's New Deal used government spending in an effort to end depression, British governments relied upon deflation and cut government spending; their American counterpart was Herbert Hoover. The Labour Party, twice in office with minority support in the House of Commons, had no more success than the Conservatives in seeking to revive the economy. When the full force of the world depression hit England in 1931, Labour was in office. The Prime Minister, Ramsay MacDonald, responded by forming a national government with Conservative, Liberal, and a minority of Labour leaders. MacDonald was expelled from the Labour Party for his action; this did not prevent his coalition government from receiving the greatest popular and parliamentary majority in modern English history at the general election of October, 1931.

Notwithstanding the country's economic difficulties, the commitment of political groups to constitutional action through existing institutions of government remained unaffected. This was demonstrated most clearly by the nonviolent general strike of 1926. When union leaders saw that their actions had potential revolutionary implications, they disowned them. The strike, which was notable for its peacefulness, collapsed. At a time when Fascist or Communist parties or both were challenging authority in Germany, Italy, France, and Spain, British Communist and Fascist parties mustered tiny followings to little political effect. Stanley Baldwin, who dominated government for most of the 1930s, consciously saw his task as upholding an old Conservative ideal of lessening social and political tensions, rather than using his party's strength to pursue a course that might risk violent reactions.[27]

During World War II the country's domestic political priorities altered greatly. The total war of modern technology, in Anthony Eden's words, exposed weaknesses in the nation's social life "ruthlessly and brutally." [28] After a near disastrous

[27] On the moderation of Labour, see especially Alan Bullock, *The Life and Times of Ernest Bevin,* Vol. I (London: Heinemann, 1960). For a contemporary account, see J. M. Gaus, *Great Britain: A Study of Civic Loyalty* (Chicago: University of Chicago Press, 1929). Note also Robert Benewick, *The Fascist Movement in Britain* (London: Allen Lane, 1972).

[28] House of Commons, *Debates,* Vol. 355, Col. 757 (December 6, 1939). All references to *Debates* are to the 5th series.

experience in a government coalition in World War I, Labour leaders bargained for a full measure of authority before taking office in Winston Churchill's national coalition of 1940. National unity was sought not only through Churchillian exhortations but also through major policy changes intended to provide "Fair shares for all" in circumstances of total war and total mobilization. Out of the coalition emerged the Beveridge Report on Social Welfare, the Keynesian Full Employment White Paper of 1944, and the Butler Education Act of 1944. These three measures – the first two named after Liberals and the third after a Conservative – remain major landmarks of the mixed-economy welfare state today.

The "fair shares" emphasis was continued by the election of a Labour government under Clement Attlee in 1945. It maintained rationing and controls in efforts to see that everyone shared the postwar austerity required to rebuild the economy. The National Health Service was established, providing free medical care for all. The mines, gas, electricity, the railways, road transport, and the steel industry were nationalized, in the hope that the industries would prove better for workers and consumers through public ownership and would more readily contribute to the achievement of the government's economic goals. By 1951 the Labour government had exhausted the list of policy innovations on which there was agreement within the party. Its economic policies had yet to produce prosperity; austerity and rationing were still required six years after the end of the war. In 1951 a much reformed Conservative Party under Winston Churchill was returned to power by the electorate.

For more than two decades since, Conservative and Labour governments have sought to combine economic prosperity and a generous provision of public services for the electorate. The 1950s saw a marked rise in living standards, after years of wartime scarcity and postwar austerity. Standards of living once thought the privilege of a relative few became widespread. Some observers interpreted the boom in mass consumption as the start of a "classless" society. Aided by rising prosperity, the Conservatives won general elections by unprecedented increases in their parliamentary majorities in 1955 and 1959.

The expectations of a continuous and easy rise in prosperity were dashed in the 1960s. The Conservative government, and the Labour government of Harold Wilson elected in 1964, faced rising expectations for private consumer goods and for such public services as education, housing, and pensions. They found the nation's economic resources inadequate to meet all these claims.[29] The Conservative government turned to the Common Market and to economic planning, abandoned a decade earlier in reaction against wartime controls. In opposition, Labour MPs argued that Socialism provided a better means to plan the economy in an era of technological change. The economic hopes of the 1964–1970 Labour government were shattered by a classic economic problem: how to maintain a booming domestic economy without simultaneously risking the devaluation of the pound because of domestic inflation. The Wilson government turned to deflationist measures for a remedy. While deflation succeeded in forcing up unemployment and reducing economic growth, it did not secure the balance of payments. In 1967 the Labour government devalued the pound and intensified its deflationary measures. In 1970 Labour was defeated by the biggest swing of votes in the postwar era. The Conservative government, returned under Edward Heath, entered office promising to avoid the mistakes of its predecessor. The difficulties of the Heath administration show that the country's economic problems are not the result of partisan mismanagement, but reflect greater structural difficulties. Entry into the Common Market in 1973 was a tacit admission that the problems of Britain's economy were too great for a British government to solve alone.

A MIXED INHERITANCE

History constrains any British government. While at the time they occurred, past events were not inevitable, today they must be taken as given, limiting what any British government

[29] For discussion of the ups and downs of government economic policy, see successively revised editions of Samuel Brittan's work, *Steering the Economy* (Harmondsworth: Penguin, 1971).

can do. The influence of the past is not completely determinant. For example, at any time since the outbreak of the troubles in Northern Ireland in 1968, the British government has been free to choose among very different policy alternatives. There is one thing that the government cannot do: avoid responsibilities arising from the Anglo-Irish Treaty of 1921.

The extent to which the past constrains the present is not a constant; it varies from policy area to policy area. For example, housing policy makers are greatly constrained by history, because the houses that can be built in any one year constitute but a few per cent of the nation's total housing stock. Nine-tenths of all Englishmen must live in houses that were not built under the government of the day. The housing stock that the government inherits is mixed, combining good modern and Victorian houses, as well as century-old slums and poorly built and planned newer houses. On the other hand, high-standard houses built today become part of the nation's future stock of houses. The continuity of policy so often evident in British politics allows a particular government to start a new policy with the expectation that its benefits will compound in the future. At the same time, it compels a government to place a ceiling on expectations of immediate change; it cannot write off overnight the inheritance of the past.

The state of the economy today illustrates how the inheritance of the past mixes assets and liabilities. The early industrialization of England in the late eighteenth and early nineteenth century gave the country great industrial resources and an especially great advantage in international trade. In the middle of the nineteenth century England was more than the world's greatest industrial nation; it was the world's only industrial nation. The industrialization of England generations before that of other nations meant that its annual rate of economic growth could be low, yet its aggregate resources great, because of the length of time in which growth compounded. (The United States has enjoyed a similar historic advantage.) While early industrialization was a great economic asset, the value of this asset has declined through time. By surpassing England in gross national product per capita in the 1960s, European countries have demonstrated that later industrialization can be an advantage, if combined with a higher annual rate of economic growth.

In the course of time, assets can turn into liabilities. For example, England's industrial preeminence owed much to the achievements of the coal, textile, and shipbuilding industries. Changes in technology have made obsolete historic investments in factories and labor skills. The spread of industrialization to other countries, sometimes supported by British capital and British machinery, has lost export business, as former customers now produce goods once imported from England. By contrast with countries such as Spain, Turkey, and Mexico, where the governments seek to industrialize agrarian and handicraft economies, in England the problem is that of "remodernizing" an industrial society, developing new industries capable of absorbing the labor made redundant by industrial decline, and earning money lost by contracting markets for traditional exports.

The contribution of Old England to contemporary politics is most evident in the implicit assumptions fundamental to the conduct of government. Englishmen take for granted rule by a central authority based in London, just as they expect their governors to consider that their powers, while great, are not unlimited. Englishmen also take their national identity for granted. While there are nationalist movements intermittently active in other parts of the United Kingdom, within England there is no such thing as a Yorkshire or Lancashire or Kentish nationalist party. Not least in importance is the avoidance of Protestant vs Catholic conflict within English society and, latterly, the avoidance of clerical vs anticlerical disputes that persist in Italy, France, and other European societies.

The contributions of modern England to the state of England today are mixed. First, members of the old governing class successfully incorporated the populace in representative government. While politicians and voters may disagree about the ends of policy, they agree about the means of resolving disputes. Second, administrators developed a framework of institutions capable of meeting the unprecedented problems of environmental change arising from industrialization. Subsequently, they expanded institutions to provide the services of a modern welfare state. Third, there is a legacy committing government to continuous involvement in many areas of social life. Some of the commitments are based upon popular expectations; others are enshrined in statute books. The gradual accumulation of welfare-state legislation entrenches many citizen claims upon the state. It also commits a large proportion of government revenue to policies that no politician would seriously think of rejecting, for fear of electoral repercussions. The fourth contribution is negative. The inability to resolve major problems of the British economy has left contemporary governors the accumulated deficit of decades of economic change, which have reduced the country's position relative to other major industrial nations and worsened it in relation to the claims that government would like to make upon national resources.

When the inheritance of the past is viewed as benign, its persistence provides great reassurance to governors and governed. One great premise of English politics is the assimilation of past and present. Doctrines recommending the radical rejection of past achievements for the sake of an unknown and untested future have had little appeal to Englishmen, who have preferred to adapt obsolete political institutions rather than abolish them. Such a preference most obviously applies to the monarchy. This symbol of the continuity of England's government has changed greatly in its practical significance through the centuries. The line of inheritance is far more tenuous than is conventionally admitted. The monarchy has passed from Tudors to Stuarts to the House of Orange and then the House of Hanover by a series of dynastic accidents and political pressures. As recently as 1937 Edward VIII was forced to abdicate because the King wished to marry a divorced American against the advice of Parliament.

The confidence that is engendered by past success can become complacency. In the early 1960s articulate Englishmen in many walks of life began to attack established practices and cry for change. To the question – "What's wrong with Britain?" – many different answers have been given. Each answer emphasizes the need to change rather than continue practices inherited from the past. Parliament, the civil service, and the parties have been included in the criticisms. In 1964 a Labour government was elected, pledged to modernize Britain. In 1970 a Conservative government was elected, pledged to do the same — although Conservative ambitions differ significantly from those of Labour. Notwithstanding the rhetoric of change, neither party sought to introduce revolutionary change in British politics or society. In office, both parties have found that the constraints of the past — both positive and negative — are greater than anticipated when out of office.

The insular character of English politics is reflected by the tendency of those taking part in the "condition of England" debate to treat England's problems as unique. This is not the case. Other nations have problems too. An American journalist, Anthony Lewis, has succintly put England's mixed inheritance into perspective:

> Of course there are things wrong with Britain today. What seems unjustified is any national sense that in these sins Britain is worse than other countries, and must therefore suffer. A moment's consideration of the United States, with its terrifying problems of war, and poverty and social division, should make clear the absurdity of any such guilty notion . . . In Britain, after all, the problem is only money.[30]

Most Englishmen have enough perspective on their past, and their present — and on other countries — to accept the idea that while conditions could be better, they could also be worse. Given great past advantages, the implicit premise of political change becomes the assimilation of past and present, rather than the radical rejection of the past on behalf of an unknown and untested future. The spirit is summed up in the motto of Lord Hugh Cecil's study of conservatism: "Even when I changed, it should be to preserve." [31]

30 "QE2 and Other Sore Points," *Sunday Times,* January 12, 1969.
31 *Conservatism* (London: Williams & Norgate, no date, c. 1912), p. 243.

CHAPTER III

The Constitution of the Crown

> *"On all great subjects," says Mr. Mill, "much remains to be said," and of none is this more true than of the English Constitution. The literature which has accumulated upon it is huge. But an observer who looks at the living reality will wonder at the contrast to the paper description. He will see in the life much which is not in the book; and he will not find in the rough practice many refinements of the literary theory.*

THE CONVENTIONAL WAY to describe a government is by its constitution. This can hardly be done in England, because there is no written constitution. At no time in the past was there a break with tradition so great that the governors had to meet, like former colonialists after a successful revolution, and write down how they were to be governed henceforth. Englishmen often refer to a mixture of Acts of Parliament from the thirteenth century onward, judicial pronouncements, habitual customs, and conventions about "the rules of the game" as their constitution. After an attempt to collect documents to give a written description of the constitution, one author concludes, "It would be foolish to suppose that this mode of systematizing the material gives a complete picture of the British Constitution." [1]

[1] Leslie Wolf-Phillips, *Constitutions of Modern States* (London: Pall Mall, 1968), p. 182.

The absence of a written constitution is considered a great advantage by many who write about British politics. It is said to permit government to adapt its actions and institutions to changing circumstances and demands, without the procedural difficulties that a written constitution, such as the American, imposes. Given the medieval origins of government in England, there has been great need for changing established institutions at many times in English history. Flexibility arises from vagueness about the powers and procedures of government. When there is a major dispute about the actions of the government of the day, both sides can appeal rhetorically to "constitutional" principles. Neither can refer to any document that binds the actions of government. Disputes are resolved initially by superior political power. As the immediate cause of controversy recedes into the past, all sides of the controversy usually come to accept yesterday's disputed actions as part of today's constitutional practice.

The authority of British government does not derive from a semimythical compact between citizens, as in America, where the constitution is ordained and established by the actions of "We, the people." The authority of government is embodied in the Crown. This does not mean that the monarch of the day personally determines the major activities of what is referred to as Her (or His) Majesty's Government. Instead, the Crown serves as a collective symbol of institutions of the state. For example, government property is held in the name of the Crown, rather than in the name of someone as transitory as a Prime Minister, something as abstract as the state, or as diffuse as the people of England. In the law courts, criminal actions are similarly entered as the case of *Regina* (i.e. Queen Elizabeth II) against the person accused of offending against the Queen's peace.

The question thus arises: What constitutes the Crown? No simple answer can be given.[2] A major study of constitutional law defines the Crown as "the sum total of governmental

[2] See Geoffrey Marshall, *Constitutional Theory,* Ch. 2 (Oxford: Clarendon Press, 1971); and W. J. M. Mackenzie, "The Civil Service, the State and the Establishment", in Bernard Crick, editor, *Essays on Reform* (London: Oxford University Press, 1967).

powers synonymous with the Executive." But these terms are then said to be extralegal, that is, not customarily used in statutes.[3] Defining the Crown is important in legal proceedings because of the immunities granted the Crown's servants, arising from the feudal doctrine that a lord could not be sued in his own courts. Acts of Parliament usually state whether a public authority partakes of the Crown. But sometimes the position is not clear-cut; it is possible for a public body to be regarded as pertaining to the Crown in some respects, but not in others. Today, as in Bagehot's time, there is confusion between the dignified parts of the constitution (that is, conventional doctrines) and efficient parts (the informal understandings and procedures operating within government). The doctrine of the Crown exemplifies this contradiction. It also reflects Bagehot's view that the dignified parts help sanctify popular allegiance by tradition and myth, while the efficient parts enable government to work easily.[4]

THE WHITEHALL MACHINE

British government could continue for months without new legislation, but it would collapse overnight if hundreds of thousands of civil servants stopped administering prosaic laws concerning taxes, pensions, housing, health, and other responsibilities of the welfare state. Because English government is centuries old, the accumulation of laws is especially great. Because it is "big" government, even a middle-rank civil servant may be responsible for a staff of several thousand people or for spending tens of millions of pounds. Only if these duties are executed routinely — that is, quietly and effectively — will the most prominent members of government have the time and opportunity to debate and make new policies.

In everyday English, the term government can be used with a variety of modifiers. One may speak of the Queen's government in order to emphasize persisting and nonpartisan features. Using the name of the Prime Minister of the day, e.g.,

[3] E. C. S. Wade and A. W. Bradley, *Constitutional Law* (London: Longman, 8th edition, 1970), pp. 171 ff, 678 ff.

[4] W. Bagehot, *The English Constitution,* pp. 4 ff.

the Heath government, emphasizes personal and transitory features. Reference to a Labour or Conservative government emphasizes partisanship. The phrase government officials usually refers to civil servants rather than elected politicians. Collectively, the executive agencies of government are often referred to as the Whitehall machine, or simply Whitehall, after the London street in which many major government offices are located. Downing Street, the home of the Prime Minister, is a small lane off Whitehall, and the Palace of Westminster – the home of both the House of Commons and the House of Lords – is at one end of Whitehall. The term "Parliament" can refer to the elected Chamber alone, the House of Commons, as well as to both the House of Commons and the House of Lords. The term "Westminster" can refer collectively to Prime Minister, Parliament, and civil servants in Whitehall. The historic clustering of government offices in Westminster symbolizes the centralization of government, just as the increasing dispersion of government offices throughout London symbolizes the growing complexity of "central" government.

The reigning monarch, as distinct from the Crown, is almost exclusively concerned with dignified aspects of government.[5] The duties of Queen Elizabeth II are few in relation to "her" government. The Queen must give formal assent to laws passed by Parliament, but she may not state publicly her opinion about legislation. The Queen is also responsible for naming the Prime Minister and dissolving Parliament before a general election. In these actions, the Queen is expected to act consistently with the will of Parliament, as communicated to her by the leaders of the governing party of the day.

The Queen receives major government papers, including reports of Cabinet meetings. She usually receives the Prime Minister once a week to discuss current affairs. The monarch has the opportunity to encourage the Prime Minister or to warn him about points that Cabinet deliberations have over-

[5] For the best-informed description, see the study by Dermot Morrah, Arundel Herald Extraordinary, *The Work of the Queen* (London: Kimber, 1958).

looked. No Prime Minister in modern times has suggested that he followed a policy because of the monarch's wishes. The efficient as apart from the dignified responsibility for government remains with elected politicians.

The institutional responsibilities of the Queen are necessary, even if unimportant. In the absence of a hereditary monarch, England might have a president, like Germany or Italy, to commission each new government and to undertake ceremonial tasks. In the absence of a monarch or a figurehead president, the ceremonial duties and the symbolic aura of the head of state would be invested in the Prime Minister of the day. There are few Englishmen who would wish to make such a change.

The ceremonial role of the Queen as head of state consumes a substantial portion of royal time. The Queen or other members of the Royal Family appear at a great range of public functions, from horse races and air shows to the laying of cornerstones for new local government buildings. The Royal Family is also in demand for goodwill tours overseas. Because these time-consuming tasks are performed by the Royal Family, leading elective politicians have more time for the efficient work of government. The differentiation of roles also establishes a clear distinction between "national" and "partisan" aspects of government. In America, by contrast, the President is not only head of state, but also head of a political party.

In times past, the monarch's right to name the Prime Minister was more than a mere formality. Today, the Queen's choice of a Prime Minister is dictated by the decision of the majority party in the House of Commons. Conservative and Labour MPs each elect a leader from among their number in the Commons. As soon as the result of a general election is known, the Queen is expected to send for the leader of the winning party, and entrust him with forming a Cabinet. Because his party has a majority in the Commons, his Cabinet should have the confidence of the elected chamber of Parliament. The monarch's responsibility for naming a Prime Minister becomes a problem only in the absence of others to take responsibility for the decision. A problem could arise in the event that no party held a majority of seats in the House of Commons. In such circumstances, more than one party leader might think himself qualified to lead a coalition government; the last Parliament to lack a majority party was elected in 1929. The resignation of a Prime Minister during the life of a Parliament has happened three times since 1945, each time when the Conservatives were in power. Until 1965, the Conservative Party had no procedure to elect a leader in such circumstances. The Queen, acting through her private secretary and advised by senior members of the Conservative government, had to take responsibility for choice. In 1957, the naming of Harold Macmillan to succeed Anthony Eden was the subject of some controversy; in 1963, the naming of Sir Alec Douglas-Home to succeed Macmillan was even more controversial. In 1965 Sir Alec announced arrangements for electing a leader by the parliamentary party. Edward Heath shortly thereafter was elected Conservative party leader on a contested ballot of his colleagues in the House of Commons. Harold Wilson had similarly been elected Labour leader in 1963 on a second ballot by Labour MPs.

The powers and prerogatives of the Crown are in effect vested in the Cabinet.[6] The Cabinet was described by Walter Bagehot as the efficient secret of the English constitution, securing "the close union, the nearly complete fusion of the executive and legislative powers." [7] Fusion results from the fact that Cabinet ministers come from the majority party in the House of Commons, thus assuring control of legislation, while concurrently they are the executive heads of the major departments of central government. By contrast, American politicians are constitutionally debarred from simultaneously being Congressmen and members of the presidential executive. Because the Conservative and Labour parliamentary parties vote as cohesive blocs, no Cabinet is likely to be turned out of office by losing a vote of confidence. British government is thus best referred to as Cabinet government or party government rather than parliamentary government.

Cabinet endorsement is the strongest sanction a policy can

[6] For the historical evolution of these institutions see John P. Mackintosh, *The British Cabinet* (London: Stevens, 2nd edition, 1968); and Hans Daalder, *Cabinet Reform in Britain, 1914–1963* (London: Oxford University Press, 1963).

[7] Bagehot, *The English Constitution,* p. 9.

have short of embodiment in an Act of Parliament. Because of the growing volume of government business, a large and increasing proportion of decisions of public interest do not go to the Cabinet for determination. Decisions are taken within departments, by Cabinet committees, or by ad hoc meetings of ministers, in which the Prime Minister may participate. These extra-Cabinet decisions can be vetoed by the Cabinet. While this rarely happens, ministers must bear their colleagues in mind because, whoever issues instructions, the whole of the Cabinet is collectively held responsible to Parliament for everything that is done in its name. The convention of collective responsibility requires all ministers to give public support to a decision, or at least refrain from making public criticism. If a minister does not wish to go along with his colleagues, he must resign or confine his criticisms to occasional unattributed leaks to the press. Cabinet ministers usually go along silently with colleagues in other departments in return for receiving collective endorsement of many of their own departmental actions. The result is a large measure of dignified unity, muffling though not stifling private controversies within government.

Within the Cabinet, the Prime Minister occupies a unique position. Sometimes he is referred to as *primus inter pares* (first among equals). But, as Winston Churchill once wrote, "There can be no comparison between the positions of number one and numbers two, three or four." [8] As leader of the majority party in the House of Commons as well as chairman of the committee of leading party politicians in the executive, the Prime Minister personally represents the fusion of legislative and executive authority. The Prime Minister can present government policy to his parliamentary party as the collective judgment of the party's leaders in the Commons. He can tell his Cabinet colleagues that his views reflect the wishes of the great majority of the party's MPs in the Commons. His status in one place reinforces his status in another.

[8] Winston S. Churchill, *Their Finest Hour* (London: Cassell, 1949), p. 14. The most judicious summary of evidence is in A. H. Brown, "Prime Ministerial Power," reprinted in Mattei Dogan and Richard Rose, *European Politics* (Boston: Little, Brown, 1971). See also Anthony King, editor, *The British Prime Minister* (London: Macmillan, 1969).

While the Prime Minister is not popularly elected, in dealings with his parliamentary supporters he can invoke electoral sanctions against those who challenge him. The personalization of politics in the press and on television makes the Prime Minister the most visible symbol of the governing party.[9] A popular Prime Minister can claim support as a necessary condition of the party's winning the next general election. Even when unpopular, a determined Prime Minister can suggest that the struggle required to unseat him would do the party far more electoral damage than could be offset by the personality of a new leader. For example, Harold Wilson threatened critics in the Parliamentary Labour Party with expulsion and almost certain electoral defeat:

> All I say is "watch it." Every dog is allowed one bite, but a different view is taken of a dog that goes on biting all the time. If there are doubts that the dog is biting not because of the dictates of conscience but because he is considered vicious then things happen to that dog. He may not get his license renewed when it falls due.[10]

As chairman of the Cabinet, the Prime Minister can, in Clement Attlee's words, "extract the opinion of those he wants when he needs them." Votes are virtually never taken in Cabinet. A discussion is concluded by the Prime Minister's summing up. In Attlee's words:

> The job of the Prime Minister is to get the general feeling — collect the voices. And then, when everything reasonable has been said, to get on with the job and say, "Well, I think the decision of the Cabinet is this, that or the other. Any objections?" Usually there aren't.[11]

After a Cabinet meeting is over, it is up to the Secretary of the Cabinet to prepare a minute, in consultation with the Prime Minister. The minute becomes the recorded decision. As formal resolutions do not come before the Cabinet and

[9] See the data presented by Martin Harrison in David Butler and Michael Pinto-Duschinsky, *The British General Election of 1970* (London: Macmillan, 1971), p. 208.

[10] Quoted in *The Times,* March 3, 1967.

[11] Quoted in Francis Williams, *A Prime Minister Remembers* (London: Heinemann, 1961), p. 81.

discussion may emphasize many points, there can be significant leeway in recording what will be said to have been decided.

As the chairman of the Cabinet, the Prime Minister is its authorized spokesman when it is not meeting.[12] The Prime Minister can, if he wishes, make statements that collectively commit his Cabinet colleagues or require those in disagreement to resign or overthrow him. In crisis situations, when there is little or no time to call Cabinet meetings, the Prime Minister can deal personally with affairs, consulting or advising ministers in affected Cabinet departments as he thinks best. The Prime Minister is most on his own in foreign affairs because, as efficient head of the government, he negotiates with the leaders of America, Russia, and the Common Market countries with considerable domestic freedom of action. Most Prime Ministers since 1945 have shown more interest in foreign policy than in domestic policy. The Prime Minister can make statements on behalf of "his" government in domestic policy too, but he must usually consult affected ministers before making a statement because they should be better informed in matters affecting their department than he is. When two ministers are at loggerheads about a domestic policy that affects both their departments, either may turn to the Prime Minister to arbitrate their differences.

The political authority of the Prime Minister is greatly strengthened by his powers of patronage. In addition to appointing about twenty Cabinet ministers, he appoints sixty or more MPs to junior posts, in charge of minor departments outside the Cabinet or in variously titled subordinate posts within departments, e.g., minister of state, undersecretary of state, or parliamentary secretary. Collectively, these ministers constitute the front-bench of the governing party. In addition, another thirty or so backbench MPs act as unpaid parliamentary private secretaries to individual ministers; the job of a parliamentary private secretary is to keep his min-

[12] For views of a Prime Minister by two of his Cabinet ministers see Patrick Gordon Walker, *The Cabinet* (London: Cape, 1970); and Richard Crossman, *Inside View* (London: Cape, 1972).

ister in touch with back-bench (rank-and-file) opinion in the House of Commons. As the work of government has grown, the number of ministerial appointments has also increased. In 1900 ministerial jobs were given to 42 of the 402 MPs in the governing Conservative Party. In 1967 Harold Wilson had 122 MPs in jobs as ministers, junior ministers, or as parliamentary private secretaries. This number totaled one-third of the membership of the Parliamentary Labour Party.[13] It also constituted two-thirds of the numbers required to give the Prime Minister a majority if a vote of no confidence were moved against his actions in the Parliamentary Labour Party. Any Prime Minister can at will alter the number and status of jobs that he awards, without reference to Cabinet colleagues or Parliament. Wilson was particularly adept at inventing new titles in an attempt to balance the status of various political groupings within the 1964–70 Labour Cabinet.

The patronage power of the Prime Minister is very important because all ministerial appointees, including the most junior, are expected to support the Prime Minister privately and publicly. Because the Prime Minister has sole discretion to sack ministers, failure to give support can lead to a minister's losing office. The hope of preferment encourages back-bench MPs wishing office to support the Prime Minister. In making ministerial appointments, the Prime Minister is formally free to name or exclude anyone he wishes. In practice, a Prime Minister must include most of the major parliamentary politicians of his party. In this way he ensures that potential critics and successors are publicly bound to support him, because they are jointly responsible for all that the Cabinet does. The more widely a Prime Minister distributes jobs among various groupings within the parliamentary party, the broader his base of support. Many MPs regard office as a fair exchange for support. But the policies and ambitions that lead men into Cabinet can lead them to resign. A minister who resigns on an issue of policy always runs the risk that his colleagues find that they can govern without him. But a resigna-

[13] See Richard Rose, "The Making of Cabinet Ministers," *British Journal of Political Science,* I:4 (1971), Table 1.

tion does not inevitably blight a rising minister's career. The ups and downs of political events may retrospectively make his resignation look justified, or a Prime Minister may decide that it is not prudent to allow a major party figure to remain untrammeled by responsibility indefinitely. While most ministers who resign have gone into oblivion, a few, such as Winston Churchill, Anthony Eden, and Harold Wilson, have risen to the Prime Ministership subsequent to resigning or refusing office.[14]

The formal powers of the Prime Minister change slowly if at all, but the effective significance of the office varies according to the way in which the incumbent of the moment defines his role and the political circumstances of the day. Woodrow Wilson's words about the American president are equally apt in England; a chief executive can strive "to be as big a man as he can." Individual Prime Ministers set very different sights.[15] Clement Attlee, for five years deputy Prime Minister in wartime and Labour Prime Minister from 1945 to 1951, took the part of a nonassertive spokesman for the lowest common denominator of views within the Labour Cabinet. This self-denying role kept him apart from the clash of personalities among his senior ministers. Unobtrusively and often effectively, he could carry his Cabinet by stating views succinctly in ways that invited little controversy. When Winston Churchill succeeded him in 1951, he was almost 77 years old and in ill health. Churchill wished to remain in office to conduct foreign affairs; he exerted little influence in domestic policy, and was increasingly remote from his Cabinet. By comparison, Dwight D. Eisenhower after his heart attacks was both more vigorous and more assertive in his role as American president. Anthony Eden, notwithstanding relative youth and long experience of office, failed to define a role for himself in domestic politics. In foreign affairs, he took initiatives without consulting colleagues, leading to the Suez War of 1956. Eden's health broke

[14] See J. A. Cross and R. K. Alderman, *The Tactics of Resignation* (London: Routledge, 1968).

[15] Every postwar Prime Minister to date has published a memoir recounting his view of his work, except for Sir Alec Douglas-Home and Edward Heath.

when the attack was halted, and he resigned. His successor, Harold Macmillan, was ready to intervene strategically in both domestic and foreign policy; exceptionally, he had held major offices in both policy areas. Macmillan's directives were not so frequent as to cause friction with his Cabinet. After five years in office, however, political setbacks and ill health weakened Macmillan's ability to set policy guidelines; his resignation on health grounds in October, 1963, was welcomed. Sir Alec Douglas-Home, his successor, had the good health to take an active role in government, but lacked any knowledge of economic affairs, then the chief political problem of government. Sir Alec was also distrusted by many Cabinet colleagues because of the way in which an inner-party caucus had secured him the post.

Both Harold Wilson and Edward Heath assumed office committed to an activist definition of the Prime Minister's job. In 1964, Wilson encouraged British journalists to compare him with John F. Kennedy, perceived in London as a powerful doer of things. Mr. Wilson's fondness for publicly praising his achievements led critics to describe him as more interested in managing the public relations of government than its policies. Edward Heath entered office in 1970 with the declared intention of stressing "action not words." Heath stated major objectives, both domestic and in Common Market policy. By his concern with the reorganization of the Whitehall machine, Heath showed a wish to enhance the powers available to the Prime Minister of the day. Events have since shown that Heath's thorough preparation did not anticipate all the problems that face a party in office.

A sharper picture of what the Prime Minister is and is not can be obtained by comparing his office with that of the American president. The president is directly elected by the nation's voters for a fixed term of office. A Prime Minister, by contrast, is chosen by his colleagues in the Commons for an indefinite term. He is as likely to enter office through the resignation of his predecessor midway between elections as he is to enter office by leading his party to electoral victory. Popular endorsement, reinforced by a fixed term of office, makes the president more secure than a Prime Minister in negotiating with partisan colleagues. But the Prime Minister is stronger in the legislature, because he is the elected leader of the majority party there. The president, by contrast, can only negotiate with Congress; he cannot prove that the fate of Congressmen depends upon support for his policies. The president is, however, the undoubted leader of the federal executive. The most commanding phrase in the American executive is: "The President wants this." The equivalent phrase in Whitehall is: "The Cabinet has decided that." The Prime Minister, while the chief spokesman for the Cabinet, cannot ignore the views of his colleagues there, for if he loses the confidence of his Cabinet ministers, they may seek to supplant him, and all ministers have a common interest in opposing the issuance of Prime Ministerial *diktats*. The Prime Minister has an advantage over the president, in that his office places him at the top of a hierarchical pyramid of institutions, embracing local as well as central government. By contrast, the president must struggle to enforce wishes through a set of institutions that divide powers between federal, state, and local governments as well as separating the legislature, the judiciary, and the executive.

Every Prime Minister must live with the fact that, while he is on top of the Whitehall machine, the number of things he can himself do is limited by the number of hours in the week. (See pp. 329 ff. for the limits of his role.) The number of things that can be done by "his" government is determined by what is done within the departments that individual members of Cabinet head.

If the Cabinet is the keystone of the arch of central government, then the departments are the building blocks. Every Cabinet decision must be administered through a department, or by interdepartmental collaboration. Moreover, the limited amount of Cabinet time results in the great bulk of decisions being taken within the departments, especially if the subject matter is not expected to be a matter of political controversy. An individual minister's standing in Cabinet depends upon his ability to show in discussions with other ministers that he knows the answers to questions and criticisms from colleagues and, when necessary, can coordinate actions with other departments. From time to time, politicians or professors suggest that the involvement of Cabinet ministers in departmental affairs prevents the Cabinet from becoming a long-range planning agency. These critics usually advocate a small Cabinet of half a dozen men to act as overseers of Whitehall. No Prime Minister has accepted this view, except in wartime government. The majority have agreed with Herbert Morrison that "a Cabinet without departmental ministers would be deficient in that day-to-day administrative experience which makes a real contribution to collective decisions." [16]

There is no agreement among Prime Ministers or political scientists about the best way in which to organize the work of government or classify government departments. The last major review of the departmental structure of government, Lord Haldane's Report of 1918, noted two alternative principles: division in terms of client groups, such as pensioners, employees, or Welshmen, or organization according to the services to be performed, e.g., dividing responsibility for children among Education, Health, and custodial sections of the Home Office.[17] Every Cabinet has had some departments organized primarily in terms of clients, and other departments organized by services. As of October, 1973, departments were as follows:

Economic Affairs – The Treasury; the Department of Trade & Industry; Employment; Posts & Telecommunications; Agriculture, Fisheries & Food.

External Affairs – Foreign & Commonwealth Office; Defence; the Chancellor of the Duchy of Lancaster, responsible for Common Market relations.

Social Services – Health & Social Security; Education & Science (including the Paymaster-General, responsible for the Arts).

Environmental and Regional – Environment (including English Local Government, Housing, and Transport); the Scottish Office; the Welsh Office; the Northern Ireland Office.

16 Lord Morrison of Lambeth (Herbert Morrison), *Government and Parliament* (London: Oxford University Press, 3rd edition, 1964), p. 48.

17 For classification schemes, see W. J. M. Mackenzie, "The Structure of Central Administration", in Sir Gilbert Campion *et al.*, *British Government since 1918* (London: Allen & Unwin, 1950).

Law — Lord Chancellor's Office; Home Office; the Attorney-General and the Solicitor-General for England & Wales; the Lord Advocate and the Solicitor-General for Scotland.

Managerial and Nondepartmental — Leader of the House of Commons (job doubled with the nondepartmental portfolio of Lord President of the Council); Civil Service Department (job combined with Lord Privy Seal and Leader of the House of Lords); Parliamentary Secretary of the Treasury (i.e., Chief Whip in the House of Commons).

The compound labels and parentheses indicate the complexities of departmental structure. This is accentuated by the readiness of Prime Ministers to put new labels on old or rearranged government functions, or to abolish old titles by merging responsibilities in "superdepartments" like Environment.

One reason why departmental titles and duties can easily be altered is that government departments are not usually single-purpose institutions with a clear hierarchy of tasks, but rather an agglomeration of more or less related administrative units that have been brought together by government expansion, fission, and fusion. For example, the creation of a new department, such as the Ministry of Technology launched by the Labour Government in 1964, meant placing a newly styled Cabinet minister on top of a rearranged collection of government institutions previously responsible to a variety of ministers. Reciprocally, the abolition of the Ministry of Technology by the Conservatives in 1970 did not mean the wholesale dismissal of civil servants, but rather the reassignment of the parts of the Ministry of Technology to other ministries. The reason for the creation of the ministry was the same as the reason for its abolition: The Prime Minister of the day thought that a new institutional framework would better carry out policies in the field.[18]

The limiting consideration in the creation of a government department is the political controversy that its work will probably generate. A department cannot be any larger than a sin-

[18] For a discussion of these changes, see Sir Richard Clarke, *New Trends in Government* (London: HMSO, 1971).

gle minister can answer for in the Cabinet and in the House of Commons. For example, a department dealing routinely with a heavy volume of work, like the Post Office, required so little ministerial attention that its work was "hived off" to a separate Post Office Corporation outside the departmental framework of Whitehall. Reciprocally, as the troubles in Northern Ireland became progressively greater following the civil rights demonstrations of 1968, the duty of monitoring events there shifted from a junior minister to the Home Secretary, and then led to the creation of a separate Northern Ireland ministry. The ability of a minister to answer for a department depends in part upon the coherence of its subject matter. For example, Education & Science concerns a number of readily integrated services, whereas Environment or the Home Office concern very disparate and difficult-to-relate policies. The smaller and more homogeneous the groups being served by a department, the more coherent its work becomes. For example, the centralization of agriculture pressure groups makes the Ministry of Agriculture, Food & Fisheries, much more easily administered than the Department of Trade & Industry, which lacks comparably centralized business pressure groups. The danger of having a well-organized narrow client group is that the minister may become its captive if its appeal is politically powerful. If he has many different groups making demands upon him, he can decide how to play one off against another.

Old established departments such as the Treasury and the Home Office illustrate another important proposition: the differences between Whitehall departments. The Home Office has a staff of approximately 25,000 and the Treasury, 1,000. The Home Office has many tasks that can be kept administratively separate: police, fire, prison, drugs, cruelty to animals, control of obscene publications, and race relations. The Treasury, by contrast, has a few major interrelated tasks: management of the economy, protecting the balance of payments, and control of public expenditure. Because of the importance of its tasks, the Treasury has one-quarter more senior civil servants than the Home Office. The Home Office has more staff because of the much greater volume of its detailed routine work. The job of Home Secretary is thus much more burdensome. More paper work is required, and the Home Secretary is always vulnerable to adverse publicity, e.g., if a convicted murderer escapes from prison or a newspaper stirs up concern with drug taking. Responsibility for the economy is much more diffuse, and the Chancellor of the Exchequer has a ministerial colleague, the Chief Secretary, to carry most of the burden of managing public expenditure.

The two departments also vary greatly in procedure and style.[19] In the Home Office, there is a tradition of advice moving slowly up through the civil service hierarchy, with recommendations reflecting concern with consistency in the details of administration. For example, when the abolition of capital punishment was being debated, one Senior Home Office official opposed it on the grounds that it would be manifestly unfair to those who had already been executed. In the Treasury, by contrast, the Chancellor is more likely to receive a variety of opinions from his civil servants, and they, in turn, are likely to be as varied and changeable in their outlook as academic economists. Not least in significance is the difference in power. A Home Secretary, by virtue of his domestic responsibilities, can expect that his decisions will usually be enforced. By contrast, any Chancellor of the Exchequer has to accept that whatever he decides could be upset by international economic trends over which British government has no control.

Whatever his department, a Cabinet minister has a multiplicity of constitutional duties. First, he must represent his department in Cabinet, securing the endorsement of Cabinet colleagues for administrative and legislative actions of his department. Second, a minister must answer in Parliament for what his department does. Even if he disapproves and knew nothing about a departmental action, he must stand up for it in Parliament, because constitutional theory (if not organizational theory) stipulates that a minister, and not a civil ser-

[19] For an insider's view, from which some of the above material was drawn, see Roy Jenkins, "The Reality of Political Power," *Sunday Times*, January 17, 1972.

vant, is responsible for every action of government.[20] If the issue is a minor one, he may escape personal blame; if minor errors frequently recur, MPs may not take so lenient an attitude. Ironically, if the error is a major one, a minister may be saved from resignation because his colleagues in Cabinet, who share responsibility, will rally round to maintain confidence in the government. The minister may suffer subsequently by removal from office in a Cabinet reshuffle. A minister must also consult those most affected by his department's work, meeting delegations and inspecting departmental field offices, or seeing "on the ground" what local authorities or other assisted agencies are doing with their funds from central government. In between these tasks, a minister must also take decisions, many about minor matters requiring little more than a quick glance at the top note in a file of papers, but others of immediate or long-term significance. The greater the span of responsibilities of a department, the more a minister appears important, yet the more remote he may be from the point where decisions are taken for which he will get the credit or the blame.

Every Cabinet minister is assisted by several junior ministers assigned to his department by the Prime Minister. Junior ministers are sometimes delegated the oversight of substantial chunks of departmental work, such as race relations or prisons in the Home Office or university affairs in Education. But a junior minister cannot take a major decision of political significance. The doctrine of individual ministerial responsibility formally fixes the whole responsibility for the department upon its chief minister. While the doctrine has been increasingly infringed by the growth of large departments, no Cabinet minister can remain indifferent to his possible blame for errors made by his subordinates.

Civil servants perform the great bulk of the work done in the name of a Cabinet minister. There are substantial legal and theoretical problems in defining precisely the boundaries of the civil service in British government. The Tomlin Commission defined them as "servants of the Crown, other than

[20] See S. E. Finer, "The Individual Responsibility of Ministers," *Public Administration,* XXXIV (Winter 1956).

holders of political or judicial offices, who are employed in a civil capacity, and whose remuneration is paid wholly and directly out of monies voted by Parliament." But a legal textbook notes that in order to determine whether a given public official is a civil servant, "The facts of each appointment must be considered." [21] The Tomlin Commission's definition is particularly deficient, in that many people paid by public moneys, e.g., university professors and students in receipt of grants for studying at universities, do not think of themselves as civil servants, nor are they considered such.

The half-million people employed by the Civil Service Commission to handle the paper work and politics of central government are divided into strata unequal in size and significance. The smallest and highest stratum is the administration group. Until reforms were put into effect in 1971, this group was divided into a small administrative class, totaling about 2,500 persons at the top of the civil service, and a much larger executive class, concerned with administration of a politically nonsensitive kind. The merger of the two categories in a single administrative group has not ended the distinction in the character of the work done – nor has it altered the outlook of those recruited under the old arrangements and currently occupying the great majority of senior positions in Whitehall. Hence, the term "administrative class" will be used to refer to those 4,600 civil servants occupying posts at principal grade or above in the administration group; senior civil servants are those 1,700 persons in the post of assistant secretary or above.[22] In all, the civil service has about 60,000 staff undertaking executive class work, e.g., administering the payment of social service benefits. It has about 60,000 professional, scientific, and technical staff engaged in fields as different as engineering, accountancy, psychology, soil conservation, and keeping of museums. The largest numbers are clerical staff, assigned to

[21] E. C. S. Wade and A. W. Bradley, *Constitutional Law*, p. 218. See also, W. J. M. Mackenzie, "The Civil Service, the State and the Establishment."

[22] The Diplomatic Service is separately recruited. Its work differs in some respects from that of the home civil service discussed here, but it has a similar organizational hierarchy.

typing and filing letters and doing work with little discretion or responsibility. The civil service also includes about 200,000 industrial workers, primarily in defense work, such as making munitions.[23] While there is a significant number of professional civil servants whose salary is commensurate with that of senior civil servants, the expertise that makes them professionals has traditionally confined them to specialized tasks. The motto of the administrative class has long been: "The expert should be on tap but not on top."

The work of the administrative class is political, though civil servants usually deny that they are politicians, because of the partisan connotations of the term. Their work is political because they are not so much concerned with the details of management as they are with the implications of alternative choices and differing opinions about what government should do. It is also political inasmuch as officials are often expected to make public choices, albeit on relatively minor matters, without reference to their minister.[24]

One major concern of a senior civil servant is to look after "his" minister. The line separating administration and policy is not clearcut. It is up to civil servants to decide what problems and papers go up to the minister for decision and which do not require his sight before disposition. The most senior civil servants administer little; much of their time is spent screening materials for possible ministerial attention. They are also concerned with reviewing bulky departmental files and recommendations that come up from their juniors. Civil servants are expected to advise on the administrative practicability of any policy proposals. An active minister may have his enthusiasm dampened by a chilling note stating that a pro-

[23] For copious details of civil service staff size, see the report of The Fulton Committee, *The Civil Service,* Vol. IV, *Factual, Statistical and Explanatory Papers* (London: HMSO, 1968). The five volumes are henceforth cited as The Fulton Committee. For subsequent developments, see the Annual Report of the Civil Service Department, first issued in 1969. A general review of the post-Fulton civil service is given by John Garrett, *The Management of Government* (Harmondsworth: Penguin, 1972).

[24] For excellent sketches of how civil servants and ministers work together, see Maurice Kogan, *The Politics of Education* (Harmondsworth: Penguin, 1971).

posal is administratively impracticable. Such a statement is not a veto of ministerial action, but it is advice which cannot lightly be ignored. Civil servants are also expected to be on the alert for potentially awkward political consequences in activities of the department, to alert the minister if a public controversy threatens, and to provide him with arguments in defense of the department if a political storm breaks out.

A second major concern of senior civil servants is to look after the coordination of affairs of state. A civil servant reports to a minister. But he is also a servant of the Crown, that is to say, he also has a commitment to see that the Queen's government is carried on with economy, ease, and equity. If a minister wishes to "pull a fast one" on his colleagues in other Whitehall departments, his civil servants may quietly alert their colleagues in other departments or in the Cabinet Office, to ensure that his efforts are unsuccessful. Usually, coordination of government occurs without any conflict between ministerial and wider Whitehall loyalties. The civil service heads of the Whitehall departments meet weekly to discuss the coordination of government business, thus shadowing at official level the work of the Cabinet. Civil servants from different departments sit together on many committees concerned with interdepartmental affairs. At these committees they can agree to actions that will be consistent with their criteria for good government, secure in the knowledge that few ministers will then try to overturn what committees have already agreed. Civil servants also have a career incentive to cooperate with their opposite numbers from other departments. Administrative-class officials expect to be posted from department to department during the course of about forty years in Whitehall. People whom they face from opposing positions in one interdepartmental committee may be close colleagues another year.

Ministers and civil servants are both deeply involved in what two students of the Treasury have described as "political administration." [25] Within a department, their shared responsibility gives them common concerns. As civil servants rise in

[25] See Hugo Heclo and Aaron Wildavsky, *The Private Government of Public Money* (London: Macmillan, 1974).

the administrative hierarchy, they gain skill in performing politicians' roles and anticipating what their minister will have in mind. Reciprocally, as ministers gain experience, they learn to accept or anticipate the problems that administrators will raise about politically attractive initiatives. Civil servants usually write Cabinet papers and can substitute for ministers in negotiations with local authorities, pressure groups, nationalized industries, and other bodies outside Whitehall. Ministers and civil servants are best differentiated by the fact that the former owe their Whitehall position to party and electoral fortunes, whereas the latter owe their jobs to nonpartisan recruitment and promotion.

Ministers and civil servants usually work well together because their roles are complementary. A minister looks to his civil servants for statements of the pros and cons of alternative policy options. He also wishes them to devise ways to introduce new policies consistent with his own and his party's wishes. A minister expects his civil servants to provide him with arguments that he can use to impress listeners when representing the department in public or elsewhere in Whitehall. Most ministers express satisfaction with the advice they receive from their civil servants, and only a small fraction are very critical. The chief complaints from ministers about civil servants are that they tend to be cautious and consensual in putting forward a standard "departmental" viewpoint. Civil servants expect a minister to provide clear and meaningful guidelines for decisions delegated to them. They expect a minister to be politically effective in fighting the department's case for more resources and influence in Cabinet and elsewhere. Their chief complaints are that ministers often procrastinate in taking a decision or fail to take any decision at all, or that they argue badly in Cabinet briefs in which the department has carefully set out its case.[26]

Changes in the scale of government affect ministers and senior civil servants equally. Whitehall today passes far more legislation, spends a far larger proportion of the national income,

[26] See Bruce W. Headey, *The Job of Cabinet Minister* (Glasgow: University of Strathclyde Ph.D., 1973), especially Ch. 6.

and undertakes far more topics of significance to society than before World Wars I and II. The character of Whitehall's work is also changing. The growth of the mixed-economy welfare state has meant that government is increasingly responsible for a wide range of specialist activities, such as health care and industrial research. In addition, it is involved in positive management or encouraging managers on a scale unprecedented prior to World War II. While the size of the Cabinet has remained almost constant, from 1929 to 1966 the number of administrative-class officials increased from 1,100 to 2,500, and the number of executive-class civil servants increased more than fivefold to 83,600, as did those in the chief professional, scientific, and technical categories, rising to 84,900.[27]

These changes have, in turn, been paralleled by alterations in the institutions and procedures of Whitehall. The movement for change began in the 1960s and has not ended yet. Ministers have been less ready to accept personal responsibility for mistakes of their departments, and individual civil servants have occasionally been identified by name in the press for actions regarded as commendable or culpable. The increase in the number of ministers in each department and the recruitment of temporary advisers from outside Whitehall have reduced the lonely eminence of the responsible minister of a department. Moreover, the permanent secretary of the department is less likely today to be the sole channel for advice to the minister from very senior civil servants. Civil servants or outsiders with professional expertise are more likely to be found directly advising ministers, and technical tasks are being "hived off" from departments and placed in the hands of accountable public officials. The number of specialist classes in the civil service has been reduced, and a new Civil Service Department established specifically to manage the personnel work of government. Ministers in both parties have been ready to encourage changes that they perceive give them a wider range of advice on policy and increase their political influence. But any catalogue of trends in political administration risks exaggerating the speed and extent of change. Perma-

[27] See The Fulton Committee, Vol. IV, p. 271.

nence, not rapid change, is of the essence of a civil service. When men spend forty years with one employer, there are real constraints upon the speed with which outlooks can change. Moreover, comparison shows that many steps regarded as "major" moves toward politicizing Whitehall look like a reaffirmation of nonpartisanship and anonymity, when viewed from the perspective of Washington.[28]

One reflection of the climate for change in the Whitehall of the 1960s was the appointment of a committee under Lord Fulton, a university head, to examine the structure, recruitment, and management of the civil service. The committee compiled and published a great quantity of detailed information. Its hearings and the arguments it received strengthened a climate of opinion conducive to change. The recommendations of the committee, issued in June, 1968, were limited to matters concerning civil servants alone. Comments on the relationship of civil servants and ministers were explicitly ruled out by the Prime Minister's statement of terms of reference. Of this restriction, the Fulton Committee noted tersely, "We found at many points of our inquiry that this imposed limits on our work." A civil servant commented that this omission meant that change will be a "botching up operation," intended to ensure that "given the highly restricting and artificial conventions within which civil servants are obliged to work, they manage remarkably well." [29]

It is particularly noteworthy that major criticisms that the Fulton Committee advanced of the civil service are applicable to ministers too. For example, ministers, like civil servants, are generalists; they are not expected to have expertise or professional skills relevant to their departments. The constitutional distinctions between the responsible minister and junior min-

[28] See Lewis A. Gunn, "Politicians and Officials: Who is Answerable?" *Political Quarterly* XLIII:3 (1972) especially p. 260, and Maurice Wright, "The Professional Conduct of Civil Servants," *Public Administration* LI (Spring, 1973).

[29] See the Fulton Committee, Vol. III:2, *Surveys and Investigations,* p. 23; and *Report of the Committee,* Vol. I, pp. 94 ff, 107. See also G. W. Jones, "The Eclipse of Fulton," *New Society,* August 17, 1972; and Peta Sheriff, "Factors Affecting the Impact of the Fulton Report," *International Review of Administrative Science,* XXXVI:3 (1970).

isters are rigid, just as the divisions between civil servants and ministers and within the civil service are rigid. Neither MPs nor civil servants have training or experience of the management of large organizations, except what they learn "on the job." Ministers are shuffled from department to department in response to the political exigencies of the moment. There is little attention given to developing subject-matter expertise among junior ministers or among promising administrative-class civil servants.[30]

Because the Whitehall machine is run by a combination of ministers and civil servants working hard six or seven days a week,[31] anything that affects one part has implications for the whole system of executive government. If the calibre or skills of the civil service deteriorate, this affects what the Cabinet can achieve. If a Prime Minister or his Cabinet is uncertain or unrealistic in setting policy objectives, this affects what civil servants can achieve. When one falters, the whole falters. Insofar as the skills of civil servants are not adequate to today's problems, then the aggregate capability of government is diminished. Insofar as ministers have similar shortcomings, then the Whitehall machine will operate below capacity and below the very high levels of achievement desired by politicians.

THE ROLE OF PARLIAMENT

In its dignified aspect Parliament is very impressive. The Palace of Westminster, the meeting place of the House of Commons and the House of Lords, is a familiar symbol throughout the world. Parts of the building date back to the eleventh century; the bulk is of Victorian Gothic design, as massive as it is nonutilitarian. Officers of the House emphasize its dignity by wearing elaborate formal dress, including wigs. The late Aneurin Bevan, a left-wing Labour MP, described his first impression of Parliament as a church dedicated to "the most conservative of all religions – ancestor worship."[32]

[30] The Fulton Committee, Vol. I, pp. 11 ff.

[31] Cf. the detailed accounts of the Rt. Hon. Ernest Marples and Lord Strang, reprinted in Richard Rose, editor, *Policy-Making in Britain* (London: Macmillan, 1969).

[32] Aneurin Bevan, *In Place of Fear* (London: Heinemann, 1952), p. 6.

In terms of efficient power, Parliament is not so impressive, because its role in policy making is strictly limited. The Cabinet controls its proceedings; by convention, the Leader of the Opposition is also allowed to fix topics for debate on a limited number of days. The Prime Minister can be sure that any proposal his government puts forward will be promptly voted on in Parliament and voted on in the form desired by the executive, for the government drafts legislation and controls amendments. Furthermore, the Cabinet enjoys the powers of the purse. The budget prepared by the executive is debated at length in Parliament, but it is not altered in this process.

The limited influence of Parliament is made clear by a comparison with the United States Congress.[33] In America each of the houses of Congress controls its own proceedings, independently of the other and of the White House. When one party controls the presidency and the other Congress, claims of party reinforce autonomy. An American president can ask Congress to enact a bill, but he cannot compel it to vote on a measure, and he risks the possibility that a bill he asks for may come to him for signature with amendments that reduce or destroy its value to the White House. Last and not least, Congress can vary presidential requests for appropriations up or down. The budget that the president presents is not a final document but an attempt to get Congress to provide funds for programs of the executive departments. Congressmen invoke their budgeting powers to monitor closely executive activities throughout the year. In each of these instances Parliament lacks the powerful checks upon the executive that Congress has.

The domination of the executive over the legislature in Britain is a consequence of party discipline in the House of Commons. MPs of the majority party support Cabinet motions (and vote against those of the opposition) in order to maintain their party in control of the executive. Defeat on a vote of confidence would mean the fall of the Cabinet. MPs with ministerial ambitions are rarely given posts if they fre-

[33] For an institutional comparison, see Kenneth Bradshaw and David Pring, *Parliament and Congress* (London: Constable, 1972).

quently vote against those who control patronage. Moreover, those who elect an MP expect him to follow the party line; should an MP resign from the party and seek reelection as an independent, he will almost inevitably be rejected by those who had voted for him as the official party nominee. A survey of MPs found that three-quarters thought party discipline "just about right." In the blunt phrase of a Labour MP, George Darling:

> There is a lot of nonsense talked about party discipline, usually by so-called Liberals who haven't got a party and have the quaint notion that if they had it would work effectively as a sort of anarchists' federation.[34]

The strength of party discipline is such that a party can govern with a very small majority in the House of Commons. For example, from October, 1964, to March, 1966, the Labour government held office though it had but 317 of 630 seats in the Commons.

Within each party, discipline is most strongly endorsed by front-benchers, that is, MPs with a role as a minister or as a "shadow" spokesman on the subject for the opposition. Front-bench leaders of the parties are glad to have their positions endorsed by the feet of their back-bench MPs, tramping through the division lobbies of the Commons, even if some MPs do not endorse a measure with their hearts and minds too. MPs feel at ease voting with their colleagues, even if they consider a measure dubious. They accept the norm that partisans should vote together. To vote against the party line requires commitment to a specific political position strong enough to overcome diffuse claims of group loyalty.

Individual back-bench MPs can rebel against the party whip by abstaining or, less often, by voting against the party whip — as long as they know that such action will not bring down their government because imitated by many of their colleagues and the opposition. Party leaders are, however, always nervous about a decline in their parliamentary ma-

[34] Quoted in Rudolf Klein, "What MPs Think of their Jobs," in Bernard Crick, *The Reform of Parliament,* (London: Weidenfeld & Nicolson, 1st edition, 1964), p. 212.

jority, for this indicates publicly a loss of confidence in their leadership. In anticipation of rebellions by its own back-benchers, the governing party of the day is prepared to give way on a few features of already announced legislation to produce a united front in the Commons. Opposition leaders are prepared to moderate their views too. Very occasionally, as in the debate on entry to the European Common Market in 1971–72, the government must consider that abstentions plus votes cast with the opposition by its MPs might defeat a motion of confidence.[35] Both the government and the opposition usually experience several "rebellions" each year, in which a dozen or more MPs abstain or vote against the party whip. Ironically, the larger the majority of a governing party, the more likely it is to experience rebellion, because MPs know that by withholding support they caution rather than defeat their leadership. Many MPs will rebel against their leadership at least occasionally. Those who have most electoral security and least hope for ministerial office are especially likely to rebel; the normal sanctions of discipline mean less to them.[36]

The party line on voting in the Commons is stated officially in a weekly memorandum issued by the Chief Whip. The principal job of the Chief Whip and his assistants is to maintain a two-way flow of communication between back-bench and front-bench MPs. The Chief Whip can advise the party leader in advance of incipient rebellion. While a Prime Minister usually feels sure of a majority if a vote of confidence is pressed, he cannot strain the loyalty and confidence of his back-benchers "too often," because the Cabinet's political support in the party rests on the maintenance of vocal and uncoerced back-bench approval as well as on votes produced by the whips.

The opposition party, no matter how well it is disciplined,

[35] See Uwe Kitzinger, *Diplomacy and Persuasion*. On back-bench influence generally, see Ronald Butt, *The Power of Parliament* (London: Constable, 1969 edition).

[36] See Robert Jackson, *Rebels and Whips* (London: Macmillan, 1968); and John E. Schwarz and Geoffrey Lambert, "Career Objectives, Group Feeling and Legislative Party Voting Cohesion," *Journal of Politics*, XXXIII:2 (1971).

has virtually no hope of altering government policy by its own actions, nor can it hope to win a division in the Commons. Even if the governing party loses a division because of mismanagement by its whips, the decision can always be revoked by another vote the following day when the whips will inevitably have the party's majority present. The minority party in the Commons accepts defeat in every major parliamentary division for up to five years (the maximum statutory life of a contemporary Parliament), because it hopes for victory at the next election. It will then be able to exchange its powerless minority status for the assets of office.

In the course of a parliamentary year, the House of Commons spends far more time talking than voting. Up to half the time of the Commons is spent discussing government motions. In addition to legislation, the government must find time to arrange debates about subjects in which policy is not yet crystallized, e.g., population growth, as well as time to justify crisis action in foreign and economic affairs. About one-fifth of the time is given to the opposition to initiate debates criticizing government action or inaction. About one-sixth of the Commons's time is spent discussing motions brought forward by individual MPs, many on matters unrelated to party. The rest is absorbed by a miscellany of proceedings. The parliamentary year is longer than a British university year; the Commons meets for about 160 to 175 days annually, usually five days a week.[37]

A typical House of Commons day allows MPs to discuss a variety of topics in different procedural forms.[38] The day may begin with a morning committee meeting, although MPs with jobs outside the House object to this sacrifice of "working" time. At 2.30 P.M. the House assembles for prayers and, after procedural matters, departmental ministers answer parliamentary questions, of which they have been notified in advance by MPs of both parties. At 3.30 P.M., ministers, opposi-

[37] For details on parliamentary procedure, see, e.g., Norman Wilding and Philip Laundy, *An Encyclopedia of Parliament* (London: Cassell, 1968); and *Second Report from the Select Committee on Procedure, 1970–71* Session (London: HMSO, H. C. 538, 1971).

[38] See D. E. Butler and J. Freeman, *British Political Facts, 1900–1968,* pp. 124–5.

tion leaders, or back-benchers may raise exceptional or urgent items for brief discussion. For instance, the Prime Minister may make a statement concerning an international crisis and answer a few questions about it. Usually by 3.45 P.M. the House is dealing with its customary business, discussing pending legislation, or debating general policy questions. At 10 P.M. major debates normally end. The last half hour of each parliamentary day is reserved for an individual back-bencher to air a grievance in an adjournment debate and receive a reply from a junior minister. At all times, the intricate procedural formalities stand in contrast to the intimacy and informality of manners within the Palace of Westminster. A visitor not only sees the Royal Mace resting on the center table of the Commons, but also the feet of many Cabinet ministers, who slump down on the front benches to rest while listening to debates. During debates, members may shout interjections, heckle, or break into fits of laughter or loud protest.

The variety of parliamentary procedures for discussing public questions is important; many problems of contemporary government cannot be managed by Acts of Parliament. Problems of economic growth, industrial disputes, the balance of payments, troubles in Northern Ireland, environmental planning decisions, and a host of foreign affairs and defense questions are usually handled by decisions expressed in Cabinet or ministerial directives, rather than by Acts of Parliament. The decisions taken often require reference to an Act of Parliament, but it may be a measure passed years or centuries ago. MPs debate after the event the wisdom of discretionary decisions taken by the executive. They review, in advance of enactment, bills that propose legislation concerning many minor matters such as the carriage of goods by sea or the amendment of the copyright act, as well as major matters, such as rents, the structure of local government, or an industrial relations act. Two centuries ago Parliament could, by means of private bill legislation, concern itself with administrative details. A century ago it could introduce fundamental changes by deliberating at length about measures fully controlled by legislation, such as the reform of the franchise.[39] Today, legislative

[39] See S. A. Walkland, *The Legislative Process in Great Britain*, pp. 12 ff.

action is peripheral to many of the responsibilities of government. The policies that a Cabinet frames — in economics and foreign affairs especially — are not legal statutes, but rather statements of intentions that the government will strive to realize by actions of departmental ministers and civil servants. Parliament debates the expressions of intent and the degree of government success in realizing these intentions.

The first and foremost function of MPs is weighing men rather than weighing measures. MPs continually assess their colleagues as ministers and potential ministers. A minister may win a formal vote of confidence but lose standing among colleagues if his arguments are demolished in debate, or if he shows little understanding of the case that his civil servants have briefed him to argue. The clublike atmosphere of the Commons also permits MPs through the years to judge the personal character of their colleagues, separating those who merit trust from those who do not. By this continuing assessment of men, MPs make uncoerced judgments of the Cabinet and Opposition leadership. While this is not recorded in division lists, journalists often reflect the intangibles of confidence in their parliamentary reports.

The legislative role of Parliament is a second function. Laws are called Acts of Parliament, but they are prepared by lawyers in Whitehall acting on instructions from civil servants carrying out ministerial directives. The general principles of bills are decided by ministers, and details are discussed at length with affected and interested parties. Before a bill becomes law it must pass through a lengthy process of parliamentary scrutiny.

When a minister first announces a bill to the House of Commons, he does so briefly without debate in what is called the first reading. The bill is published and amendments received. The bill next comes before the House in a second-reading debate on its principles. The bill is discussed in detail and amendments considered. Major bills are usually debated by the Committee of the Whole House (all MPs meeting under slightly different rules of procedure). Lesser legislation is considered by standing committees containing only a fraction of the House; party discipline is effective there. If a bill has been to a standing committee, the House debates the report containing its decisions. If a bill has already been debated by the Committee of the Whole House, another debate is not necessary. The report stage is the last one at which amendments of substance can be added in a bill's progress through the Commons. Of the hundreds of amendments offered annually, more than five-sixths are minor or technical. Nearly all the amendments accepted by the Commons are on motions moved by the government to tidy up ambiguities or anomalies revealed by scrutiny in debate.[40] After amendments are disposed of, a third reading follows. The bill then goes through similar stages in the House of Lords. If passed there, it becomes an Act of Parliament by receiving the royal assent; this is now a formality. If the Lords make amendments, the bill returns to the Commons for further consideration. If the Lords refuse to pass a bill certified by the Speaker of the House of Commons as a money bill, it nonetheless becomes law within a month after it leaves the Commons. Less urgent but important bills can be enacted into law if twice approved by the Commons, even if the Lords reject them twice in successive annual sessions. The House of Lords can thus delay but not defeat a bill.

A third function of Parliament is to scrutinize the administration of laws. Since new legislation constitutes a minute portion of the law that Whitehall is administering at any one time, this is a substantial task. An MP may write directly to a minister, questioning a seemingly anomalous or unfair departmental decision or policy called to his attention by a constituent or a pressure group. If the MP is not satisfied with the results of this review, he can raise the issue at question time in the Commons.[41] MPs can also raise administrative issues at greater length in the daily adjournment debate. The knowledge that dissatisfaction with a private reply can lead to public

[40] See Valentine Herman, "Backbench and Opposition Amendments to Government Legislation" in Dick Leonard and Valentine Herman, *The Backbencher and Parliament* (London: Macmillan, 1972).

[41] See D. N. Chester and N. Bowring, *Questions in Parliament* (Oxford: Clarendon Press, 1962); Anthony Barker and Michael Rush, *The Member of Parliament and his Information* (London: Allen & Unwin, 1970), pp. 140 ff; and John Rose, "Questions in the House," in Dick Leonard and Valentine Herman, *The Backbencher and Parliament*.

debate ensures that correspondence from back-bench MPs is given special attention within the minister's private office. The minister may reaffirm departmental policy so convincingly that his questioner will not wish to pursue the matter further. He may decide to alter policy to avoid a repetition of embarrassing questions on a point. In more than one-fifth of adjournment debates, a minister makes a positive response to his critic.[42] If a minister is persistently in trouble with backbenchers on administrative issues and fails to convince his colleagues by his replies, the Prime Minister may resolve the difficulty by changing the minister. Since 1967, MPs can request the Parliamentary Commissioner for Administration (also known as the Ombudsman, after his Danish prototype) to investigate complaints about maladministration by central government departments. Many fields of inquiry are excluded by the Commissioner's terms of reference; in his first two years of work nearly three-fifths of all complaints received were rejected as outside his jurisdiction. The Commissioner's findings are reported to Parliament for debate. He has no power to order the reversal of a government decision.[43]

The House of Commons also uses committees to scrutinize administration. A small group of men can give more time to an issue than can be given on the floor of the House. Moreover, committees can interview civil servants and other experts, as well as receive written reports. One type of committee is primarily concerned with reports from expert staff about matters of administration. For example, the Public Accounts Committee, always chaired by a leading Opposition MP, reviews government expenditure after the event, publicizing instances of waste and financial mismanagement. Its existence as a watchdog is a caution to administrators of public money. The Statutory Instruments Committee scrutinizes

[42] See Valentine Herman, "Adjournment Debates in the House of Commons," in Dick Leonard and Valentine Herman, *The Backbencher and Parliament.*

[43] Cf. Frank Stacey, *The British Ombudsman* (Oxford: Clarendon Press, 1971); Rudolf Klein's review, *New Society,* November 11, 1971; and Roy Gregory and Alan Alexander, "Our Parliamentary Ombudsman," *Public Administration,* L (Autumn 1972), p. 331.

regulations laid down by the executive under powers delegated by Act of Parliament. It can call the attention of the House to statutory instruments that it believes inconsistent with parliamentary practice and legislation. A Select Committee on Expenditure, introduced in the 1970–71 session of Parliament, reviews the long-term expenditure implications of the annual government budgets, as well as examining the priorities established in the budget. It has yet to establish itself as effective in publicizing or influencing expenditure policies of the executive. The Select Committee on Nationalized Industries scrutinizes a major field of public administration not amenable to normal forms of parliamentary investigation, because nationalized industries are managed by boards appointed by ministers. Select committees are also established on an ad hoc basis to deliberate upon such matters as electoral law reform, or to inquire into unusual events, such as a parliamentary scandal.

In response to demands by back-bench MPs and academics, a series of specialist committees was established on an experimental basis, commencing in 1966. These have concerned such matters as Science and Technology, Scottish Affairs, Overseas Aid, Education and Science, Race Relations, and the Parliamentary Commissioner. Back-benchers tend to favor specialist committees.[44] Front-benchers, and especially serving ministers, generally oppose powerful committees because they do not wish to encourage additional parliamentary criticism of their work. Ironically, as committees move from discussion of detail to more general questions of political principle, ministers can feel more secure because on questions of confidence in policy, party discipline predetermines the committee's verdict.

A fourth function of MPs – what Bagehot called "the expressive function" – is to voice political ideas, privately as well as publicly. Within the governing party, ministers usually talk informally with back-benchers prior to making major decisions on legislation; each minister has a parliamentary private

[44] Anthony Barker and Michael Rush, *The Member of Parliament and his Information,* pp. 149 ff. See also, contributions by Nevil Johnson and H. Victor Wiseman in A. H. Hanson and Bernard Crick, editors, *The Commons in Transition* (London: Fontana, 1970).

secretary to collect views about departmental policy from back-benchers. Both parliamentary parties have specialist committees that meet privately; these committees shadow government departments. If rebuffed in private conversations and meetings, back-benchers can carry their disagreements to the floor of the Commons, putting down early-day motions critical of their leaders. While these motions are not debated, they will get publicity if a substantial number of MPs sign.[45] MPs can also speak against their own front-bench in a debate, even though the whips will expect them to vote with the minister in the division that ends it.

Bernard Crick has argued that Parliament has a fifth function, that of sustaining a continuous election campaign by placing facts and fancies before the electorate.[46] The government can use parliamentary publicity to mobilize consent for policies that require popular participation, e.g., economic growth. The opposition can use Parliament to influence the electorate to withdraw its consent, and the governing party may alter policies in anticipation of a general election defeat. Parliamentary debate may also have what Bagehot called a "teaching function," educating voters in the meaning of important public issues and relating specific problems to more general political values.

The weakness in theories of the impact of Parliament on popular opinion is the assumption that voters are as interested in Parliament as are MPs or professors of politics. There is much evidence to the contrary. The average daily sale of *Hansard,* the journal containing a verbatim report of parliamentary debates, is about 2,000 copies. Only the quality newspapers read by one-tenth of the electorate report in any detail speeches made in the Commons. Radio and television news programs often use stories based on parliamentary debates, but as cameras and tape recorders are barred from the Palace

[45] See Anthony Barker and Michael Rush, *The Member of Parliament and his Information,* and S. E. Finer, H. B. Berrington, and D. J. Bartholomew, *Backbench Opinion in the House of Commons, 1955–59* (Oxford: Pergamon, 1961).

[46] *The Reform of Parliament* (revised 2nd edition, 1970), p. 238. See also S. H. Beer, "The British Legislature and the Problem of Mobilizing Consent," in Elke Frank, editor, *Lawmakers in a Changing World* (Englewood Cliffs, N.J.: Prentice-Hall, 1966).

of Westminster, their reports are secondhand. One reason why broadcasting is barred is that many MPs fear that broadcasting authorities would regard only the high spots of a day's debates as newsworthy. MPs gain a mass audience by leaving the Palace of Westminster to record their views for a broadcast. The public's lack of interest in parliamentary debate is matched by that of MPs. A survey found that only one-sixth of back-benchers regularly listen to their colleagues make speeches; another two-fifths regularly listen to speeches on topics of interest. Less than one-third of MPs read or skim *Hansard*. The majority rely on press reports to tell them what is said on the floor of the House.[47]

A newly elected MP, contemplating his role as one among 635 [48] individuals in the House of Commons, immediately notices the advantages that election brings. Remarks that went unnoticed when he was a private citizen now almost automatically appear in print. He is able to direct inquiries to any branch of British government and expect prompt, courteous, and full answers. As an MP, he will have the opportunity to meet people in many different walks of life, and travel at government expense or at the expense of an interest group. A person wishing to augment his income can find that Parliament opens opportunities for free-lance journalism and a variety of part-time consulting posts. The Palace of Westminster also provides most of the facilities of a first-class London club.

By the time an MP has drawn his first year's salary, he has begun to note the shortcomings of parliamentary life. The pay is calculated to permit MPs without outside earnings "to live and maintain themselves at a modest but honourable level." [49]

47 See Anthony Barker and Michael Rush, *The Member of Parliament and his Information*, pp. 135 ff; Ronald Butt, *The Power of Parliament*, ch. 15; and David Butler and Donald Stokes, *Political Change in Britain*; p. 425.

48 The redistribution of seats to accommodate population shifts increases the total size of the Commons to 635 MPs in the Parliament to be elected in 1974 or 1975.

49 See *Report of the Committee on the Remuneration of Ministers and Members of Parliament* (London: HMSO, Cmnd. 2516, 1964), paragraph 35; and, latterly, *Remuneration of Ministers and Members of Parliament* (London: HMSO, Cmnd. 4836, 1971). On back-bench life generally, see Peter G. Richards, *The Backbenchers* (London: Faber, 1972).

The expense allowance of MPs often fails to cover costs arising from maintaining a home in London and in a constituency distant from London. Back-bench MPs and Opposition front-benchers lack the personal staff that Congressmen enjoy. Office and secretarial facilities are grudgingly made available and may involve extra expense. The lack of services for MPs reflects the historic definition of the role as a part-time job for a wealthy person. A 1967 survey found that two-thirds of Conservative MPs had part-time jobs, whereas three-quarters of Labour MPs made politics their sole occupation.[50] Conservatives usually argue that work outside the Commons keeps them in touch with the "real-world" problems of an ordinary citizen. Labour MPs argue that it is a full-time job to keep in touch with the world of politics. Differences in occupational backgrounds also help explain party differences in MPs' attitudes. A Labour MP who was formerly a teacher or a coal miner cannot carry on his work while simultaneously sitting in the Commons; a Conservative barrister or company director can.

Once in the House, every back-bencher is faced with a wide choice of alternative roles. He may decide to do no more than meet the whip's expectations of a party loyalist, voting as the leadership decides, without taking part in deliberations about policy. If he does wish to be more than a name in a division list, an MP must decide whether to make his mark by brilliance in debate, willingness to attend routine committee meetings as an acknowledged spokesman for a pressure group, or in a nonpartisan way, e.g., as a House wit or chairman of its kitchen committee.[51]

The chief political role open to every MP is that of advocate. MPs can use the facilities of the House of Commons to publicize causes that they feel are neglected or misunderstood. Individual MPs have become known as advocates for causes as disparate as world government (not yet realized), a revolving toothbrush (realized without legislation), or abortion law

[50] See Anthony Barker and Michael Rush, *The Member of Parliament and his Information,* p. 373.

[51] See Richard Rose, *People in Politics,* pp. 98 ff.

reform (realized without implicating the parties in a controversial matter). MPs may get together with like-minded colleagues to form "ginger groups" to push the Labour leadership left or the Conservative leadership to the right, according to their ideological views. Many MPs are recognized spokesmen for an interest group. Some represent interests with which they were identified long before entering Parliament. An accountant may speak for an association of accountants, and a former miner may receive financial aid from the National Union of Mineworkers. An MP can accept a retainer to advocate a point of view in Parliament as long as he declares his interest before speaking. An MP is usually expected to speak for constituency interests, though his constituents accept that party discipline will prevent him from voting with a constituency interest against the party policy when these are in conflict. An MP can use the grievance procedures of Whitehall to speak (or write letters on behalf of) individually aggrieved constituents. Most MPs also hold "surgeries" ["clinics"] in their constituency at least once a month. Constituents can attend to pour out personal problems to a sympathetic listener, even if it is a problem that central government cannot put right.[52] When in his constituency, an MP visits party officials to make sure that whatever their views, they do not voice grievances about the work of their MP.

Ironically, the one role that an MP will rarely undertake is that of legislator. Each year the government sets aside a small amount of time for MPs to introduce private members' bills. MPs ballot for this privilege. Because government support is not assured, only 40 per cent of these bills pass, an average of about eight a session.[53] A number are noncontroversial measures, concerning such things as unsightly litter or miscellaneous provisions of law reform. A substantial number of private members' bills concern issues so controversial that neither front-bench will take responsibility. For example, the legaliza-

[52] See Robert E. Dowse, "The MP and his Surgery," *Political Studies*, XI:3 (1963); Anthony Barker and Michael Rush, *The Member of Parliament and his Information*, pp. 173 ff.

[53] See Dick Leonard, "Private Members' Bills since 1959," in Leonard and Valentine Herman, *The Backbencher and Parliament*.

tion of abortion and homosexuality and easier grounds for divorce were private members' bills. Many reform measures take years to pass because, without whips to enforce discipline, groups of MPs can obstruct a bill as successfully in the Commons as their counterparts can in Congress.

The House of Lords, the upper chamber of the British Parliament, is unusual because it is primarily a hereditary institution. In addition to hereditary peers, whose recent or remote ancestors have been ennobled for their activities, the Lords include up to eleven judges sitting as Lords of Appeal in Ordinary, twenty-six bishops of the Church of England, peers who have had hereditary titles conferred for their public services, and, since 1958, distinguished men and women appointed to life peerages. (Members of the Royal Family are disqualified from sitting in the Lords, although holding titles.) Hereditary peers constitute the majority of members of the Lords, but they do not dominate its proceedings. About one-third of the hereditary peers attend the Lords less than once a year. Only one-seventh of the Lords attend at least half its sessions. Many of the active peers are retired members of the House of Commons, who find the three-afternoons-a-week pace of the Lords suited to their advancing years. Life peers, numbering more than 150 members of the Lords, can speak from extraparliamentary experience in varied walks of life: industry, finance, trade unions, education, and the mass media.[54]

Like the House of Commons, the Lords is an electoral chamber, weighing men as fit or unfit for ministerial office. Because of the high average age of peers, few expect office; only in the Conservative ranks are there younger peers seeking to establish themselves politically. Since 1963 the most politically ambitious can disclaim a hereditary peerage and stand for the House of Commons. Because convention requires that every minister be a Member of Parliament, a seat in the Lords can be given a minister brought in from outside Westminster to

[54] For attendance figures, see Bernard Crick, *The Reform of Parliament,* revised 2nd edition, p. 137, and J. R. Vincent, "The House of Lords," *Parliamentary Affairs,* XIX:4 (1966).

contribute his expertise to government. Once in office, the minister will have to prove his worth in debate in the Lords, an audience less difficult than that of the Commons but able to observe failure if an outsider does not adapt himself to Westminster ways of thought. The absence of any constituency responsibility gives a peer an advantage in a post requiring much traveling, such as the Foreign Office, or in a post in which freedom from constituency pressures might be useful, such as race relations.

The Lords' power to reject bills passed by the House of Commons was formidable until the Parliament Act of 1911 abolished its unlimited right of veto, substituting instead the power to delay the enactment of legislation. Since the Parliament Act of 1949, this delay can be little more than one year. The power of delay is specially significant in the year before a general election – though governments try to avoid controversial legislation in this period. The Lords wish to avoid rejecting measures from the Commons, because this raises questions about their status. The Lords cannot claim to represent the nation, because they are neither elected popularly, nor are they drawn from anything like a cross section of the population. Moreover, the Lords have always had a Conservative majority. Before the passage of the Life Peerages Act, Conservatives outnumbered Labour peers by about eight to one; since then, the Conservative advantage over Labour has been three to one.[55] Occasionally, the Lords have used their powers to delay the passage of a major Labour government bill, or to oppose a nonparty measure, e.g., the abolition of capital punishment; incidentally, opinion surveys showed the Lords more nearly reflected public opinion than the elected Commons. The use of delaying powers is exceptional; the threat of their use occasionally worries a government, especially a Labour government.

The Lords can initiate or amend legislation. The government of the day often introduces legislation in the Lords if it deals with technical matters, such as the consolidation of

[55] See Bernard Crick, *The Reform of Parliament,* revised 2nd edition, p. 108.

previous Acts of Parliament or law reform. Other Lords' bills deal with nonparty matters, such as legislation affecting animals. The government of the day can use the Lords as a revising chamber to incorporate amendments suggested in debate in either chamber. Members of the upper house can also introduce private peers' bills. In three sessions from 1968 to 1971 the Lords' initiated on average nineteen bills annually.[56]

Like the Commons, the Lords can discuss public issues without reference to legislation. The government or opposition may initiate a debate on foreign affairs, or individual backbenchers may raise on their own initiative such topics as pornography or the future of hill farming. Peers may use their right to question ministers to scrutinize administration. Because peers have no electoral constituency, it would be considered constitutionally improper for peers to interfere with elections to the Commons. Press coverage is slight. A peer who wishes to influence public opinion is more likely to get publicity if he makes his remarks on a public platform outside the Palace of Westminster than if he records his thoughts in the little-read House of Lords *Hansard*. Debates in the Lords have their chief audience within Westminster. A survey of peers found that 56 per cent thought civil servants regularly noted what the Lords said, and 44 per cent thought ministers paid attention to their deliberations. The House of Commons was reckoned to be less attentive: only 7 per cent thought MPs regularly paid heed to Lords' debates. Subsequently, a survey of MPs found them distant and unenthusiastic about the Lords. Five-sixths of Labour MPs paid little or no attention to its debates, and half the Conservative MPs said the same.[57]

The limited influence of both Houses of Parliament has led to much discussion of the reform of Parliament by MPs, active peers, and students of politics. In the early 1960s, some writers acted as if parliamentary reform might resolve the problems

[56] See Ivor Burton and Gavin Drewry, "Public Legislation: A Survey of the Session 1970/71," *Parliamentary Affairs*, XXV:2 (1972), pp. 126, 145 ff.

[57] See Anthony Barker and Michael Rush, *The Member of Parliament and his Information*, pp. 144–47; and Peter Bromhead and David Shell, "The Lords and their House," *Parliamentary Affairs*, XX:4 (1967), pp. 342 ff.

facing the country. Less ambitious proponents of change argued that the increased involvement of government in so many spheres of life required an increased role for the House of Commons as the representative of the governed. MPs have demanded more information about what is going on in Whitehall. The case for greater collective facilities has been reinforced by a claim for greater facilities for individual members: a proper office, a full-time secretary, a proper expense allowance, and even, some argue, a political assistant.[58] The publicly provided facilities of an American congressman are the envy of many British MPs. The demand for change has come particularly from younger MPs who see the role as a full time job: They wish to make their job as interesting and important as possible.

The demands for reform have resulted in many minor changes in Parliament since 1964.[59] MPs are gradually getting better office space, secretarial assistance, and more generous expense allowances. The establishment of a number of specialist committees has given MPs more opportunities to scrutinize administration and policy, but has brought rebuffs from the executive. For example, committees have been denied full-time staff assistance or funds for much travel. The specialist committees have yet to establish themselves securely within Parliament, let alone to demonstrate strength *vis à vis* Whitehall. Procedural reforms allow more time for MPs' voices to be heard but do not necessarily give them more to say.

Reform of the House of Lords has been at a standstill since 1963. In 1968, the Labour government proposed a bill to alter the Lords substantially; among other things, the government of the day was to be given substantial patronage powers to ensure it a working majority in the Lords at all times. Backbench MPs in both parties forced the government to withdraw its awkwardly drafted bill.[60] Ironically, the hereditary basis of

[58] For discussions of MPs' views, see Anthony Barker and Michael Rush, *The Member of Parliament and his Information*, pp. 378 ff.

[59] For a variety of studies of reform, see A. H. Hanson and Bernard Crick, editors, *The Commons in Transition.*

[60] See Bernard Crick, *The Reform of Parliament,* revised 2nd edition, ch. 5 ff. For the earlier Lords, see P. A. Bromhead, *The House of Lords and Contemporary Politics, 1911–1957* (London: Routledge, 1958).

the Lords so weakens it that it can survive unreformed. No government has feared the Lords sufficiently to give a high priority to the complex task of altering it. Peers wish to avoid a head-on clash with the government of the day for fear it may force a final solution.

Reform proposals have languished because proponents of reform disagree about what part Parliament should take in government. Some reformers believe that Parliament should have powers to prevent executive actions, whereas others simply wish greater powers to scrutinize and criticize. The former group wishes to transfer power from Whitehall to the House of Commons; the latter, to improve the work of Whitehall by correcting its oversights and errors at the Palace of Westminster. Reformers also disagree about the role of an individual MP. Some assume that being an MP is a full-time job and that facilities should be appropriated. Others argue that day-and-night immurement in the Palace of Westminster would make MPs very remote from those they claim to represent. Proposals to reform the House of Lords reveal a similar division of outlooks. Labour MPs wish to weaken it by reform, whereas many Conservatives and peers wish reform to strengthen the Lords.

The most important obstacle to reform reflects the greatest grievance of back-bench reformers: The power of decision rests with the Cabinet and not with the House of Commons as a whole. Whatever MPs say in opposition or on the back-benches, once in Cabinet office they argue that the present powers of Parliament are all that the executive can allow or afford. Back-bench MPs of both parties thus develop skepticism of the executive. Only one-sixth think that ministers wish to see them well informed about the work of Whitehall. The great majority think that ministers prefer to limit MPs' knowledge of what goes on inside Whitehall.[61]

The result is that the Whitehall machine, rather than Parliament, is the prime law-making body. A government can be virtually certain of getting a major piece of legislation ap-

[61] Anthony Barker and Michael Rush, *The Member of Parliament and his Information,* p. 363.

proved by Parliament within a single annual session. In the course of a year, a government can pass thirty to forty bills.[62] In an emergency, it can pass a major bill in weeks or days. Parliamentary scrutiny of administration is a potential restraint upon busy ministers and mammoth departments, but the time available for scrutiny is limited. The dilemma of critics is that time can be used to scrutinize administration in detail or to criticize the principles underlying government measures. The latter course has broader significance – but it also has less immediate chance of changing the actions of government.

Parliament restrains government in two major ways. First, back-bench MPs, especially in the governing party, continually voice demands that the government "do something" about an issue or clamor that "the public will not stand for" what the government is proposing to do about an issue. MPs have many opportunities to make their views heard, privately as well as publicly. Although MPs sometimes make the government alter its course, they cannot dictate what response the government makes to their pressure. MPs can only demand action in general terms, or denounce specific government initiatives without enacting alternatives in their own right.

The second constraint upon government arises from the limited amount of parliamentary time available for legislation in a year. The work of government has increased greatly in the past century, but the number of hours that the House sits annually has varied little. It sat an average of 1,178 hours a year in 1885–94, and 1,275 hours annually, 1955–1964. The procedures of the Commons make the introduction of a major bill a lengthy and tiring effort for the minister involved. He must be prepared to explain and defend it clause by clause as the House discusses it in principle and in technical detail. MPs waiting unsuccessfully for time to speak in a major debate have as their counterparts Cabinet ministers waiting to get authorization from the Cabinet to put a major bill forward

62 See Ivor Burton and Gavin Drewry, "Public Legislation: 1970/71," and article, on earlier sessions by the same authors, *Parliamentary Affairs,* XXIII:2 (1970), and XXIII:4 (1970).

in Parliament. Some three-hundred proposals are put to Cabinet annually by ministers; only one-sixth succeed in gaining a place in the year's parliamentary timetable.[63] The dignified procedures of Parliament become an efficient limit upon the work of Whitehall. But the power to limit the executive is not the power to direct it.

THE ROLE OF LAW

The role of law is narrowly defined in England today. In centuries past, judges enunciated the doctrine of "the rule of law" in efforts to restrain royal absolutism. In the twentieth century, English judges have adopted a self-denying policy. They do not consider themselves arbiters of what government may or may not do. Instead, they assert that it is up to Parliament (acting under the direction of the Cabinet of the day) to decide what government can do. Unlike courts in America, English courts claim no power to declare an Act of Parliament unconstitutional, nor will they accept a claim that an act should be set aside because it conflicts with a previous Act of Parliament, or what claimants describe as natural rights. English judges believe that "an unwritten constitution must be constantly made and unmade," but they want no part of the job: "That is for Parliament and the electorate".[64] The final court of appeal is political rather than judicial.

Instead of providing judicial review of the constitutionality of an act, as is done in America, the courts determine whether the executive acts within its statutory powers. If its action is *ultra vires* (i.e., outside its powers), the courts can order central government or a local authority to desist from an action because of a lack of statutory authority. The courts can also quash an action if it is undertaken in a procedurally improper manner. But if a statute delegates discretion to a public authority, the courts do not question the reasonableness or motives with which the executive exercises its discretion. Even

[63] See D. N. Chester, "The British Parliament, 1939–66," *Parliamentary Affairs,* XIX:4 (1966), p. 429; and Lord Morrison of Lambeth, *Government and Parliament,* Ch. 11.

[64] Louis L. Jaffe, *English and American Judges as Lawmakers* (Oxford: Clarendon Press, 1969), p. 4.

if the courts rule against the executive, the effect of a judgment can be canceled by a subsequent Act of Parliament giving statutory sanction to actions that the courts had found lacking in authority. The government can also retrospectively provide statutory justification for what the courts ruled should not be done. For example, in 1965 the Burmah Oil Company won a law suit claiming government compensation for property damaged in World War II. The government promptly passed a retrospective act abolishing the grounds for claiming compensation. On February 23, 1972, a Northern Ireland High Court, in deciding a case brought by a minority MP, John Hume, declared that the British Army had no authority to carry out a variety of actions against civilians in Ulster. That afternoon the Home Secretary introduced a bill in the House of Commons to legalize British Army actions retrospectively. The bill, overriding the Court's judgment, was approved by both Houses of Parliament the same day.[65]

Judicial avoidance of political matters is specially noteworthy inasmuch as the highest court is a committee of the House of Lords, consisting of the Lords of Appeal in Ordinary. These law lords are entitled to participate in debates and divisions of the upper chamber. When they do speak or vote, it is usually about legal matters. Even when judicial opinions have drawn attention to defects in existing statutes, law lords have hesitated to campaign to modify defective statutes.[66] The task of suggesting amendments and improvements in the large mass of statute law that has accrued through the centuries belongs to the English Law Commission, established in 1965. Most of these statutes, like the great majority of cases coming before courts at all levels of jurisdiction, concern criminal cases or civil actions far removed from major questions of constitutional law.

The desire to keep the courts out of politics is also shown in the field of industrial relations. Once unions gained legal recognition and immunities, their leaders opposed the use of

[65] See House of Commons, *Debates*, Vol. 831, Cols. 1285–1454 (February 23, 1972).

[66] See Gavin Drewry and Jenny Morgan, "Law Lords as Legislators," *Parliamentary Affairs*, XXII:3 (1969), p. 236.

legislation to establish trade union rights enforceable through the courts, and opposed granting employers rights enforceable through the courts. Trade union officials have suspected that judges would be unsympathetic with the aims and procedures of unions and have also disliked the cost and risk involved in court action. Employers have not sought judicial resolution of industrial disputes because they have not considered it likely, on balance, to improve industrial relations. When the Conservative government introduced a novel Industrial Relations Act in 1972, it also established a specialized court to avoid involving ordinary courts with this politically explosive subject. When union members defied the initial rulings of the special Industrial Relations Court, the judges and law officers of government went to exceptional lengths to minimize problems arising from the strikers' unwillingness to accept the law.

An Englishman who believes that the government has denied him basic rights will find it difficult to get the courts to redress his grievance.[67] There are no primary rules in the unwritten constitution or in constitutionlike documents that the citizen can invoke in pleading his rights against an Act of Parliament. The United States Constitution entrenches individual rights as superior to statute law in its Bill of Rights. By contrast, the English Bill of Rights of 1689 is primarily concerned with limiting royal power *vis à vis* Parliament and ensuring a Protestant crown. As long as the government has statutory authority for its actions, the courts will uphold them. The government's statutory powers can be so broad as to sanction almost anything, as wartime examples illustrate. In 1940, Parliament passed in one day an Emergency Powers (Defence) Act that empowered the government to compel persons "to place themselves, their services and their property at the disposal of His Majesty." In the wartime case of *Liversidge* v. *Sir John Anderson,* the courts ruled that a statute could delegate to the minister the power to detain anyone whom he suspected of conduct prejudicial to public safety, without answering to

[67] For discussions of civil liberties and the law, see Harry Street, *Freedom, the Individual and the Law* (Harmondsworth: Penguin, 1963); and David Williams, *Keeping the Peace* (London: Hutchinson, 1967).

the court for the reasonableness of his action. In 1968 a Labour Government enacted a bill to restrict the entry to Britain of persons of Asian origin domiciled in Kenya, notwithstanding the fact that they held British citizenship. A member of the Labour Cabinet, R.H.S. Crossman, later commented that the measure "would have been declared unconstitutional in any country with a written constitution and a Supreme Court." [68]

In the great majority of cases in which Englishmen believe the government is acting wrongly, the point at issue is not a charge of treason or the denial of *habeas corpus* but some point of administration concerning welfare benefits, planning permission for a house, or similar questions. The ancient doctrine that the Crown can do no wrong has created difficulties for the adjudication of disputes in which the government or its agents is one of the parties. Many of these problems were resolved by the Crown Proceedings Act, 1947, which allowed the Crown to be sued by ordinary legal processes in a number of instances. But Crown privilege can still be claimed to prevent the production of documents if the executive deems this against the public interest. As government is involved annually in hundreds of thousands of administrative actions giving potential grounds for grievance, administrative tribunals have been established to hear complaints by citizens against a government department. These specialized tribunals deal with problems such as land and property, pensions and national assistance, the health service, the military, transport, and income tax. The Council of Tribunals, established in 1958, oversees the procedures that these quasi-judicial bodies use.[69]

The powers of British government are constrained in spite of rather than because of formal institutions of the law. Englishmen voice fewer complaints about the denial of civil liberties or due process of the law than do citizens in many

[68] "Understanding the Profusion of Shrinking Violets," *The Times*, September 6, 1972.

[69] See, e.g., J. A. G. Griffith and Harry Street, *Principles of Administrative Law* (London: Pitman, 4th edition, 1967); and H. W. R. Wade, *Towards Administrative Justice* (Ann Arbor, Michigan: University of Michigan Press, 1963).

countries with written constitutions, bills of rights, and established procedures for judicial review. In the words of Lord Wright in the Liversidge case:

> In the Constitution of this country, there are no guaranteed or absolute rights. The safeguard of British liberty is in the good sense of the people and in the system of representative and responsible government which has been evolved.[70]

The role of the police further emphasizes the importance of mutual trust between governors and governed. The police work on the assumption that their authority will be generally accepted, and those they seek to apprehend are outlawed socially as well as being outside the criminal law. A long tradition of nonviolence allows police to patrol unarmed; criminals are expected to be unarmed too. To an extent that is outstanding in any international comparison, the police in England are regarded with respect. A national survey found that more than 90 per cent of the English people consider the police helpful, polite, fair, efficient, and honest.[71] This does not mean that policemen are never criticized. Those in frequent contact with the police, whether professional criminals, social deviants, or organizers of extremist political demonstrations, often regard the police antagonistically. They cite instances in which the discretionary authority of the police is used in ways that are wrong by the standards of deviants or wrong by more widely held public standards. The crucial point here is that individual policemen guilty of wrongdoing are considered atypical by the mass of the population, rather than normal figures in an urban landscape.

In England, unlike troubled European societies, the government has no paramilitary security force to compel obedience to the law, or anything like the American National Guard for use in the event of domestic political disorder. Eng-

[70] G. Le May, *British Government, 1914–1953* (London: Methuen), p. 332.

[71] See the report of an Opinion Research Centre poll in the *Sunday Times,* December 21, 1969. For fuller views, compare the Royal Commission on the Police (London: HMSO, Cmnd. 1728, 1962), and Jenifer Hart, "Some reflections on the Report," reprinted in Richard Rose, editor, *Policy-Making in Britain.*

land's insular position made the Royal Navy its prime armed service; by its nature, the Navy could not deploy its force for use within Britain. The Army is almost never used to enforce public order within England. It is used domestically as a source of ready manpower in an emergency, whether a flood, a railway wreck, or a strike in a major public service.

The British Army has been trained for use in outposts of empire in other continents; hence, it has always been a dispersed as well as a relatively small force. Historically, an army officer's career has not been regarded as a professional commitment to military values and military concerns. Instead, it has traditionally been a job that a gentleman could hold without losing social status, and an aspiring gentleman could take to enhance his status. Because British soldiers have been gentlemen as well as officers, they have never constituted a military clique within government — nor have retired soldiers in the House of Commons or the House of Lords formed a significant military lobby.[72] The historic complaint about the British Army is that it has been more concerned with the social status of regiments and of officers within regiments than with their technical capabilities. Reforms introduced since World War II have made the military more professional, albeit in circumstances in which the army's place in public life has been declining.

The importance of English attitudes in maintaining law and order is best demonstrated by a comparison with Northern Ireland, the most disorderly part of the United Kingdom. Westminster has never been successful in efforts to import English institutions of police, courts, or military organization into any part of Ireland, because these institutions can operate only with the full consent of the population. Consent has not been granted by Irish Republicans, and has been given contingently by Ulster Protestants determined to maintain their own political hegemony. The initial Westminster reaction to the civil rights disorders in Ulster was to encourage the Northern Ireland government to imitate English procedures.

[72] See Simon Raven, "Perish by the Sword," in Hugh Thomas, editor, *The Establishment* (London: Blond, 1959).

For example, following the 1969 Belfast riots, the Hunt Committee on the Royal Ulster Constabulary recommended that the police divest themselves of arms and change their uniform color from Irish green to English blue. Its recommendation failed to bring order. The British Army increasingly adapted its attitudes to Irish circumstances. In August, 1971, the British government was justifying internment of hundreds of Catholics suspected of subversive opinions or activities, even though this violated the European Convention of Human Rights. The government argued that internment was being carried out under the authority of an Act of Parliament. By February, 1973, it was interning Protestants too. Such actions show the inability to export England's rule of law to all parts of the United Kingdom.[73]

GOVERNING STYLE

A century ago Bagehot described British government as simple: "The ultimate power upon all questions is in the hands of the same persons." By contrast, American government was seen as composite: "The supreme power is divided between many bodies and functionaries." [74] American government is still composite, but British government is no longer simple. Today, British government is best characterized as "mixed" government. Whitehall departments have a mixture of functions, writing laws, administering them, and overseeing the adjudication of resulting disputes. Parliament is more concerned with the conduct of the executive than with the drafting of bills. The courts assess how the executive applies laws; they do not judge whether Parliament has the power to act. The operation of this mixture of institutions is affected by the style of governing,[75] as well as by formal structures.

The mid-Victorian faith in simplicity remains important today in how men think and act. Englishmen, especially those who work in Westminster, believe that there ought to be a

[73] See Richard Rose, *Governing without Consensus,* Chs. 4, 15.

[74] W. Bagehot, *The English Constitution,* p. 201. See also, Malcolm Shaw, *Anglo-American Democracy* (London: Routledge, 1968).

[75] See, e.g., Richard A. Chapman and A. Dunsire, *Style in Administration* (London: Allen & Unwin, 1971).

single place of decision. Whether it be Parliament, the Cabinet, or the Prime Minister's office is a secondary point. Public officials act as if their powers are as great and as centralized as their responsibilities imply. Notwithstanding the buffetings to which every British government is subjected by external pressures, belief in the power of government remains strong.

One reason why British government can still appear unitary is that it is in many crucial respects still run as a small-scale institution. The center of government is not dispersed along the Thames as the United States federal government is dispersed along the Potomac. Instead, it is drawn together in Whitehall. While civil servants and ministers are not expected to reside in Whitehall (except for the Prime Minister and a few very senior colleagues), they spend most of their waking hours together there, developing an intimacy like that found within an Oxford college or an American college fraternity, rather than resembling something as sprawling as the metropolitan University of London or the University of California. Within this village, everyone knows everyone else. Ministers may find the life of the small-scale society unpleasant, as they compete against each other for scarce resources: money, parliamentary time, press headlines, and Prime Ministerial favor. Civil servants can take a different view; while ministers (and governments) come and go, they remain forever.[76]

The ethos of Whitehall is set by civil servants rather than ministers, because they are more numerous as well as more durable. At any one time, there are likely to be about one-hundred ministers and seventeen times as many senior civil servants working in Whitehall. Of these, it can be reckoned that only thirty or so ministers carry much political influence; they must work in tandem with about three-hundred civil servants.[77] The hundreds of thousands of civil servants meant to carry out the decisions of the several hundred top people are

[76] For illustrations of the foregoing, see Hugh Heclo and Aaron Wildavsky, *The Private Government of Public Money*.

[77] See F. M. G. Willson, "Policy-Making and the Policy-Makers," in Richard Rose, editor, *Policy-Making in Britain,* and Sir Richard Clarke, "The Number and Size of Government Departments," *Political Quarterly,* XLIII:2 (1972), p. 174.

kept at arm's length by considerations of protocol and hierarchy within government.

In the small world of Whitehall, civil servants are not anonymous. Each has a reputation to maintain with his peers and with the civil service superiors who determine his promotion. What is it that gives him a good repute? First and foremost, he must be trustworthy. He will be scrupulously honest in money matters and in keeping private his knowledge of public affairs. Second, he will not try to "pull a fast one" on his colleagues in other departments by withholding information that makes his department look bad or is in the interest of his colleagues in other departments to know. A senior civil servant should also be considered reliable; predictability of actions is important when time is pressing, and a short conversation cannot discuss everything. Coordination can best occur if officials in each department know what their colleagues elsewhere expect them to do. Soundness is another cardinal virtue. A civil servant who repeatedly voices "clever" but controversial ideas may become a bore because more experienced hands will have to explain, for the nth time, why his particular idea is not desirable or simply "not practical politics." Intelligence is demonstrated by showing an awareness of the complexities of a problem, by finding one more snag than anyone else has found, or finding one more objection to an awkward proposal for change. Whitehall (like much English university education) prizes the critical intelligence, rather than the mind skilled at constructing things, whether in the area of civil engineering or of new techniques for managing the economy.

The knowing impassive figure of the mandarin is the symbol of the English civil service, just as the symbol of his Washington counterpart is the aggressive athlete, the man with "clout." "Why are your officials so passionate?" a British Treasury official once asked presidential advisor Richard Neustadt.[78] Neustadt turned the question around, asking why British civil servants are so dispassionate about the outcome of their activities. He concluded that American civil servants

[78] Richard E. Neustadt, "White House and Whitehall," in Richard Rose, editor, *Policy-Making in Britain,* p. 292.

care about policies because their careers are wrapped up with the success of their departments and, even more, their reputation for getting things done. To win a political battle is to advance personally, as well as to advance the commonweal. In England, by contrast, civil servants know that, come what may, their minister will get the credit (or the blame) for the outcome of their negotiations. They are personally detached because they have no career stake in the outcome of what they are doing. Their general reputation for following the Whitehall code is more important than the outcome of any specific struggle for policy. The style of governing is that of the relaxed amateur, rather than that of the determined, ruthless professional. British civil servants do not play to win; the important thing is how you play the game.

Whitehall civil servants are perennially skeptical of politicians' claims to reform the world within the lifetime of a single Parliament. Their daydream of paradise is not of megalomaniac power, but of a world in which there are few decisions to make, because ministers, MPs, and subjects have left them undisturbed in the orderly administration of routine affairs of state. In the words of Sir William Armstrong, permanent head of the civil service, the chief danger in government is not "that obstructive bureaucrats will drag their feet" but that ministers' "optimism will carry them into schemes and policies which will subsequently be seen to fail – failure which attention to the experience and information available from the service might have avoided." [79] An experienced minister, Roy Jenkins, describes a great problem of government as knowing when to accept departmental advice and when to reject it. Jenkins reflects that any minister "will occasionally regret, amongst decisions which could have gone one way or the other, both those made with advice and those made against it." [80]

Both ministers and civil servants see themselves as men with great responsibilities. Ministers are ultimately responsible to the electorate; immediately, they are responsible to their col-

[79] Sir William Armstrong, "The Role and Character of the Civil Service," text of a talk at the British Academy, London, June 24, 1970, p. 21.

[80] Roy Jenkins, "The Reality of Political Power."

leagues in Cabinet and to their patron in Downing Street. The longer they remain in office, the more they are likely to develop a sense of responsibility to their department and its servants; it is their position as head of a department that gives them status in government. Civil servants are ultimately responsible to the Crown; immediately, they are responsible to their minister and to the head of the civil service. While civil servants have little personal contact with party politics and even less with the electoral hurly-burly of representative government, they also have a keen sense of responsibility to the public interest – as they see it. The public provides the intended beneficiaries of government policies. But the public is distant from the world of Westminster. Immediately, civil servants, MPs, and ministers must respond to the demands of their offices and to the demands that each makes upon the other if the Queen's government is to be carried on.

CHAPTER IV

Political Culture and Legitimacy

It is the dull traditional habit of mankind that guides most men's actions and it is the steady frame in which each new artist must set the picture that he paints.

THE POLITICAL CULTURE of England consists of those values, beliefs, and emotions that give meaning to politics.[1] Political values are important because conceptions of a desirable state of society can justify action and direct political choice. The values of Englishmen cannot be isolated from their political beliefs and emotions. For instance, freedom of speech may be regarded as a value in itself, or it may be upheld because it is believed to lead to the best choice of public policy, or it may be cherished because of emotional attachment to a norm that is traditional in England. The political culture is a more or less harmonious mixture of the value preferences, beliefs, and emotions of a citizenry.

The cultural outlooks of Englishmen are not inherited in a biological sense, but they are transmitted from generation to generation. Through a process of political socialization, Englishmen learn about events of the remote past and political

1 For a fuller discussion, see Richard Rose, *People in Politics*, pp. 39 ff; Dennis Kavanagh, *Political Culture* (London: Macmillan, 1972); and Lucian W. Pye and Sidney Verba, editors, *Political Culture and Political Development*.

outlooks formulated before they were born (See Chapter V). As each citizen matures, he accumulates a range of politically salient experiences, thus learning at firsthand what to expect from government. With elderly citizens, this knowledge may derive from experience of British government in the very different circumstances of England before World War I. To refer to outlooks learned in the past as "traditions" suggests they are derived only from the distant past. But in England, traditions may have originated in preindustrial society, in an era of Victorian prosperity, or more recently.

Political outlooks not only reflect past events but also influence what Englishmen believe ought to happen in the present and the future. The idea of "oughtness" intentionally blurs empirical and normative expectations. For example, Englishmen think that there ought to be a general election, even if the governing party will probably lose, because no government in the past has illegally prolonged its stay in office. Yet they also think this ought to happen because it is morally right that a government, especially an unpopular government, should periodically submit itself to electoral judgment. Even when expectations are unambiguously clear, they do not necessarily determine events. Twice in this century, in the exceptional circumstances of wartime, governments have postponed general elections with the consent of all parties in Parliament.

In social science as in everyday speech, the word culture may refer to attitudes about such varied things as taste in music, child-rearing practices, or how to behave in social relations. The boundaries between political outlooks and attitudes concerning other aspects of social life are not rigid. Only if one focuses on a few basic questions can a political culture be analyzed in any detail. Unfortunately, political scientists do not agree about the most important subjects of political culture. In this chapter, two questions have been selected for special attention. The first is: Why do citizens give allegiance to political authority? The second is: Who should exercise this authority? The first question concerns the legitimacy of the regime, and the second the definition of representative government.

Many of the attitudes that are the stuff of culture are what

Sidney Low called "a system of tacit understandings." [2] They are tacit because they are taken for granted. Ordinary citizens do not speak the language of political theorists or political sociologists. Nor are they accustomed to articulate what they think of government or why they think as they do. The discussion that follows draws upon a mixture of materials – survey data, unobtrusive measures of behavior, philosophical speculation, and personal observation – in an effort to depict the political culture of England today. It gives particular attention to the views of the politically active minority of Englishmen. This group is not only more articulate about its various political outlooks, but also has above average influence upon government.

ALLEGIANCE TO AUTHORITY

Of all the attitudes that affect government, the most important are those concerning allegiance to political authority. Authority is fully legitimate if citizens support the regime and comply with its basic political laws, that is, laws that the governors say must be obeyed as a condition of the survival of the regime. If people refuse to support the regime but comply with its laws, then it is coercive. A regime that loses both the support and compliance of its citizens is heading toward the repudiation of its authority.[3]

Ascertaining diffuse support for political institutions is very difficult. Support for a regime is not a judgment about the effectiveness or efficiency of government. People may simultaneously give diffuse support to their form of government, while making many specific criticisms of how it works. There is the risk of confusing a desire for reforming particular institutions, for instance, Parliament or the Prime Ministership, with unconditional rejection of authority. Reform may assist in maintaining a regime. In Northern Ireland or France, where authority has been in dispute and regimes subject to change, it is meaningful to ask people whether they support the current regime or prefer another form of political authority. In

[2] Sidney Low, *The Governance of England* (London: Ernest Benn, revised edition, 1914), p. 12.

[3] See Richard Rose, *Governing without Consensus*, Ch. 1.

England the continuity of authority makes the question inconceivable to many and hypothetical to nearly everyone.

Evidence from surveys of citizens attitudes toward authority indicates overwhelming support for the English regime, that is, the form of government in England. For example, a survey taken in connection with the reform of local government found that 94 per cent believe that government by elected representatives is a very good or fairly good way of governing; only 3 per cent think it is not a good way to run the country. Equally strong support was given for representative institutions in local government. At a higher level of abstraction, only 5 per cent of persons with opinions said "democracy" (a term usually applied to British government) was bad; the great majority endorsed it as permitting government by the people or guaranteeing freedom.[4] High levels of support for the regime were found by similar questions asked in an English loyalty study. The popular view of institutions is shared by MPs. Interviews with MPs by Robert Putnam found that only 2 per cent thought there should be a major change in the form of government; the alterations most frequently mentioned were reforms to improve existing procedures.[5]

Englishmen are also ready to comply with basic political laws. The concept of a political crime or a crime against the state is unknown in England. People who violate laws are considered to be "antisocial"; the most reprehensible criminals are guilty of crimes against society. The idea of using violence to change the government is not found within the English political culture. For this reason the English loyalty survey could not ask meaningful questions about the endorsement of political crimes, as can be done in Northern Ireland. Englishmen were asked whether there are ever any circumstances in which it would be all right to break the law; 46 per cent said there are. But the circumstances cited were either explicitly humanitarian, for instance, "to help someone," or else remote from politics, for instance, "if you found someone else with your wife." Only one-fifth said that it would be all right to

[4] Committee on the Management of Local Government, Vol 3, *The Local Government Elector* (London: HMSO, 1967), pp. 66 ff.

[5] See Robert D. Putnam, *The Beliefs of Politicians* (New Haven: Yale, 1973).

break a traffic law, evade income tax, or steal food if in need. When asked about a conflict between laws and individual conscience, the majority said a person should comply with the law; only 27 per cent said that conscience was a justification for violating any law.[6] It is extremely rare for anyone charged with breaking a law to admit legal culpability but to claim that his conscience morally justified such action.

The actions of Englishmen provide strong evidence of their willingness to comply with basic political laws. The last time that a major English political group endorsed unconditional resistance to basic political laws was before World War I. The Conservative party in opposition gave succor to Ulster Protestants arming themselves to fight, if need be, against the passage of Irish Home Rule by a Westminster Parliament. In 1912, Bonar Law, the Conservative party leader, denounced the British Liberal government as "a revolutionary committee which has seized upon despotic power by fraud."[7] The General Strike of 1926 was nonviolent, and the interwar economic depression passed more peaceably than in America or continental Europe.

The political party most in disagreement with other parties today – the Communist Party of Great Britain – does not advocate rejection of laws and organize for armed insurrection, as its continental counterparts have sometimes done. Instead, it advocates working through established parliamentary and economic institutions. It has sustained this policy even though its electoral efforts have had derisory results. Its "peak" support occurred in 1945, when the Communists won 0.4 per cent of the vote; in 1970, the party's candidates won 0.1 per cent, and none of its 58 candidates gained as much as one-eighth of the vote in his constituency. Surveys of Communist voters have found that individual Communists differ little from Labour activists in their acceptance of the institutions of authority. The British Communist Party's record since its foundation

[6] See Richard Rose and Harve Mossawir, "Voting and Elections" *Political Studies,* XV:2 (1967), for a full presentation of results cited in this chapter.

[7] Quoted in Robert Blake, *The Unknown Prime Minister* (London: Eyre & Spottiswoode, 1955), p. 130. More generally, see George Dangerfield, *The Strange Death of Liberal England* (London: Constable, 1936).

caused one writer to describe it as "overwhelmed by the British political culture and forced to accommodate to the country's political tradition." [8] Self-proclaimed Fascists appear from time to time, but their failure to gain recruits for "strong-arm" squads is their most noteworthy feature.[9]

Acts of Parliament are almost invariably carried out by the voluntary consent of citizens. Law enforcement does not require the massing of large numbers of uniformed and secret police. In proportion to its population, England has internal security forces one-third smaller than those of America, West Germany, France, or Italy.[10] Even when individuals or groups disagree on fundamental political issues, civil disobedience or subversion is hardly even counseled. Instead, Englishmen believe that they should exercise their right of freedom of speech to voice opposition openly within the law. For example, in every war for the past century there has been a vocal and educated minority opposing the conflict. During the Suez War of 1956, the leader of the Opposition, Hugh Gaitskell, told the Commons that the Labour Party would be:

> . . . bound by every constitutional means at our disposal to oppose it. I emphasize the word "constitutional." We shall, of course, make no attempt to dissuade anybody from carrying out the orders of the government, but we shall seek, through the influence of public opinion, to bring every pressure to bear upon the government to withdraw from the impossible situation into which they have put us.[11]

When a few supporters of unilateral nuclear disarmament advocated civil disobedience as a method for advancing their views in the 1960s, they found that even within this radical

[8] Robert Kilroy-Silk, in a book review in *Political Studies,* XVIIII:4 (1970), p. 557. See also D. T. Denver and J. M. Bochel, "The Political Socialization of Activists in the British Communist Party," *British Journal of Political Science,* III:1 (1973).

[9] See Robert Benewick, *The Fascist Movement in Britain* (London: Allen Lane, 1972); and George Thayer, *The British Political Fringe* (London: Blond, 1965).

[10] Charles L. Taylor and Michael C. Hudson, *World Handbook of Political and Social Indicators,* Table 2.5.

[11] House of Commons *Debates,* Vol. 558, Col. 1462 (October 31, 1956). More generally, see Leon D. Epstein, *British Politics in the Suez Crisis.*

group, unlawful political action failed of support.[12] Their failure stands in contrast to the contemporaneous achievements of White Citizens' Councils and black militant groups in America.

To note the readiness of Englishmen to comply with basic political laws is not to say that every Englishman obeys every law at all times. The number of indictable crimes reported to police each year was 34 per 1000 people in 1971; there is also an equal proportion of motoring offenses, drunkenness, or similar nonindictable charges.[13] Fast driving, burglary, or homicide can be identified as "antisocial" actions, but they are not crimes against the state. When workers engaged in strikes in 1972 in defiance of the Industrial Relations Act, the government criticized the strikers for violating the law, and the strikers criticized the government for passing the law, but neither union leaders nor Cabinet ministers claimed that the incidents were a generalized challenge to established political authority. There are isolated incidents in which anarchists or other groups intentionally attack government buildings or public officials. But by international standards, their numbers are few. That such challenges can occur within the framework of United Kingdom government is indubitable. Northern Ireland provides a recurring example of what can happen to British government when it lacks the full support and compliance of its subjects. The unilateral declaration of independence by Southern Rhodesia in 1965 provides another example of the successful repudiation of the authority of the United Kingdom. Both examples are literally and figuratively "un-English."

Explanations of the allegiance of Englishmen are of many types. The writings of English political philosophers offer one potential source of explanation. For centuries political philosophers have concerned themselves with the question of political authority. While the most famous are long dead, many practical men who claim to learn only from their own experience are, as J. M. Keynes said, slaves of the ideas of dead (and often long discredited) theorists.

[12] Christopher Driver, *The Disarmers* (London: Hodder Stoughton, 1964); and Frank E. Myers, "Civil Disobedience and Organization Change," *Political Science Quarterly,* LXXXVI:1 (1971).

[13] *Social Trends,* Vol. 3, p. 156.

The ideas of great philosophers cannot provide an explanation for a common outlook among Englishmen today because the best-known philosophers have disagreed so much about the nature and justification of political authority. In England there is nothing like a "Lockean consensus" attributed by some scholars to the United States. Thomas Hobbes, writing at the time of the seventeenth-century English civil war, saw society tending toward the "war of every man against every man." Government must, if need be, compel compliance, so that public order (and much else) could be secure, he declared. The ability of a regime to assure order was itself a reason for giving it support. John Locke, writing almost contemporaneously with Hobbes, had a very different view of authority, claiming that it should rest upon the agreement of intelligent and independent men seeking to secure their natural rights by collective political action. Edmund Burke, an eighteenth-century observer of the American and French revolutions, sought to reconcile contrasting views. Burke emphasized the importance of tradition as a sanction for consent: "People will not look forward to posterity who never look backward to their ancestors." Yet he also accepted the need for change: "A state without the means of some change is without the means of its conservation." Writing in the early years of the Industrial Revolution, Jeremy Bentham emphasized the improvement of social conditions by the conscious reform of government. Bentham's touchstone was "the greatest happiness of the greatest number" of the citizenry. John Stuart Mill, who began writing under the influence of Bentham, also argued for individual rights. Mill held that the state could demand compliance with laws only when this was necessary to restrict individual behavior to avoid greater harm to others.

It might be more correct to explain allegiant outlooks in part as a result of the *absence* of certain extreme schools of political philosophy prominent in other European countries. For example, modern England has produced few who glorified reactionary or authoritarian government on nationalist or religious grounds. The absence of totalitarian philosophies greatly reduces the number of actions that might be considered politically subversive. For example, the work of artists may be discussed in terms of political values by art critics; artists who are out of sympathy with the government are not censored or imprisoned for creating "antiregime" art, as in the Soviet Union. England has not produced notable writers who endorsed violent revolution or who, like Rousseau, advanced philosophical arguments against the very idea of the state. Even Walter Bagehot, a wordly wise journalist, did not emulate Machiavelli by glorifying the pursuit of power. Instead, he celebrated the conditions necessary to maintain government by consent.

While most Englishmen are likely to be ignorant of the "great books" of political philosophy, they will have some knowledge of how government has worked in the past. Older Englishmen know about it from personal experience. Younger Englishmen may learn from school history or oral history. Additionally, they may adopt attitudes without knowing the traditional origin of what they learn from their elders. Traditional experience cannot, however, explain allegiance to the regime, because traditions contain an even greater range of events and morals than the literature of political philosophy. For example, regicide is traditional. Well-placed Englishmen have been committing treason against the Crown at least since the time of Thomas à Becket in the twelfth century. Lowly Englishmen have been revolting against the Crown at least since Wat Tyler's peasant rising of 1381. W. J. M. Mackenzie summarizes the contrasting "lessons" of history in three models. The model most used in public discussion is liberal: English people govern themselves through responsible parliamentary government. Another model drawn from history is elitist: Political power reflects social and economic power. A third model is that of dissent: Englishmen recognize and, after the event, often endorse the views put forward initially by a few who were speaking according to their conscience against the majority.[14] Because many English disagreements are much more remote in time than their American, French, or German equivalents, their contemporary salience is dulled.

[14] W. J. M. Mackenzie, "Models of English Politics," in Richard Rose, editor, *Studies in British Politics,* 2nd edition, p. 55.

The existence of a common national identity is often advanced as a reason for allegiance to government. Englishmen have an unusually well-defined sense of identity, developed through centuries of island life. Because an Englishman takes his Englishness for granted, individual politicians may be accused of being incompetent but not of being un-English (or "un-British," if they are Scottish or Welsh). Their loyalty to authority is assumed. The American phenomenon of the politician's claim to be 100 or 200 per cent American is unknown on the part of the English, as is anything like a House Un-American Affairs Committee seeking out subversives as the cause of the nation's ills.[15] Ironically, the efforts of Enoch Powell to stir up national consciousness are hamstrung by Powell's own origins. His name betrays his Welshness. By identifying himself with the cause of Ulster Protestants, Powell has further emphasized that his concept of "Britishness" embraces a far more heterogeneous population than the average Englishman would recognize as "his own kind." Powell's appeal is negative, lying in a rejection of black immigrants. This is illustrated by the weakness of anti–Common Market propaganda of a xenophobic sort in comparison with racialist anti-immigrant propaganda. So secure are Englishmen in their personal and national identity that ineptitude does not stimulate a fear of national disintegration, a fear afflicting many newly formed nations. The outlook is summed up in the phrase: "There will always be an England." Confidence in national identity is as impressive when it is an obstacle to adaptation as it is when easing the assimilation of change.

While a secure national identity is important in removing one possible challenge to authority, it is not sufficient to account for allegiance. People may be confident of their national identity, as the French are, yet disagree about the constitution that should govern their collective fate. Moreover, the regime that governs England also claims authority over the three non-English parts of the United Kingdom. Cen-

[15] See Edward A. Shils, *The Torment of Secrecy* (London: Heinemann, 1956); and Herbert H. Hyman, "England and America: Climates of Tolerance and Intolerance," in Daniel Bell, editor, *The Radical Right* (New York: Doubleday, 1963).

turies of peace between England and Wales and Scotland contrast strongly with the centuries of battle between England and Ireland. One cannot claim that English people are well suited to govern a multinational Kingdom, or that identification with Britain always encourages allegiance. In generation after generation, Ulster Protestants have been ready to resort to armed insurrection against Westminster, justifying revolt as the only means of maintaining their "Britishness." [16]

Symbols of England's past are sometimes invoked as determinants of present allegiance. "Traditional" symbols can date from nineteenth-century England, as does most of the present Palace of Westminster, or have medieval origins to sanctify them, as with some procedures in Parliament. Bagehot noted a century ago that within the dignified appearance of traditional government, English politicians for generations have been busily "interpolating the new reality." Such representations of authority as the flag and the national anthem are everywhere understood and accepted, as "symbols of England's greatness." Even efficient institutions, such as Parliament and general elections, may have symbolic significance. It can even be argued that these institutions of representative government are overrated as efficient agencies of governing and underrated as symbols.

There is no doubt that Englishmen respond with positive emotions to government. The Civic Culture survey found that when Englishmen were asked in 1960 what gave them most pride in their country, 46 per cent mentioned political institutions, by comparison with 7 per cent in Germany and 3 per cent in Italy. Only Americans were more likely (85 per cent) to show pride in their government.[17] It can be argued that the very high American figure reflected an "overly" emotional attitude toward authority; an Englishman may not be so articulate because he confidently takes his government for granted.

The monarchy is the most prominent and personal symbol of authority. Public opinion reacts positively to this symbol.

[16] In Ulster, "Britishness" is a symbol of Protestantism, see e.g., A. T. Q. Stewart, *The Ulster Crisis* (London: Faber, 1967).

[17] Gabriel Almond and Sidney Verba, *The Civic Culture* (Princeton: Princeton University Press, 1963), p. 102.

For example, when the Gallup Poll asked people whether they would perfer a queen or a president as head of state, 80 per cent endorsed the monarchy and 12 per cent a president.[18] Some social scientists – particularly Americans – have argued that the traditional, personal, and quasi-religious associations of the Crown make it a specially powerful influence upon allegiance. In an area as little documented and as charged with emotion as the monarchy, social scientists should move warily, rather than deferentially or aggressively.[19]

Survey evidence rejects the hypothesis that the Queen is a major influence upon allegiance. The English loyalty survey found that 78 per cent thought the Queen had little or no influence upon government as against 13 per cent who thought she had a lot of influence and 2 per cent who believed she had too much.[20] Extensive open-end interviews with a subsample of Englishmen interviewed in the Civic Culture study found that only one-quarter referred to any role of the Queen in the efficient activities of goverrnment.[21] Two-fifths regarded the monarchy as a favorable symbol of the unity of society. Said a widow in Derby: "I hold with the royal family. You look to the head of the country. Keeps the country together, having royalty to look up to. They set such a good example." Some who favor the monarchy stress the need for a head of state. Said a housewife in Leeds: "You've got to have somebody at the head. It might as well be her." The few who object to the monarchy on general grounds object to the institution, not to

[18] *Gallup Political Index,* No. 138 (London: 1972), p. 8. On earlier antimonarchial republican sentiments, see Kingsley Martin, *The Crown and the Establishment* (Harmondsworth: Penguin, 1963).

[19] Cf. Edward Shile and Michael Young, "The Meaning of the Coronation," *Sociological Review,* Vol. I (1953); Norman Birnbaum, "Monarchs and Sociologists," *ibid.,* Vol. III (1955); and Fred Greenstein *et al.,* "Queen and Prime Minister – the Child's Eye View," *New Society,* October 23, 1969.

[20] In addition to survey data in the loyalty survey, see also J. G. Blumler *et al.,* "Attitudes to the Monarchy," *Political Studies,* XIX:2 (1971).

[21] Data coded by the author from 111 open-ended British Life History questionnaires kindly made available by Gabriel Almond and Sidney Verba.

individuals. This point was made explicit by a housewife in the Potteries, who said: "I don't think there is any need for them. They are outdated and a waste of money. I have nothing against them personally."

While the majority who react to the Queen do so in emotional terms, their emotional responses are limited, even shallow. Individuals with strong emotions about the Queen – for or against – are atypical. Few show any interest in the royal family as individuals. The institution rather than the personality is the basis for respect. This was unambiguously demonstrated when King Edward VIII was hurriedly forced to abdicate in 1937, because of his intention to marry an American divorcée. Popular regard was immediately transferred to his brother, who became King George VI.

The trouble with explaining allegiance by reference to symbols is that there is no way to separate a potential cause from a potential effect. One can as easily say that the Queen is a popular symbol because she is the head of a fully legitimate regime as argue that the Queen causes support and compliance. Similarly, the regard in which Englishmen hold their flag, their community, their traditions, and their institutions can be a consequence of centuries of legitimate government rather than a cause of it. There is nothing compelling in the existence of symbols per se. In Northern Ireland the same symbols stimulate conflicting reactions from Republicans and from those proclaiming loyalty to the Crown.[22]

In the English loyalty survey, each respondent was asked to express his view of why people should be allegiant, by agreeing or disagreeing with a series of statements often advanced as reasons for supporting government or obeying laws. The most frequently endorsed justification is in terms of rational choice: It's the best form of government we know. A majority also emphasize popular endorsement: It's the kind of government the people want, and the inevitability of authority: We've got to accept it. Justification by tradition ranks least in importance. The only other justification that fails of endorse-

22 Richard Rose, *Governing without Consensus,* p. 244.

TABLE IV.1 *Justifications for Supporting the System of Government (in percentages)*

	Agree	*Disagree*	*Don't know*
It's the best form of government we know	77	19	4
It's the kind of government the people want	66	25	9
We've got to accept it whatever we think	65	32	3
It usually provides the right things for people	49	40	10
It's good because it is traditional	44	49	7

Source: Richard Rose and Harve Mossawir, "Votings and Elections," in *Political Studies*, XV:2 (Oxford: Clarendon Press, 1967), p. 190. Reprinted by permission.

ment by at least half the respondents is the argument that government usually provides the right things for people (Table IV.1).

When Englishmen are asked to explain why they obey laws, they find many reasons for compliance. More than half endorse practical arguments – laws are generally sensible, and you will be punished if you break laws – and also arguments that bespeak confidence in the regime that administers law – laws are fairly enforced, made by elected representatives, and by people who know what one ought to do (Table IV.2).

Collectively, these survey responses emphasize the absolute value of legal procedures and a rational calculation of instrumental satisfactions and the avoidance of punishments.[23] Traditional emotions do not appear to be important determinants of the allegiance of the majority of Englishmen. As the justifications are not mutually exclusive, the minority who regard tradition and emotion as important can give allegiance on these grounds. Thus, a liberal may endorse government because it is elected, and a traditionalist because it is an agent of Her Majesty the Queen. Because most Englishmen endorse

[23] See Max Weber, *The Theory of Social and Economic Organization* (Glencoe, Illinois: Free Press, 1947).

TABLE IV.2 *Justifications for Obeying Laws (in percentages)*

	Very good	*Not very good*	*Don't know*
Laws are generally sensible	90	8	2
Laws are fairly enforced	75	18	5
Laws are made by people we elect	75	20	5
You'll be punished if you break laws	74	22	4
People who make the laws know what you ought to do	64	29	6
Everyone has always done so	45	51	4

Source: Richard Rose and Harve Mossawir, "Voting and Elections," in *Political Studies*, XV:2 (Oxford: Clarendon Press, 1967), p. 191. Reprinted by permission.

a multiplicity of justifications for authority, allegiance can be maintained on a multiplicity of grounds. If the government of the day has difficulties in providing the right things for people or in making laws considered sensible, authority can be justified on other grounds.

THE SCOPE OF AUTHORITY

The legitimacy that Englishmen confer upon government generally does not give unlimited authority to their governors. From the time of the Magna Carta in 1215, Englishmen have expected the Crown to limit the scope of its authority. While the Tory version of the history of England stresses the development of the powers of the Crown, the Whig version is the story of winning liberty from royal despotism. The establishment of civil liberties in the modern sense can be dated from before the commencement of franchise reform in 1832.[24] Unlike most of his continental neighbors, the Englishman of today has never been the subject of authoritarian rule, whether by a government of his own people or by an occupying army.

The courts do not determine the scope of government's au-

[24] See T. H. Marshall, *Citizenship and Social Class* (Cambridge: University Press, 1950), pp. 14 ff.

thority, because there is no written constitution denying legality to stipulated types of laws; this is in marked contrast with judicial interpretation in the United States. The constraints upon government are practical, not legal. Parliament, it used to be said, can pass any law except one that makes a man a woman.[25] The main constraints upon government are cultural. Government's authority is not limited by law but by popular beliefs about what it can legitimately do and what it is not right for it to do. For example, four centuries ago it was considered right for the government to prescribe or proscribe religious observances, and little more than a century ago it was considered right to confine some public benefits to persons belonging to the state church. Today, both bishops and politicians believe that a policy of "noninterference" in each other's affairs is the right way to define the relationship of church and state.

In the absence of a legally entrenched bill of rights guaranteeing the liberties of Englishmen, individuals must depend upon cultural norms to limit the actions of the government. The long-established belief in freedom of speech is an effective inhibition against censorship in all matters except those affecting national security. Laws governing public meetings and demonstrations give substantial leeway to protest groups to put forward their views within the law.[26] Allegations that the government infringes on individual liberties are heard less often in England than in America. For example, during the "cold war" British Communists continued to enjoy nearly all the liberties of other British subjects, notwithstanding the discovery from time to time of Soviet penetration of government security. Unconcern with legal guarantees of liberties is also shown by the limited interest of governments – both Conservative and Labour – in passing laws conferring legally enforceable rights upon citizens. This reluctance is most no-

[25] Entry to the European Common Market creates treaty obligations which may lead to judicial review of Acts of Parliament. See Sir Leslie Scarman "Law and Administration: a Change in Relationship," *Public Administration,* L (Autumn 1972).

[26] See David Williams, *Keeping the Peace.*

ticeable in race relations. By contrast with Washington, Westminster has been very slow to pass antidiscrimination legislation, and the laws it passes provide few judicial remedies for grievances of black Britons.[27]

Increasingly, Englishmen expect to regulate their morality without reference to government, and government has reduced the scope of moral legislation. Even before a series of permissive legislative acts in the 1960s, the enforcement of moral norms by statute law was limited in scope. For example, while America and Scandinavian countries were experimenting with the legal prohibition of alcohol to curb drunkenness, England adopted the simpler tactic of requiring the closure of public houses at specified hours each day. No British government has ever sought to curb completely the ordinary citizen's desire to gamble if he wishes. Laws have regulated forms of gambling and the organization of gambling as an industry. In the 1960s, laws against homosexual relations between consenting male adults were repealed, and censorship of books, films, and plays was virtually abandoned. Abortion was legalized in 1967, further reducing the scope of legislation affecting private morality.[28]

Throughout the past century, British government has been expanding the scope of welfare policies. The expectation of communal provision for welfare dates from medieval times. Industrialization brought reform of the institutions of welfare administration, as Englishmen moved from the countryside to cities. The expansion of national wealth and the creation of a mass electorate were followed by the expansion of welfare services under Liberal, Conservative, and Labour governments. Today Englishmen expect to enjoy the benefits of the welfare state whether they are poor, well-to-do, or of average income. The government of the day is expected to make provision for health, education, and social services for everyone in need. Need is not defined in economic terms but by one's con-

[27] See Bob Hepple, *Race, Jobs and the Law in Britain* (Harmondsworth: Penguin, 1970 edition).

[28] See Peter G. Richards, *Parliament and Conscience* (London: Allen & Unwin, 1970).

dition of life: a child needs education, as an elderly person needs a pension.[29]

While Englishmen agree about many things that the state ought to do (e.g., provide schools and police services) and many things it ought not to do (e.g., regulate tastes in food or reading matter), there is always political controversy about points at which the line should be drawn between state intervention and nonintervention. For example, both the Conservative and Labour parties have found practical and normative difficulties in determining the extent to which government should exercise authority in the field of industrial relations. After trade unions gained freedom from restrictive nineteenth-century laws, they became committed to the belief that court-enforced legislation would work against their interests by limiting the right to strike or penalizing those who struck against the wishes of the government of the day. Employers have tended to accept this view because conflict between trade unions and government would only further complicate labor-management negotiations. The trade unions showed how much they valued freedom from legislation – whether it was intended to be beneficial, like the American Wagner Act, or to be restrictive, like the American Taft-Hartley Act – by threatening to bring down the Labour government in 1969 if the government carried out its announced intention of enacting an industrial-relations bill. The unions have since endorsed various forms of industrial action in efforts to secure repeal of the Industrial Relations Act passed in 1972 by the Conservative government.[30] The limited scope of their dispute with government about union autonomy is indicated by the fact that concurrently the unions expect the government to intervene in the labor market to maintain full employment.

One reason why the scope of government is limited is that

[29] For an Anglo-American comparison, see Hugh Heclo's chapter in Richard Rose, editor, *Lessons from America*. More generally, see T. H. Marshall, *Social Policy* (London: Hutchinson, 1967 edition).

[30] See e.g., Hugh Clegg, *How to Run an Incomes Policy and Why we Made Such a Mess of the Last One* (London: Heinemann, 1971); and Peter Jenkins, *The Battle of Downing Street* (London: Charles Knight, 1970).

Englishmen do not believe in the unlimited power of intellect to resolve political problems. The Conservative Party has emphasized the limits of rationalism since the days of Edmund Burke; it even issues pamphlets that scorn those whose political policies are found "by the light of their naked intellect." While the Labour Party emphasizes the application of reason to politics, it usually does so through plans involving piecemeal social engineering to achieve specific aims. The flights of the left wing of the Labour Party into the realm of grand socialist theory have not led to the repudiation of antiintellectual norms; rather, they have tended to bring intellectuals into disrepute within the Labour Party. There remains substantial popular support for Bagehot's view: "What we opprobriously call stupidity, though not an enlivening quality in common society, is nature's favorite resource for preserving steadiness of conduct and consistency of opinion." [31] Repeated surveys of party leaders indicate that voters are more likely to criticize party leaders for being "too clever by half" than to praise them for their intelligence.[32] MPs too are skeptical about intellectual grand designs. A survey found that 87 per cent of MPs made no reference whatsoever to a future ideal state of society when discussing important issues. Instead of stressing blueprints of the future, MPs consider the administrative practicality of public policies and the immediate "political acceptability" of their desired policy.[33]

All views about the scope of authority change through time. In the nineteenth century rights of property were considered almost inviolate, even against the claim of the government to regulate safety in mines or factories. In the 1920s and 1930s virtually no one expected the government to solve problems of unemployment by economic intervention. Today both politicians and voters expect the government to act to prevent

[31] W. Bagehot, *The English Constitution,* Ch. 1. See also *Some Principles of Conservatism* (London: Conservative Political Centre, 1956), p. 3.

[32] Notwithstanding this, four of the last five Prime Ministers have held good honors degrees from Oxford. Cf. David Butler and Donald Stokes, *Political Change in Britain,* pp. 379–80.

[33] See Robert D. Putnam, "Studying Elite Political Culture: the Case of 'Ideology,' " *American Political Science Review,* LXV:3 (1971), pp. 659–61.

unemployment. Expectations of government planning of the economy have fluctuated within both parties. Since 1945 Labour and Conservative governments have announced intentions to plan the economy; subsequently governments of each party have announced that they could not achieve their planned goals. Government initiatives generate experiences from which people learn that what was once thought "impossible" or "undesirable" is practicable or attractive. In this way welfare-state measures have gradually expanded in scope. The failure of successive British governments to fulfill their plans for the economy shows that experience can sometimes lead citizens to expect less rather than more from government.

Nearly every Englishman expects government to influence his life in some way. In the English loyalty survey, only 11 per cent of respondents said that government had no effect on their lives. Among those perceiving some effect, 48 per cent said that government had a lot of influence, and 28 per cent said it had a little influence. The most frequently cited examples of government influence were economic policy, welfare measures, and taxes. When people were asked whether they thought government actions made things better or worse, responses showed cautious optimism: 37 per cent said that government usually made things better and 13 per cent that government usually made things worse. The largest group – 44 per cent – thought the impact of government varied from situation to situation.[34]

Whatever the governors may hope, the governed do not expect politics to affect their central personal concerns. Englishmen are not distrustful of the state, but they do not see themselves as dependent upon it. When the loyalty survey asked each respondent to name the main concern of himself and his family, most mentioned a problem that could be seen in political *or* personal terms. For example, a person's income, housing, health in old age, or the education of his children are affected by both government policies and individual actions. When asked what group outside the family could help most with their chief concern, 71 per cent saw no place other

[34] Richard Rose and Harve Mossawir, "Voting and Elections," pp. 183 ff.

than the family to turn. Even though this question was asked immediately after a series of questions about government, only one-seventh of concerned persons said they might look to government or other political institutions for help. Good government is unobtrusive government. By doing what Englishmen have come to expect, it maintains popular support. By not being expected to do everything, it can avoid the odium of totalitarian authority as well as the blame for many frustrations.

WHOSE AUTHORITY?

Regimes are run by small groups of governors. But they hold power because in some sense they claim to represent the governed. Before considering the recruitment of governors and influences upon decisions, one must ask who is expected to govern and what justifications are advanced for these expectations. Some theories of representation emphasize normative values. Ideally, who ought to govern? Others stress empirical concerns. Given the existing characteristics of society and government, who will succeed to office? At least seven different sets of expectations can be identified.[35]

1. The most traditional theory emphasizes the independence of the Crown from popular pressures. Government, deriving its authority from the ancient and unlimited prerogatives of the Crown, exists to advance the common good; government is not intended to discover the common good by elaborate opinion-sounding devices. In the words of L. S. Amery, who gave contemporary restatement to an ancient doctrine, government is "the active, initiating, and governing element." Since the advent of universal suffrage, the mass of the population has become involved in government, but in a responsive rather than a directive manner. In Amery's words, England is governed "by consent and not by delegation"; government is "for the people, with, but not by, the people." In such cir-

[35] For much fuller discussions of theories of representation, see A. H. Birch, *Representative and Responsible Government* (London: Allen & Unwin, 1964); and S. H. Beer, *Modern British Politics* (London: Faber, 2nd edition, 1969).

cumstances, the Cabinet has a "primary responsibility to the Crown as the embodiment of the unity and continuity of our national life." [36] The outlook is summed up in the epigram, "The government's job is to govern." The Crown view of government is popular with any party in office, because it provides a justification for the government's doing what it wishes. Reciprocally, any opposition is less happy with it, because their opponents enjoy the prerogatives of Her Majesty's government.

2. Theories of government by the few differ greatly in the way in which the choice of the few is justified. The historic importance of government by hereditary noblemen has made contemporary social scientists conscious of the potential importance of deference to governors selected by birth. But successive survey studies have demonstrated one thing unequivocally: The proportion who defer to politicians on grounds of birth is no more than about one-tenth of the electorate. Moreover, even among working-class Conservatives – the group considered most prone to a deferential outlook – individuals are more likely to be "secular" or "pragmatic" rather than deferential.[37] These studies do not refute the significance of deferential outlooks in the nineteenth-century transition to universal suffrage but rather measure the distance between 1867 and contemporary England.

Predemocratic belief in the inequality of political influence is expressed today in theories that emphasize reciprocal and differing political rights and obligations. Those at the top of the hierarchy of authority – whether in government, education, or other spheres of social life – are expected to have achieved their place by merit, and to justify their eminence by having regard to the welfare of all who depend upon them. The model, feudal in its original assumption of a lord's caring for his retainers, can be fitted to a society where merit is measured by education, not landed acres. Contemporary Conserva-

[36] L. S. Amery, *Thoughts on the Constitution* (London: Oxford University Press, 2nd edition, 1953), pp. 3 ff.

[37] See Dennis Kavanagh, "The Deferential English: a Comparative Critique," *Government and Opposition,* VI:3 (1971), and the sources cited therein.

tism may be said to be about inequality. For example, Harold Macmillan, when Prime Minister, could assert:

> Human beings, widely various in their capacity, character, talent and ambition, tend to differentiate at all times and in all places . . . To deny the bold, the strong, the prudent and the clever the rewards and privileges of exercising their qualities is to enthrone in society the worst and basest of human attributes: envy, jealousy and spite.[38]

Inequality justified by educational merit is most evident in recruitment for the civil service. Adolescents and young adults are recruited on the basis of competitive examination. Those with the highest academic attainments enter a career leading to the most senior administrative posts; those with lesser attainments enter technical or clerical posts. The most difficult jobs are considered to require the most intelligent recruits.[39]

3. Liberal theories of representation emphasize the importance of the individual citizen's role in government. MPs are meant to represent constituencies in which each individual has a vote of equal value. In turn, ministers of the Crown are expected to be responsible to the House of Commons. Thus, at only one remove, individual electors could claim to control – if not positively direct – government. Liberalism was originally a normative philosophy justifying nineteenth-century reform, and then a not unrealistic description of how the reformed government operated. Today it is most significant as a justification for the importance of choosing government through a general election. There still remain areas of public life where every adult citizen is not equal in law. For example, it was not until 1965 that a government committee recommended abolishing a property qualification for jury service and making every citizen qualified to judge his peers. The jury list finally became based on the electoral roll in 1972.[40]

[38] *The Middle Way: 20 Years After* (London: Conservative Political Centre, 1958), p. 9.

[39] Cf. Michael Young, *The Rise of the Meritocracy* (Harmondsworth: Penguin, 1961); and Robert A. Dahl, *After the Revolution?* (New Haven: Yale, 1970).

[40] See *Report of the* (Morris) *Departmental Committee on Jury Service* (London: HMSO, Cmnd. 2627, 1965).

4. Collectivist theories of representation emphasize the importance of group solidarity rather than individual choice. If an individual cannot hope to see his personal views reflected exactly in the complex process of government, his group can be represented by spokesmen. Socialists have stressed the representation of class interests through trade unions and the Labour Party. Some have sought to confine the group to a single class. For example, Frank Cousins, a leading trade unionist, once declared to a Labour party conference, "We represent Britain, we represent the working class of Britain and they are Britain." [41] The collectivist approach, like the doctrine of the power of the Crown, emphasizes the unrestricted authority of group leaders. This raises important questions about who group leaders represent. For example, a Labour government would claim to represent the whole country if its views were endorsed by two-thirds of its MPs, even though such a majority within the party could represent little more than one-third of the whole House of Commons.

5. A variant of the collectivist view is the theory of governing by group consultation. All interests affected by a policy are granted the right to be consulted before the government acts. Those who are not organized will be represented by altruistic sympathizers or self-appointed spokesmen. Those who participate in consultations are expected to accept government decisions once taken, even if they are not consistent with their demands. The significance of collective consultation is evidenced by the extent to which the government, though formally centralized and powerful, reduces its freedom of action by appointing committees consisting largely of representatives of affected groups to advise it on policy.

6. Duopolistic choice, a theory propounded by Joseph Schumpeter as a description of postwar British government, combines elements of several preceding doctrines.[42] Schumpeter saw government as conducted by a few, the teams who lead the two major political parties. Individual voters can exercise

[41] *Labour Party Conference Report* (London, 1962), p. 182.

[42] *Capitalism, Socialism and Democracy* (London: Allen & Unwin, 4th edition, 1952).

choice between the two parties at general elections. Between general elections, the winning team can exercise the power of the Crown, restrained only by prudential considerations of securing reelection within five years. In the duopolistic model of party competition, it is the producers (the teams of party leaders) rather than the consumers (the voters) who structure political alternatives.

7. In the Whitehall theory of government, the minister and his civil service advisors represent the public interest, as against the sectional demands of pressure groups.[43] Most of the time-consuming negotiation with pressure groups and the evaluation of their demands is done by civil servants. Insofar as men in Whitehall do not need to consult with those outside, the theory is like that of Amery, but stresses the civil service more than ministers. The doctrine not only downgrades the importance of Parliament, but also the importance of the executive, because of the vagueness of "the public interest" and the political weakness of civil servants in controversial areas. W. J. M. Mackenzie has suggested that this doctrine can foster "the ungovernable interests," because civil servants in Whitehall lack the ability to enforce their own terms against many major interests in society. The metaphor of monarchy comes full circle in Mackenzie's comment:

> The state is submerged by the interests; it continues, but only as a form of contest. The so-called government is like a medieval king amid the barons' wars. His body is a symbol and a prize; the factions strive to possess it, but as soon as one succeeds, its success creates a coalition against it, and the cycle begins again.[44]

The coexistence of many different theories about who should govern does not result in conflict about the regime, because many of these doctrines are not mutually exclusive. For example, individual preferences can be expressed at general elections, as in the liberal theory, and collective interests advanced by parties and pressure groups. The civil service

43 See A. H. Birch, *Representative and Responsible Government,* pp. 165 ff.

44 W. J. M. Mackenzie, "Models of English Politics," p. 59.

may concurrently resist group demands and policies immediately popular with the electorate, as harmful to the long-term "public interest." The existence of institutions capable of accommodation to more than one theory of representation helps sustain legitimacy, placing institutions outside many conflicts between parties and pressure groups.

Popular beliefs about who should govern reflect a pluralistic outlook. In the English loyalty survey, more than half the respondents said that the Prime Minister, Members of Parliament, big business, the press, and trade unions had a lot of or too much influence.[45] MPs' views of who should govern are also pluralistic. MPs think that voting and showing an interest in politics are sufficient to occupy an ordinary citizen; only 14 per cent think the average voter should take more part in politics. In reply to questions about popular participation, from 61 to 91 per cent of MPs endorse liberal as against oligarchic sentiments (Table IV.3).

The term *trusteeship* perhaps best characterizes the form of representation prevailing in England today. Writing before World War I, A. L. Lowell described governors as retaining many political privileges from an earlier time, holding them "by the sufferance of the great mass of the people, and as trustees for its benefit." Members of Parliament act as virtual representatives of a wide congeries of interests in society, some justified by their numbers (e.g., pensioners or consumers), and some by their strategic influence upon public policy (e.g., trade unions in key industries, and City bankers). In turn, front-bench leaders act as trustees for the party in and out of Parliament. Just as MPs expect Parliament to lead public opinion, so the majority of MPs think a party's leaders should take the initiative; only 20 per cent say that a leader should primarily be responding to his followers' views. Those in authority are expected to use their powers, subject only to intermittent and general judgments. In the words of a Labour MP:

> The essential thing in a democracy is a general election in which a Government is elected with power to do any damned

[45] Richard Rose and Harve Mossawir, "Voting and Elections," p. 185.

TABLE IV.3 *MPs' Attitudes toward Citizen Participation in Government (in percentages)*

Attitudes (Liberal opinion in parentheses)	*Endorse Liberal opinion*	*Endorse Oligarchic opinion*
People ought to be allowed to vote even if they cannot do so intelligently (Agree)	91	9
Certain people are better qualified to run this country because of their traditions and family background (Disagree)	81	20
Every citizen should have an equal chance to influence government policy (Agree)	81	19
A few strong leaders would do more for this country than all the laws and talk (Disagree)	77	24
In this complicated world the only way we can know what is going on is to rely on leaders or experts who can be trusted (Disagree)	71	29
Few people really know what is in their best interests in the long run (Disagree)	61	40
It will always be necessary to have a few strong, able people actually running everything (Disagree)	61	39

Source: Derived from R. D. Putnam, *The Beliefs of Politicians* (New Haven: Yale University Press, 1973), Table 16.2.

> thing it likes and if the people don't like it, they have the right to chuck it out.

A Conservative Member with an aristocratic background endorses the same view in a characteristic mock diffident manner:

> Well I can't think of any other practicable method. I mean, I personally consider myself capable of coming to decisions without having to fight an election once every four or five years, but on the other hand, the people must be allowed to feel that they can exercise some control, even if it's only the control of chucking somebody out that they don't like.[46]

[46] See Robert D. Putnam, *The Beliefs of Politicians,* Part III. Cf. A. L. Lowell, *The Government of England,* Vol. II (London: Macmillan, 1908), p. 508.

CULTURE AND SUBCULTURE

The Earl of Balfour, writing an introduction to Bagehot in 1927, asserted: "Our whole political machinery pre-supposes a people so fundamentally at one that they can safely afford to bicker: and so sure of their own moderation that they are not dangerously disturbed by the never-ending din of political conflict." [47] Yet neither Balfour, nor latter-day social scientists writing about "consensus" (i.e., unanimity of views) make clear what it is that the English people are fundamentally at one about.

The foregoing survey of cultural attitudes shows that there is a consensus of support for the institutions of the regime and compliance with basic political laws. Moreover, while Englishmen do not agree about who should govern, they agree about how their governors should be chosen. The ability of Englishmen in times past to resolve disagreements without disrupting the regime has caused Englishmen to expect to continue to do so today. Culture, while important as an intervening influence, is not uniquely determinant.

Consensus about a very few political attitudes coexists with continuing disagreement about major issues of contemporary politics. The several norms described above are consensual because they do *not* determine specific positions on policies. Disagreement about policies can be conducted peaceably because the participants agree about the institutional procedures that will be used to resolve their differences. To the ordinary party politician, it is the differences that are important rather than the common allegiance. Disagreement about public policy is reflected in almost every survey of political attitudes taken in Britain (see Table IX.2, p. 304). Insofar as politics is about conflicting choices, a question that showed unanimity would, by definition, concern an issue above politics or one so basic that it was the foundation upon which everyday politics rested.

Any attempt to typecast individual Englishmen by their cultural outlooks faces difficulties because an individual need not integrate his views with the logical rigor of an ideology or a

[47] "Introduction" to W. Bagehot, *The English Constitution*, p. xxiv.

social-science construct. For example, the authors of *The Civic Culture* described three "ideal-type" cultural outlooks: the participant citizen, the loyal undemanding subject, and the parochial person remote from government. A substantial majority of Englishmen cannot be classified in terms consistent with the outlooks described by the authors. They reflect a mixture of cultural values, beliefs, and emotions.[48]

Political parties provide concrete institutional expression for differences in political outlooks. Party differences in England do not extend to disagreement about the regime. At a minimum, party outlooks may differ in a single value, such as equality, liberty, or continuity with the past. The differentiation of partisan subcultures does not mean that there is disagreement about every matter of political relevance. Moreover, divisions in political outlooks can be found within as well as between the political parties.

The political outlook of the Conservative Party is broad and tolerant, like that of the Church of England toward theology; the Labour Party, by contrast, smacks of the Welsh chapel, where quarrels about theology are evidence of the importance given doctrines. Within the Conservative ranks one can discern some who are natural conservatives. They have a clear-cut approach to social change: They are against it. The known is always preferred to the unknown; the present is good (or bad) enough. Laissez-faire Conservatives look forward to a day when nineteenth-century principles of the market economy are once more established by what would be reactionary measures: the repeal of welfare-state legislation. The largest group of Conservatives in government are adaptive. They take the ambiguous position of favoring the existing order – in so far as possible. They are ready to make changes to preserve existing institutions of government. Occasionally, as in the case of entering the Common Market, Conservatives favour policies that promise greater rather than fewer changes. This strategy is justified, in the words of Lord Hailsham, as making use of

48 The proportion who were mixed is from 63 to 87 per cent, depending upon classification criteria. See Richard Rose and Harve Mossawir, "Voting and Elections," p. 191.

"the true lessons taught by their opponents." Conservatives, he argues:

> . . . see nothing immoral or even eccentric in catching the Whigs bathing and walking away with their clothes. There is no copyright in truth and what is controversial politics at one moment may after experience and reflection easily become common ground.[49]

In the Labour Party left-wing Socialists emphasize the party's traditional commitment to the nationalization of industry and a distinctively neutralist foreign policy. As against this view, revisionists have argued for a nondoctrinaire but interventionist approach to economic issues and alliances with like-minded foreign countries. During periods of Labour government, a third approach is also prominent: "Socialism is what the Labour Government does." [50] The differences between the pledges of the Labour Party in 1964 and the achievements of the 1964–70 Labour government have intensified differences among groups within the party, notwithstanding Harold Wilson's avowed purpose of acting as a reconciler of party differences. In the 1970s, all groups of the party have begun to converge in emphasizing redistributive aspects of welfare policies, providing more benefits for the poor from greater taxes upon the well-to-do. The party has not, however, advocated income equality. Some Labour policies emphasize popular sovereignty, usually "welfare-oriented" policies for the good of the most numerous group, manual workers. Another set of policies is not related to class, but stresses the rights and needs of minorities, e.g., sexual deviants, gypsies, drug addicts, etc.[51] The very inclusiveness of ideas within the party is reflected by its constitutional aim (Clause IV.5) to promote "political, social, and economic emancipation" for workers "by hand or by brain," that is, 99 per cent of the

[49] Quintin Hogg (intermittently, Lord Hailsham), *The Conservative Case* (Harmondsworth: Penguin, 1959), p. 16. For ambiguities in Conservative outlooks, see Richard Rose, "Tensions in Conservative Philosophy," *Political Quarterly,* XXXII:3 (1961).

[50] Peter Jenkins, *The Battle of Downing Street,* p. 101.

[51] See John Gyford and Stephen Haseler, *Social Democracy: Beyond Revisionism* (London: Fabian Research Series No. 292, 1971).

population. However controversial the policies of the Labour Party, they are not based upon doctrines of class conflict.

The outlook of liberalism is not confined to members of the Liberal Party but can be found among partisans supporting the two major parties as well. Insofar as liberalism stands for individual rights and individual participation in political activity, it could be argued that political developments and the growing interest in the relationship of individuals to the state has made liberal concerns specially significant. Conservative and Labour Party supporters will often endorse Liberal Party views; reciprocally, the Liberal Party may advocate some policies also to be found in Labour programs and others to be found in Conservative documents. The Liberals complain that their electoral weakness results from the fact that everyone who thinks like a liberal does not vote Liberal. The party's critics claim that the outlook of the party is so vague and encompasses so many conflicting viewpoints that it deserves no distinctive following because it is unclear what the party stands for.

From a perspective focusing on the authority of the regime rather than issues of current controversy, the important feature of English politics is the acceptance by all parties of the regime's legitimacy. Political differences are reconcilable. Most MPs see conflicts of interest as limited, rather than as "zero-sum" conflicts in which one side must lose what the other gains. This outlook is illustrated by the way in which an MP calmly characterizes his partisan opponents:

> Well, they're different men with different policies, and some of them I quite like. They seem decent chaps, but I don't know . . . I don't agree with their policies.[52]

The chief challenge to political authority today is more likely to be found in the economic system. Financiers and industrialists, as well as trade union leaders, wish to limit government intervention in their economic affairs. In pursuing economic goals, businessmen or trade union leaders may act

52 Robert D. Putnam, "Studying Elite Political Culture," p. 677; Putnam, *The Beliefs of Politicians*, Part II.

in opposition to government expectations. For example, during a sterling crisis a part-time director of the Bank of England told a private client to sell sterling short, noting, "This is anti-British and derogatory to sterling but, on balance, if one is free to do so, it makes sense to me." [53] In a similar fashion, trade union leaders have repeatedly rejected government pleas to cooperate in wage regulation. In 1966, Frank Cousins asserted, "If we are having a free-for-all, my people are part of the 'all.' " [54] Given such noncooperation, British governments must either accept limits on their economic authority or risk noncompliance with their laws. The failure of Labour and Conservative governments to secure agreement upon a wage policy at many times since World War II has led a sociologist, John Goldthorpe, to argue that "the most far-reaching implications of inequality for the integration of British society occur not in the political sphere but rather in that of economic life." Wage policies cannot be agreed in industry because of a lack of agreement about what is a "fair" wage; disagreements are reflected in disputes among unions about appropriate differentials within the working class, as well as in disputes focusing on differentials betwen manual and nonmanual workers. For a government to seek to enforce standards of "fair wages" and "fair labor practices" where consensus is lacking "would carry the very real threat of extending economic into political instability." [55]

At any given point in time, many values, beliefs, and emotions in the political culture will be shared, because inherited from a common past. But when change occurs, there will inevitably be differences in the readiness of different parties to assimilate new ideas. English political parties are specially noteworthy for their readiness to assimilate ideas from their opponents.[56] When an election transfers complete control of government, the winning party maintains nearly all the legis-

[53] Quoted in W. J. M. Mackenzie, "Models of English Politics," p. 60.

[54] *Labour Party Conference Report, 1966,* p. 223.

[55] John Goldthorpe, "Social Inequality and Social Integration in Modern Britain," *Advancement of Science* (December 1969).

[56] For a tabular depiction of change through time, see Richard Rose, "England: a Traditionally Modern Culture," p. 104.

lation of its predecessor. A readiness to assimilate past, present, and future is even found among those seeking to change society. An interview study of innovative young professionals found they use the language of the future when talking of modernization, but they seek to join this with the values of the past. When asked what they most admired and disliked about England, a majority explicitly stated that the things they liked most about their culture – moderation, tolerance, a capacity for compromise, and continuity – were also the cause of what they most disliked: resistance to change.[57]

[57] Erwin C. Hargrove, *Professional Roles in Society and Government: the English Case* (Beverly Hills: Sage Professional Papers in Comparative Politics, 01–035, 1972).

CHAPTER V

Political Socialization

People who learn slowly learn only what they must. The best security for a people doing their duty is that they should not know anything else to do.

THE VALUES, BELIEFS, AND EMOTIONS of the political culture are transmitted from generation to generation through a series of socialization experiences in the family, at school, and at work. The political outlooks of Englishmen today reflect attitudes learned early in life as well as responses to contemporary events. Socialization experiences influence the "antisystem" outlook of the youthful radical as well as the positive allegiance of ordinary Englishmen. Because of the continuity of English social institutions, many norms antedate the birth of an individual.

Most agencies of political socialization are not exclusively or primarily political in intent. Parents teach their children about many things besides politics, and there are very few couples in England who would have children "for the good of the party." Schools are established to teach children reading, writing, arithmetic, and other skills valued in nonpolitical contexts, as well as to instruct future citizens. Neighbors may affect political outlooks, but a house is rarely chosen on political grounds. Only political parties claim to be social institutions primarily concerned with political socialization.

Political socialization is a continuing process. When an Englishman begins to learn about politics in childhood, he may first respond emotionally to the monarch, or he may acquire information before he can evaluate it or respond to it emotionally. By the time a person becomes 18, the age at which he can vote, he has already developed many political predispositions. But adult political behavior is not necessarily determined by these predispositions. Adult life provides many opportunities to make new discoveries about politics and to learn from experience as a politically active or politically apathetic citizen. In addition, political events may force an individual to alter his views and actions. For example, a person who is predisposed to vote for the Liberal Party will have to adopt another party if the Liberals fail to contest the parliamentary constituency in which he lives. Individuals are always potentially open to learning new ideas or altering old ones. While political socialization is a continuing process, what is newly learned often reinforces what was learned previously.

Content is more important than process to an Englishman. What an Englishman learns about politics has greater significance than how he acquires his outlook. In England a history of legitimate government emphasizes support for authority and compliance with basic political laws; in Bagehot's phrase, Englishmen hardly "know anything else to do." Allegiance to authority is thus a cause not a consequence of the pattern of political socialization. In Northern Ireland, the same institutions socialize youths into conflict.[1]

Experiences in socialization affect the political division of labor. Children learn early that people differ from each other; gradually, these differences become recognizable in political contexts. A young person becomes aware not only of differences between political parties and political roles but also of the part he is expected to take in politics. In this chapter, particular attention is given to the way in which socialization differentiates persons into Conservative and Labour support-

[1] See Richard Rose, *Governing without Consensus*, Ch. 11, "Socialization into Conflict," and James L. Russell, *Civic Education of Secondary Schoolboys in Northern Ireland* (Belfast: Community Relations Commission, Research Paper No. 2, 1972).

ers. Attention is also given to the way in which contrasting patterns of socialization may differentiate citizens into a small, actively involved minority and a larger, less interested group of citizens. Chapter VI then analyzes intensively how each of these groups participates in politics.

WITHIN THE FAMILY

The family comes first in point of time. Political attitudes learned there are related to primary family loyalties. A shop-keeping widow in Nottingham in a life-history interview explained her party loyalty thus:

> We worked like slaves as youngsters and then we hadn't enough money to have holidays like the upper classes. It made me feel there was a law for the rich and a law for the poor. I didn't see why holidays should be only for the rich. I have always sided with Labour to get fairness for all.

This woman was a lifelong Labour supporter even though she thought the Conservative Party right in its approach to the major political problems of the past 35 years. But to have voted Conservative would have meant going against her child-hood memories and the politics of her father, who was "red-hot Labour." This she could not do.

The influence of parents upon children is most readily measured by examining the persistence of party loyalty from generation to generation. Politics does not need to be charged with deep emotional overtones for children to follow the cues offered by their parents. For this influence to operate, parents must show enough political interest to make clear to their children what the family's party is. This does not always happen (Table V.1). In less than half the cases, the party preference of both parents is remembered and the same. In 29 per cent of the cases one parent provided a cue for adult party preference. The remaining 30 per cent provided no guidance or conflicting cues. Adults whose parents were both Conservative tend to be Conservative, and those with both parents Labour tend to be Labour. But the relationship is not invariant; in 39 per cent of cases in which parents agreed in their party, their offspring rejected their choice.

TABLE V.1 *The Persistence of Party Identification within the Family (in percentages)*

	Respondent				
	Con.	*Lab.*	*Lib.*	*None*	*Total*
Both parents:					42
Conservative	67	15	6	12	
Labour	10	71	6	14	
Liberal	39	33	18	10	
One parent unknown, other:					29
Conservative	55	30	7	8	
Labour	19	61	9	12	
Liberal	43	28	18	11	
Parents disagree	40	37	13	9	6
Neither parent's choice known	33	42	11	14	24

Source: David Butler and Donald Stokes, 1964 British Election survey.

A simple theory of intergenerational determinism fails because such a large proportion of the electorate does not acquire a lasting party identification in the family; only 25 per cent of voters hold the same party identification as both their parents, and another 14 per cent follow the cue of the one parent whose preference they know. The majority acquire a party identification without parental direction or in opposition to it. Politically, the most important point to note is that slightly less than half the support for the Conservative and Labour parties is, as it were, delivered by the obstetrician. Because the majority of each party's supporters has not "inherited" partisanship, each party has an incentive to seek recruits; once gained, they cannot be regarded as inevitable lifelong supporters.

Parental influence is most evident when a child born into a politically active family enters politics. This is the equivalent of going into a family business. The eldest son of a hereditary peer knows that he is guaranteed a seat in the House of Lords if his father predeceases him. Sir Anthony Wagner, Garter King of Arms, argues that a hereditary House of Lords is desirable because a peer may be groomed from childhood for adult political leadership. This view is rejected by the 55 per cent of Englishmen who favor the abolition of hereditary titles. Attitudes differ on party lines; 67 per cent of Labour supporters are against hereditary titles compared with 43 per cent of Conservatives.[2] The number of members from political families is disproportionately high in every Cabinet. In Mr. Wilson's first list of appointments in 1964, 10 of the 43 men named to ministerial posts had parents sufficiently involved in public life to merit notice in their own biographies. Among Conservatives in 1970, 7 of the 18 Cabinet ministers had family ties with politics, as did 15 of 23 ministers outside the Cabinet. Prime Ministers, too, are disproportionately drawn from political families. Winston Churchill's ancestors had been in the Commons or the Lords since the early eighteenth century. His son and grandson (as well as two sons-in-law) have also sat in the Commons. Harold Wilson's parents and grandparents, though never in Parliament, were also keenly interested in politics; he claims, "I was born with politics in me."[3]

Within the home, boys and girls learn about differences in sex roles; these are potentially significant politically. In adulthood men are more likely to be involved in "class-conscious" activities as manual laborers and as members of trade unions. In fact, the differences between men and women in partisanship is slight; the level of Conservative support among women is 2.5 per cent higher than that of men. This reflects age differences in the profile of men and women; women live longer and the elderly are more likely to be more Conservative.[4]

Women differ from men in their likelihood of holding public office. Only 12 per cent of local government councillors are women, even though being a councillor is a role in which family obligations are a limited handicap, and freedom from full-

[2] See Sir Anthony Wagner, "Hereditary Peers Defended," *The Times*, January 30, 1969; and National Opinion Polls, *Monthly Bulletin* (June 1972), p. 27.

[3] Quoted from, "The Family Background of Harold Wilson" in Richard Rose, editor, *Studies in British Politics*, p. 79.

[4] See Richard Rose, "Britain: Simple Abstractions and Complex Realities," Table 23 in Richard Rose, editor, *Electoral Behavior: A Comparative Handbook* (New York: Free Press, 1974); and, more generally, Robert E. Dowse and John A. Hughes, "Girls, Boys and Politics," *British Journal of Sociology*, XXII:1 (1971).

time employment (the status of half of England's women) is a positive asset.[5] In parliamentary politics, women constituted 5 per cent of candidates at the 1970 election, and 4 per cent of MPs. The majority of women MPs are usually Conservative when the Conservatives control the House, and Labour when that party is in control. The Prime Minister is expected to appoint one woman to Cabinet; this reflects their proportion in the Commons, though not in the electorate. The same explanation cannot be offered for the small proportion of women appointed to boards in the nationalized industries, some of which directly affect consumer as well as producer interests.[6]

The level of political interest among women is similar to that among men; 40 per cent say they are very or quite interested in politics and 54 per cent of men show such an interest. The much lower rate of political participation among women cannot be explained in attitudinal terms. It results from a combination of institutional influences, both political and social. Marriage and child rearing occupy many women in the years when young men can build the foundations for a political career. When a woman seeks nomination for Parliament, she is likely to face prejudice against a woman MP among some involved in selecting candidates for a parliamentary seat.[7] The proportion of women in Parliament is, however, rising. In the seven interwar elections, the first of which was held after women gained the franchise in 1918, an average of seven women were elected; in the eight elections since 1945, the average has been 24.

Political attitudes and activities are not identical from generation to generation for two very different reasons. First, the historical circumstances in which people learn about politics

[5] See Louis Moss and Stanley Parker, *The Local Government Councillor* (London: HMSO, 1967), p. 15.

[6] See *Women in Politics* (London: Conservative Political Centre, 1970); Pamela Brookes, *Women at Westminster* (London: Peter Davies, 1967); and "The Man who Champions the Women," *The Times,* January 17, 1972.

[7] See Michael Rush, *The Selection of Parliamentary Candidates* (London: Nelson, 1969), pp. 61 ff, 222 ff. Cf. National Opinion Polls, *Monthly Bulletin* (February 1970), p. 5.

change from generation to generation. Today's parents are likely to have begun learning about politics in a period of interwar depression and postwar austerity. Their children are learning about politics at a time when prosperity is expected. Grandparents formed party allegiances when there was a choice of three parties: Conservatives, Liberals, and Labour. Differences in historical experience influence profiles of party support among age groups: the oldest voters tend to be Conservatives. This is because of the weakness of Labour at the time when today's elderly first formed party attachments and because middle-class voters, who are disproportionately Conservative, are longer lived.

A second source of generational differences is the greater volatility of youth. More young voters are usually Labour voters than their elders, but they also tend to move in the direction that their elders are swinging. In at least two postwar elections, a majority of young people have favored the Conservatives. As young people become older, their party loyalties become more fixed, for the experience of one election tends to reinforce previous experiences. Among the youngest generation of voters interviewed by Butler and Stokes in 1964, 31 per cent very strongly identified with a party; among the oldest, 56 per cent were very strong in their party identification.[8]

Any attempt to extrapolate the political future from generational political differences requires careful qualification. Age-related differences are matters of degree, not kind. Often the difference in degree is small. Parties and pressure groups normally draw some support from people of all ages. Groups that are specifically in one age bracket, like the National Union of Students or organizations of pensioners, represent minority groups within the population. Moreover, students, like the elderly, are in transition. The lowering of the voting age to 18 before the 1970 election indicated a political recognition that young people today differ from their elders in their readiness to claim adult political responsibilities. Yet, when the election was held, class not age was the more important determinant of young voters' party choice. In every age group, a majority of

[8] David Butler and Donald Stokes, *Political Change in Britain,* pp. 54 ff.

the working class voted Labour, and a majority of the upper middle class voted Conservative.[9]

SCHOOLING

An English child first leaves the immediate surroundings of his family to go to school. When he leaves school, he is ready to go to work, and sometimes he is of voting age. Schooling thus intervenes between family and adult influences. Social theorists differ in the extent to which they regard schooling as reinforcing family influences or as an independent influence. They also differ about the extent to which people, once they leave school, can be expected to change their outlooks as adults. In English politics, there is no formal educational requirement for voting or holding public office. Education is thus neither a necessary nor a sufficient claim to holding political position. Most university graduates do not seek public office, and the majority of graduates who seek election to Parliament are defeated.[10]

When a national system of education was founded in the late nineteenth century, schools were expected to provide instruction in religion and morality, teach vocationally useful skills, keep children from early entry to the labor market, and ensure that those given the vote would have sufficient literacy to follow public affairs. Today schools teach reading, writing, and arithmetic to infants, and more abstruse subjects, such as Latin, Greek, physics, and calculus, to adolescents. Schools devote little time to formal instruction in politics. Only one-quarter of English adults interviewed in the Civic Culture study said their schools encouraged pupils to discuss current political questions; this is one-half the proportion who discuss politics in American schools.[11] There has been no need for educators to make their children Englishmen, as American

[9] See Richard Rose, "Britain: Simple Abstractions and Complex Realities," Table 22; and Philip Abrams and Alan Little, "The Young Voter in British Politics," *British Journal of Sociology*, XVI:2 (1965).

[10] This calculation includes Liberal candidates. Among the two major parties, a majority of graduates standing for the winning party are elected, and a majority of graduates standing for the losing party defeated.

[11] See Gabriel Almond and Sidney Verba, *The Civic Culture*, p. 333.

schools have sought to make Americans of children from multilingual backgrounds. English schoolchildren (and their teachers) take their Englishness for granted. In the words of one elderly life-history respondent, school taught patriotism "in the form of prayers and history."

Many secondary schools offer a course about the British Constitution as an optional subject of study.[12] In this course, textbooks and examination questions concentrate upon easily memorized topics, such as the institutions and procedures of government; party political issues are usually avoided. The subject is not among the most popular. The influence of such instruction is doubtful. For example, Geoffrey Mercer compared pupils taking an ordinary-level examination in Modern Studies, which covers current affairs topics as well as institutions of government, with pupils in the same schools not studying politics. Mercer found that the formal study of political issues had very little effect on youthful political outlooks. The chief influences upon youthful political efficacy are self-expressed political interest, age, and intelligence. Pupils do not look to their school curriculum to stimulate political interest, nor does the curriculum stimulate interest when this is not already present.[13]

English schools, like American schools, teach "life adjustment" as well as academic subjects. Implicitly as well as explicitly, schools help young people prepare for adulthood by indicating behavior and attitudes appropriate to adult life. This role raises questions about the extent to which young people (or their elders) wish to adjust to society or alter it. The answers given reflect broad political values rather than narrow pedagogic views. Education is the subject of political dispute between Socialists, believing that education can change society, and Conservatives, believing that education can and should maintain existing conditions. Politicians differ as parents too. A majority of Conservative MPs send their children

[12] Cf. articles in the journal *Teaching Politics*, published by Longman from 1972; and D. B. Heater, editor, *The Teaching of Politics* (London: Methuen, 1969).

[13] See Geoffrey Mercer, *Political Education and Socialization to Democratic Norms* (Glasgow, Strathclyde Occasional Paper No. 11, 1973).

to private fee-paying schools, and a majority of Labour MPs send their children to state schools.[14] Both sides agree in assuming that schools are important causal influences in the formation of adult outlooks.

The English[15] educational system has always emphasized inequality. The great majority of the population has been considered fit for only a minimum of education. In the words of one participant in the nineteenth-century debate on educating Englishmen:

> Any attempt to keep the children of the labouring classes under intellectual culture after the very earliest age at which they could earn their living would be as arbitrary and improper as it would be to keep the boys at Eton and Harrow at spade labour.[16]

The minimum age for leaving school was twelve in 1902, fourteen in 1918, and fifteen in 1944; it was raised to sixteen in 1972. The majority of English adults left school at the earliest possible legal opportunity. Free secondary education was not introduced until 1944. The proportion of young people in full-time higher education today is rising, but only because it was historically low; it was 1 per cent in 1902 and 2 per cent in 1948. Highly educated people, a small minority of Englishmen, are expected to play an important part in politics. Lord Hailsham, speaking as minister of Education, has argued.

> Equality of opportunity in education or life does not mean either equality of performance or ability or uniformity of character. The object of education is to bring out differences just as much as to impose standards, and the democracy of the future will not be a drab mass of second-rate people in which distinction of intellect or character is decried as egg-headness. It will be a society governed by its graduates — science and arts and

[14] See Michael Parkinson, *The Labour Party and the Organiaztion of Secondary Education, 1918–1965* (London: Routledge, 1970); and Brian Jackson, "Parents in Parliament," *Where?* (Autumn 1964).

[15] The discussion that follows explicitly excludes Wales and Scotland.

[16] Quoted in a review by Royden Harrison in *New Society,* December 2, 1971, p. 1107.

social sciences — and largely run by people who put public service in front of enjoyment, profit, or leisure.[17]

The organization of secondary education has assumed that the majority of children are not capable of passing an academic type examination. The free secondary schools introduced by the 1944 Education Act were of two major kinds, academic grammar schools and secondary modern schools. At the age of eleven, pupils have been sorted by education authorities into a quarter who are judged capable of benefiting from an academic grammar school education and three-quarters who are not. The minimum passing standard for the ordinary-level examination taken by sixteen-year-olds is set on the assumption that it will be too hard for 60 per cent of all pupils, including the overwhelming majority of secondary modern pupils. Initially, secondary modern schools were meant to offer an education different from that of grammar schools, rather than inferior to them. But headmasters, teachers, and parents have judged them by academic achievements, the one standard on which secondary modern schools could not hope to match the grammar schools. Children assigned to secondary modern rather than grammar schools are said to have "failed" the eleven-plus examination.

In the 1950s and 1960s, a combination of Socialists and educational sociologists (sometimes, the same persons) campaigned to end "segregation" in secondary schools by abolishing the eleven-plus examination and establishing comprehensive secondary schools catering to adolescents of all levels of intelligence. Selection at eleven was criticized as unfair because it did not make allowance for the academic handicaps that working-class children sometimes have. The tendency of grammar schools to emphasize middle-class aspirations while secondary modern schools emphasize other outlooks was attacked as inconsistent with the ideal of a common citizenship.[18] Conserva-

[17] "A Society Governed by Graduates," *The Times,* January 24, 1962.

[18] Cf. Central Advisory Council for Education, *15 to 18* (London: HMSO, 1959); Frances Stevens, *The Living Tradition* (London: Hutchinson, 1960); and Brian Jackson and Dennis Marsden, *Education and the Working Class* (London: Routledge, 1962).

tives opposed any nationwide change in policy, arguing that each local education authority should make its own choice. The 1944 Education Act allowed local authorities to establish comprehensive schools if they wished, but most Labour local authorities had not done so.[19] In October, 1965, the Labour government requested all local authorities to reorganize secondary education to abolish the eleven-plus examination. After the return of a Conservative government in 1970, a new circular was issued, rescinding the Labour policy and emphasizing local option once again. (See below, pp. 358 ff.) The proportion of young people in comprehensive schools has been growing.[20] Within comprehensive schools, young people are not required to have a common education. Pupils may be streamed into courses with differing occupational prospects by their own selection of academic or nonacademic subjects. Alternatively, they may be streamed by their teachers on the basis of ability.

Secondary schools discriminate on grounds of social status as well as intelligence. Public schools (that is, private, fee-paying, and often boarding institutions) accept pupils of a wide range of intellectual abilities. Pupils have one thing in common: parents who will pay high annual fees for tuition. Boarding schools allow young people to be raised among their social peers rather than among a heterogeneous set of neighbors. Entrance to the most prestigious public schools, such as Eton, may be aided by family connections. The brightest of public schoolboys at the best schools are likely to receive an academic education superior to the average state secondary school, while at the poorest of public schools they are likely to receive an education inferior to that of the state schools. Public schools were developed in Victorian times from medieval foundations to provide an education and character training

[19] For the viewpoint of ministers, see Maurice Kogan, *The Politics of Education*. For case studies, see Paul E. Peterson, "British Interest Group Theory Re-examined," *Comparative Politics*, III:3 (1971); and Richard Batley, Oswald O'Brien, and Henry Parris, *Going Comprehensive* (London: Routledge, 1970). Cf. Raphaella Bilski, "Ideology and the Comprehensive Schools," *Political Quarterly*, XLIV:2 (1973).

[20] See *Social Trends*, Vol. 3, pp. 127 ff for detailed educational statistics and trends.

suitable for the sons of gentlemen and of those who wished their sons to become gentlemen even though they were not of such status themselves.[21] At that time, gentlemanly status was an important qualification for holding major public office. These historical influences remain important. Public schools normally stress group solidarity within the school and exclusiveness in relation to those outside the school. The pattern of authority within the school is meant to prepare boys to conform to group norms as well as to act as leaders. Approximately 5 per cent of young persons attend public schools or their equivalents. The great majority of former public schoolboys seek careers in industry or commerce, which have the most numerous job opportunities. Only a small proportion of them aspire to a career in the civil service or in older professions traditionally associated with politics.[22] There are thus substantial differences in aspirations even within the public school sector of secondary education.

Higher education further differentiates young people. The proportion of pupils leaving secondary school with at least the minimum qualification for university entrance has gradually been rising; in 1970, it was 14 per cent of all adolescents. Less than half proceed to higher education. About half of these go to university, another quarter to colleges of education, and the remainder to a variety of full-time and part-time institutions, such as polytechnics. By comparison with American states (or with Scotland), England has historically had few universities. As recently as 1956, half of English students at university were attending one of three places: Oxford, Cambridge, or the University of London. A university degree was not required for entry into many professions, such as the law, or for an officer's commission in the Army, nor was it considered an asset in business. In the 1960s the demand for university education rose greatly. This reflected a higher birthrate, a higher proportion of young people staying at secondary school to take qualifica-

[21] See Ian Weinberg, *The English Public Schools* (New York: Atherton, 1967); and Rupert Wilkinson, *The Prefects* (London: Oxford University Press, 1964).

[22] Cf. Public Schools Appointments Bureau, *News Bulletin*, No. 143 (Summer, 1972), pp. 11–15.

tions for university entrance, and a higher value placed upon a degree. Even at the end of a decade of expansion, young people in university constituted less than 5 per cent of their age group.[23] Expansion "swamped" the ancient universities with new foundations: sixteen of the thirty-three English universities today were founded between 1961 and 1967. The bulk of young graduates today are not from institutions with a distinctive social status and manner. To be a graduate is no longer synonymous with being a gentleman.[24]

Differences in schooling imply differences in adult life. These most obviously affect occupational choice. A doctor or a teacher requires a formal educational qualification in order to follow his career. A businessman, a bookmaker, or a truck driver does not. The literature of political socialization states clear hypotheses about the expected political influence of education. The more educational advantages a person has, the more likely he is to: (1) favor the party most closely identified with the educationally advantaged, the Conservatives; (2) show interest in politics; (3) be active in politics. Because education affects occupation and this in turn affects position in the class structure, education can be important indirectly as well as directly. But there is a danger of reducing the study of political socialization to the study of schooling. Education may simply reinforce parental influences. Additionally or alternatively, latent and manifest political teaching may be of as little consequence as some more academic parts of the curriculum.

A few American social scientists have argued that differences in English schools will create antiregime outlooks among some young people. The evidence in the preceding chapter shows that this has not happened in preceding generations. The argument for growing disaffection is based on the absence of 100 per cent endorsement of reputed norms of democracy by English schoolchildren. It can be argued that this "two cheers for democracy" approach shows a realistic assessment of the limits

[23] On the consequences of university expansion for student numbers, see Richard Layard, John King, and Claus Moser, *The Impact of Robbins* (Harmondsworth: Penguin, 1969).

[24] Cf. Margaret Stacey, *Tradition and Change* (London: Oxford University Press, 1960), p. 14.

of government.[25] The chief English study of youthful attitudes indicates that partisanship, not schooling, is the chief influence upon overall evaluations of government.[26]

Education is positively related to party preference: The more education a person has, the more likely he is to vote Conservative. This is true when class is held constant. Among the upper middle class, those with further education to age seventeen or beyond are 5 per cent more likely to favor the Conservatives than those with the state minimum of education. Within the lower middle class the difference is 10 per cent, and among the working class, those with higher education are 18 per cent more likely to favor the Conservatives. But class differences are much more important that educational differences. Among upper-middle-class persons with a minimum of education, 66 per cent are Conservatives; among working-class people with the same education, 35 per cent are Conservatives.[27] Length or type of education has little influence upon interest in politics; it can explain less than 1 per cent of the variation between those most and least interested. The Civic Culture survey found that Englishmen with more education were slightly more likely to feel a sense of political efficacy, but these differences are less than those found in the United States.[28]

Education is most clearly related to active participation in politics. The more education a person has, the greater the possibility that he can go higher up the political career ladder. Englishmen with a minimum of education constitute nearly three-quarters of the electorate but less than half the number of local government councillors, and less than one-tenth the number of MPs, ministers, or administrative civil servants.

[25] Cf. Jack Dennis *et al.*, "Support for Nation and Government among English Children," *British Journal of Political Science*, I:1 (1971); and Dennis Kavanagh, "Allegiance among English Children: a Dissent," *ibid.*, II:1 (1972). Note also, Paul R. Abramson and T. M. Hennessey, "Beliefs about Democracy among British Adolescents," *Political Studies*, XVIII:2 (1970).

[26] See Ted Tapper, *Young People and Society* (London: Faber, 1971), pp. 136 ff.

[27] Richard Rose, "Britain: Simple Abstractions and Complex Realities," Table 10.

[28] See Giuseppe di Palma, *Apathy and Participation* (New York: Free Press, 1970), Tables IV, 1–4.

Reciprocally, those with a maximum of education, the 2 per cent with a university degree, constitute more than half the MPs, ministers and high-ranking civil servants (Table V.2). The preeminence of university graduates among the ranks of senior civil servants is hardly surprising, given the recruitment of these officials by competitive academic examination. Education also greatly affects membership of the House of Commons, which has no educational qualification for entry. The Labour party, claiming to represent working-class interests, draws more than half its MPs and ministers from the very small fraction of its supporters who are university graduates.

Education is neither a necessary nor a sufficient cause of a political career. It is not necessary, because at every rank some persons enter without any formal academic qualifications. This is most notable in local politics; it even applies to a few administrative civil servants who have worked their way up from the lower ranks. Higher or prestigious education is not a sufficient determinant of a political career. An exhaustive study of pupils at Winchester, one of the best of public schools, found that only 3.3 per cent of its former schoolboys entered Parliament or local politics in the nineteenth century; and among former Wykehamists, from 1890 to 1922 less than 1 per cent entered Parliament. The armed services and business have claimed the largest proportion of Wykehamists.[29] This finding, which is even more applicable to less well-known public schools, demonstrates that educational advantages assist a person who wishes to enter politics but do not provide sufficient motivation to make a person seek a political career.

Education often reflects family background and, in the case of public schools, social status independent of formal learning. For example, in this century eleven of sixteen Prime Ministers have been university graduates. But five of the eleven graduates were born into aristocratic families, and two of the five nongraduates were born into well-connected political families. One must therefore separate the influence of family and of schooling. One way to do this is to examine the proportion of

29 See T. J. H. Bishop, with Rupert Wilkinson, *Winchester and the Public School Elite* (London: Faber, 1967), pp. 66 ff.

TABLE V.2 *Educational Differences by Political Role (in percentages)*

Highest level of education	*Voters*	*Local Councillors*	*MPs*		*Ministers*		*Administrative civil servants*
			Con.	*Lab.*	*Con.*	*Lab.*	
University	2	9	64	51	80	65	71
Other further education	4	6	2	10	0	2	17
Military, commercial, etc.	3	4	—[a]		7	0	—
Public or direct-grant school	5	18	24	2	12	2	—
Grammar school	9	12	10	16	0	9	—
Technical, intermediate	5	5	—	1	0	5	10
Elementary, secondary modern	72	45	—	19	0	16	2

Sources: Voters and Councillors, Louis Moss and Stanley Parker, *The Local Government Councillor*, Vol. 2 (London: HMSO, 1967), p. 27; MPs derived from D. E. Butler and M. Pinto-Duschinsky, *The British General Election of 1970* (London: Macmillan, 1971), p. 301; ministers calculated by the author from *Who's Who* data on Conservatives of Cabinet rank appointed in 1970, and Labour ministers appointed in 1964. Civil servants include persons promoted from lower ranks; based on A. H. Halsey and Ivor Crewe, *The Fulton Committee*, Vol. III (1), pp. 64ff.

[a]Data not available.

those in politics whose education is prestigious and meritocratic (i.e., attended both public school and university), purely prestigious (public school only), purely meritocratic (grammar school and university), or lacking both prestige and high merit.

Table V.3 emphasizes the differences between Conservative and Labour politicians, as well as between politicians and those who elect them. Leading civil servants are university graduates and often have a prestigious secondary education. The median Conservative MP and minister has "jam on one side and butter on the other," that is, he has a public school education and he has earned a university degree. The modal Labour MP has no education to brag about, whether viewed in terms of prestige or merit. But the modal Labour minister has an education that is both prestigious and meritorious. Whatever the party or office, a politician whose only asset is passing examinations and winning scholarships is at a disadvantage compared with those who have been to public school or, in the case of the Labour Party, those whose very lack of education gives them an "ordinary" status. Educational differences between Labour MPs and ministers increased during the

TABLE V.3 *Prestige and Merit in the Education of Politicians (in percentages)*

	MPs		*Ministers*		*Administrative civil servants*
Type of education	*Con.*	*Lab.*	*Con.*	*Lab.*	
Pure merit	13	33	12	26	44
Pure prestige	24	2	19	2	—[a]
Prestige and merit	51	18	68	39	56
Neither	12	46	0	33	—[a]
Numbers	330	287	41	43	—[a]

Sources: MPs derived from D. E. Butler and M. Pinto-Duschinsky, *The British General Election of 1970* (London: Macmillan, 1971), p. 301; ministers calculated by the author from *Who's Who* data on Conservatives of Cabinet rank appointed in 1970, and Labour ministers appointed in 1964. Civil servants include persons promoted from lower ranks; based on A. H. Halsey and Ivor Crewe, *The Fulton Committee,* Vol. III (1), pp. 64ff.

[a]In default of full details, all civil servants are classified as if graduates.

six-year life of Harold Wilson's administration. By 1970 graduates outnumbered nongraduates in the Labour Cabinet by a margin of 17 to 4. Jim Callaghan, one of the most senior Labour ministers, could complain that his life was "less complete than it might be" because he had not gone to university.[30]

Another way to examine the influence of schooling in political socialization is to study differences among children currently in school. This approach appeals to those who believe in education as a means of "engineering" social change. While little can be done about the effect of education upon those who have already left school – virtually the whole of the adult electorate – state control of education offers opportunities to change the socialization of those now in school and, even more, of their younger brothers and sisters.

A study by Ted Tapper of the political outlooks of fourteen-year-olds in a variety of English secondary schools, from a prestigious direct-grant grammar school to secondary modern and comprehensive schools, provides survey evidence to test the relative influence of different types of schooling as against parental influences. The data show that party preferences are most sensitive to socialization influences. Youthful partisanship is scarcely influenced by educational factors; parents' party preferences account for nearly all of the 43.7 per cent of explained variance in party preference.[31] A total of 37 per cent of young persons described themselves as interested in politics. Here again, parental influences are most important. Interest in politics is also associated with a young person's academic ability, as indicated by how long he expects to remain in school. Together, these influences explain 25.7 per cent of the variation in youthful political interest.

Education might be expected to influence youthful political aspirations most. Just as different types of secondary schools have been organized to prepare young people for contrasting occupational roles, so might they prepare children for con-

[30] "Farmer Jim from the JC ranch," *The Guardian,* June 6, 1970.

[31] All findings from Tapper's work are based upon this author's AID analysis of the original data, weighted to adjust his respondents to proportions in different types of secondary schools at the time of field work.

trasting adult roles as citizens. When asked about political activities, 42 per cent of youthful respondents could see themselves in a political position; the role of MP was most often chosen. But, contrary to the theories of educational sociologists, differences between the majority without political aspirations and those with such aspirations cannot be explained by parental or schooling factors. Influences that collectively accounted for more than two-fifths of the variation in party preference and one-quarter of the variation in political interest account for only 7.6 per cent of the variation in political aspirations among Tapper's sample.

The relative unimportance of secondary school influences for political outlooks is also evidenced by a study comparing pupils at Winchester, a very prestigious public school, and Taunton grammar school. The researchers found that responses to questions about politics revealed similar patterns in these two different types of schools. The authors conclude: "The special features of public school education do not produce any striking effects on political attitudes."[32]

Generalizing about the political effects of university education is difficult because the population of students changes rapidly, given the three-year length of the degree course. The wave of student protests that began at the London School of Economics in 1967 has not reached the scale of student demonstrations in America, France, or Germany. English students have tended to protest about student concerns and events within universities. They differ from students in America, where protests have often concerned political issues that also affect those outside the universities, e.g., race relations and the Vietnam war.

Studies of student attitudes prior to the protest era found students more dissatisfied politically and more ready to support Labour than would be expected of young people of predominantly middle-class background. Attitudes differed according to the student's subject of study. Students in social sciences have

[32] Quoted from Denis McQuail, Liam P. O'Sullivan, and W. G. Quine, "Elite Education and Political Values," in Richard Rose, editor, *Studies in British Politics,* p. 98.

tended to be the most pro-Labour or "left" in political outlook, and engineers the most conservative. Similar differences in political outlooks are found among teachers of the social sciences as against the sciences and engineering.[33] Because students in English universities usually choose their field of study *before* entering university, one cannot say that studying in different faculties causes youthful rebellion, but rather that rebellious young people are attracted to some academic subjects and conservatives to others. Whether these outlooks will persist through adult political life is an open question. A wave of left-wing sentiment swept Oxford and Cambridge in the 1930s, but it evaporated soon after World War II. The extent of change that student politicians undergo is illustrated by the fact that many members of Mr. Wilson's Labour Cabinet of 1964–70 had been contemporaries of his at Oxford in the 1930s; in their student days, these ministers had belonged to the Labour, Liberal, Conservative, and Communist parties. Harold Wilson himself was in the Liberal Club.

Schooling has a limited effect upon political attitudes because, at most, it is an intervening influence. English schools have reflected social differences among parents. Parental outlooks influence party preferences and interest in politics. An academic or nonacademic secondary education does little to alter or reinforce parental influence. Schooling exerts influence at a point relatively remote in time from the political world in which adult English people find themselves today. For example, the median voter at a general election has left school a quarter-century before polling day. Whether the school emphasizes an ethic of service in high public office, as Winchester does, or lesser aspirations, as do the majority of state secondary schools, makes little difference to young persons in school. The concept of citizenship, implying equality independent of educational achievement, appears to dominate political learning at this stage in life. A young person learns of common rights and duties rather than about differences in political

[33] See e.g., *Students in Society* (Manchester: University Union, 1963); and A. H. Halsey and Martin Trow, *The British Academics* (London: Faber, 1971).

roles and duties. The differences become prominent when young people move from school to adult life.

CLASS

To speak of class as an influence is to invoke a concept as diffuse as it is meant to be pervasive; sometimes it is used as a label for the cumulative effect of all socialization experiences. Occupation is the most commonly used definition of class in England; it will be the definition employed henceforth in this study.[34] To group people together in terms of a single economic attribute does not necessarily mean that they are identical in every other respect. A coal miner usually lives in a mining village where his occupation is integrally related to a whole network of social relations with family, friends, and neighbors. But a civil servant from the North of England, working in central London but living in a suburb outside it, may find his work relationships divorced from other present and past ties. To infer political differences from occupational differences is to assert something that must be proven or disproven.

Nearly every definition of occupational class places about two-thirds of Englishmen in the working class and one-third in the middle class. In politics it is particularly important to distinguish differences among nonmanual workers. The handful of upper-class people living solely on inherited capital are less significant than the 5 per cent of upper-middle-class people who dominate the professions and large organizations, including government. The "middle" middle class, holding less important positions in business and industry, is larger than what is above it. The lower middle class in routine white-collar jobs is equal in size to the other two sections of the middle class combined. Within the working class, sociologists often discriminate between skilled, semiskilled, and unskilled groups. Studies of voting and political recruitment show differences

[34] For an historical review of changing sociological indicators, see Mark Abrams, "Some Measurements of Social Stratification in Britain," in J. A. Jackson, editor, *Social Stratification* (Cambridge: University Press, 1968). More generally, see W. G. Runciman, *Relative Deprivation and Social Justice* (London: Routledge, 1966).

between the upper middle class and the lower middle class. Substantial political differences are not found among strata within the working class.[35]

Using occupational criteria to assign people to classes has the disadvantage of ignoring the influence of subjective attitudes. In T. H. Marshall's definition, "The essence of social class is the way a man is treated by his fellows (and, reciprocally, the way he treats them), not the qualities or the possessions which cause that treatment."[36] Subjective class assessments differ from objective assessments based on occupation. Surveys consistently find that nine-tenths or more of the population are prepared to place themselves in one or another class category. But about one-third subjectively place themselves on the "wrong" side of the class line defined by sociologists. Because more people upgrade than downgrade themselves, the subjective class structure shows the middle class about equal in size with the working class.[37] Differences in objective and subjective class rankings arise because the criteria people use to place themselves are much more heterogeneous than the sole criterion of occupation. Some working-class people use Socialist standards to assign people to classes by their contribution to social well-being. They rate farmers, doctors, and coal miners higher than company directors, accountants, or civil servants.[38]

Insofar as preadult experiences are important, a person's class may be determined by his father's occupation rather than his own. In many cases, an adult will have the same level of occupation as his parent. If he rises or falls in class, he may wish to retain the political outlook learned in childhood. Al-

[35] For copious tables showing class-related differences in politics, see Richard Rose, "Britain: Simple Abstractions and Complex Realities," and "Class and Party Divisions: Britain as a Test Case," *Sociology,* II:2 1968).

[36] T. H. Marshall, *Citizenship and Social Class,* p. 92.

[37] A different set of questions used by David Butler and Donald Stokes, *Political Change in Britain,* Chs. 4–5, give differing proportions of class identifiers. Their distribution has not been replicated by any other British survey known to this author.

[38] See Michael Young and Peter Willmott, "Social Grading by Manual Workers," *British Journal of Sociology,* VII:4 (1956).

TABLE V.4 *The Influence of Class upon Party Preference (in percentages)*

	Con.	*Lab.*	*Other, none*	*Difference, Con.-Lab.*	*Total*
Prof'l & business middle class	70	22	8	+48	15
Lower middle class	54	37	9	+17	22
Working class	38	51	11	-13	63

Source: 1970 Gallup Poll data.

ternatively, the experience of moving up or down the social ladder may result in tensions pushing an individual to political extremes. The extent of social mobility depends in part upon the number of classes into which people are grouped: one careful analysis found 50 per cent of Englishmen are nonmobile working class and 15 per cent nonmobile middle class. The socially mobile Englishmen constitute 25 per cent of the population; 19 per cent have moved into the middle class from working-class childhoods and 7 per cent are downwardly mobile into the working class; another 9 per cent could not be classified.[39]

Whatever measure is used, class differences are expected to result in significant differences in party preference and in political interest and participation. Those differences not only reflect the importance of what Weber called "life chances in the market"; [40] they also reflect indirectly the interaction of this economic factor with other socialization experiences.

The influence of present occupational class upon party preference has been documented by every voting study ever undertaken in England (Table V.4). Three qualifications must be made. The first is that a proportion of the electorate has no party preference or prefers the Liberals, a non-class party. Within the working class, this nonaligned group almost prevents Labour from being the party of a majority. Second, the

[39] See Paul Abramson, "Intergenerational Social Mobility and Partisan Choice," *American Political Science Review,* LXVI:4 (1972).

[40] See H. H. Gerth and C. Wright Mills, *From Max Weber* (London: Routledge, 1948), pp. 180 ff.

relationship between class and party is asymmetrical. The middle class is more strongly Conservative than the working class is Labour; the most homogeneous category is the upper middle class. A third qualification follows from this: The relationship between party and class is partial, not complete.[41]

The relationship between class and party increases when one takes into account the parental class of voters. Englishmen in the same class as their parents are likely to be Conservative if middle class and Labour if working class. Upwardly mobile Englishmen will favor the Conservatives, but by a lesser margin than those born into the middle class. A plurality of downwardly mobile Englishmen are Labour, but they are less strongly Labour than are those born in the working class. They also tend to favor their new class less strongly than upwardly mobile people favor theirs. The effect of social mobility remains when one controls for differences in parents' party preference within each class. Working-class children from Conservative homes are more likely to be upwardly mobile than those from Labour families.[42]

One reason for the limited relationship between class and party preference is that Englishmen differ in the degree to which they regard class as salient to their everyday concerns. When Butler and Stokes asked people *whether or not* they think of themselves as belonging to a particular class, the proportion answering yes varied from 50 to 60 per cent. On this basis, the electorate must be divided into three groups: those who think of themselves as middle class, those who see themselves as working class, and those who do not articulate a sense of class consciousness, unless pressed to do so by a survey interviewer. According to this study, the largest single category of Englishmen consists of persons who do not think of themselves in class terms.[43]

When the figures in Table V.5 are examined by reading

[41] See Richard Rose, "Britain: Simple Abstractions and Complex Realities."

[42] Recalculated from data in Paul Abramson, "Intergenerational Social Mobility, and Partisan Choice," Tables 1–2.

[43] I am indebted to Lewis Morrison, a Strathclyde student, for suggesting analyzing the data in the manner shown in Table V.5.

TABLE V.5 *Subjective Class Identification and Party Preference (in percentages)*

	Con.	*Other, none*	*Lab.*	*Totals*
Middle class identifier	8.5	4.2	2.4	15.1
Low class salience	19.3	11.6	15.6	46.5
Working class identifier	8.5	7.2	22.7	38.5
Totals	36.3	23.0	40.7	100

Source: David Butler and Donald Stokes, 1964 British Election Survey, combined answers to Q. 69a and Q. 69a*.

across the rows, one finds that among the consciously middle class, Conservatives outnumber Labour voters by 3½ to 1. Among the consciously working class, Labour voters outnumber Conservatives by a ratio of 2½ to 1. Among those for whom class is not particularly salient, the Conservatives have a 6-to-5 advantage. When the figures are examined by reading down the columns, one finds that more than half the Conservative vote comes from persons for whom class is of low salience. The same is true for nonvoters and those who support the Liberals and other parties. Less than one-quarter of the Conservative vote comes from persons who consciously see themselves as working class, and an equal proportion from those who see themselves as middle class. Among Labour voters, more than half are consciously working class and only one in 16 sees himself as middle class. Taken together, the figures in Table V.5 show that 42.8 per cent conform to "class-typical" roles, as middle-class Conservatives, working-class Labour voters or persons refusing these party alternatives and not regarding class as salient. "Class deviants" (i.e., consciously working-class Conservatives and consciously middle-class Labour) are 10.9 per cent of the total electorate.

More complex theories of the influence of class emphasize the role played by class-specific institutions, for instance, trade unions, in socializing people into political attitudes. For example, persons who belong to a trade union are expected to be more likely to vote Labour than are those whose nominal class position is not reinforced by involvement in a class-specific organization. Approximately half the working-class families in England have one or more members who belong to a union. This relationship within the working class is reflected by differences in political outlooks. Among manual workers in trade unions, 60 per cent favor Labour; a plurality of lower-middle-class union members also favor Labour. The reciprocal attitude also exists: those who are in the working class but do not belong to trade unions are divided evenly between the Conservative and Labour parties. Unions can indirectly influence political attitudes because their bargaining power collectively strengthens the influence of individual manual workers. The Civic Culture survey found that manual workers in England are almost as likely to be consulted by their employers about job decisions as are white-collar workers. In turn, this correlates with an individual's belief that he can influence government.[44] In extreme instances, trade-union action can cause a government to subsidize a firm to maintain thousands of jobs or even to nationalize an industry.

The distinctive housing patterns of English society make it possible to study the political effect of living in a socially homogeneous neighborhood.[45] One-third of English families live in municipally owned council houses. Council houses are usually grouped together in substantial numbers. This clustering not only creates individual identification with the council estate but also makes persons identifiable as council tenants by those who live elsewhere. About four-fifths of council-house tenants are of the working class. In 1970, 63 per cent of working-class council tenants supported Labour, as against 40 per cent of working-class voters who owned their own homes. Among the lower middle class, a majority of council tenants favored Labour and a majority of home owners favored the Conservatives.

[44] Gabriel Almond and Sidney Verba, *The Civic Culture,* pp. 364 ff; see also David Butler and Donald Stokes, *Political Change in Britain,* pp. 154 ff.

[45] See Richard Rose, "Britain: Simple Abstractions and Complex Realities," Table 14–16.

The influence of neighbors is also found at the level of the parliamentary constituency. Constituencies are not necessarily "natural" social units; the average English constituency had 64,000 electors in 1970. Working-class people who live in safe Labour constituencies, surrounded by working-class neighbors are much more likely to vote Labour than are manual workers in marginal constituencies. In safe Conservative constituencies, where the middle class is most numerous, the response of working-class voters to community pressures results in a plurality voting Conservative. Lower-middle-class voters are equally likely to respond to community norms. Only upper-middle-class voters are little affected by the political coloration of the area in which they live. The influence of neighbors is better measured by types of housing or parliamentary constituencies than by urban-rural differences. Rural areas are not distinctly agricultural; mills, factories, and mines can be intermingled with farms. Further, there are middle-class wards within the most industrial of English cities. In consequence, once allowance is made for differences in the social composition of constituencies, urban-rural differences have little independent effect upon party preferences.

Analyzing the relationship of class and political participation is difficult, because full-time politicians are, by definition, in middle-class jobs. Trade union officials too are engaged in nonmanual work. The influence of class is most apparent when one examines the occupational class of the parents of politicians. Because national political roles are prestigious upper-middle-class jobs, no one in Parliament can be said to be downwardly mobile, unless one wishes to suggest that Sir Alec Douglas-Home lost prestige when he resigned his earldom to become Prime Minister in 1963. Educational data show that the great majority of Conservative MPs come from comfortably middle-class homes. Politics neither raises nor lowers their occupational status. The Labour Party, by contrast, has always drawn a significant proportion of its MPs from working-class families. Educational changes since World War II have created a third type of Labour MP, a person born into a working-class home but with an assured middle-class career because he is a university graduate. The administrative civil service draws disproportionately upon the offspring of middle-class families, because it recruits primarily from the universities, whose students are disproportionately of the middle class. The higher the political office, the greater the likelihood that it will be filled by someone who began his working life in a middle-class job (Table V.6). One-fifth of the nation is employed in professional or managerial tasks, but 45 per cent of councillors and more than half the MPs and ministers in both parties began their working careers at this level.

TABLE V.6 *The Occupational Background of Politicians (in percentages)*[a]

		MPs		*Ministers*		
Class	*Councillors*	*Con.*	*Lab.*	*Con.*	*Lab.*	*Nation*
Professionals	16	41	54	50	55	8
Managers, business	29	35	10	22	5	11
Lower middle class	12	2	5	0	0	16
Manual workers	19	1	26	0	41	56
Farmers of all kinds	15	9	0	6	0	4
Armed forces	2	7	0	11	0	1
Other, none	7	4	4	11	0	4

Sources: Concillors and national figures from *Management of Local Government*, Vol. 2, Tables 1.7, 1.10; MPs recalculated from data given by D. E. Butler and M. Pinto-Duschinsky, *The British General Election of 1970* (London: Macmillan, 1971), p. 302; ministers, 1964 Labour Cabinet and 1970 Conservative, calculated by the author.

[a]Occupation is based on early adult occupation. Manual workers in the Labour Cabinet were trade union officials immediately prior to entering Parliament.

Leading Labour politicians, even more than Conservatives, are drawn from the professions, especially teaching, the law, and journalism. Stated negatively, Labour politicians have virtually no experience as managers of large organizations. Because trade unions can sponsor candidates by giving cash support to members nominated as candidates, a substantial number of Labour MPs and 1964 Cabinet ministers have been of working-class origin. But the proportion drawn from working-class occupations has declined steadily from the party's foundation.[46] In 1906, 86 per cent of Labour MPs were from working-class backgrounds. Since 1945, the proportion has been less than half, reaching 26 per cent in 1970. Moreover, at the 1970 general election, more than two-fifths of the MPs returned with trade-union sponsorship were not themselves working-class people; they were adopted by unions seeking to strengthen their political voice in Parliament.

While class differences do affect party loyalties and, even more, recruitment into active political roles, they do not lead to the development of political outlooks based upon assumptions of class conflict. When people are interviewed about their attitudes toward class-related issues, differences are found within the middle class and within the working class; the two groups are not cohesive and opposing in views. A majority of people in each class think it difficult to rise in the English class system, but this is not perceived as a major source of frustration. When asked to say whether one class is happier than another, 69 per cent think that people are equally likely to be happy in either class. Among those who think one class happier, those in each class see themselves as happier than the other class.[47] A majority of voters say that they do not think there is bound to be political conflict between the classes. After an intensive analysis of questions about party images, Butler and Stokes conclude that approximately one-fifth of the electorate base their party choice on class concerns. But fewer still see politics in terms of mutually exclusive (as distinct from differing) class interests.[48] Survey evidence also shows that a clear majority of voters rejects the idea that class interests are defined by the social characteristics of their MPs. They think it much more important that an MP should live in the constituency that elects him than that he should be of the same social class as most of his electoral supporters.[49]

[46] See Richard Rose, "Class and Party Divisions: Britain as a Test Case," pp. 131–32.

[47] See National Opinion Polls, *Bulletin,* No. 109 (June 1972), pp. 17–18.

[48] See David Butler and Donald Stokes, *Political Change in Britain,* pp. 91 ff.

[49] See a survey on public attitudes to Parliament, commissioned by Granada Television in 1972 from National Opinion Polls for the program "State of the Nation Parliament."

International comparisons further emphasize the limited influence of class upon political loyalties in England. Studies testing the relative political influence of such basic social characteristics as class, religion, age, sex, and education, have found that in England class explains less variation in party loyalties than basic social characteristics explain in France, Germany, Italy, the Netherlands, Belgium, or Scandinavian countries.[50] In most continental countries, religious or secular outlooks are stronger determinants of party loyalties than class is in England. By European standards, Englishmen are noteworthy for the relative weakness of class as a determinant of party loyalties.

THE CUMULATIVE EFFECT

In the course of a lifetime, every Englishman is subject to a great variety of social experiences; some emphasize differences between him and his fellow citizens, whereas others emphasize an identity of concerns. Until the past decade, racial differences were not a basis for differential socialization, because virtually the whole English population was white. In this century, religion has been rapidly declining in significance, both socially and politically. Today, differences in religious socialization are not translated into significant political differences. Moreover, more than 95 per cent of the English population is Christian and nearly 90 per cent Protestant. The increasing numerical preeminence of England within the United Kingdom makes differing national identities of limited aggregate significance today. At the time of the first census in 1801, England contributed 53 per cent of the United Kingdom's population; today it constitutes 83 per cent of the United Kingdom. Within England, four-fifths of Englishmen live in urban areas, and more than one-third of those living in areas classified as rural are close enough to a city to commute daily for work.[51]

[50] See Richard Rose, "Introduction," *Electoral Behavior: A Comparative Handbook*.

[51] The figures are derived from Richard Rose, "Britain: Simple Abstractions and Complex Realities," Table 25, weighted to allow for the effect of commuting from nominally rural areas to urban jobs. See *Social Trends*, Vol. 2, p. 134.

The cumulative effect of these influences is a society that is very homogeneous in terms of race, religion, national identity, and urban life-style. European societies such as France, Germany, Belgium, and the Netherlands – not to mention America and Canada – are by contrast pluralist. In these societies, social groups are more nearly equal in size along each dimension of social differentiation, and more dimensions of social structure are politically salient, such as race in America and language in Belgium and Canada.

Englishmen are said to differ politically along class lines, because class-related differences are the only differences substantial in size and political salience. The greatest degree of partisanship is shown by the smallest social groups within English society: middle-class rural Protestants (Conservative advantage, 45 per cent) and middle-class rural Catholics (Conservative advantage, 43 per cent). The largest group – urban Protestant manual workers – shows an almost even division of partisanship; the Labour advantage in this group is 9 per cent.

The relative importance of different socialization influences can be summarized by examining how much influence each has upon political outlooks, giving precedence to those experiences that come first in time. With a powerful computer, one can use a statistical technique known as AID (Automatic Interaction Detector) to see how much influence a variety of social factors could have on party loyalties. In Table V.7 a national adult sample of British voters is divided successively by generation, sex, and other socialization categories, in the order that these influences are likely to affect voter preferences. The influence of four adult factors – union membership, housing, region, and religion – is considered at the end of the analysis. At each socialization stage one can compute the amount of variation in party preference produced by each additional influence.

Cumulatively, more than half the explained variation in party preference can be accounted for by early childhood influences. Neither generation nor sex explains as much as one per cent of the variation. But father's class and, independent of class, parent's party preference are of substantial importance,

TABLE V.7 *The Cumulative Effect of Socialization Experiences (in percentages)*

Stage	*Division*	*Conservative proportion, Con.-Lab.*	*Variation explained at each stage*
1. Generation	Born pre-1914	53	0.9
	Born, 1914+	43	
2. Sex	Male	46	0.1
	Female	48	
3. Father's class	Middle	71	8.8
	Working	36	
4. Father's Party	Conservative	76	13.8
	Labour	19	
	Other, none	52	
5. Education	Academic	73	3.7
	Minimum	41	
6. Current class	Middle	74	7.7
	Working	30	
Other influences			
7a. Union membership	Yes	27	–
	No	59	
b. Housing	Owners	65	1.2
	Tenants	36	
c. Nation	England	48	0.7
	Non-England	41	
d. Religion	Church of England	50	1.3
	Other	40	
Total			38.2

Source: David Butler and Donald Stokes, 1964 British Election Survey, analyzed by the author with AID (Automatic Interaction Detector) III.

together accounting for more than half the total variation explained. Attendance at school beyond the minimum required has little additional effect upon party preference. In adult life, current occupational class shows up as the influence of most additional importance. (If one had to pick a single influence, current class would be the most powerful; its effect is lessened here because allowance has been made for influences preceding it.) The analysis also shows how important all of these influences are collectively. They explain 38.2 per cent of the major party preferences of voters; 61.8 per cent of preferences must be explained by other factors independent of those discussed here.

One reason for the absence of homogeneous class voting is that a majority of Englishmen do not have a set of socialization experiences consistent with the ideal-type definitions of class. Models of class determinism presuppose that working-class people have a minimum education, have a trade-union member in the family, rent their home, and think of themselves as belonging to the working class. Middle-class people are expected to have the opposite set of experiences. In fact, only 21 per cent of the British electorate meets all of these ideal-type criteria. Moreover, middle-class Englishmen are more likely to conform to their class stereotype (12 per cent) than are manual workers (9 per cent). The median middle-class Englishman has three of the four attributes expected to reinforce the influence of a nonmanual job. The median working-class Englishman has two. The experience that most unites the working class is a minimum of education; that which is most often lacking is membership in a trade union. As the number of reinforcing attributes increases, the likelihood grows of an individual's voting for the party typical of his class. The extent to which individuals have a cross-class mixture of socialization experiences helps explain contrasting political preferences among people nominally assigned to the same occupational class.[52] The greater homogeneity of experiences within the middle class helps explain the greater cohesion of voters there.

The absence of mechanical consistency in political socialization can also be explained by changes in the institutions involved in the process. In party politics, the collapse of the old Liberal Party and the subsequent organizational growth of the Labour Party have altered the alternatives among which voters can choose. A new party preference has been forced upon those brought up in Liberal homes, who find no Liberal candi-

[52] Cf. *Ibid.*, Table 13. See also Elizabeth Bott, *Family and Social Network* (London: Tavistock, 1957).

date in their constituency. Because women were not given the vote until after World War I, more than one-quarter of women voting in the 1970 general election reached the age of political awareness before women had the right to vote. Another group first voting in 1970, those eighteen to twenty-one years old, exercised political rights that had been conferred upon them only a few months before. The political controversies of the 1970s indicate that changes in the institutions and processes of politics will continue, forcing many adults to "relearn" or "rethink" established political ideas.[53]

Youthful socialization is most important in the recruitment of a small proportion of Englishmen into national political roles. Those in national politics are better born, better educated, and better employed than the average Englishmen. As one goes up the ladder of office holders from voter to councillor, MP, senior civil servant, and minister, the social differences between governors and governed increase. Yet the same evidence also shows that there is no single course of entry into political life.

Socialization influences the probabilities of political action; it does not determine them with certainty. Because socialization is a continuous process, individuals remain open to change in their political outlook at any time in adult life. The likelihood of change depends upon the degree of an individual's involvement in politics. The mass of English people are carried forward by inertia in whatever political role they find themselves. They have enough interest and knowledge to vote, but not enough involvement readily to learn new political roles and ideas. By contrast, the minority who are full-time politicians undergo intense explicitly political experiences. Preadult and parapolitical influences are likely to be most important for those least involved in politics. Among political participants, socialization into the role of politician is likely to override other influences. This is illustrated by the entry of a party of new men into office. The new governors can alter the policies of government. But accession to office may also

[53] David Marsh, "Political Socialization: the Implicit Assumptions Questioned," *British Journal of Political Science* I:4 (1971).

alter the men. Lord Balniel, the heir to one of the oldest titles in Britain, has noted that existing patterns of politics are preserved "not so much by the conscious efforts of the well established, but by the zeal of those who have just won entry, and by the hopes of those who still aspire." [54]

[54] Lord Balniel, "The Upper Classes," *The Twentieth Century* No. 999 (1960), p. 432.

CHAPTER VI

Recruiting Participants

The principle of popular government is that the supreme power, the determining efficacy in matters political, resides in the people – not necessarily or commonly in the whole people, in the numerical majority, but in a chosen people, a picked and selected people. It is so in England.

EXAMINING WHO DOES and does not participate in politics broadens understanding of the relationship between government and society. At most, socialization can only predispose individuals to take part in politics. Whether or not a person actively participates in politics depends upon procedures for recruiting participants as well as upon individual aspirations. For example, in the early nineteenth century civil servants were recruited on the basis of kinship and friendship with political patrons. Today they are recruited by examination. Each procedure gives special advantage to a minority – but the basis of choice and the anticipated political consequences are different.

Before analyzing how politicians are recruited, one must first ask: Who are the politicians? If a politician is defined as an individual whose actions influence choices between alternative public policies, then a housewife may be a politician influencing economic policy by her market-place reaction to prices. In this study, politicians are defined by their role and not by their office; they are individuals who expect and are expected to participate in policy making. Ministers and MPs are, by virtue of their office, politicians, as are senior civil servants. Individuals holding important offices outside government, for instance, trade union officials, heads of important export firms, or national newspaper editors, intermittently take a politician's role when they participate in deliberations about central government policy. They differ from ministers in that ministers devote all their time to a political role, whereas these other individuals are only intermittently active in politics.[1] In addition, individuals whose full-time employment gives them no political standing may follow politics as an avocation, becoming activists in their local community, with a voluntary office on the town council or in the local branch of a party or trade union.[2] At election time the great bulk of Englishmen temporarily become politicians, voting to decide who will represent them between elections.

Once active in politics, whether on a full-time, intermittent, or voluntary basis, an Englishman undergoes intensive socialization in his role. This experience differentiates all politicians, whatever their social origins, from nonpoliticians. Political socialization in institutions outside of government, for instance, in the family, in school, or at work, can at most influence predispositions. Role socialization within political institutions, for instance, local government, party organizations, or the Palace of Westminster and Whitehall, is "on-the-job" learning. An individual's political career depends upon his ability to do what is expected of him. These expectations are not so much the product of individual ideas as they are a consequence of the chief institutions of government.

In this chapter the recruitment of politicians is analyzed in terms of the institutional opportunities provided for individual participation in politics and the differential response of Englishmen to these opportunities. The first section considers the extent to which members of the peripheral public, that is,

[1] For a full discussion of the roles of politicians, illustrated with British and American materials, see Richard Rose, *People in Politics*, Chs. 3–4.

[2] Local government employees (but not elected councillors) are involved full-time in public affairs. While the leading officials in the largest towns are paid as highly as very senior civil servants, the bulk have nondiscretionary duties; to avoid complications, these officials are excluded from further discussion in this chapter.

those without a full-time political office, take a political role in their local community. The second considers socialization into the most important central political roles. The extent to which high social or economic status is converted into political office is reviewed in the third section. The significance of a process that "selects in" some people and "selects out" others is considered in the final section.

THE PERIPHERAL PUBLIC

Every Englishman has a multiplicity of roles in society today. He is spouse and parent, worker and consumer, and taxpayer and beneficiary of public services. Any analysis of political recruitment risks distorting the significance most individuals give to political activities. Most Englishmen do not view their lives in terms of what can be achieved in political roles. Instead of speaking of individuals as voters, it would make more sense to speak of the behavior of ordinary individuals in electoral situations. The role of voter or citizen is not the chief defining characteristic of Englishmen.

The largest portion of the population have strictly peripheral political roles, whether they are nominally involved in politics as members of pressure groups or are outside the boundaries of organized participation except for casting an occasional vote. The members of the peripheral public are linked to central politics by local activists who claim to represent them and by the field staff of central government, whose offices (e.g., the post office, the employment exchange, the army recruiting station, or the constituency party) are a local outlet for central political institutions. In every Western nation the peripheral public and local activists constitute the majority of the citizenry. Problems of scale and specialization make it impossible for the majority of people to participate full-time in central political roles. The ordinary citizen can either seek a relatively active role in his local community,[3] or a relatively less important role in the national political system.

[3] See L. J. Sharpe, "Theories and Values of Local Government," *Political Studies,* XVIII:2 (1970); Dilys M. Hill, *Participating in Local Affairs* (Harmondsworth: Penguin, 1970); and L. J. Sharpe, "American Democracy Reconsidered," *British Journal of Political Science,* III:1–2 (1973).

TABLE VI.1 *Involvement in Local Politics*

Level	*Estimated number of people*	*Estimated % of electorate*	*Source*
Consumer of local government services	39,200,000	98	LGE, p. 44
Votes at local election	16,800,000	42	LGE, p. 78
Knows name of council chairman/mayor	11,200,000	28	LGE, p. 24
Very interested in local affairs	8,000,000	20	CAS, p. 29
Ever contacted local councillor	6,800,000	17	LGE, p. 17
Confident of influencing local council	4,800,000	12	LGE, p. 75
Knows date and place of council meeting	3,200,000	8	LGE, p. 54
Member, reorganized local council	21,695	0.05	

Sources: LGE = Mary Horton, *The Local Government Elector*, Vol. 3 (London, HMSO). CAS = *Community Attitudes Survey: England*.

Nearly every Englishman sees himself as a consumer of local government services, but knowledge and interest, two attitudes conducive to effective participation in local politics, are limited (Table VI.1). In a survey commissioned to provide information for the reform of local government structure, one-quarter of the respondents could name their local mayor or council chairman, and one-fifth said they were "very interested" in what goes on in their local area. Only one-tenth said that they had ever attended a local council meeting, and fewer knew the usual date and place of their local council meetings.[4]

By comparison with Americans, an Englishman has fewer opportunities to vote at the local level, for he normally casts a ballot at only one local election; he is not concurrently a voter in local, county, and state elections, as well as a voter in school board and sewer district elections. An Englishman is offered no opportunity to vote for legislative or institutional reforms in local referendums, nor is there a public ballot on

[4] Mary Horton, *The Local Government Elector* (London: HMSO, Vol. 3).

tax increases or bonds to finance capital expenditure for local services, as happens in many American local jurisdictions. When local government elections are held, a voter expresses his preference for councillors to represent his views; the senior administrative officials of local government are appointed rather than elected, as often happens in America. The concentration of authority in the hands of a small council of elected persons and a large body of professional local government civil servants makes the town hall mirror arrangements found in Whitehall.

The majority of Englishmen are passive subjects, not active participants in local politics. Less than half vote at local elections; in half the wards, seats are uncontested, so that an election is unnecessary. A total of 26 per cent said they had been in touch with local authority officials within the year. The problems that lead people to their council office are housing, welfare services, education, and such environmental services as refuse collection. Local councillors are sought out less often. When people were asked whether they might succeed if they tried to influence a local council decision, 36 per cent said they would not bother trying and another 18 per cent said they would be unsuccessful: 46 per cent thought they might be able to exercise influence.[5]

About one in twenty Englishmen has at some time thought of taking an active part in local politics by standing for local office. Less than half of those have ever in fact held local office. The limit to participation is not electoral defeat, but the unwillingness of potential community leaders, when it came to the point, to stand for election. People exclude themselves from local politics for three major reasons: 36 per cent lack the time or the health to do the work, 32 per cent lack the self-confidence and temperament, and 24 per cent lack knowledge and interest in local politics.[6]

A seat on the local council represents the height of partici-

[5] See M. Horton, *The Local Government Elector*, Ch. 2, and Louis Moss and Stanley Parker, *The Local Government Councillor* (London: HMSO, Vol. 2, 1967), p. 45.

[6] See M. Horton, *The Local Government Elector*, Chs. 5–6; Cf. L. Moss and S. Parker, *The Local Government Councillor*, Chs. 4, 9.

pation for an amateur politician. Because the job is unpaid, councillors are expected to remain in the workaday world outside politics; the average councillor spends about twelve hours a week on political work. Studies of local councillors find that most achieve a high degree of satisfaction from their work. Some see council work as a complement to other community activities; some see it as compensation for a dull job; others, such as retired persons and housewives, see council politics as a substitute for full-time employment. Because of the limited willingness of people to enter council politics, a determined Conservative or Labour activist has a reasonable chance in most parts of the country to become a councillor.

The government commission that sponsored these surveys of citizenship rejected the argument that the best way to reform local government was decentralization, increasing the number of elective offices, and bringing local government closer to the consumers of its services. Instead it decided to amalgamate local authorities into larger units, resulting in fewer elective posts and a higher ratio of electors to representatives. The new councils take power in 1974. The amalgamation of smaller authorities is intended to improve the efficiency and effectiveness of local government services. The most succinct justification is provided in the conclusion to a research report on participation in the unreformed government of Tyneside:

> The present structure does not sacrifice efficiency for the sake of participation. It sacrifices both for no reason at all. If it is possible to see a path to greater efficiency, the fear that it might destroy a vigorous and extensive pattern of participation turns out to be imaginary. Participation is already feeble and confined to a minority. If, on the other hand, a high level of participation is desired, it is by no means enough to maintain the present system of local government. On the contrary, an active search is needed for new modes of activity that will engage the energies of those who now are indifferent or disenchanted.[7]

The extent to which an individual is reckoned to participate in central government depends upon the definition of

[7] Henry Parris, *Participation in Government: A Study of Tyneside* (Durham: University Politics Department, 1970) pp. 50–51.

participation. If governors are to live up to their name, everyone must participate, even if only as a compliant subject. Virtually everyone participates if participation is defined as paying taxes and drawing benefits. The mixed-economy welfare state provides benefits at every stage of life, from maternity and children's allowances through schooling, housing, and health to a pension in old age and a death benefit for the next of kin. More than five-sixths of the population live in a household drawing a weekly money benefit from the state.[8]

Parliamentary elections provide the one opportunity an Englishman has to participate directly in central government. Virtually every British citizen eighteen years old or over is eligible to vote. Citizens of Commonwealth countries (e.g., Australia and Zambia) and of the Irish Republic are also entitled to vote while residing in Britain.[9] The burden of registration is undertaken by local government officials, and registers are revised annually to maintain accuracy. Election day is not a legal holiday, but the wide dispersal of polling stations, the compactness of the territory, and the individual sense of citizen duty result in a high turnout of voters by comparison with American standards, though not by European comparisons. In the seven general elections since 1950, turnout has averaged 78.1 per cent; when figures are adjusted to allow for the effect of mortality and other technical considerations, the average turnout is 82.4 per cent.[10] Turnout has been falling since 1959 but remains much higher than in an American presidential election. Many who do not vote at an election are prevented from doing so by temporary illness or holidays. There is no substantial group of people who persistently refuse to vote because of apathy or disaffection. Englishmen are well advised to vote when a parliamentary elec-

[8] Calculated from *Social Trends,* Vol. 3, pp. 91–93. Note that the proportion of voters enjoying benefits is lower than the proportion of the population, because many families receiving benefits are drawing family allowances for children below voting age.

[9] See H. W. Wollaston, *Parker's Conduct of Parliamentary Elections* (London: Knight, 1970 edition), p. 40 ff.

[10] For details on turnout, see Richard Rose, "Britain: Simple Abstractions and Complex Realities," Table 5.

tion is held. Casting a ballot for a single candidate for one seat in the House of Commons is a person's only chance to participate in a nationwide election.

For the majority of English people, voting is a duty; only 18 per cent in the loyalty survey agreed with the statement that "you don't have to vote unless you feel like it." The majority said they have no emotional involvement in election campaigns. This attitude does not arise from a lack of confidence in elections. Most of them think that elections offer voters a real choice between parties, that most people think about how they vote, and that voters do have a big influence on government. Only 12 per cent of respondents showed a marked distaste for the electoral system.[11]

Between elections Englishmen can be vicariously involved in national government by taking an interest in politics. Nine per cent of the electorate say they are "very interested" in politics outside an election campaign; at the other end of the scale, 14 per cent describe themselves as "not at all interested" in politics. When voters are asked to identify major party politicians, the median respondent names three persons; only 5 per cent can name three Conservative, three Labour and one Liberal front bencher.[12] While there are class differences in political involvement, because of size the working class constitutes a majority of those very interested in politics, as well as of those not at all interested.

Political parties provide one means by which individuals can participate in national politics. Both the Conservative and Labour parties maintain constituency associations throughout England, and the Liberals wish to do so. There are no restrictive entrance rules; the parties seek as many members as are willing to join. With a little initiative or effort, a person can find himself ward secretary of his local party or a member of its general management committee. The great majority of

11 See Richard Rose and Harve Mossawir, "Voting and Elections," pp. 187 ff.

12 See Mark Abrams, "Social Trends and Electoral Behaviour," *British Journal of Sociology,* XIII:3 (1962), p. 234; and National Opinion Polls, *Monthly Bulletin* (February, 1970).

Englishmen identify with a political party, but they are not so strong in their adherence as to become members. Both political parties define membership in terms of dues paid to constituency organizations. In the Labour Party, nearly nine-tenths of the party's 6,222,000 members are affiliated by trade-union headquarters; some of these members do not know that they belong to the Labour Party. Party dues are paid as part of union dues. Trade unionists automatically become party members unless they take the trouble to contract out of their union's wholesale application to the Labour Party. In 1972 the Labour Party reported 703,000 nominally affiliated individuals who joined independently of paying union dues. The Conservatives do not claim to know how many members they have. A study of constituency associations conducted before the 1970 election [13] estimated the actual number of individual members of the Labour party at 350,000 and of the Conservative Party, 1,600,000. The Liberals have perhaps 50,000 members. For most party members, paying annual dues is their maximum participation in politics.

Another measure of political involvement is participation in local political activities, from voting to standing as a candidate for public office. One survey found 7 per cent engage in at least five of ten common political activities. A majority of these activists vote, help in fund-raising efforts, urge people to vote, hold office in an organization, advise people to get in touch with an MP, make public talks, and present their views to an MP. The activists are almost evenly divided between Conservative and Labour supporters. The activists are not an exact social cross section of the population but include substantial numbers from all ages, classes, educational backgrounds, and both men and women. One researcher concludes that the activist is distinctive in what he *does* rather than for what he *is*.[14]

Many Englishmen indirectly participate in politics by belonging to organizations that consistently or intermittently act

[13] See David Butler and Michael Pinto-Duschinsky, *The British General Election of 1970,* pp. 265, 279.

[14] See Robert Worcester, "The Hidden Activists," *New Society,* June 8, 1972.

as political pressure groups. These range in character from an anglers club concerned with the pollution of a local stream to the Automobile Association, representing motorists. An estimated 61 per cent of the population belong to at least one organization; 9 per cent belong to four or more groups. The most popular organizations are leisure, social, and sports clubs, but 19 per cent report that they belong to an "issue" organization, that is, a trade union, a professional association, or a public body or committee. A total of 14 per cent are officers or committee members of a voluntary association. Although educated people are most likely to belong to an association, a majority of people in all age and educational strata belong to a voluntary association.[15]

In the 1970s ad hoc and extraparty protest groups have appeared in local and national politics. Many of these groups reflect localized concern with a single issue, whether it involves conditions in a university or a local council's failure to assure pedestrian safety at a busy crossroads. The concentration of politics in London has made it possible for London-based protest organizations to appear as nationwide organizations, because they protest in the national capital. In a country of 55 million inhabitants, it is not especially difficult to attract several hundred people to a protest meeting on almost any kind of issue. One requires a cause, a speaker with a name or a recognizable status, and money to hire a hall and advertise the meeting. Local protest groups may be able to recruit very widely within an area affected by a new highway or sewage problem, but they are unlikely to seek or gain many recruits outside the range of those immediately affected. The Campaign for Nuclear Disarmament, active in protesting against British foreign policy in the 1960s, has persisted long enough to permit analysis of its recruits. In a study appropriately entitled *Middle Class Radicalism,* Frank Parkin found that CND protesters believed in the efficacy of their marches and leaflet campaigns, as well as in the importance of the symbolic gesture of dissent. Three-quarters came from Labour or "left" homes; they were thus not in revolt against parents. But they

[15] See Mary Horton, *The Local Government Elector,* pp. 113 ff.

TABLE VI.2 *Involvement in National Politics*

	Estimated number of people	*Estimated % of electorate*
Electorate, 1970	39,342,000	98
Voters, 1970	28,345,000	72
Organization members	24,000,000	61
Receiving weekly cash benefit	18,600,000	47
Party members, all categories	8,000,000	20
Official post in organization	5,500,000	14
Very interested in politics	3,500,000	9
Political activists	2,750,000	7
Individual party members	2,000,000	5
MP, senior civil servant	4,000	0.01

Sources: As cited in footnotes of text. Some figures are derived from survey estimates, others are precise counts; all have been rounded off.

could hardly be called representative of the electorate generally.[16]

The majority of Englishmen participate in national politics only if voting or belonging to a voluntary organization is taken as a sufficient token of activity (Table VI.2). At most, it might be taken as a sign that people think they can influence public affairs by their actions. But the Civic Culture survey found that while 62 per cent believed themselves able to influence government if they tried, only 6 per cent claimed they had ever tried to exert influence.[17] A number of indicators converge in showing 5 to 14 per cent of the electorate regularly involved in politics. If holding elected office is the measure of being a politician, the proportion drops below 1 per cent. By this standard one could argue that the proportion of the adult population actively participating in politics in England today is scarcely higher than it was before the passage of

[16] Frank Parkin, *Middle Class Radicalism* (Manchester: University Press, 1968). Because protest groups are usually ad hoc and localized, they are difficult to document. *New Society* often carries comments about these groups.

[17] Gabriel Almond and Sidney Verba, *The Civic Culture*, p. 186; original codebook responses for Q. 29.

the great nineteenth-century democratic franchise reforms. The limited number of politicians is not unique to England. America and other Western nations are also divided politically into a relative few who are very interested in politics and a much larger less interested mass.

CENTRAL POLITICAL ROLES

There are two contrasting approaches to the study of central political roles. Prescriptively, one might first define a job in terms of specific tasks, then consider how individuals might be recruited to meet the qualifications for them. This is the approach of management theory. Alternatively, one might proceed inductively, analyzing the attributes that influence the recruitment of Englishmen to leading political roles, and then ask: Given their skills, what kind of job can they do? Because of the constraints that history and contemporary conventions place upon political recruitment in England, the inductive approach is preferable.[18]

The holders of central political roles can be grouped under three broad headings: Cabinet ministers, senior civil servants, and intermittent public persons. Members of Parliament are not, by that very fact, central to government; they become so by attaining ministerial position. Ministers must be elected to Parliament, then selected for promotion. Civil servants first compete by examinations and then gain promotion by seniority plus selection. Some intermittent public persons depend upon patronage for appointment to public bodies, while others owe their prominence to holding office in major pressure groups independent of government.

Three generalizations can be made about those in central political roles. Experience is positively valued. Starting early on a path that can lead to political eminence is almost a precondition of success. Civil servants normally enter Whitehall immediately upon taking a university degree in their early twenties. Aspiring Cabinet ministers are advised to gain entry to the House of Commons at an early age, because an MP

18 Much of what follows on ministerial recruitment is drawn from Richard Rose, "The Making of Cabinet Ministers."

must accumulate seniority in the House of Commons before gaining a ministerial post. For example, members of Edward Heath's first Cabinet in 1970 were on average thirty-four years old upon entering the Commons and fifty-one upon appointment to office. In the first Cabinet of Harold Wilson in 1964, the average Labour appointee had entered the House at thirty-eight and was fifty-six when appointed minister. Ministers outside the Cabinet and intermittent public persons also serve long apprenticeships before gaining political eminence. For example, a trade union leader will usually enter his trade in adolescence and require thirty to forty years to reach the general secretaryship of his union. In making appointments to the chairmanship of ad hoc government committees, government departments consider age evidence of sound judgment.

A second recruitment consideration is that Englishmen who seek leading political roles are not expected to start at the bottom in local politics and work their way gradually to the top in London. Instead, early in his career an individual must gain "cadet" status for a central political role, then gradually accumulate seniority and skill. The process might be described as "working one's way sideways" inasmuch as seniority will carry a person a substantial distance forward. The process is most evident in the senior civil service. Virtually no one is recruited from the ranks of local government. Similarly, cabinet posts are never given to individuals by virtue of their stature in local or regional politics, as might happen in a federal country. Moreover, very few individuals who gain prominence in central political roles have previously established themselves as leaders in local politics. Among MPs, 71 per cent have not had local government experience prior to election to Parliament. Among Cabinet ministers the proportion is higher.[19] The local councillor's office is the high point of a peripheral citizen's participation; membership in Parliament is the beginning point for a central political role.

A third influence upon recruitment is geographical. MPs,

[19] See Michael Rush, *The Selection of Parliamentary Candidates,* pp. 60, 181; and Peter G. Richards, *The Backbenchers,* p. 22.

senior civil servants, and most intermittent public persons spend all their working life in London. Jobs outside London are regarded as in a backwater. In industry and finance as in trade unions, London is the center. MPs are not required to have lived in the constituency that nominates them or to take up residence there upon election. Among Conservative candidates selected for winnable constituencies, 22 per cent had a direct constituency connection; in the Labour Party the proportion is little more than one-quarter.[20] A defeated MP or candidate can move to another constituency to reenter the House and maintain his national status.

Election to the House of Commons is virtually a precondition for becoming a Cabinet minister. MPs are self-recruited, in the sense that aspirants for a parliamentary nomination are expected to put themselves forward. They are selected, in that nomination for winnable or safe seats involves competition among aspirants for the favor of the local party's selection committee. A young man anxious to take a central political role does not need to become an MP. He can make a more certain career in Westminster by winning entry to the administrative civil service in his early twenties. Both Harold Wilson and Edward Heath were administrative civil servants before seeking entry to the House of Commons. Two of the five other post-1945 Prime Ministers showed sufficient academic ability to have won entry to the senior civil service instead of the Commons if they had wished.

The motives leading men to seek election to Parliament are multiple, mixing public and private concerns.[21] Case studies, statistical analyses, and novels have been written about the trials of entering the House of Commons. An MP, his parliamentary agent, his wife, and his biographer might each emphasize a different motive. One thing is certain: Ambition for power is not the sole motive. The majority of candidates at each general election are defeated, not elected. With the Liberal

[20] See Michael Rush, *The Selection of Parliamentary Candidates*, pp. 74, 181.

[21] Note the catalogue of motives in Sir Lewis Namier, *The Structure of Politics at the Accession of George III*, (London: Macmillan, 2nd edition, 1957), Ch. 1.

Party, defeat is so likely that the party's headquarters "discourages any potential candidate who indicates he is interested in standing because he hopes to get into Parliament." A study of Conservative and Labour candidates found that more than three-quarters of those defeated nonetheless considered their campaigns enjoyable and satisfying.[22]

Once elected, at least three-quarters of MPs can count on a career of fifteen years or longer in the Commons, because most parliamentary seats are safe against electoral tides.[23] National influences determine the movement of much of the floating vote. A local MP is limited in his ability to increase (or decrease) his majority. It is, moreover, unusual for a sitting MP to be denied the party's renomination. MPs with long service automatically join a pool of individuals potentially qualified for a ministerial post when their party has a parliamentary majority.

In promoting individuals to a ministerial post, a Prime Minister may use any of three criteria: representativeness, loyalty, or competence. An MP may be offered an appointment as a representative of women, Scots, or of a political tendency within the parliamentary party. Even factional opponents may be offered posts, to gain their silence through collective responsibility. Loyalty to the Prime Minister is important to counterbalance potential opposition in the Cabinet and to encourage back-bench MPs in the belief that loyalty brings rewards. Competence is an abstract term. It begs the question: Competence in what – parliamentary debate? administration? the subject matter of the department?

The discretion that a Prime Minister can exercise in recruiting ministers is limited by the fact that he has upwards of one hundred jobs to distribute among approximately two hundred MPs. The remainder of his back-benchers are ruled out of consideration by parliamentary inexperience, old age, ideo-

[22] See Dennis A. Kavanagh, *Constituency Electioneering in Britain* (London: Longmans, 1970), pp. 81 ff; and Jorgen Rasmussen, *The Liberal Party: A Study of Retrenchment and Revival* (London: Constable, 1965), p. 212.

[23] See Jorgen Rasmussen, "The Implications of Safe Seats for British Democracy," *Western Political Quarterly,* XIX:3 (1966).

logical extremism, personal unreliability, or even lack of interest in office. An analysis of Conservative and Labour MPs in the period 1918–59 found that a chief requirement for securing office was survival in the Commons. A majority of all MPs elected three times or more achieved a ministerial post.[24] A Prime Minister is likely to spend as much time deciding what posts are to be offered individual MPs as he is in deciding which MPs are to be offered something.

Experience of the Commons does not lead naturally to the work of a minister, as preparatory school leads to public school. The chief concerns of an MP are dealing with people and talking about ideas. These attributes are useful in Whitehall too, but a minister must also have other skills: an idea of how to handle the paper work required by a major administrative post; ability to appraise policy alternatives, the consequences of which will not be clear until long after he has left office; and a capacity to relate political generalities to the specifics of a technical problem. A minister may find the transition from the back benches to government almost as great as that required by his initial election to Parliament.

An MP joining the government is usually first appointed to a junior ministerial post. Because the convention of ministerial responsibility places authority in one man, a junior minister will usually be given little responsibility by comparison with political overlords or senior civil servants. The job of a junior minister is not intended as a training ground for Cabinet ministers,[25] as a junior executive post in nongovernmental organizations can be a conscious apprenticeship for higher responsibilities.

When ministers are asked what they think their task is, nearly every minister makes some reference to involvement in policy and to maintaining parliamentary support for his department's work. Half think it important to protect or advance their department against other departments in Cabinet deliberations. Half emphasize the importance of main-

[24] See P. W. Buck, *Amateurs and Professionals in British Politics, 1918–59* (Chicago: University Press, 1963), pp. 114 ff.

[25] See D. J. Heasman, "Ministers' Apprentices," *New Society*, July 16, 1964.

taining morale and efficiency within their department. One-third stress the need for public relations work among pressure groups and the general public. Differences in defining the job lead to differences about the skills considered most important in recruiting ministers. Half think that a good minister is a man with a specialist's ability to handle Parliament and a gifted amateur's approach to the problems of his department. But the other half think that a specialist's knowledge of a department's tasks, plus general managerial ability, is most important.[26]

The recruitment of ministers from among MPs ensures that they have had ample experience to meet one of their important tasks: handling parliamentary business. By comparison with their counterparts in the old Commonwealth countries of Canada and Australia as well as in America and the Fourth Republic of France, British ministers tend to be younger on first election to Parliament, but must wait much longer before entering the Cabinet (Table VI.3). British MPs are also noteworthy because of the relatively high proportion who have held no public office – whether executive or administrative – prior to entering Parliament.

The recruitment of ministers does not provide men with substantial knowledge of the subject matter of their department. The restriction of appointments to established MPs prevents a nationwide canvass for men with specialists' skills for particular posts. Little more than one-tenth of ministers are appointed to departments where they can claim some specialized knowledge.[27] The one way in which a minister can be sure of learning about a department's work is to learn on the job. The amount of time required to learn the ropes of a department varies with its complexity. Anthony Crosland, a Labour minister with an unusually analytical mind, has reckoned: "It takes you six months to get your head properly above water, a year to get the general drift of most of the field, and two years really to master the whole of a department." A Fulton Committee study reckoned that the time

[26] See Bruce W. Headey, *The Job of a Cabinet Minister,* Ch. 3.
[27] *Ibid.,* pp. 124 ff.

TABLE VI.3 *Comparative Patterns of Ministerial Recruitment (in percentages)*

	Britain	*USA*	*Canada*	*Australia*	*4th Republic France*
First elected before age 40	48	38	37	44	44
No prior public office	65	28	52	51	51
10 years in House before first Cabinet post	67	–[a]	24	12	18
Age at entry, Cabinet (median)	50–54	50–54	50–54	45–49	45–49

Source: Derived from Joseph A. Schlesinger, "Political Careers and Party Leadership," in Lewis J. Edinger, editor, *Political Leadership in Industrialized Societies* (New York: John Wiley & Sons, 1967).
[a]Category not applicable.

from appraising a policy to implementing a solution could be as much as five years. But the conventions of Prime Ministerial patronage result in the frequent reshuffling of ministers from department to department. From 1955 to 1970 the average minister in major departments stayed 2.2 years in one office. The rate of ministerial turnover has been increasing since 1900; it is one of the highest in Western nations. In seven-eighths of the instances in which a minister is moved, he goes to a job in a department where he has no previous experience. The process of "on-the-job-learning" must start again.[28]

The recruitment of ministers has come under criticism as part of a general cry for the reform of government. Industrialists argue the need for more businesslike ministers; economists, the need for more economic expertise; and some academics praise the American system of "in-and-outers," that is, persons who move between policy making for the federal executive and managing large organizations outside Washington – whether state government, universities, or profit-making

[28] Cf. Richard Rose, "The Making of Cabinet Ministers," pp. 407 f, Crosland's discussion in Maurice Kogan, *The Politics of Education*, pp. 155 ff, and The Fulton Committee, Vol. II, p. 20 ff.

companies. In 1964 Mr. Wilson named five individuals without previous parliamentary experience to ministerial posts. This practice had previously been followed only in wartime emergencies, when men with management experience were required to run the administrative apparatus of modern war. The most prominent appointee (and the only one to enter the Commons rather than the Lords), Frank Cousins, resigned less than two years after his appointment. Mr. Heath did not emulate the tactic in 1970. In an historical review of the recruitment of ministers, F. M. G. Willson concludes, "The pattern not only remains overwhelmingly similar to that established over the last hundred years, but if anything moved slightly towards more orthodoxy in terms of parliamentary and administrative experience." [29]

The recruitment of senior civil servants has been a controversial subject for generations. Most of the controversy has concerned the class origins of recruits to the Home Civil Service and, even more, to the Foreign Office. Less attention has been given to the skills required of recruits. Lord Macaulay stated the traditional view in commenting on civil service reform in the middle of the nineteenth century:

> We believe that men who have been engaged up to twenty-one or twenty-two in studies which have no immediate connection with the business of any profession, and of which the effect is merely to open, to invigorate and to enrich the mind, will generally be found in the business of every profession superior to men who have, at eighteen or nineteen, devoted themselves to the special studies of their calling.[30]

The view was endorsed by Harold Wilson a century later in the recommendations of the Fulton Committee for civil service reform.[31]

[29] "Entry to the Cabinet, 1959–1968," *Political Studies,* XVIII:2 (1970), p. 238; and by the same author, "The Routes of Entry of New Members of the British Cabinet, 1868–1958," *Ibid.,* VII:3 (1959).

[30] Quoted in Anthony Sampson, *Anatomy of Britain* (London: Hodder & Stoughton, 1962), pp. 222–23.

[31] House of Commons, *Debates,* Vol. 773, Col. 1553 (January 21, 1968). For the most thorough details of the recruitment of civil servants, see A. H. Halsey and Ivor Crewe, The Fulton Committee, Vol. III (1).

Candidates for entry to the administrative class could take examinations in such subjects as Greek Composition, Classical Archeology, Welsh History to 1536, Old English, the History of the German Language, or Spanish Literature to 1525. History and classics graduates took the entrance examination out of all proportion to their numbers in the universities – and showed themselves exceptionally able in their academic specialties (Table VI.4). The prominence of these two subjects reflects their importance in the academic curriculum of secondary schools. For generations bright schoolboys were expected to be bright at classics.

TABLE VI.4 *Educational Specialties of Civil Service Recruits, 1948–1968 (Administrative Class, Home Civil Service– in percentages)*

Subject	*1948–56*	*1957–63*	*1964–68*
History	32.4	31.0	29.4
Classics	20.9	23.5	10.7
Economics, politics, and philosophy	20.0	18.0	14.2
Modern languages	8.7	7.8	10.6
English literature	5.7	5.7	7.9
Law	4.0	4.2	3.4
Science and engineering	1.1	3.3	7.1
Mathematics	2.3	1.2	2.0
Other	4.9	3.9	14.4
None	0	0.6	0.2
Number	527	332	493

Sources: *Recruitment to the Administrative Class* (London: HMSO: Cmnd. 232, 1957); Civil Service Commissioners, *Report*, (London: HMSO, annual), and *The Method II System of Selection* (London: HMSO, Cmnd. 4156, 1968).

The Fulton Committee claimed that civil servants should be recruited because they had "relevant" knowledge of the work of government, "minds disciplined by the social studies, the mathematical and physical sciences, the biological sciences or in the applied and engineering sciences." It did not, however, indicate why scientific or engineering subjects should, of themselves, be more relevant to the work of Whitehall administrators than history or classics. The Committee's uncertainties about what a civil servant should know were revealed when the Committee failed to agree about a straightforward way to test for "relevant" knowledge.[32] The Civil Service Commission has since remedied this deficiency. Candidates for the highest administrative posts are now examined for their ability to summarize lengthy prose papers; to resolve a problem by fitting specific facts to general regulations; to draw inferences from a simple table of social statistics; to follow logical diagrams; and to display verbal aptitude.

Because bright young men enter the civil service with few specialized skills and spend decades before reaching senior posts, socialization into the roles assumes specially great importance. Civil service recruits, whether their fathers were coal miners or members of the aristocracy, are expected to learn what to do by following the procedures used by those senior to them. Senior civil servants determine the promotion of their juniors. Cooption ensures the transmission of established assumptions about *how* government work should be transacted; it need not imply agreement about *what* should be done in particular policy areas. An individual gains promotion because he knows how things should be done and not because of his views about policies. He is inoculated against deep involvement in subject matter by frequent postings from post to post; the median administrator is 2.8 years in a particular job.[33]

The recruitment of senior civil servants is sometimes criticized for rewarding "generalists," people who lack specialists' skills in economics, sociology, law, or the sciences. The criticism is wide of the mark. Civil servants are specialists in a difficult and abstruse field: the management of Whitehall. Their knowledge of public administration extends far beyond what can be learned in textbooks. They know how to deal with the Treasury in annual negotiations about departmental esti-

[32] See The Fulton Committee, Vol. I, pp. 27 ff; and Appendix E, especially p. 162.

[33] See The Fulton Committee, Vol. II, pp. 20 ff. On the formal training of civil servants, see E. Grebenik, "The Civil Service College: the First Year," *Public Administration,* I (Summer 1972).

mates, how to remind a minister tactfully that his preferred policy may be a political disaster, how to produce a cover-up answer for an awkward parliamentary question, and how to arrive at a departmental policy when the mind of the minister is blank.

The more sophisticated critics of the civil service do not deprecate the value of knowing how to work the Whitehall machine. But they question whether this knowledge is sufficient. The Fulton Committee emphasized that much of the work of Whitehall concerns large-scale management. While civil servants are often advising others who manage nationalized industries or local authorities, their careers do not include experience in working for government outside the departmental framework of Whitehall. Permanent Secretaries in charge of departments are likely to have less knowledge of major subject areas of administration, because their experience is concentrated in the Treasury, Downing Street, and other coordinating posts.[34] The readiness of civil servants to respond to their minister's state of mind attracts another criticism.

> The great defect of Whitehall is the shortage of long-range thinking. Ministers themselves tend to think of the lifetime of the Parliament. And the civil servant is engrossed in getting his minister through the week's work, or through the parliamentary session.[35]

Dissatisfaction can also be found within Whitehall. A study undertaken for the Fulton Committee in 1966 found that one-fifth of those recruited to the administrative class a decade earlier had resigned from the service, and another fifth were applying for jobs outside it. A later study of recruits undertaken two years after they had joined the administrative class found that about half were ready to consider leaving the civil service if a good job came up elsewhere.[36]

[34] See Maurice Kogan, *The Government of the Social Services* (London: Trustees of the Charles Russell Memorial Lecture, 1969), p. 19.

[35] Sir Dennis Proctor, himself a former Permanent Secretary, in "What's Wrong with Whitehall?" *Sunday Times,* October 1, 1967.

[36] See R. G. S. Brown, "Fulton and Moral," *Public Administration,* XLIX (Summer 1971), p. 193; R. A. Chapman, "Profile of a Profession,"

Many individuals are only intermittently involved in politics and may not even see themselves in a political role. If all persons holding government appointments were defined as political, then such diverse persons as the Archbishop of Canterbury, the Director General of the British Broadcasting Corporation, the Regius Professor of Greek at Oxford, and the Astronomer Royal would be politicians. If challenged, each would probably deny that he was a politician, yet also claim that he carried out his duties with regard for the public interest.

Tens of thousands of Englishmen are recruited into part-time government service by appointments to bodies concerned with public policy. Most part-time appointments are without salary. Civic-minded people are expected to give advice gladly on a council, committee, or commission, or assist law enforcement as a Justice of the Peace. Many members of government committees sit by virtue of full-time employment in an organization affected by the committee's deliberations. Pressure-group officials are involved in politics informally as well as formally. For example, successive Secretaries of State for Education have paid tribute to Sir William Alexander of the Association of Education Committees for his "enormous knowledge and experience of how the whole complicated mechanism of education policy works." [37] Pressure-group appointees are often balanced by having as committee chairmen a "lay gent," a person whose amateurism implies neutrality in his conduct of government work. The Treasury is said to keep a list of "the great and the good" to act as lay representatives of the public on specialist committees.[38]

A very small proportion of those in central political roles are temporary recruits to a full-time post in government. The

---

in The Fulton Committee, Vol. III (2), p. 1 and p. 13; and Peta E. Sheriff, "Outsiders in a Closed Career," *Public Administration,* L (Winter 1972).

[37] See Maurice Kogan, *The Politics of Education,* pp. 134, 174 f.

[38] See K. C. Wheare, *Government by Committee* (Oxford: Clarendon Press, 1955), pp. 15 ff; "Government by Appointment," an issue of *Planning,* XXVI:443 (London, PEP, 1960); Peter G. Richards, *Patronage in British Government* (London: Allen & Unwin, 1963).

closed-shop conventions of Parliament virtually debar anyone from moving to a prominent ministerial post without an apprenticeship in the House of Commons. In addition, the civil service has been opposed on principle to recruiting staff from outside its ranks, especially at higher levels. It is argued that such recruitment could make high-paying Whitehall jobs patronage plums to be awarded to party sympathizers. Civil servants expect that they will receive top jobs as the reward for years of accumulated seniority. In wartime, temporary civil servants have been recruited in large numbers from industry, the universities, and elsewhere, because of the great expansion of government work. At the end of the war, some remained in Whitehall and others left. In the 1970s the number of "wartime temporaries" is rapidly diminishing by retirement and death. Temporary administrative appointments of a mixture of economists and journalists were attempted by the 1964–70 Labour government. Samuel Brittan, an economic journalist turned Whitehall irregular, concluded from his experience that the contribution of any irregular is limited by the vice of his virtue: The more novel the perspective he brings to Whitehall, the greater the things he must learn in order to operate effectively within the confines of Whitehall. The more an individual learns, the less he has a distinctive contribution to make. New men by themselves cannot make a "new" style of government. To change government they must learn the strengths as well as observe the weaknesses of the old ways.[39]

No precise estimate can be made of the numbers of people intermittently involved in central political roles. The number is certainly far greater than the number of MPs or of very senior civil servants, if only because these groups are small. Intermittent public persons are recruited from a much wider spectrum of society than Cabinet ministers or Conservative MPs. For example, a study of members of Royal Commissions set up on an ad hoc basis found that 46 per cent had a family background so ordinary that they did not note their father's

[39] See Samuel Brittan, "The Irregulars," in Richard Rose, editor, *Policy-Making in Britain;* D. L. Munby, Memorandum No. 136, to The Fulton Committee, Vol. V (2); and varied comments in Hugh Thomas, editor, *Crisis in the Civil Service* (London: Blond, 1968).

status or occupation in standard biographical sources. While 42 per cent had an Oxford or Cambridge education, 30 per cent had no education beyond secondary school. Among those on Royal Commissions, less than half were drawn from the old professions, for instance, the law, civil service and Parliament, the church, landowners, or the military, even though many Royal Commissions are concerned with the reform of law, government, or other old established institutions. The varied careers of these recruits to intermittent public posts suggest that they bring to Westminster a wider variety of viewpoints than are found within the ranks of full-time politicians.[40]

The varied forms of intermittent political participation can best be shown by giving short biographies of a few well-known public figures.

> *Lord Fulton.* Born 1902 into an academic family. Educated at Dundee High School, St. Andrews and Oxford universities. Oxford don. Wartime temporary civil servant. Ministry of Fuel and Power. Head of University College of Swansea, 1947–59. First head, new University of Sussex, 1957–67. Chairman of sixteen government or nonprofit committees or councils, including Committee on the Civil Service, Education in Hong Kong and in Sierra Leone, and board for mining qualifications. Governor, BBC. Chairman of the British Council. Knighted, 1964. Life peerage, 1966.
>
> *Victor Grayson Hardie Feather.* Born 1908. Educated at local Bradford school to age of fourteen. Employee, Cooperative Society. Joined Trades Union Congress staff, 1937, General Secretary, 1969–1973. Adviser on trade-union reorganization in Greece, Berlin, India, and Pakistan. Member of committees on reorganization of local government in England; overseas information service; National Economic Development Council. Council Member, BBC, British Council, Consumers Association, Advertising Standards Authority, British Productivity Council, Civic Trust. Director, National Building Agency. Commander, Order of the British Empire, 1961.

40 Calculated from data in Charles J. Hanser, *Guide to Decision: the Royal Commission* (Totowa, N.J.: Bedminster Press, 1965), Appendix 3, based on an analysis of members of every sixth Royal Commission, 1900–1964.

Andrew Akiba Shonfield. Born Tadworth, Surrey 1917. Educated at St. Paul's School and Oxford. War service Royal Artillery 1940–46, staff officer Major. *Financial Times* 1947–57. Economic Editor, *The Observer,* 1958–61. Royal Institute of International Affairs (Director of Studies) 1961–68; Director since 1971. Chairman, Social Science Research Council, 1969–71. Member, Royal Commission on Trade Unions; Foreign and Commonwealth Office Committee on Overseas Representation. British representative on European Economic Community Vedel Committee 1971–72. BBC Reith Lecturer, 1972. Author, *Modern Capitalism,* etc.

Different as the careers of these three public persons are, all have two things in common. None has ever been a candidate for elective office, nor held a post as an established civil servant. Their absence from conventional categories of politicians does not make them any the less involved in central political roles.

POLITICIANS AND SOCIETY

Defining political activity in terms of roles leaves in question the importance of government office as against positions of power in The City of London, trade unions, the mass media, or other status-conferring institutions. A public official may not be able to decide, without approval by various veto groups, what government will do in a given area. But formal office is a necessary if not sufficient cause for government action. A public official can also act as a veto group of a particularly important kind. A "do-nothing" Cabinet minister may frustrate many pressing demands upon his department.

Traditionally, the leaders in English society were simultaneously leading social, political, and economic personages. Aristocrats born into high social status could claim seats in Parliament by virtue of noble birth, financial eminence by virtue of inherited wealth, plus such riches as might be added by their own efforts. When the chief tasks of government were no more than traditional tasks, social leaders could easily double in leading political roles. The Industrial Revolution not only created specialized economic institutions but also increased the specialized work of government.[41] The twentieth century has accelerated the rise of the full-time professional politician, just as it has brought professionalization to many other social roles, from sport to scholarship. Hence, in contemporary England it is necessary to ask: To what extent are those who have achieved high social status or economic positions recruited into politics? This is not a question about the social origins of politicians but rather about the political inclinations of those in high nonpolitical positions.

Today, the qualities and achievements that confer social status are multiple and diverse. There does not appear to be any agreement about what it is that puts "top" people on top.[42] Prestige can be accorded persons on grounds as different as traditional honor (the Queen), statesmanship (a former Prime Minister, in old age), television personalities (David Frost), and achievement in sports, whether one is a jockey in the sport of kings or a football hero in the sport of the working class. People with very different criteria of prestige live without conflict because they do not meet. For example, in a community study in rural Oxfordshire, the wife of an Army colonel welcomed a newcomer to a village of five hundred with the statement that, except for three families, "nobody" lived in the village, that is, there was no one else significant in terms of her criteria of status. In working-class communities, people with middle-class attributes may find themselves similarly isolated.[43]

Individuals with high social status cannot claim to speak in the name of the government by virtue of their celebrity. They may claim the right to tell the government what to do in a public speech or a private conversation. But this right is also claimed by vocal political activists, whatever their social status. Social leaders must translate their diffuse status into specific public office in Westminster or Whitehall. This is especially the case with those whose celebrity gives them the prestige of

41 See J. M. Lee, *Social Leaders and Public Persons* (Oxford: Clarendon Press, 1963).

42 See National Opinion Polls, *Monthly Bulletin,* No. 109 (June 1972).

43 Margaret Stacey, *Tradition and Change,* p. 145. See also Brian Jackson and Dennis Marsden, *Education and the Working Class,* pp. 53 ff.

a leader but confers no organized followers, for instance, a hereditary peer. Some lords who have renounced their peerage in hopes of gaining election to the House of Commons have learned the hard way that they do not have enough political following to gain nomination or election to the Commons.

To gain authority within government, an individual must transfer his high social status into political position. But interest in politics is a minority taste among persons of high social status. For example, the proportion of hereditary peers attending and speaking in House of Lords debates is lower than the active proportion of newly appointed and life peers.[44] The proportion of arts graduates seeking to enter the senior civil service is but a small fraction of each year's crop of graduates. Similarly the proportion of Etonians in Cabinet is but a small fraction of Old Etonians in London society at any one time.

The incentives for translating diffuse status into political position must be weighed against drawbacks. For a person of high social status, the title of MP confirms but may not enhance his prestige. A politically important position in the civil service may be looked upon as less prestigious than a politically unimportant post in the Royal Household. In status terms, political life is most rewarding to those who lack high inherited status. For them, to become an MP is to rise in status. For some people even being a defeated parliamentary candidate can confer prestige.[45] To move from an Oxford arts degree – awarded to thousands annually – to a post in the civil service is to gain in meritorious prestige. Because of its traditional status, an administrative job in the prison section of the Home Office would have more social status than managing a radio factory, because the former work is for public good, not private profit.

Politics does not attract people of high status because of its financial rewards. An MP's salary of £4,500 is much less than that of senior civil servants or of many political journalists.

[44] See Bernard Crick, *The Reform of Parliament*, p. 137.

[45] See Dennis Kavanagh, *Constituency Electioneering in Britain*, pp. 81 ff.

The duties of the post result in substantial extra expenses which are often not covered by existing expense allowances. Some MPs claim that half or more of their salary is spent in discharging the duties of their office. A Cabinet minister's salary (£13,000) is not high by comparison with salaries paid persons with similar responsibilities outside government. The heads of nationalized industries are paid more than the Prime Minister – and even then may complain that their pay is less than they could earn in private industry. In private industry success usually brings valuable capital gains. A politician cannot realize money profits when the "stock" of his party rises. When it falls, he loses both office and official salary.

The nature of political work and of politicians today constitutes a disincentive for high-status people to enter politics. In the days before franchise reform, office holding could be considered a form of noblesse oblige. Now it means seeking favor among the democratic mass. Individuals may prefer to pursue less controversial and plebian activities. This is especially true of urban government. A study of local notables in Bristol found that 73 per cent had never thought of seeking election to the local council, and only 11 per cent had become councillors. They avoided politics because of a dislike of party politics; many also held councillors in low esteem as a group.[46]

The chances of an individual's converting diffuse social status into a political role are most evident among the ranks of Conservative MPs. Since 1945 wealthy Conservative parliamentary aspirants have not been able to use their money to buy a nomination; they must compete for the favor of a constituency association. A very disproportionate number of Conservative MPs are former public schoolboys (Table V.1). They enter the Commons because their social bearing is thought appropriate by the local activists who control the nomination; the nominators are often, in status terms, one notch below the nominee. The advantage of a public school background is greatest for Etonians. Approximately one-fifth of all Conserv-

[46] See Roger V. Clements, *Local Notables and the City Council* (London: Macmillan, 1969), pp. 51, 156 ff; and D. C. Miller, "Decision-Making Cliques in Community Power Structures," *American Journal of Sociology*, LXIV:6 (1958).

ative MPs are Old Etonians.[47] By contrast, Labour MPs and civil servants tend to be recruited from less prestigious but still middle-class backgrounds.

Once an individual has been recruited into politics, his prestige is not so much measured by his social origins as by his political accomplishments. A councillor will have more prestige than a ward secretary. MPs have more political prestige than councillors, and those ministers or former ministers sworn into the Privy Council take precedence over back-bench MPs. The civil service provides an even larger number of status gradations and status symbols. The most successful of politicians and civil servants raise their social status by earning honors or titles for their political and public services. A Prime Minister can receive a hereditary earldom on retirement, and MPs may receive a peerage or a knighthood. Rising in the hierarchy of the civil service is marked by a succession of honors, including knighthoods and peerages. Honors can soften the blow of forced retirement. A Cabinet minister fired for inefficiency or old age can be consoled with a peerage. The honors list, issued twice a year by the monarch on the advice of the Prime Minister of the day, can also be used to provide incentives for those recruited to undertake arduous intermittent public duties. When asked what he would do with his newly conferred middle-rank honor, one public person smiled and said, "Work to improve it."

While there is a substantial literature about the business interests of MPs and, on the Labour side, the trade-union affiliations of MPs, there is no comparable literature about the political interest (or lack of interest) of those in leading economic positions. Any systematic analysis of the political involvement of economic leaders must start by noting the very heterogeneous nature of leadership positions in the economic system. They range in extremes from nonexecutive directorships of banks or insurance companies to full-time direction of a factory or full-time leadership in a trade union.

[47] The higher his social status, the more likely a Conservative is to be adopted for a safe seat. See Michael Rush, *The Selection of Parliamentary Candidates,* pp. 83 ff. On Etonians, note the remarks by Lord Boyle, in Maurice Kogan, *The Politics of Education,* pp. 71–72.

Within most leadership positions in the economic system, intensive specialization is a chief characteristic of recruitment and career advancement. A study of industrial managers concludes, "All in all top managers have not had marked experience outside industry, outside their own firm, or outside their own line of work." [48] This statement is equally applicable to the trade-union world, Cooperative societies, the City of London, retailing, and manufacturing industries. Most steel men, for example, have worked all their lives in the steel industry. They are not intermittently steel men and politicians: their very lack of political skills has been demonstrated by the "unprofessional" (in the political sense) nature of their campaign against nationalization. Of the 164 directors of the dozen steel companies that were privately owned prior to nationalization in the late 1960s, only five had ever been MPs. The only company with a board of directors having substantial political experience had acquired this asset by recruiting very senior former civil servants.[49] Most businessmen have little time to give to politics. Businessmen can denounce Conservative governments for refusing to follow "businesslike" policies for the sake of votes. In England, by contrast with America, the ideology of businessmen is less a positive assertion of free-enterprise values than it is a dislike of the machinery of state intervention and controls. Trade-union leaders have historically shown greater confidence and interest in politicians of a Labour stripe. But unions nonetheless have established incompatibility rules. A trade-union leader cannot sit on both the General Council of the Trades Union Congress and the National Executive Committee of the Labour Party. A full-time trade-union official cannot enter the House of Commons as a Labour MP and expect to remain important in the direction of his union. Leading officials of nationalized industries, though appointed by government and subject to guidance from the Cabinet, usually maintain a low political profile.

In order to undertake a political career, a person must forgo the expectation of conventional business success. Since 1900,

[48] R. V. Clements, *Managers* (London: Allen & Unwin, 1958), p. 151.

[49] See Richard Rose, *Influencing Voters* (London: Faber, 1967), pp. 147 ff.

only eight businessmen and four trade unionists have been among the forty-nine men to have held office as Prime Minister, Chancellor of the Exchequer, or Foreign Secretary. In Mr. Wilson's first Cabinet, no one could be described as a businessman by occupation; seven were trade unionists. By the time Mr. Wilson left office, his Cabinet had become more professionalized; there was but one trade unionist. In Mr. Heath's first Cabinet, three ministers were businessmen by occupation; none was a trade unionist. No leader from the business world has been a senior minister since the war. Similarly, only two leading trade-union officials have sat in Labour Cabinets since 1945. Industrial firms and City banks, like trade unions and Cooperative societies, are not anxious to see able young men in their employment seek parliamentary careers. When this happens, it is usually assumed that the aspiring politician will lose his chance of promotion to high office in his employing organization. Just as the House of Commons is jealous about the need for a minister to have served an apprenticeship on the back benches, so those in industry, in commerce, and in the trade unions expect a man to have acquired experience in economic affairs before being rewarded with a top position.

The occupational careers of politicians differ from those of many comparable middle- and upper-income groups. Senior civil servants are most distinctive, for few have worked for a profit-making company before entering Whitehall. Many Cabinet ministers are best described as full-time politicians, having invested their early working years in building up a career in politics instead of in the business world. A majority of MPs prefer professional jobs to jobs in large organizations. Professional work, for instance, as a journalist, a lawyer, or a public-relations consultant, can often be combined with political work. Election to the Commons may even raise the fee a professional man can command. Other professional jobs, such as that of a teacher, can be dropped if an individual enters Parliament and then resumed again upon defeat. Conservatives have long appeared to think that an army officer, retiring with a pension in his mid-forties after twenty-one years in the forces, can readily move from serving the Queen in the Army to serving the Queen in Parliament. Conservative and Labour MPs differ in that the former tend to belong to "commercial" professions, for instance, accountancy and the law, where income and employment patterns associate them with leading businessmen. Labour MPs tend to belong to "welfare" or "service" professions, for instance, teaching, the lower ranks of the civil service, etc., where work is less well paid or involves employment by a nonprofit organization. Among the sixth of MPs with careers as company executives, directors, or wealthy gentlemen of leisure, nearly all are Conservative MPs.[50] Politicians and students of politics may feel that political leaders are superior to economic leaders – but businessmen, economists, and trade unionists may believe the opposite. Those with inherited social status may feel superior to both and disdain a career in politics or industry. The attractions of public office may be weighed against the attractions of other work and found wanting. Even more important, the attractions may not even be considered, because of the repute of politics or because of an Englishman's positive interest in things nonpolitical. Political, economic, and status leaders may each be amazed that the others regard their rewards as worth seeking.

Intensive apprenticeship is a prerequisite for success in many aspects of English life today. Just as a Cabinet minister must usually spend years as an MP, so a bishop must serve as clergyman, a general as a lieutenant, a professor as a university lecturer, a managing director as a manager working under the authority of others, and a film star spend time, perhaps, as a struggling actor. The result of specialization is that leadership positions are today far more differentiated in England than they were at the beginning of political reform, when the local lord might also appoint the clergyman, lead the militia, sit as a magistrate, and send his son to the House of Commons, while himself attending debates in the House of Lords. After years of interviewing men in leading positions in many different areas of English life, Anthony Sampson concluded:

> My own fear is not that the Establishment in Britain is too close, but that it is not close enough, that the circles are over-

[50] See David Butler and Michael Pinto-Duschinsky, *The British General Election of 1970,* p. 302.

lapping less and less, and that one half of the ring has very little contact with the other half.[51]

SELECTIVE RECRUITMENT

The extent to which political recruitment is selective depends upon the size of the political class within society. Nothing could be more selective than a parliamentary election that results in one person's becoming Prime Minister of a country of 55 million people. Yet nothing is considered more representative, because this is the one occasion in which every adult Englishman can participate in politics with equal effect for his vote. The greater the scope of activities defined as political, the greater is the number of people who must participate in politics. A totalitarian definition makes it a political act for a TV viewer to go into the kitchen for a cup of tea when a party political broadcast appears. Growing government intervention in the economy has made company directors and shop stewards at least intermittently politicians. Their economic position gives them freedom to act independently of government. Workers can vote with their feet by an unofficial strike. Businessmen can vote with their pocketbooks by investing money outside the United Kingdom.

There is more than one place in Table VI.3 where one can draw the line between politicians and those outside politics. For example, if officers of organizations are considered to be at least intermittently politicians, because their representative status enables them to voice pressure-group demands, more than five million citizens are politicians. Even if one reduces the total to activists or to those who have stood for election to local or national office, there remains the "as many as/but only" problem. Does one say, "as many as 2,750,000 people are political activists," or does one say, "but only 2,750,000 people are political activists"? By any criterion other than a totalitarian one, active participants in politics constitute a limited but significant fraction of the Crown's subjects.

51 Anthony Sampson, *Anatomy of Britain,* p. 632 and end papers. If Sampson had included leaders in local government, Wales, Scotland, and Northern Ireland in his "British" study, the lack of contact would be greater.

The most analyzed features of political recruitment in England are those concerning the social origins of politicians. Whatever the criterion chosen – age, sex, occupation, or education – politicians differ in profile from those whom they represent politically. Success in national politics, like success in polo, is ultimately due to skill and training. But the opportunity to develop such skill and the predisposition to play the game depend only in part upon natural aptitude. They depend also upon general social characteristics and particular family and personal circumstances.

A critic of the patterns of political recruitment prevalent today has argued that it has changed so little since the first Reform Act that Sir Alec Douglas-Home, Harold Macmillan, Clement Attlee, and Hugh Gaitskell would all have been at home in any Parliament since 1832. While true, this criticism misses perhaps the more significant point. For more than a century, national political roles have been open, albeit with unequal opportunities, to persons from heterogeneous backgrounds. For instance, Benjamin Disraeli, born in a Jewish family at a time when Jews were denied the vote, became the great leader of the mid-Victorian Conservative Party. One might argue that Victorian politics was sufficiently open to men of talents so that persons born into families of no particular social standing, such as Harold Wilson, Roy Jenkins, Edward Heath, and Enoch Powell, would also have been at home in Parliament then.

The recruitment of politicians, especially MPs, selects a mixed lot of persons, viewed in terms of social origins. If the good fortune of Old Etonians in gaining nomination in safe Conservative seats is regarded as a form of class nepotism [52] in that party, then the trade-union sponsorship of candidates of working-class origin in safe Labour seats can also be seen as class nepotism, albeit favoring a different class. When Sir Alec Douglas-Home was taunted with the claim that he owed his Prime Ministership to being the fourteenth Earl of Home, he replied by saying that Harold Wilson might equally be ac-

[52] See H. R. G. Greaves, *The British Constitution* (London: Allen & Unwin, 2nd edition, 1948), p. 164.

cused of being the fourteenth Mr. Wilson. Both comments are correct, insofar as they emphasize that each man owed his political eminence to a distinctive family upbringing. Senior civil servants are less mixed in social characteristics than are MPs, because of the importance placed upon formal education in recruiting for the civil service. The growing importance of university education in recruiting Cabinet ministers accounts for one of the most striking changes in the social characteristics of politicians: the decline of working-class ministers in the Cabinets of Labour governments.[53] Working-class people remain, however, a majority among those most interested in politics; their greater numbers more than offset a slightly lower level of interest in politics among manual workers.

Comparisons between British MPs and United States senators bring out distinctive characteristics of the recruitment process in each political system.[54] In Britain politicians are much more likely to have come from working-class families or to have been industrial workers than are politicians in America. Whatever their class, British MPs are likely to be city dwellers. By contrast, United States senators are much more likely to come from farm families and to have grown up in small towns. The preponderance of lawyers among United States senators is not matched in the House of Commons. On the other hand, the lesser educational gulf between lawyers and the mass of the population in America contrasts with the gulf between the Oxford and Cambridge education of many MPs and ministers and the minimum state education of the mass of the electorate.

The contrast between the egalitarian basis of the electoral franchise and the selective nature of political recruitment is undoubted. Its political significance is, however, controversial.[55] An argument for economy of effort requires some selec-

[53] See Richard Rose, "Party and Class Divisions: Britain as a Test Case," p. 154.

[54] Compare the data cited here with that in Donald R. Matthews, *U.S. Senators and their World* (Chapel Hill: University of North Carolina, 1960), Ch. 2.

[55] For a general discussion of the criteria for recruiting governors, see Robert A. Dahl, *After the Revolution?* (New Haven: Yale, 1970).

tion of persons to specialize in political roles. The need for competence justifies selection for some posts by criteria that favor university graduates. Yet considerations of communication between electors and elected – by imaginative sympathy as well as by face-to-face dialogue – argue for the importance of selecting some politicians because they are, in one or more senses, like the electorate.

One thing is certain. Knowledge of the social origins of politicians in England does not produce any confident prediction of individual political attitudes. If social origins were determining, then Conservative MPs would hardly ever disagree, because they are socially similar. To assert such determinism would be to deny the existence of politics – that is, disagreement about issues – within the Conservative Party. Yet the Conservatives are never all of one mind. For example, in the late 1950s Harold Macmillan suffered the resignation of three Old Etonians from his government on political grounds. Their replacements were also Old Etonians. In the Labour Party, disagreements are frequent, but they are not easily related to social characteristics. The radical left-wing MP from a public school and Oxford background is as familiar as the working-class MP with a conservative, right-wing outlook on many major public issues. Some argue that Labour politicians from social backgrounds similar to that of the bulk of Labour voters are more conservative politically, because less secure socially. It is undoubtedly true that a major objective of two interwar Labour governments under Ramsay MacDonald was not to change society, but to prove that Socialists could govern just as well as (and even, just like) the well-born.[56]

Debates about the recruitment of politicians cannot be resolved by stating that competence should be the criterion for selection. This begs the question: What is competence? In recruiting for the civil service, academic achievement is the customary sign of competence. Experience is highly valued for

[56] Cf. "Mr. Gunter says Intellectuals control Labour," *The Times*, February 17, 1972; Robert J. Skidelsky, *Politicians and the Slump;* V. L. Allen, "The Ethics of Trade Union Leaders," *British Journal of Sociology*, VII:4 (1956); and Egon Wertheimer, *Portrait of the Labour Party*, (London: Putnam, 1929).

promotion. Seniority not only provides an impersonal basis for selection but also is proof that an individual has undergone lengthy socialization into the norms of Whitehall. MPs gain preferment by demonstrating to the Prime Minister and the Chief Whip that they can conform to the expectations specific to parliamentary and party politics. They gain promotion by demonstrating skills specific to Whitehall and Westminster and not by conforming to the expectations of their former public school headmaster or their parents.

The openness of the political class to new recruits, however unlikely their backgrounds, has caused changes in the social characteristics of politicians to be gradual. This gradualness has made it easy to transmit informal norms of political behavior from generation to generation. The importance of past outlooks is intensified by the lengthy period of role socialization that career politicians must undergo. Civil servants spend two decades (virtually all their adult lifetime to date) being socialized into Whitehall norms *before* moving to senior posts. MPs undergo role socialization for a decade or more before becoming important ministers. This continuity helps make the routine work of government, including party politics, move forward easily. Each politician knows what he can and cannot do, within the confines of his current role, and what he must do if he wishes promotion. The resulting stability is no less impressive if it is viewed as an obstacle to change when unfamiliar political problems arise.

CHAPTER VII

Communication and Non-Communication

A parliamentary minister is a man trained by elaborate practice not to blurt out crude things.

COMMUNICATION IS THE HYPHEN that joins distant parts of the political system. The government wishes its subjects to know what is expected of them and also wishes detailed information about popular needs and activities. Citizens wish government to know what they want or, at least, what they will not stand for. Because politics is about differences in opinion, communication does not of itself resolve conflicts of choice; noncommunication is as likely to be decisive. A minister cannot act if he has no knowledge that a problem exists. Reciprocally, a voter can easily ignore the wishes of "his" party, if he does not know where it stands on an issue.

Political communication is simple in outline form: Who says what to whom how? [1] A sender transmits messages through one or more channels (or media) to an audience. The status of the sender affects the attention paid to what is said and the confidence that his audience will have in his message. A Cabinet minister usually commands far more attention than an

[1] See Richard Rose, *People in Politics,* Ch. 5, Jeremy Tunstall, editor, "Introduction" to *Media Sociology* (London: Constable, 1970), pp. 5 ff, and Lord Windlesham, *Communication and Political Power.*

ordinary voter. In previous generations, those with high status in London society enjoyed special opportunities to communicate with politicians. Today, society figures have been eclipsed by television personalities and newspaper columnists. Partisan status is also important: An individual will sooner believe a back-bench MP of his own party than a front-bench spokesman of his opponents. Messages can be classified by the way in which they combine values, facts, and emotional symbols. For example, Acts of Parliament are often commands to do or refrain from doing things; other messages may simply be for information only. The channels of communication include public media, such as the press, television, and public meetings, and private media, such as letters and conversations in the corridors of Whitehall. The larger the audience, the less the likely political influence of its individual members. Only at election time does a mass audience determine what happens. Those with central political roles concerning a particular decision are often few enough to fit into a large meeting room in Whitehall.

The liberal model of English politics demands a great flow of information between governors and governed. The greater the supply of information, the better informed the public and, as the public is expected to be the ultimate arbiter of policy, the better the policies of government. In the liberal model, government is expected to supply information freely to the governed because the public has "the right to know." The Whitehall model of communication, by contrast, has a very different view of supply-demand relationships. Information is assumed to be a scarce commodity and, "like all scarce commodities, it is not freely exchanged." [2] Publicity is thought to be costly, not only because of the time required to carry out extensive public-relations campaigns but also because public discussion of difficult policy questions might interfere with private negotiations in Whitehall between spokesmen for affected pressure groups. Many laws and Whitehall conventions assume publicity is "not in the public interest." [3] In the words

[2] Sam Brittan, *Steering the Economy,* p. 29.
[3] The title of a book by David Williams (London: Hutchinson, 1965).

of David Butler, an academic and media commentator on politics, "conducting the whole business of advising and policy-forming in public just wouldn't work." In the blunter words of a Foreign Office official: "It is no business of any official to allow the government to be embarrassed. That is who we are working for. Embarrassment and security are not really two different things." [4]

The relative costs and benefits of secrecy and publicity differ from political issue to political issue. The greater the numbers who will be required to cooperate in a policy to make it work (e.g., voluntary wage and price restraint), the greater the need to publicize policy objectives and the reasoning behind it in hopes of mobilizing consent. The fewer the numbers involved in carrying out a policy, the less publicity that need be given. This principle applies not only to technical matters affecting small numbers of people, but also to decisions with broad impact taken by a small central group, for instance, decisions about interest rates or foreign policy.

The roles of communicator and audience are often exchanged. Those who speak often, like MPs, are also expected to listen to those who seek to influence them. Those who usually listen, like voters, can speak at elections. The dynamics of policy making often require politicians to propose a course of action, then listen for reaction from those affected. Once the reaction is heard, they can speak again, revising ideas in the light of what they have learned in a continuing feedback process.

Every political figure, whether minister or citizen, is part of both horizontal and vertical communications networks. Horizontal communication involves persons of a similar political status, such as Cabinet ministers, meeting together. Vertical communication involves communication between individuals differing in their political status. For example, a minister for local government must ensure that his views reach down to the local council office. Reciprocally, a citizen's views must

[4] A statement by John Welser in a 1970 Official Secrets Act trial, quoted in Anthony Sampson, *The New Anatomy of Britain* (1971), p. 369. See also, David Butler, "Cabinet Secrets," *The Listener,* February 29, 1968.

travel up to where decisions are taken. The sections of this chapter gradually move the focus of attention up the vertical hierarchy from the general public to the public media and then to Whitehall.

The greater the number of levels and channels in the communications process, the greater the opportunity for distortion. Insofar as messages move simultaneously through many channels, redundancy makes it less likely that a message will be lost, though it increases the burden of monitoring information. The greater an Englishman's political involvement, the more complex his communications network will be. In theory, this offers him more information. But it also offers greater difficulty in attending to all the information that flows to, around, or by him.

PUBLIC OPINION

Traditional discussions of the role that public opinion ought to play in government assume that members of the public have opinions to communicate and that no difficulties need necessarily arise in the translation of public opinion into public policy. The assumptions are belied by the evidence.

Every survey of public opinion first divides citizens into two groups: those who have an opinion about a given issue, and those who do not. The proportion of "opinionated" citizens is likely to be highest for issues immediately concerning the great mass of the population. For example, when people are asked whether or not they are satisfied with their standard of living, 99 per cent state a view. When they are asked to evaluate the performance of government in handling different issues, the proportion of "don't knows" rises; occasionally, the don't knows are the largest group. When voters are asked to choose between alternative policies, rather than simply give a global endorsement of what is done by the powers that be, the proportion of don't knows tends to be even higher.[5] Moreover, if the same question is put to the same person at two different points in time, there is a pos-

[5] See, e.g., Gallup Poll, *Political Index,* No. 147 (October 1972), pp. 161, 168.

sibility that he will give a different answer, even though no major political events have occurred to cause a change in outlook. The degree of uncertainty and instability indicates that some opinions expressed are almost random responses to passing events (including an opinion survey), and not opinions held strongly enough to justify action with long-term consequences.[6]

Insofar as opinions are meant to be based on knowledge,[7] there is good reason for some Englishmen to withhold judgment on issues of the day. In nineteenth-century England, it was probably easier for the electorate to understand issues than it is today. There were fewer big political problems facing a government at any one moment. Often the response demanded of government required a decision in principle, for instance, whether or not to reform the franchise. By comparison, the electorate today spans the whole mass of the adult population. Problems defined as political are more numerous. The alternatives among which the government must choose are complex, and many choices involve highly technical considerations. In such circumstances, it is not surprising that many voters are less concerned with informing themselves about the means, for instance, the economic policy most likely to succeed, and are more concerned with stating priorities about the ends, for instance, the achievement of steady prices and a rising standard of living.

Knowledge of politics reflects interest in politics; the more interested a person is, the more likely he is to hold opinions about issues. There are many reasons for citizens not to take an interest in politics or even to avoid discussing the subject. Englishmen may feel that talking about politics leads to arguments, threatens friendships, or reveals civic ignorance. Low interest may also reflect reasoned calculation. Anthony Downs has argued that because the ordinary individual can exercise

[6] See David Butler and Donald Stokes, *Political Change in Britain,* Ch. 8.

[7] Classical philosophers did not regard information as a requirement for political participation. See Jay G. Blumler, "Does Mass Political Ignorance Matter?" in *Publics et Techniques de la Diffusion Collective* (Bruxelles: l'Institut de Sociologie, 1971).

so little political influence, it is uneconomical for him to spend substantial sums and many hours each week reading books, papers, and periodicals specializing in political information. Instead, the best "value-for-money" strategy is to delegate responsibility for gathering information to full-time politicians.[8] A citizen then need only acquire sufficient information about competing parties to choose between them. This knowledge he may gain free, by living where one political party is constantly referred to as the party for "people like us." Because political news circulates widely and freely by television, by the press, and in conversations during election campaigns, an individual will be reminded of voting and which party best suits his predispositions. During election campaigns, more than half the electorate talks about political events. In between elections, levels of interest drop; the proportion of persons saying they have "not much interest in politics" rises from 30 per cent to 47 per cent, and of those saying they have a "good deal" of interest falls from 34 per cent to 16 per cent.[9]

When individuals hold views on public issues, their opinions can affect their voting behavior only if one party is perceived as different from and superior to the other in its policies. In order to avoid giving offense to sections of the electorate, British party leaders sometimes avoid taking up a clear position on a current issue (Table XI.1). Voters may impute policies to their favored party, in order to avoid inconsistency between party choice and issue preference. In a Gallup survey asking voters to evaluate the parties in terms of their competence to handle each of nine major issues, an average of 31 per cent of British respondents said they didn't know which party would do best.[10]

The public debate about British entry to the European Common Market – a seemingly straightforward question – illustrates the several difficulties that arise in efforts to relate public opinion to government. When the issue was first

[8] *An Economic Theory of Democracy* (New York: Harpers, 1957) especially Part II.

[9] See David Butler and Donald Stokes, *Political Change in Britain*, 1963 Survey, Q. 31; and 1964 Survey, Q. 7.

[10] *Political Index*, No. 147, pp. 160, 162.

mooted in the early 1960s, the don't knows were sometimes the single largest group; respondents with no opinion or no knowledge often formed an absolute majority of the electorate. In the subsequent decade, the proportion of don't knows decreased as the Common Market became the object of much discussion in the media. But the division of opinions fluctuated greatly. Prior to entry in 1973, the proportion endorsing entry to the Common Market fluctuated from a high of 71 per cent in July 1966 to a low of 16 per cent in November 1970, according to the Gallup Poll.

At the time of the 1970 general election, voters had no choice of pro and antimarket parties, for all three were then in favor of entry. The Labour and Conservative parties subsequently took up contrasting positions, but MPs within each party disagreed among themselves about whether the terms negotiated were satisfactory or not. As the parties shifted in and out of government and altered their position on the Common Market, the views of voters altered. Voters with shifting, uncertain, or confused opinions could claim with justice that their outlook reflected the views expressed by party leaders. When the country entered the Common Market, the median Englishman was literally a don't know; those with opinions were nearly evenly divided, 39 per cent for entry, and 45 per cent against.[11] Confusion was not confined to the ranks of the less informed. A survey of university economists was equally unclear in its implications: 40 per cent favored entry on economic grounds, 42 per cent were against, and the median economist was undecided.[12] In the midst of such uncertainties, there was one person who was without doubt of his view: the Prime Minister, Edward Heath. He knew what he wanted: British entry to the Common Market. Britain joined.

A general election is the principal occasion at which the majority of the public "speaks" its mind. Elections, however,

[11] See Gallup Poll, *Political Index*, No. 149 (December 1972) p. 205; and *British Attitudes towards the Common Market*, 1957–1971 (London: Gallup Poll). More generally, see Uwe Kitzinger, *Diplomacy and Persuasion.*

[12] See, e.g., "The Dons who want to go to Market," *The Observer*, October 24, 1971.

are blunt instruments infrequently used. Counting votes can decide who governs. But it does not say what the governors should do. Election results communicate no more than a rough judgment for or against a party. For propaganda purposes the new Cabinet may speak of receiving a mandate – as if every voter necessarily read and agreed with their preelection proposals before casting his ballot. On a few issues, a majority of a party's voters can have more confidence in the party they vote against than in the party they vote for (Table IX.2, p. 304). The doctrine of an electoral mandate is a dignified symbol rather than an effective means of expressing popular opinion.

When the majority of Englishmen speak out politically, they use actions not words. Popular sayings about "voting with your feet" or "voting with your pocketbook" have real meaning in economic policy. A trade union can take strike action after the government of the day – Conservative or Labour – declares that a strike is not in the "national" interest. Workers hear this argument, just as an unfortunate Minister of Labour cannot avoid noting their rejection of his plea. Company directors can similarly act against government economic policy. They can withhold investment at times when the government wishes to stimulate investments, and push investments when the government wishes to curb this form of spending. Businessmen expect the government to reinforce verbal pleas for investment by such market mechanisms as tax incentives.

Collectively, citizens can voice demands for welfare services by actions undertaken without political intent. For example, when people who have relied upon public transport buy automobiles, the extra traffic they add to the road constitutes a demand that something be done about the road network that they help overload. When people have larger families, the resulting rise in the number of small children creates pressure for the increased provision of a whole host of child-related public services. Because of the importance of the nation's age structure for the demand of education and of welfare services, forward projections of population are a persisting government concern.[13]

[13] See, e.g., Jean Thompson, "The Growth of Population to the End of the Century," *Social Trends,* Vol. 1 (1970).

An Englishman can communicate his views about public policy by choosing among three types of market behavior: exit, voice, and loyalty.[14] A citizen who disagrees profoundly with government policy may exit from the country, emigrating to Australia, Canada, or elsewhere. In fact, emigration rates are low. Individuals with sufficient resources and initiative can exit from the effects of a single policy. For example, parents dissatisfied with the government's comprehensive policy for state secondary schools may send their children to an independent fee-paying school instead. An unemployed worker, dissatisfied with progress on government schemes to end unemployment in his locality, may move to another region where a job can be found. In many circumstances a citizen cannot avoid the effects of public policy. For example, many home-owners cannot afford to move elsewhere if an annoying road is built at the bottom of their garden. Such individuals protest, hoping that it will divert the route or gain sufficient compensation to finance moving from the house. When individuals who disagree with a government policy find that they cannot escape its jurisdiction and the protests they voice are rejected, loyalty becomes important. A citizen must show by his actions that he is prepared to comply with the law, even if he dislikes it, or place himself outside the bounds of the loyal citizenry.

PUBLIC MEDIA

The media, as their name implies, are the means of communication. The media rarely create the events they report as news. Among the chief media, television is the most popular means of following political news; it is preferred by 48 per cent of Englishmen; 20 per cent prefer newspapers, 19 per cent private conversations, and 5 per cent radio.[15] Englishmen do not rely upon one medium of political communication exclusively. Intentionally or incidentally, most Englishmen are exposed to politics through radio, television, and the press. Moreover, everything that a citizen views, reads, or hears is

14 See Albert O. Hirschman, *Exit, Voice and Loyalty* (Cambridge, Mass.: Harvard University Press, 1970).

15 David Butler and Donald Stokes, *Political Change in Britain*, p. 220.

evaluated in the light of his own firsthand experience, whether relevant or remote.

The major media are large and complex industries. Politics is not the sole concern of publishers and broadcasters. Communicators may be concerned most of all with audience ratings, profitable balance sheets, or proficiency in technical skills. Very few media specialize in political content, and many news and feature stories are remote from the world of Westminster. Technical considerations, for instance, the availability of visual materials to illustrate TV news, also affect how the media operate.

Television and radio (collectively described as broadcasting) are highly centralized but competitive channels of political communication. The British Broadcasting Corporation provides two network television services and four radio services throughout the United Kingdom. Its regional branches provide local programs, especially in non-English parts of the kingdom. Local radio stations, inaugurated in England in 1967, are a specialized news medium on a noncommercial basis. The Independent Broadcasting Authority licenses fifteen companies to produce programs for regional audiences; they exchange programs to provide network services. Independent Television News covers central government and international news for the IBA stations. Commercial local radio stations are also commencing under IBA auspices.

Because of technical limitations on channel availability and economic limitations on program competition, the broadcasting industry is subject to government licensing. The BBC's Board of Governors is appointed by the government, as are the members of the Independent Broadcasting Authority. Each body operates under a government charter, subject to periodic review and renewal. Because the BBC depends for much revenue upon the license fee required of each household receiving programs (in 1973, £7), the government can affect operations by its readiness to permit this fee to rise. The annual profits of independent television companies, derived primarily from advertising, are affected by financial provisions of their licenses. Moreover, the periodic renewal of a license is not automatic. In 1967, the authority refused to renew the license of one program company, TWW (Television West and Wales) and altered the scope of broadcasting by other companies, to encourage program companies to respect IBA directives.

Because broadcasting authorities are subject to government control of charters, and the control of government can change hands just before a charter is up for renewal, companies have a substantial inducement to report politics impartially. Moreover, statutes require the companies to maintain a fair balance between differing points of view. At one time, broadcast comment on issues being debated in Parliament was not allowed; they were treated as though they were under consideration by a court. This inhibition no longer applies; the views of the main political parties are presented by typical and atypical spokesmen. The bias toward caution in choosing commentators is balanced against the view that novelty makes news. After the 1970 general election campaign, a study found that BBC-1 divided its news coverage almost equally among the two major parties, with 46 per cent for the Conservatives and 42 per cent for Labour; the Liberals received 10 per cent of attention and other candidates, 1 per cent. Independent Television News acted similarly, with the Conservatives 2 per cent ahead of Labour. Parties and candidates are not permitted to purchase time to advertise themselves. The parties are allocated time for party political programs on radio and television roughly in accord with their electoral strength. This allocation continues between elections too. In nonelection periods, BBC television devotes 6 per cent of its viewing time to straight news and another 16 per cent to documentaries and information programs. This equals the time devoted to films and light entertainment.[16]

The general public trusts the impartiality of the broadcasting media. In one national survey, only 9 per cent attributed any political bias to BBC news, and 7 per cent attributed bias to ITN. Weekly current affairs programs are similarly considered impartial.[17] This confidence is not shared by all politi-

[16] See *BBC Handbook 1973* (London: BBC, 1972), p. 47, and Martin Harrison, "Broadcasting," in David Butler and Michael Pinto-Duschinsky, *The British General Election of 1970*.

[17] See Marplan, *Political Index* (London: January, 1970), Table 5.

cians. One set of complaints is nonpartisan. It alleges that the broadcasting authorities do not give enough time to programs that the viewers ought to watch, that is, programs concerning Parliament. Yet MPs themselves have been singularly unhelpful in providing live programs. Repeatedly they have rejected proposals to permit the televising or filming of Commons debates. Politicians' complaints against television may also be motivated by the hope that unpopularity rests not with themselves but with those who communicate news about them. Harold Wilson's unusual interest in the media, described by one BBC official as a "mixture of contempt and fear," put a particular strain upon broadcasters and politicians when Wilson was Prime Minister.[18]

There is no agreement among broadcasting staff about the best way to treat political news. The BBC today still reflects the ethos of Lord Reith, the director-general during its formative years between the wars. Lord Reith once commented, "It is occasionally indicated to us that we are apparently setting out to give the public what we think they need – and not what they want – but few know what they want and very few what they need." Lord Reith's high-minded ethic has resulted in few people "at the top of the Corporation knowing, or indeed caring, what the audience makes of the service it receives."[19] Competition from commercial television for audiences has made some BBC staff more audience conscious. But this has only intensified differences within the BBC. In a study of the BBC current-affairs staff in the 1966 election, Jay Blumler found a "sacerdotal" approach among a group who saw elections as intrinsically important events and the BBC as the priestly intermediary between politicians and people. "Pragmatic" producers, by contrast, wished to report the election only insofar as events were newsworthy. An airplane crash or a bank robbery could be given more prominence than a Cabinet minister's repetition of a denunciation of his opponents.

[18] John Grist, *The Listener,* July 2, 1970. For general discussion, see Martin Harrison, "Broadcasting," and the sources cited therein.

[19] See Tom Burns, "Public Service and Private World," *The Sociology of Mass Media Communicators* (Keele, Staffordshire: Sociological Review Monograph No. 13), p. 71.

As the campaign progressed, the communicators agreed on one thing: Politicians, rather than broadcasters, were the would-be manipulators of public opinion, because of their efforts to influence campaign coverage. The communicators saw themselves, rather than MPs, as public watchdogs guarding against manipulation of the media.[20]

Studies of audience reaction to political television emphasize how little effect programs have upon political outlooks. People judge programs in the light of their prior party loyalty; they do not choose a party in response to their current program preference. Long-time Conservatives like Conservative programs best, and veteran Labour supporters like Labour programs best – regardless of program content. A reanalysis of BBC audience-research studies shows that in each campaign since 1959 viewers' reactions have become consistently less favorable. This has happened notwithstanding the effort that parties have made to produce "popular" party-political broadcasts at election time (Table VII.1).

The expectations that viewers bring to televised politics are several. Some hope the programs will provide guidance for voting; others wish to be informed about what politicians are thinking, gain reinforcement for their partisan loyalty, or seek excitement in an election race. Programs can alter voters' impressions of individual political personalities – though not necessarily for the better. For example, in 1964 Harold Wilson altered public perception of his personality, but the change emphasized "malevolent dynamism." [21] The less well-known the personality or, in the case of the Liberals, the less well-known the party, the more important television becomes as a means of increasing popular awareness, if not popular appeal.

By contrast to America, Canada, and many continental European countries, the press is centralized to an unusual degree. Morning newspapers printed in London can circulate

[20] See Jay G. Blumler, "Producers' Attitudes towards Television Coverage of an Election Campaign," in Richard Rose, editor, *Studies in British Politics*.

[21] Jay G. Blumler and Denis McQuail, *Television in Politics* (London: Faber, 1968), p. 243.

TABLE VII.1 *Average Reaction Indices for Party Election Broadcasts*

	Ratings by BBC viewing panels[a]											
	Supporters				*Opponents*				*Uncommitted*			
Party broadcasts of:	*1959*	*1964*	*1966*	*1970*	*1959*	*1964*	*1966*	*1970*	*1959*	*1964*	*1966*	*1970*
Labour	74	72	67	63	44	42	38	32	57	57	48	44
Conservative	73	66	65	65	45	38	38	34	55	53	48	41
Liberal	69	71	66	60	51	53	50	42	55	58	55	47

Source: Jay G. Blumler, "Information and Democracy" (Bucharest: IPSA Round Table, 1972), p. 17. Reprinted by permission.
[a]100 is most favorable rating.

throughout England thanks to special night transport facilities. London-based papers account for two-thirds of daily newspaper circulation and nearly all Sunday newspaper circulation.[22] The concentration of production is made necessary by the high costs of newspaper operation. Revenue is greatly affected by advertising. A popular newspaper will have difficulty breaking even financially with a circulation of one million. National papers with circulations smaller than one million require a specialized readership justifying premium advertising rates. As recently as fifty years ago, England had many more daily newspapers. Production costs were cheaper, and many political groups owned papers to provide propaganda outlets, and sometimes make profits. The Trades Union Congress sponsored a daily newspaper on behalf of the Labour movement from 1923 until financial pressures forced it to stop in 1962. Today, no national daily paper is tied to a political party financially, though none is without political bias in its editorial columns. Lord Beaverbrook, the publisher of the *Daily Express,* once claimed, "I ran the paper purely for the purpose of making propaganda and with no other object." But he quickly qualified this statement by adding, "I do not think a paper is any good for propaganda unless you run it as a commercial success." [23]

The label *news*paper gives a very partial description of the contents of the press. About two-fifths of the space in a newspaper is devoted to paid advertisements. Of the remaining space, about one-half is devoted to news stories, as against features, pictures, and other material. Approximately one-third of this space, that is, about 10 per cent of the total paper, is devoted to political news, domestic and foreign.[24] The popular papers further reduce their editorial content by using

[22] See Winston Fletcher, "Britain's National Media Pattern," in Jeremy Tunstall, editor, *Media Sociology,* p. 80.

[23] Quoted in Colin Seymour-Ure, *The Press, Politics and the Public* (London: Methuen, 1968), p. 95. On the economic history of the press, see Lord Francis Williams, *Dangerous Estate* (London: Grey Arrow, 1959); and, for trends, D. E. Butler and J. Freeman, *British Political Facts,* Ch. 19.

[24] See Colin Seymour-Ure, *The Press, Politics and the Public,* Tables 13–14.

large headlines and printing stories in type so bold that the number of words per column inch is few. Only the readers of the four serious papers are offered comprehensive coverage of the day's news.

The contents of the press are very much related to their readership profiles. A paper's editorial characteristics give each paper an image and a loyal following not unlike that of a political party. A paper's partisan bias is also part of its image; the newspaper-reading public has a definite perception of a paper's politics, however much an editor protests its independence (Table VII.2). The most important difference between the readership of papers is educational rather than political; a paper's news and editorial comment may presuppose a readership that seeks information or a readership seeking simplification and entertainment. The four serious morning papers have the lowest circulations. The four popular papers have the highest circulations. Differences in educational profiles are related to differences in the class basis of readership. A paper

TABLE VII.2 *National Daily Newspaper Readership*

	Paid circulation[a]	*% of Readers adult*[a]	*% of Readers working-class*[a]	*% of Perceived partisanship*[b]
Popular papers				
Mirror	4,279,000	33	78	80 Labour
Express	3,341,000	23	59	69 Conservative
Sun	2,699,000	24	80	75 Labour
Mail	1,702,000	12	51	63 Conservative
Serious papers				
Telegraph	1,433,000	9	20	72 Conservative
Times	340,000	3	20	74 Conservative
Guardian	339,000	3	22	51 Conservative
Financial Times	188,000	2	17	–

Sources: a = *National Readership Survey, January-December, 1972* (London: Joint Industry Committee for National Readership Surveys, 1973). Reprinted by permission. b = Derived from Marplan, Political Index, (January 1970), Table 6. Percentages refer to persons with an opinion about the paper's partisanship, whether or not readers.

with a higher proportion of working-class readers will have more readers with a minimum of education.

The nationwide importance of London-based newspapers and the gulf between the serious and the popular papers stratify media readership. In pretelevision days, radio was similarly stratified, with Light, Home, and Third programs, appealing to lowbrow, middlebrow, and highbrow audiences respectively. Television has tended to homogenize broadcasting, because high production costs create pressures favoring "mass" audiences. A survey of civil servants illustrates the stratification of readership. Among administrative-grade officials, 88 per cent read *The Times,* 72 per cent the *Telegraph,* and 36 per cent the *Guardian.* Only one-quarter read a popular paper. By contrast, among the clerical grade, the majority read a popular paper; only one-quarter read the *Telegraph,* and 4 per cent *The Times.* Senior civil servants are also prominent among the audience for specialized weekly periodicals offering news and comment. Whereas only a few per cent of the adult population read a serious weekly, 88 per cent of administrative-grade civil servants do. *The Economist* is read by 68 per cent, and *New Society,* specializing in welfare services and social problems, is second, being read by 33 per cent.[25]

Political reporting is highly centralized. The crucial man is the paper's lobby correspondent, who usually writes the paper's main political news story each day. Because he mixes daily with politicians on a privileged basis in Westminster, he can claim to write with authority. In the dramatic words of one writer, "A minister can get in touch with all the British press that matters simply by arranging to go into the lobby room." A lobby man learns to report parliamentary news by learning how politicians think. He spends fifty to sixty hours a week working in and around the Palace of Westminster. Learning to think like a politician does not lead lobby men to identify strongly with party positions; professionalism breeds detachment. A 1968 survey of lobby correspondents found that they divided evenly into three groups: Labour,

[25] See A. H. Halsey and I. M. Crewe, *The Fulton Committee,* pp. 32 f.

Conservative, and those who voted Liberal or abstained. Parliament is the lobbyman's professional life. Total involvement makes for informed reporting of Parliament. In the words of one correspondent:

> The most common form of political journalistic practice . . . is to put oneself in the place of the politicians, consider their problems and work out the answers . . . With experience and judgment it is possible to be right about ultimate decisions in a high proportion of cases.[26]

Like back-bench MPs, a lobby man has limited time for Whitehall departments. He depends for the most part upon ministers to provide background to government policy, whether the issue is technical or not. Specialist correspondents in such fields as economics, defense, and education provide supplementary coverage of public affairs, basing their stories on technical experts in and out of government, rather than MPs. The lobby man, a paper's chief political correspondent, cannot act as a watchdog in Whitehall because he "stands guard in the wrong place." [27]

Media men not only transmit news from government to the general public, but also originate information in editorials, in the comments of columnists, and in the remarks of television personalities. The policy that a newspaper expresses in its editorials is made in close quarters, but very different quarters from that of the parliament lobby. The complexities of modern publishing not only prevent a newspaper owner from frequent interventions in decisions about editorial policy but also limit the time a paper's editor can devote to enunciating views. William Rees-Mogg, editor of *The Times,* has reckoned that his job is "acting as the leader of an executive team." He writes one editorial a week and would like to write more, "but it's fairly difficult to get a long enough patch of the day clear enough." If a lobby man runs risks of having his

[26] All quotations in this paragraph from Jeremy Tunstall, *The Westminster Lobby Correspondents* (London: Routledge, 1970), pp. 20, 64, 59 ff, and 35.

[27] Colin Seymour-Ure, *The Press, Politics and the Public,* pp. 176 ff, p. 311. Cf. Jeremy Tunstall, *Journalists at Work* (London: Constable, 1971).

perspective affected by too close contact with politicians and events, the occupational hazard of an editorial writer is detachment. Involvement in the daily routine of a newspaper office plus heavy reading in fields of special interest allow limited time to confront at firsthand the problems about which editorial writers pronounce. The content of the day's editorial page is likely to be decided by intraoffice discussion in the light of the paper's past position and readership. In face-to-face discussion, idiosyncratic influences enter. An experienced editor, Donald McLachlan, concluded from an account of the making of editorial policy, "What the effect of this on the public is I do not know." [28]

The influence of the press upon the political outlooks of its readers is not independent of other influences. A reader's views will be affected by his class and his party loyalty as well as his paper; class may influence the choice of both party and paper. If a person chooses a newspaper because it accords with his established party preference, partisanship determines readership. Voters from Conservative families are more likely to read pro-Conservative papers as adults, and those from Labour families, pro-Labour papers. Subsequently a person is more likely to remain loyal to his original party if he has chosen a newspaper which will continually expose him to his party's viewpoint.[29]

Both the press and broadcasting influence the agenda of political discussion by their criteria for deciding what merits reporting and what does not. The criteria for defining political news are broad. Ministers complain that bad news is always news. Claims of success by ministers will also be printed, if the speaker has high political status. In the words of a lobby man, "You may not believe what a man is saying, but if he is Prime Minister, he has a right to have his views known." Agreement about the definition of news among journalists on different

[28] Donald McLachlan, "The Press and Public Opinion," reprinted in Richard Rose, editor, *Studies in British Politics,* p. 190; William Rees-Mogg's comments, quoted in Colin Seymour-Ure, "Policy-Making in the Press," a special issue of *Government and Opposition,* IV:4 (Autumn 1969), p. 498.

[29] Cf. David Butler and Donald Stokes, *Political Change in Britain,* pp. 232 ff; and Richard Rose, "Class and Party Divisions," p. 148.

papers and competition between papers inhibits efforts to "cover up" events definable as news.

While the criteria of political news are broad, they are not all-embracing.[30] They exclude certain types of events, as well as publicizing others. Activities are newsworthy if they are:

–Immediate (the latest economic figures, not trends of the decade).
–Novel within a familiar context (a Liberal party victory in a by-election).
–Of concern to lots of people (an increase in pensions) or to a high-status individual (an increase in the Queen's grant from Parliament).
–Factually ascertainable (a change in Cabinet ministers, rather than a changing mood of ministers).
–Close at hand (poor rubbish collection in London rather than Newcastle-upon-Tyne).
–Related to recognized areas of reporting (the wedding of a celebrity, but not the restaurant meals of a celebrity).
–Occurring when little else is happening (a politician's speech on a day when Parliament is not sitting has no competition from reports of Commons' debates).

Cumulatively, these criteria push out of prominence (or into the serious weeklies, monthlies, or books) discussions of problems that cannot meet the requirements for news. News criteria and expectations define the terms in which events are reported. A demonstration may be reported because of its potential for disorder, rather than in terms of the issue that the demonstrators are marching about.[31] Sometimes the opportunity to write a major story occurs fortuitously, because events provide a "peg" to hang it on, that is, to present information that journalists already knew about but could not find a way to print. For example, in 1963 a fluke enabled the *Sunday Times* to run a story about housing problems in Lon-

[30] The listing that follows is adapted from one appearing in that of Johan Galtung and Mari Holmboe Ruge, "The Structure of Foreign News," in Jeremy Tunstall, editor, *Media Sociology*.

[31] See James D. Halloran, Philip Elliott, and Graham Murdock, *Demonstrations and Communication* (Harmondsworth: Penguin, 1970).

don: a man who had made millions in the development of older houses became involved on the fringes of the Profumo scandal. He was therefore newsworthy. Because he had died, an unfavorable account of his property dealings could be given without risk of libel actions. The story won a prize, and the publicity led to government legislation. Politicians too have come to appreciate the possibilities of "making" news by planning events (or statements) to meet news criteria.

Although their professional interests are different, communicators and politicians need each other. Journalists need politicians as news sources. Politicians need journalists to give publicity to their views and themselves. In this process, the communications loop can be complete if it only includes politicians and journalists; members of the general public may neither note nor care about the publicity that results.

COMMUNICATION IN WESTMINSTER

The complexity of government makes communication difficult, whether one is a minister trying to find out what is going on in the lower reaches of a vast administrative empire, or a supplicant for the department's services, trying to find out what action has been taken on a request presented months ago. Central politicians are involved in vertical communications with those they represent or serve; horizontal communication keeps them in touch with the actions of other major political groups. Vertical communication is usually public; horizontal communication is usually private.

Members of Parliament are the chief constitutional channel for communicating the views of voters to government. But an MP's representative status does not reduce him to a messenger, delegated to carry local opinion to Parliament. He can present his own views as well as, or instead of, representing what he is told by his constituents. Conscience provides one justification for this. Unlike America, where Congressmen are electorally vulnerable to constituents' pressures, an MP's constituents will not reject him if he follows the party line rather than the constituency's special interests in the division lobby. Most constituents will not even know his views. In one survey, the proportion of voters who correctly stated their MP's views on four major issues varied from 12 to 26 per cent.[32]

Few citizens communicate their views to their MP. One study found that only one-tenth had ever contacted an MP. Most communications are requests for help in adjusting minor administrative decisions, for instance, adjusting a claimant's disability pension. Citizens appear to see their MP as a grievance officer rather than a delegate for constituency opinion on national issues. Constituencies give MPs a small but steady flow of mail; the median MP gets twenty-five to fifty letters a week from his constituents. MPs also meet their constituents at their constituency "surgery" where a citizen can press views or ask for assistance with a personal problem. The median MP holds a surgery more than once a month. Many of the visitors raise questions concerning local government responsibilities, such as housing. Others vent personal wrath or air a persecution complex; a psychiatric social worker might be as suitable a listener as a politician. In only a minority of cases do surgery visitors raise problems within the MP's competence. The surgery is not an occasion for lobbying on policy but for performing welfare services. The great majority find the work interesting, and a substantial proportion find helping people in this way the most valuable part of their activities as backbenchers. When MPs want to find out their constituents' views on issues, they must make a special effort by canvassing their constituents.[33]

Party headquarters do make efforts to study the political views of voters by commissioning opinion surveys. The Conservative Party before the 1959 election was the first to indicate an interest in market research. The Labour Party attacked the Conservatives for trying to "sell" policies like soap, then showed themselves more proficient in using surveys prior to

[32] David Butler and Donald Stokes, *Political Change in Britain,* p. 427.

[33] See Anthony Barker and Michael Rush, *The Member of Parliament and his Information,* pp. 174 ff; 192 ff; Rosemary Dinnage, "Parliamentary Advice Bureau," *New Society,* February 24, 1972; Robert E. Dowse, "The MP and his Surgery"; and Dennis Kavanagh, *Constituency Electioneering in Britain,* pp. 64 ff.

the 1964 election campaign. Since then both parties have commissioned opinion surveys. But these studies in no sense determine or direct the actions of politicians. Many English politicians believe that they know, by virtue of election, what ordinary voters think. They rate opinion polls well down the list of useful sources of information.[34] Politicians are also ready to ignore evidence that points in politically uncongenial directions. For example, after Labour's defeat in the 1959 election, one group within the party argued that it should not extend nationalization policies; opinion-poll evidence of the unpopularity of nationalization was cited as one among several reasons for this. Proponents of nationalization denounced both the propriety and the validity of the evidence. The Labour Party retained its commitment to nationalization, and in 1966 the Labour government nationalized the steel industry. Ironically, efforts to promote the use of opinion surveys have demonstrated the extent to which politicians are ready to ignore the views of those whose votes they seek.[35]

Government departments differ enormously in their channels of communication with the peripheral public. The two chief departments, the Treasury and the Foreign Office, have virtually no channels for communication within Britain. Their listening posts are in Paris, Brussels, Washington, and elsewhere abroad. Only through their economic policies and marketplace reactions can the public and Treasury officials "speak" to each other. A department such as Social Security has elaborate channels of communication, because it is applying government policy to thousands of individuals through local offices. The problem of such a ministry is a surplus of information. It must have fixed procedures in order to handle multitudes of individual communications. But emphasis on routine, essential in a bureaucracy, can lead officials to ignore unanticipated factors of substantial consequence in individual cases.

The Central Statistical Office seeks to provide government departments with quantitative information about the condi-

[34] See Dennis Kavanagh, *Constituency Electioneering*, pp. 56 ff.
[35] See Richard Rose, *Influencing Voters*.

tions of the English people. The sensitivity of government policy to short-term fluctuations in the economy ensures its economic reports a significant audience. It is more difficult to provide statistics about social conditions. The decennial census requires years to plan and years to publish; moreover, its scale limits the number of questions asked. The bulk of government statistical work is done within individual departments. This assures that data are collected by those most immediately concerned with their use; for example, statistics concerning children are collected in four different major departments. But it creates difficulties in making comparisons or drawing out interrelationships between separate departmental files. In 1970 the Central Statistical Office began publishing an annual volume on social trends, with chapters concerning employment, leisure, health, housing, and other areas of social policy. The editor noted in the introduction to the first edition, "An important function of *Social Trends* is to identify gaps in the statistical framework." In efforts to construct social indicators of the objectives of government, statisticians have discovered there are gaps in government objectives, that is, the purposes of a government program are not always specified clearly enough to permit statistical measurements.[36]

Since questions of morale became important in World War II, the government has sponsored social surveys. Sample surveys are a faster and more economical way to collect basic demographic information than a census inquiry. Much work is done by the Government Social Survey; some is contracted to research companies. For example, the Fulton Committee on the Civil Service had eight surveys collected as evidence. The major social survey of the civil service illustrates the obstacles facing political research. In the second paragraph of the report, the academic authors write, "Enquiry into such matters as political allegiance, religious affiliation, attitudes to career and promotion opportunities were ruled out as too delicate and difficult, even if there had been time to undertake them by valid and reliable techniques." [37]

[36] See Andrew Shonfield and Stella Shaw, editors, *Social Policy and Social Indicators* (London: Heinemann, 1972).

[37] A. H. Halsey and I. M. Crewe, *The Fulton Committee,* 3 (1) p. 1.

Many conventions, laws, and practices of British government emphasize noncommunication rather than communication. Upon occasion, a decision not to discuss an issue may stem from a political desire to avoid considering an uncongenial policy. For example, in 1964 Harold Wilson ruled that the devaluation of sterling should not be discussed in any official document, public or private, because of his wish to avoid this policy.[38] Usually public discussion is avoided because of Whitehall doctrines about how government business should be conducted. The philosophy is summarized in a White Paper entitled *Information and the Public Interest.*

> It does not follow, of course, that public consultation on tentative proposals is invariably the right course. It may result in slower decisions and slower action when prompt action is essential. Sometimes, too, conflicting views, and conflicting interests are already well known. In such cases a prolonged period of consultation will merely impose delay without any compensating advantages. Each individual case has to be considered on its merits.[39]

The government declares that it favors prior publication of information about policy matters "whenever reasonably possible." [40] Whitehall remains the sole judge of what is reasonable and possible.

The constitutional justification for the secretive character of Whitehall is the doctrine of ministerial responsibility. Everything that a department does is said to be done in the name of its minister. The convention that the department reflects the mind of a single individual has, as a corollary, that no one else can speak for the department. Both junior ministers and senior civil servants in the department are expected to make no public statement committing the department to a particular policy, unless authorized by the minister. This convention is strengthened by Section 2 of the Official Secrets Act of 1911,

[38] See Peter Jay, "Devaluation — Who was to Blame?" *The Times,* November 23, 1967; Henry Brandon, *In the Red* (London: Andre Deutsch, 1966), p. 43.

[39] *Information and the Public Interest* (London: HMSO, Cmnd. 4089, 1969), pp. 6–7.

[40] *Ibid.,* p. 7.

which makes it a crime for any person to communicate any information that he has received by virtue of being a minister or civil servant. This Act even covers such matters as a "restricted" circular from the minister to hospital authorities, asking them to convey Christmas greetings to all the staff on Christmas Eve. Libel laws are interpreted in ways that inhibit press comment on personalities, for fear of having to pay substantial damages. Occasionally, journalists get around these restrictions, but official resistance to "unreasonable" publicity remains strong.[41]

The doctrine of ministerial responsibility is inaccurate in its empirical assumptions. Time is one obstacle to communication to and from the minister. There are not enough hours in the day for any minister to read everything about the work of his department or to draft or sign every statement issued in his name. A minister must communicate his views in general terms, so that his staff can apply them in particular instances without direct communication. The complexity of government is another major obstacle to communication. A minister cannot keep abreast of all that goes on in other departments relevant to his work, and simultaneously be fully informed about what happens beneath him in his department. When departmental scandals occur, the minister is formally responsible, but he can plead with truth that he did not know about what was being done in his name. This plea can even be made on behalf of the Prime Minister. For example, Lord Denning's inquiry into the Profumo scandal in 1963 exculpated Harold Macmillan from blame on the ground that he was not told about what was going on, even after the security services became aware of Mr. Profumo's politically compromising extramarital relationships.[42] The flow of information between central and local government is also inhibited by geographical and institutional distance. In the extreme case of Northern

[41] See e.g. Colin Seymour-Ure, *The Press, Politics and the Public,* pp. 149 ff. Note also "Police Question Editor of Sunday Times," *The Guardian,* December 8, 1972.

[42] See *Lord Denning's Report* (London: HMSO, Cmnd. 2152, 1963); and Clive Irving, Ron Hall and Jeremy Wallington, *Scandal '63* (London: Heinemann, 1963).

Ireland, the Prime Minister may not take official cognizance of events reported for weeks in Belfast newspapers until someone such as Miss Bernadette Devlin camps overnight on the doorsteps of 10 Downing Street.[43]

The doctrine of ministerial responsibility, with its corollary of civil service anonymity, remains powerful because it appeals to the most important people in government: ministers and civil servants. Ministers do not wish to have news of differences within their department discussed in public for weeks or months prior to their decision. They are glad to take credit and blame for all that happens, trusting that a well-run department will more often than not make them look good by actions they do not know about in advance. Civil servants regard confidentiality as the basis of trust for the exchange of opinions and advice between them and ministers; any alteration of arrangements could be seen as raising "major constitutional issues." [44] The Franks Committee on the Official Secrets Act in 1972 recommended confining criminal liability to persons disclosing information injurious to the national interest. The testimony of very senior civil servants on the proposal emphasized Whitehall's continuing commitment to restricting public knowledge of departmental deliberations. Sir William Armstrong, head of the Civil Service, favored disseminating more information, but only with the proviso that dissemination was controlled at a single point. Only this, he said, could prevent the free flow of information from being "good, bad or indifferent, inaccurate or accurate, embarrassing or unembarrassing." Sir Burke Trend, secretary of the Cabinet, opposed publication of news of the existence of Cabinet committees because this might breach collective responsibility by leading to questions about the names of ministers who are members of the committees.[45]

[43] See Richard Rose, *Governing without Consensus*, p. 123 f.

[44] *Information and the Public Interest*, p. 10.

[45] See the report of Lord Franks' *Departmental Committee on Section 2 of the Official Secrets Act 1911* (London: HMSO, Cmnd. 5104). For a succinct summary, see Rudolf Klein's comments, *New Society*, October 5, 1972, pp. 34–35.

Collectively, these inhibitions limit press reporting of what happens inside government. A *Times* reporter has chronicled the obstacles placed in his way by the Parliamentary Commissioner's (Ombudsman's) office when the reporter sought to publicize information contained in the annual report of that office. The results of a year's investigation are reported together, so that a journalist does not have time to investigate each incident of potential news interest. The accounts often treat people and places anonymously, thus preventing a journalist from making further investigations and persons living in the affected area from knowing fully about the decision in the case. The Parliamentary Commissioner's office refuses to supply the name of the MP who, by statute, must endorse a complaint. The refusal of information arises from statutory provisions. When officials have discretion in making information available, practices vary but are usually cautious. For example, the National Council of Civil Liberties wrote separately to heads of each of forty-six police authorities in England and Wales, requesting copies of their annual report; it received eighteen in reply.[46]

MPs as well as journalists suffer from Whitehall's inhibitions about publicity. Parliamentary questions are limited in value, because questions are not permitted on many topics ranging from details of arms sales and purchases made by the National Health Service to regional figures for money invested in National Savings certificates.[47] Even when the speaker allows a question on a delicate subject, the minister involved may refuse to answer. For example, at the beginning of the Suez War, Sir Anthony Eden refused Parliament an answer to a question asking whether or not the country was at war with Egypt![48] Because only a few minutes are allowed each question, a minister can reply with a form of words that does not

[46] Tony Smythe, "Police Report," *New Society,* November 9, 1972; George Clark, "Official Secrets of Britain's Ombudsman," *The Times,* May 7, 1970.

[47] See Jim Michael, "Secretive Service," *New Society,* October 12, 1972.

[48] See House of Commons *Debates,* Vol. 558, Cols. 1452–54 (October 31); and Cols. 1620 ff (November 1, 1956).

illuminate the topic. In the opinion of a former civil servant:

> The perfect reply to an embarrassing question in the House of Commons is one that is brief, appears to answer the question completely, if challenged can be proved to be accurate in every word, gives no opening for awkward supplementaries and discloses really nothing.[49]

In response to back-bench MPs' demands to know more about what happens in Whitehall, specialist committees and the estimates committee have been expanded since 1964. Committee hearings provide opportunities for lengthy discussions between MPs and senior civil servants about some major matters of policy. But they have not altered the balance of publicity, for two reasons. The first is that the government of the day lays down ground rules restricting the powers and scope of these committees. Both Conservative and Labour governments have been cautious in extending the Commons' opportunities to learn about the work of Whitehall. The second reason is the lack of attention given deliberations by MPs and by the press. A comparison with Congressional committee hearings in Washington provides one explanation: the Commons' committees receive less publicity because they have much less power.

Faced with such constraints, 91 per cent of MPs say that they are not adequately informed about the actions of government. Moreover, five-sixths of MPs think their lack of knowledge is in part caused by ministers wishing to limit what the Commons is told. The most positive comment on the situation is an MP's remark that:

> Ministers wish to limit our power not our knowledge; there is no lack of knowledge if MPs can absorb it.

But the more typical view is that:

> The tendency of paternalism towards Government backbenchers is strong: "If you knew what I know you'd see I'm right." Meanwhile, father knows best.[50]

[49] H. E. Dale, *The Higher Civil Service of Great Britain* (London: Oxford University Press, 1941), p. 105.

[50] See Anthony Barker and Michael Rush, *The Member of Parliament and his Information,* pp. 150, 363 ff.

Noncommunication between governors and governed can create some problems while avoiding others. This point is increasingly being realized in Whitehall. The 1969 White Paper, *Information and the Public Interest,* acknowledged the desirability of "reinforcing the increasingly liberal attitude of the last few years." [51] One reason for this is pressure from groups outside Whitehall – the press, academics, pressure-group officials, and, not least, MPs – to know more about what is going on inside government. Another is Whitehall's recognition of the value of public discussion of policy alternatives in advance of decision. Discussion can anticipate criticism, remove defects from legislation, and help mobilize the consent of those consulted.

One way in which Whitehall seeks information is through ad hoc Royal Commissions and Departmental Committees, which review and recommend policies on such subjects as the press, reform of the trade unions, judicial administration, the aircraft industry, and decimal currency. A Royal Commission is often constituted when government is unable or unwilling to assume sole or immediate responsibility for a policy decision. It can acquire information; recommend a course of action likely to be agreed by the majority of affected interests appearing before it; gain public support for a policy that the government wishes to adopt eventually; or avoid or stall decisions about a controversial matter. In drafting terms of reference, the government of the day will define terms so that the Commission does not publicize issues that the government wishes to leave unexamined.

An experienced committee man, Andrew Shonfield, has described how these bodies proceed:

> Just plunge into your subject; collect as many facts as you can; think about them hard as you go along; and at the end, use your commonsense, and above all your feel for the practicable, to select a few good proposals out of the large number of suggestions which will surely come your way.[52]

[51] *Information and the Public Interest,* p. 4. But compare other comments from the White Paper quoted elsewhere in this chapter.

[52] "In the Course of Investigation," *New Society,* July 24, 1969.

Like a judge, a committee usually confines itself to listening to the views of those who wish to testify – orally or in writing – before it. It may lack time, money, staff, or inclination to undertake any other form of inquiry or research. For example, the Pilkington Committee on Broadcasting held 120 meetings in a two-year period. It listened to dozens of pressure group spokesmen, but it did not commission any sample survey of the attitudes of listeners and viewers. After it reported, a survey showed public opinion divided about a major Pilkington proposal. The pro-Pilkington stratum – those with education beyond the age of eighteen – constituted about 4 per cent of the population, and the anti-Pilkington stratum about 96 per cent of the population.[53]

Any minister who wishes to seek advice from informed opinion outside Whitehall can, by virtue of his status, easily establish contact with networks of experts who constitute a "market place of ideas" relevant to the department's work. For example, defense policy involves a feedback of information and values between government ministers, senior military officers, defense correspondents of serious papers, members of the International Institute for Strategic Studies, a few MPs of each party specially interested in defense, and spokesmen (sometimes former military officers) for firms producing armaments.[54] This network has few vertical contacts with the majority of the population. But within its horizontal level it is open to a wide variety of ideas and influences. Strictly limited communication does not necessarily result in the circulation of identical ideas.

Communication can be formalized by a department's establishing an advisory committee in which pressure-group spokesmen and experts in a field meet periodically to discuss both present and future problems facing the minister. In the 1960s, committees on economic and industrial questions were multiplied, as Whitehall sought to bring employers and trade-union

[53] Cf. *Report of the Committee on Broadcasting* (London: HMSO, Cmnd. 1753, 1962); and Harry Henry, *Public Opinion and the Pilkington Committee* (London: Sunday Times, 1962).

[54] L. W. Martin, "The Market for Strategic Ideas," *American Political Science Review,* LVI:1 (1962).

leaders together to discuss ways of making major improvements in specific sectors of the economy. The National Economic Development Council consists of representatives of the Cabinet, management, the trade unions, the nationalized industries, and one independent member. Whitehall has also sought to increase opportunities for affected urban publics to communicate their views about town planning developments before firm decisions are taken.[55]

Whitehall has also sought to improve public deliberations about its activities by making more statistical information available. Data about economic trends, including forecasts for the future, are important for industrialists trying to match investment decisions to market needs. The more important the policy, the more difficult it is to treat a forecast as a technical statistical exercise. Forecasts of economic growth are sometimes made in the optimistic hope that the forecast will become a self-fulfilling prophecy. Uncertainties about the future can be used as a justification for avoiding forecasts, when prognostication can be politically embarrassing. In 1970 a Labour Government, divided about British entry into the Common Market, issued a White Paper estimating the cost of entry at anything between £100 and £1,100 million. A Labour minister, George Thomson, who later resigned to become a European Commissioner, said that this was like saying the score of a football match would be anything from 10–0 for one side to 10–0 for the other.[56]

The classic doctrine of civil-service anonymity has been breached in that some senior civil servants are beginning to speak in public about the problems of their departments and how the departments operate. Whitehall sees this as a means of increasing public understanding and acceptance of government's work. In making public statements, however, officials "should not be drawn into expressing personal views on policy

[55] See the Skeffington Committee's Report, *People and Planning* (London: HMSO, 1969); and David Donnison, "Micro-politics of the City," in David Donnison and David Eversley, editors, *London* (London: Heinemann, 1973).

[56] See George Thomson, "The Game's the Same," *The Guardian,* July 9, 1971.

matters which could be represented as in conflict with those of their ministers, or as reflecting any political bias."[57] Ministers are also beginning to publish Green Papers in advance of White Papers. A Green Paper is intended to canvass alternative departmental responses to a current policy problem without making a formal commitment to any single one, as is the case with a White Paper. A Green Paper thus gives a minister the benefit of criticism of various alternatives before he officially commits his department.

No government document discusses informal procedures that facilitate communication. For example, ministers, senior civil servants, and journalists can communicate in "code." Information may be published if it is coded, that is, stated so that only those with private knowledge of public affairs can interpret the full significance of the message. The majority who read it will not. The report on *Control of Public Expenditure* by a committee under Lord Plowden illustrates how communication in code operates. The report was entrusted to a committee appointed by the government because the members could be relied upon not to communicate publicly what they learned by surveying government expenditure in private. It was drafted simultaneously with private memoranda; hence the committee had the option of making specific criticisms in the public print or privately. The Treasury, the chief object of criticism, made the decision about the report's publication. Following publication of the coded report, Professor W. J. M. Mackenzie, a former classicist and a wartime civil servant, published a "translation." The first paragraph of the official report reads:

> For these studies we co-opted the Permanent Secretaries of the Departments with whose expenditure we were concerned or who had special experience of the general problems under review. In some cases we sought specialist advice from outside the Civil Service. We decided, however, not to take evidence from outside bodies: our review was primarily concerned with the inner working of the Treasury and the Departments, and was necessarily confidential in character, and we decided that

[57] *Information and the Public Interest,* p. 10.

> the Group itself (except on certain specialist matters) provided a sufficient body of outside opinion to bring to bear on this task.

Mackenzie translates it thus:

> We proceeded on two principles: no dirty linen in public: outside critics are bores.[58]

The politicians' interest in publicizing their policies and themselves results in leaks of information to the media that it is not official policy to publish. A carefully planted ministerial leak may be a means to prepare the ground for a controversial ministerial announcement or to undermine support for the conflicting policies of another department. Harold Wilson as Prime Minister was even accused of leaking statements against members of his own Cabinet. Senior civil servants also brief journalists upon occasion. Technically, such disclosures are against the Official Secrets Act. But, as the Director General of the Security Service complained, "The chances of their being prosecuted . . . are minimal, if they exist at all, because they can always say that they authorized themselves to disclose the information." [59]

WHAT PRICE COMMUNICATION?

Communication is a complex and costly business. It is complex because of all the things that must fit together if governors and governed are to exchange information fully. It is costly because the price of ignorance can be great if a public policy is based upon misinformation. The cost is also great if action is delayed while a futile search is made for all the facts, or trivia are repeated endlessly in public or private consultations. Limits of time and resources make noncommunication between some the complement of communication between others. In theory everyone who needs to know will be consulted, and those who are unaffected need not be consulted. But decisions about who should and should not be informed

[58] Cf. "The Plowden Report: A Translation," represented in Richard Rose editor, *Studies in British Politics;* and the original, *Control of Public Expenditure* (London: HMSO, Cmnd. 1432, 1961).

[59] Quoted by Rudolf Klein, *New Society,* October 5, 1972.

are inevitably subjective. One characteristic of the civil service is to proliferate information within Whitehall through committee meetings and memoranda. Another characteristic is to limit communication outside Whitehall. Those "in the know" have a chance to act or react in their own interest. Those uninformed may sometimes reason that what they don't know will hurt them.

The most economical form of communication requires understanding, not talk. When individuals know each other's minds, a wink and a nod may be sufficient, or one person may put himself in another's place and take the decision that the other would have taken had he been personally informed. British government requires much "virtual" communication. MPs speak for their constituents by virtue of election, and no more precise claim to information. Ministers speak for their departments, while departmental civil servants write letters speaking for ministers. In such circumstances it is often easy for people in Westminster to mistake the echo of their own voices or the words of a trusted confidante for the views of a much larger public. In an essay on government in wartime, D. N. Chester noted how the intense concentration of effort in Whitehall facilitated horizontal communication there, while tending to isolate those involved from the general public.

> What can come to be important if one is not careful, is not how decisions affect people, but how they are thought to operate by people in the Whitehall circle. The leader or letter in *The Times* or *Economist* can become the reality by which one's actions are judged.[60]

The habits of wartime persist in peacetime. A study of the control of public expenditure by the Treasury is aptly titled *The Private Government of Public Money*.[61]

While knowledge or ignorance can influence events, perfect information cannot of itself resolve political disagreements. By definition, politics is about conflict. Canvassing views on any

60 "The Central Machinery for Economic Policy," in D. N. Chester, editor, *Lessons of the British War Economy* (Cambridge: University Press, 1951), p. 30.

61 By Hugh Helco and Aaron Wildavsky.

issue of political significance will inevitably produce arguments and evidence in support of conflicting policy choices. Ironically, the government seeks to secure information by such elaborate means as Royal Commissions when matters are least urgent. On very serious matters it may pursue a policy of studied ignorance, as in the case of Northern Ireland prior to civil rights demonstrations in 1968, because it calculates that the less known about some political difficulties the better. In many political negotiations, agreement rather than accuracy is the major objective. For example, Ely Devons has described how estimates of figures for aircraft production were not reconciled by carefully going over discrepancies between forecasts, but rather by "statistical bargaining," which had as its object the statement of a figure that all would abide by, even though it coincided with none of the estimates.[62]

Any effort to describe the imperfect market for information in Whitehall must explain why policy makers sometimes attend carefully to information, even if it is no more substantial than straws in the wind, and at other times ignore facts that appear as palpable as handwriting on the wall. What politicians want is help, not knowledge for its own sake. Busy policy makers, especially in a government as highly centralized as that of Britain, can only attend to information if the benefits are likely to be greater than the costs of ignoring it.[63] A department finds it costly to prepare detailed reports, and a minister finds it costly in time to read the flow of paper passing through his office. A policy maker's readiness to attend to communications is less a function of the quality of information and more a matter of his immediate requirements. In a political crisis, when the costs of inaction are great, then any kind of information — statistical, literary, or conjectural — will be seized upon for clues of what to do.

[62] *Planning in Practice* (Cambridge: University Press, 1950), pp. 155 ff.

[63] For a detailed statement of the argument summarized above, see Richard Rose, "The Market for Policy Indicators," in Andrew Shonfield and Stella Shaw, *Social Policy and Social Indicators*.

CHAPTER VIII

Group Pressures

The unsectional Parliament should know what each section in the nation thought before it gave the national decision.

WITHOUT ORGANIZATION, millions of Englishmen may be of the same mind politically but will have no means of expressing their views and no one to "re-present" their opinions in Westminster. With organization, the same people will have spokesmen pressing government to act. Before government acts, it will consult those who claim to speak on their behalf. English history shows, for example, how the organization of trade unions in the late nineteenth century greatly increased the political influence of millions of formerly unorganized workers. Their employers have had to come together in trade organizations too, in order to present government a case on their own behalf against the unions.

Parties and pressure groups are the most familiar types of organizations presenting demands to government. The chief distinction between the two is that pressure groups do not seek to control government by contesting elections. Because of this, pressure groups may be small in size, like the Market Research Society or the Society for the Promotion of Roman Studies. Moreover, pressure groups need not be exclusively or primarily concerned with government policy. Because a pressure group does not seek the responsibility of government, pressure group officials are always free to press demands on government from the outside. By contrast, when a party moves from opposition to office, its leaders become the recipient of demands from pressure groups as well as acting as campaigners for interests.

A clear-cut distinction between parties and pressure groups cannot be maintained in England, because of the interpenetration of the two kinds of institution. This is particularly notable in the Labour Party, which regards itself as one wing of the labor movement, complementing the activities of the trade unions and Cooperative societies. The labor movement is thus two parts pressure group and one part political party. In the picturesque words of Ernest Bevin, the Labour Party grew out of the bowels of the trade-union movement.[1] The party was founded in 1900 when trade-union leaders decided that they would need political power in order to achieve economic goals that could not be obtained by collective bargaining alone. Gradually the Socialists in the new Labour Party converted the great majority of union leaders to endorsing Socialism as a means of gaining their major objectives; these were and are both political and economic.

The relationship between the unions and the Labour Party in Britain is much closer than any such relationship found in America, where the AFL-CIO has no institutional voice or vote in the Democratic Party convention and must operate like any other pressure group. It is also different from such relationships in France or Italy, where union members may divide along political lines into Socialist, Communist, and Christian oriented unions; in Germany, the Social Democratic Party is organized independently of the unions.

Today the unions provide seven-eighths of the members of the Labour Party and about three-quarters of its income. The unions elect eighteen of the twenty-eight members of the party's National Executive Committee. They sponsored 112 of the 287 successful Labour candidates for the House of Com-

[1] *Labour Party Conference Report, 1935* (London), p. 180. For implications, see D. W. Rawson, "The Life-span of Labour Parties," *Political Studies,* XVII:3 (1969).

mons in 1970. The Cooperative societies are relatively unimportant, with only one member on the National Executive, with less than 1 per cent of the Conference vote directly in their control, and with sponsorship of seventeen Labour MPs. Trade-union branches also affiliate to local constituency parties. In some parliamentary constituencies, the local lodge of the National Union of Mineworkers is the Labour Party. In others, the party may be the most active and vocal spokesman for the labor movement. At the Westminster level, unions usually allow the Parliamentary Labour Party to represent their interests on nonindustrial matters. Moreover, union-sponsored MPs will follow the policy of the Parliamentary Labour Party rather than that of their union when the two diverge.[2] But on industrial relations issues, trade-union leaders expect to negotiate with government directly, whether it is Conservative or Labour. When Labour is in office, negotiations between union leaders and Labour ministers often reflect differences of outlook and interest between the wings of the labor movement. This was most dramatically demonstrated in 1969, when the Labour government proposed a major industrial relations bill, and trade-union leaders, acting in their own name and with the support of union-sponsored MPs, forced the bill's withdrawal.

The Conservative Party antedates the rise of industry to political influence, and its structure was established independently of business groups. Prior to 1918, businessmen divided their support between the Conservatives and the free-trade Liberal party. The rise of the Labour Party created a demand for a single "anti-Socialist" front. Since then, businessmen, fearing the return of a Labour government, have had no choice but to support the Conservative cause: The Liberals' weak position gives them little appeal to business interests. Financial contributions constitute the chief business link with the Conservative Party. There is no formal institutional connection between business groups and the Conservative Party. Moreover, there is a major distinction between businessmen

[2] See Martin Harrison, *Trade Unions and the Labour Party* (London: Allen & Unwin, 1960); and William D. Muller, "Trade Union Sponsored Members of Parliament in the Defence Dispute of 1960–1961," *Parliamentary Affairs,* XXIII:3 (1970).

who believe politics should be about a "free-enterprise" alternative to Socialism, and Conservative politicians who believe that politics should be about winning votes in a mixed-economy welfare state. Free-enterprise businessmen have withheld campaign funds from the Conservative Central Office to run antinationalization campaigns of their own. Reciprocally, Central Office has run propaganda campaigns with little reference to the free-enterprise ethic.[3] Individual Conservative MPs act as pressure-group spokesmen for a heterogeneous range of organizations, but Conservative MPs are not expected to allow this to affect their voting in the Commons.[4]

The blurring of institutional distinctions between pressure groups and parties is increased by the blurred boundaries separating the concepts of principle and interest, the reputed bases of parties and pressure groups respectively. In practice, one man may regard as an interest what another regards as a principle. The National Farmers Union, for instance, presents demands for hundreds of millions of pounds in government subsidies, but it justifies these demands by reference to social principles that place a high value on agriculture's contribution to the nation's way of life.[5] Coal-mining communities, especially in Scotland and Wales, lobby government to keep open uneconomic mines not only in order to preserve miners' jobs but also to preserve a distinctive way of life on principle. Class-conscious demands are thought by some to represent narrow interests, but these interests are also reflected in the principles of the political parties. In a standard work on English pressure groups, Allen Potter distinguishes between groups defending interests and those promoting causes or principles, but notes "the difficulties of drawing a reasonably precise line." [6] The line is further blurred by the tendency of some

[3] See Richard Rose, *Influencing Voters,* Chs. 2, 5–7.

[4] See, e.g., J. H. Millett, "The Role of an Interest Group Leader in the House of Commons," *Western Political Quarterly,* IX:4 (1956).

[5] Peter Self and Herbert Storing, *The State and the Farmer* (London: Allen & Unwin, 1962).

[6] Allen Potter, *Organized Groups in British National Politics* (London: Faber, 1961), p. 25. See also W. J. M. Mackenzie, "Pressure Groups in British Government," in Richard Rose, editor, *Studies in British Politics;* and S. E. Finer, *Anonymous Empire* (London: Pall Mall, 2nd edition, 1966).

who promote causes without financial reward to draw "psychic income" from their work.

The interpenetration of party principles and pressure-group interests can clearly be seen in the resolutions sent by activists to the annual Conservative and Labour Party conferences. Pressure-group demands unrelated to party principles appear prominently among the resolutions submitted in both parties: Constituency groups ask for better treatment for farmers, pensioners, or motorists without reference to larger ideological concerns.[7] Reciprocally, the influence of party politics in interest groups can be seen in elections to national trade union offices; elections can turn on left-wing vs moderate orientation within the Labour Party or on questions of overt or covert Communist influence. The Labour Party has sought to counter the pro-Conservative bias of medical pressure groups by maintaining its own Socialist Medical Association. The Conservatives attempt to counteract the Socialist bias of trade unions by organizing Conservative trade unionists.

Parties and pressure groups are not independent as conventional terminology implies; they are interdependent. Both are parts of a single political system, and both are concerned with advancing political demands. Controversies on particular political issues often show pressure-group officials and party politicians working together. In economic controversies, the two will usually be with their natural allies. A pressure group that has a variety of organizations as its constituent members, such as the Confederation of British Industries or the Trades Union Congress, aggregates demands and decides between competing policies in a fashion not unlike that of a political party. A party, at times, may present as a point of principle demands arising from the narrow group interests of unemployed railway workers or of manufacturers faced with declining markets.

Although pressure groups and parties are not absolutely separate, one major distinction does exist. Pressure groups do not themselves seek to win control of government by pre-

[7] See Richard Rose, "The Political Ideas of English Party Activists," *American Political Science Review*, LVI:2 (1962), and, more generally, S. H. Beer, *Modern British Politics*.

senting a slate of candidates to the electorate, as parties do. Parties also differ from pressure groups in the degree of their inclusiveness. Especially in a two-party system, parties must include people with many kinds of skills and policy concerns; they cannot be as narrow as the British Optical Association or the British Trust for Ornithology in their membership or interests.

THE ORGANIZATION OF INTERESTS

The number of potential political interests is virtually infinite, as the advent of the mixed-economy welfare state has made the government a significant influence in many areas of social life. The political culture still identifies some areas as outside government intervention, so that individuals do not expect all their needs to be met by political action. Whether and how a pressure group organizes to advance political demands depends upon the type of interest it seeks to represent, the cohesiveness of its members, and their political resources.

The variety of interests in the political arena is shown by attempts to classify pressure groups according to the claims they make on government. One authority has catalogued twenty-four different types of interest.[8] The largest single cluster concerns economic affairs: trade unions, employers' groups, professional bodies, property owners, manufacturers, and farmers. Groups concerned with the welfare of children, the elderly, the sick, and the handicapped also seek more money for their clients. Pressure groups differ greatly in the scope of their interests. A trade federation will have a broader range of concerns than a single firm that belongs to it, just as the Trades Union Congress will be concerned with industrial conditions in a wider range of contexts than is any single union. The basis of membership appeal limits the policies that concern a group. For example, the Automobile Association is not interested in foreign-policy questions, and a group lobbying on behalf of Anglo-Chinese friendship is likely to have little interest in automobiles, except when there is talk of a trade agreement with China involving motor vehicles.

8 Allen Potter, *Organized Groups in British National Politics,* ch. 2.

Trade unions and business associations are the pressure groups with the widest range of concerns.

The ease with which individuals can be organized depends in part upon the interest to be advanced. When individuals have a personal and immediate benefit to be gained from action, they are most prone to organize. This holds for doctors and lawyers as well as for miners and truck drivers. Conversely, when the interest is general and long-term, people are hardest to organize. Ironically, this means that the greater the potential numbers affected, the more difficult it is to organize a group on their own behalf. While everyone is a consumer, the membership of the Consumers Association is but 3 per cent of families in the country. Issues involving the good of all, for instance, war and peace, concern everyone. But because no one can be excluded from a peaceful outcome – even if he does nothing to bring it about – there is little incentive for individuals to join a pressure group concerned with foreign policy. An organization concerned with wages may negotiate directly with employers. Local consumer groups do not expect to negotiate with local shopkeepers about prices. Instead, they must rely on the unorganized behavior of individuals in the marketplace.

The more durable, the more frequent, the more numerous, and the more intense the contacts among individuals, the easier they are to organize for political action. Miners exemplify nearly all the characteristics that lead to organization. They usually work at mining all their lives; their work brings them into contact with fellow miners at all times; they frequently meet miners outside the pits, because they live clustered in mining villages. Because their homes are near the pits, the future of a mine becomes, in effect, the future of their community. By contrast, members of an air charter group are virtually incapable of organization, for they meet only once when waiting at an airport to board an aircraft; they have nothing in common beside a flight plan; the cheapness of charter fares even reduces the intensity of their concern to protect themselves against loss, should a charter operator default on his undertaking.

The structures of groups within the economic system illustrate the complexities besetting the translation of assumptions about common interests into pressure-group organizations. Viewed from the perspective of an economist, everyone involved in economic activity has a common interest because the economic system can be viewed as a single entity maximizing production or welfare values. While labor and business interests will sometimes agree in their economic demands, political controversy arises at the points of disagreement.

Within the profit-making sector of the economy, financial institutions in the City of London are distinctive in many respects. As major lenders of money, their interests can come into conflict with those of industrialists wishing to borrow money cheaply for investment purposes. Industrial manufacturers seek profits from the production of goods and the development of new technological skills. They are thus distinguished from retailers, who are oriented toward consumer behavior. Within the retailing field, large chain stores and small shopkeepers are often competing or in conflict. Government-owned nationalized industries are a hybrid form of economic group. Because the government owns the companies, their operations are meant to be in the public interest. Yet both Conservative and Labour governments are disturbed when nationalized industries demonstrate their public-service orientation, subsidizing consumers by selling goods and services at a loss. Cooperative societies do not pay profits to shareholders; they return profits earned to members in proportion to their purchases. Formally, they are dedicated to serving the consumer. But with rising incomes, English consumers have shown in the past two decades that they think themselves better off by buying more and more goods at cut-price chain stores. Cooperative sales have failed to grow proportionately with the rise in consumer spending. Differences between trade unions are persistently reflected in the advancement of separate wage claims, even by unions representing men working within the same industry. For example, railway workers have separate unions for locomotive drivers, clerks, and unskilled workers. Each union makes its own wage claim and has its own idea of what kind of settlement is in its particular interest.

The two largest economic groups — the Trades Union Congress and the Confederation of British Industries — are in many ways limited by their very size. The TUC seeks to represent the common interests among its more than one hundred member unions, with 9,000,000 individual members. Similarly, the CBI, organized as an amalgamation of several different business groups in 1965, seeks to represent its membership of more than 11,000 companies, 200 employers associations, and 14 very large nationalized industries. Most of the individual corporate members are also active in trade associations and the largest firms negotiate directly with government. The size and scope of these organizations make them especially useful to government departments, because the Department of Employment or the Department of Trade and Industry could not consult with all the separate organizations forming constituent parts of the CBI and the TUC. But the very inclusiveness of the organizations weakens them, for it reduces the things that all members can have in common. The limited commitment of member organizations to their parent pressure groups is shown by the limited resources provided them. CBI staff feels pressed for operating funds, although the members do not lack financial resources. The TUC has the lowest ratio of headquarters staff to union membership in the Western world.[9] Neither organization bargains on wages, because there is no agreement among unions or among employers about what wage rates should prevail within or between industries. The restricted power of leaders of the top organizations limits the agreements they can make with government. As one experienced economist has said:

> Neither the trade unions nor management have systems of private government that can send plenipotentiaries to negotiate on their behalf and commit them to settlement, save on limited

[9] See Bruce W. Headey, "Trade Unions and National Wages Policies," *Journal of Politics,* XXXII:2 (1970), pp. 428–29. For the TUC's activities, see its *Annual Report* and Congress debates. On the CBI, see Wyn Grant and David Marsh, "A Confederation of British Business?" *New Society,* November 23, 1972; and "The Confederation of British Industry," *Political Studies,* XIX:4 (1971); Stephen Blank, *Industry and Government in Britain* (London: Saxon Books, 1973).

issues and particular occasions, when the negotiators can keep in touch with their constituents as the negotiations proceed.[10]

Of all the political resources that pressure groups command, strategic location is the most significant. Location does not depend upon an organization's efforts but upon the nature of the group's activities. An organization is in a strategic position if it can quickly create a political crisis by withdrawing cooperation from government. In extreme instances, a group may "exit" from the authority of government. Bankers may move sterling outside Britain when they fear devaluation, or trade union leaders may refuse to recognize negotiating and arbitration procedures established by law. A union may also exert pressure by calling a strike if its services are critical to the day-to-day activities of society. For example, longshoremen and electricians have a strategic position superior to that of textile workers or letter carriers. England has a daily need for electricity and for food imported through the docks; it does not require a daily addition of stocks in clothing stores or the daily delivery of the mail. When government seeks to increase British exports, firms in export industries have their strategic position strengthened because the success of government policy depends on what they do. Pressure groups representing occupations with a "service" ethic, such as teachers or doctors, are constrained from exploiting their strategic position by professional norms against striking. But, as aggressive groups succeed in gaining demands from government, professional groups have become less inhibited in calling attention to their demands by showing their economic strength through strikes.

A second resource of pressure groups is the loyalty of their members. Only if members are loyal can threats and promises made by pressure-group officials be fulfilled. An official who threatens action that his members do not undertake displays weakness. In the labor movement, the leaders of major unions expect their followers on the shop floor to be loyal to the union and abide by whatever wages contract is negotiated.

[10] E. H. Phelps-Brown, "The National Economic Development Organization," *Public Administration,* XLI (Autumn, 1963), p. 245.

But there is constant pressure on national officials to secure improved terms; they fear that rank-and-file loyalty is sufficiently low to result in a wildcat strike, if members in the shops are not satisfied with what they have gained. In such circumstances a union's national officials are caught in the middle between employers and shop militants. Similarly, employers in nationalized industries may feel that they ought to be loyal to government policies calling for wage restraint, while also remaining loyal to their firm and settling wage disputes at whatever figure is mutually acceptable without regard to government policy. The limits of loyalty are especially important in multipurpose organizations. The spokesman of such an organization may talk as if his members agreed on a wide range of issues. But when their beliefs are tested by a call to action, he may find that members do not respond. They are loyal to the organization for the benefits it produces but not necessarily to its political principles. For example, although trade unions are nearly all formally on record in support of the Labour Party, about 30 per cent of union members vote Conservative.[11]

Among the many resources that pressure groups command, votes are of least consequence. No organization can claim sufficient members and membership loyalty to influence the outcome of a national election in which more than 25 million people vote. If pressure-group leaders encourage their members to vote for (or against) a particular party, they are testing whether pressure-group loyalty is stronger than party loyalty. Few pressure-group spokesmen dare take this risk. Their members usually have well-established party loyalties as well as a bundle of group interests and other loyalties that can lead them to persist in their habitual voting patterns, independently of one pressure group's position. If groups speak for regionally or locally concentrated grievances, they may seek to pressure an MP from their constituency. The last successful and visible use of a pressure-group bloc vote in English electoral politics occurred in the 1880s, when Irishmen switched

[11] Richard Rose, "Britain: Simple Abstractions and Complex Realities," Table 11.

votes in accord with their perception of which party would do most for Irish Home Rule. The concentration of nonwhite immigrants in a small number of urban areas has created conditions for localized pressures by antiimmigrant groups. But constituency studies suggest that there is not in each constituency an organized antiimmigrant pressure group responding to this common stimulus.[12]

Money is often cited as a major resource of pressure groups. The sums spent by antinationalization groups, ranging up to £1 million in an election campaign, are treated as indicators of power. Yet in 1964, the highest-spending election campaign in modern Britain, the Labour Party won. Analysis of the way in which pressure groups spent money shows, first, that much money was spent in ways irrelevant to electoral influence. It was spent to promote pressure groups with their members or to strengthen the resolve of people who were already committed Conservatives. Second, the money spent in nationwide campaigns did not appear to have any appreciable influence on the vote. Money is of declining importance in politics in England. A century ago, before laws against corruption were adopted, it could be used to buy votes; before World War II money could also be used to buy parliamentary nominations in Conservative constituencies. Today, trade union or Cooperative candidates can offer limited cash subsidies to constituency parties when seeking parliamentary nominations in safe Labour seats. Even without sponsorship, a pressure group can easily gain a parliamentary spokesman by putting an MP on a retainer. This is done openly and, as long as an MP declares his interest, there is no imputation of bribery. Party discipline ensures that the most that can be bought is a voice, not a vote in the Commons.[13]

Pressure groups with little money and a poor strategic position may seek to advance their interests by publicity. A pressure group does not invoke publicity to display its numerical strength, but the opposite: to give the appearance of popular

[12] See Nicholas Deakin, editor, *Colour and the British Electorate 1964* (London: Pall Mall, 1965).

[13] See Richard Rose, *Influencing Voters;* and J. D. Stewart, *British Pressure Groups* (Oxford: Clarendon Press, 1958).

concern and support through the multiplying effect of the media. The simplest and cheapest publicity device is to write a letter to *The Times* signed by several prominent persons. Names make news at press conferences too. If supporters have journalistic skills, articles may be written for the serious or popular press, describing the group's point of view. Staging public demonstrations is an old English custom, antedating the 1832 franchise reforms.[14] Demonstrations are difficult to organize, insofar as they require large numbers to assure substantial publicity. The Campaign for Nuclear Disarmament stages well-publicized marches against nuclear weapons; not the least reason for publicity is that the marches are held at Easter, traditionally a poor time for "hard" news.

With the rise in violent demonstrations in the Western world, the risk has risen of a demonstration's "backfiring." It may backfire upon its sponsors if demonstrators turn rowdy or violent. Alternatively, the use of force to suppress demonstrators may backfire on defenders of authority, by creating sympathy for those who are beaten. A study of a large Vietnam war demonstration converging on the U.S. Embassy in London in 1968 found that violence and the risk of violence became a central focus of publicity. The demonstration turned into a publicity "victory" for the London police, because it was handled in an orderly fashion.[15]

THE POLITICAL CONTEXT

Pressure groups exert influence within a framework of political values and institutions. The likelihood of any group's gaining wide popular support for its demands depends upon the congruence between group demands and the values, beliefs, and emotions widely diffused in the culture. One belief is accepted throughout the culture: the right of affected interests to be consulted before a government announces its decision. Lord Radcliffe, chairman of the Trustees of the

[14] See, e.g., George Rudé, *The Crowd in History, 1730–1848* (New York: John Wiley & Sons, 1964).

[15] See James D. Halloran *et al., Demonstrations and Communication.*

British Museum, could say, concerning negotiations with a minister on expansion of the Museum:

> The minister did not promise a further meeting when I left him nor did I ask for one. For myself, I should have thought it absurd to raise the question. I have been accustomed to dealing with or for government departments for a good many years now, and it would not have occurred to me in the context of this case, in which the Trustees are responsible by statute for the conduct of the Museum, that their views would be set aside and a long settled plan abandoned without even a discussion as to the reasons.[16]

The failure of the minister to discuss a decision prior to announcement was denounced by this law lord as "almost unbelievable administrative incompetence" and "not only a grave constitutional impropriety that all these agencies should be ignored and despised, but also a gross discourtesy." [17] Pressure-group officials concede that their demands will not always be met by government, but they do expect that the government of the day, whatever its party, will listen to what they have to say before making firm policy commitments. Prior consultation gives governors the chance of bargaining for the support of potential critics privately before public discussion begins.[18]

The demands of pressure groups are evaluated by disinterested parties in the light of their own values and beliefs. The more consistent pressure-group goals are with general cultural norms, the easier it is for the group to equate its interest with the national interest. The greater the clash with cultural norms, the more difficulties a group will face in securing its aims. At least six different relationships can occur:

1. Harmony between pressure-group demands and general cultural norms. In this category are groups whose aims are not challenged and whose beneficiaries command respect, affection, and support. For instance, the high regard that Englishmen

[16] Letter to *The Times,* October 31, 1967.

[17] House of Lords *Hansard,* Vol. 287, Cols. 1130 ff (December 13, 1967).

[18] Samuel H. Beer, "Representation of Interests in British Government," *American Political Science Review,* LI:3 (1957).

have for pets places the Royal Society for the Prevention of Cruelty to Animals in a favored position. It does not need to devote much of its resources to gaining popular endorsement of its aims; they are already popular. Its resources are instead devoted to the very different (and far from easy) tasks of negotiating precise details of legislation and administration with civil servants and of seeking priority for its demands in competition with others making claims on government.

2. A gradual increase in the acceptability of political values supporting pressure-group demands. For example, groups lobbying for colonial independence saw their position change in the 1950s and 1960s, as the claims of native nationalists for self-government became accepted, first within the Labour Party, and then more widely throughout the political system. Similarly, proponents of "permissiveness" in the arts and life styles generally have gained support for their views.

3. Bargaining with fluctuating support from cultural norms. Opponents of permissive legislation hope that government policies will fluctuate, rather than reflect an unreversed secular trend against their position. Fluctuations in popular support most clearly occur in response to trade-union and employer demands. While there is always some prounion and some proemployer sentiment, the balance of opinion shifts. In the 1930s it favored employers; in the 1940s, trade unions; and in the 1950s, the two groups appeared evenly balanced. The election of a Labour government in 1964 implicitly endorsed policies advocated by many unions; but after six years of Labour government, public opinion shifted away from the unions. Leaders of pressure groups with fluctuating popular support must be adaptable, pressing claims when support is high and acting defensively when their opponents are popular.

4. Advocacy in the face of cultural indifference. Indifference is a greater handicap than opposition. A pressure group fighting opposition at least has its views discussed. A group facing mass indifference will have no audience in government or outside it. For example, the National Society of Non-Smokers suffered for years from such public apathy that, although it could claim to represent 15 to 20 million nonsmokers in the country,

"the majority of them have no knowledge of this society."[19] Even after the publication of reports linking smoking with cancer, antismoking lobbies still face massive indifference.

5. Advocacy in opposition to changing long-term cultural trends. A pressure group that finds cultural norms gradually changing to its disadvantage is forced to fight a holding operation. For example, groups such as the Lords Day Observance Society were once strong enough to secure legislation regulating Sunday activities. Some of these laws remain on the statute books. In view of diminishing cultural support for the political enforcement of religious values, the Society now must concentrate on forestalling or delaying the repeal of Sunday observance laws.

6. Conflict between cultural values and pressure-group goals. Any group may advocate demands in conflict with prevailing norms in the hope that cultural values will change and its goals will be realized. But groups advocating absolute values, as pacifists do, are handicapped because they cannot bargain with opponents in hopes of partial accommodation; their goal of "all or nothing" makes even partial success appear a defeat.

While the congruence or incongruence of group demands and cultural norms is important, norms are not inflexible, especially when viewed in long-term perspective. One aim of advocates for unpopular causes is to make changes occur in the direction they favor. Moreover, legislation may itself induce changes in opinion. For example, the passage of permissive legislation by the free vote of MPs in the 1966–70 Parliament not only reflected changes in national moral standards but also was intended to make public opinion more tolerant, by giving people experience of life in a society where the state was very little concerned with the regulation of morals. The success of initially unpopular groups provides encouragement for minorities, just as the decline of such once-powerful bodies as the United Kingdom Alliance, an antidrink

[19] Allen Potter, *Organized Groups in British National Politics,* p. 87.

lobby, contains a caution. But for every minority cause that is eventually won, there are many lost causes.

Because pressure groups seek to exert influence within the established framework of politics (even when seeking to alter the framework), their activities are greatly affected by the structure of the political system. Techniques and practices customary in England would often be inappropriate in America, for the decentralized character of American government, both in Washington and at lower levels, requires the direction of influence at many political institutions, and makes American institutions more readily "permeable." By contrast, the relatively centralized nature of British government focuses attention upon Westminster and, even more, upon Whitehall.

Pressure groups give most attention to senior civil servants and departmental ministers, because the largest number of decisions of concern to pressure groups are made within a departmental context. For instance, regulations concerning industrial-injury claims in the glass industry are unlikely to be discussed at Cabinet. They can most easily be settled by negotiations between the department concerned and representatives of affected groups. In such circumstances to achieve success, employers' or workers' representatives need "only" convince departmental officials that their position is reasonable, not contrary to Cabinet policy, and not likely to cause conflict with other pressure groups.[20]

A direct approach to ministers and civil servants is the normal channel for communication between established pressure groups and government departments. The channel may be institutionalized by the appointment of group spokesmen to departmental advisory committees. It can also be acknowledged by the minister's making a friendly speech at the group's annual meeting and by the group's praising the civil servants in its annual report. Group spokesmen accept the advantages of working this way because, if they are successful, those having power to act will immediately be in accord with them. Public

[20] See *Report of the Committee on Intermediaries* (London: HMSO, Cmnd. 7904, 1950); and, for a case study, Harry Eckstein, *Pressure Group Politics* (London: Allen & Unwin, 1960).

officials prefer private approaches because these expose them to a minimum of public criticism or unwelcome publicity about complex negotiations.[21] Discussions through channels allow each side to state a point of view for negotiation, whereas public discussion may involve the exchange of inflated demands and counterclaims.

The concentration of discussions within Whitehall greatly limits the value of pressure-group ties to individual Members of Parliament. For groups such as trade unions, which have no difficulty in securing direct access to senior departmental officials, MPs are of limited importance; their initiatives may even be embarrassing at a delicate stage of negotiations. Organizations that once sought to advance their aims by lobbying MPs have found greater success can come from lobbying ministers.[22] MPs are helpful insofar as pressure groups wish to publicize claims which they believe the government will not publicly dismiss out of hand. MPs can also provide an alternative, albeit inferior, arena for advancing claims, if a pressure group finds its demands rejected in Whitehall, or if Whitehall ignores its claim to deserve consultation. Pressure groups whose work is affected by complex legislation will find it helpful to have MPs prepared to act as their spokesmen, so that the group's views can be put forward at the committee stage of legislation, when chances arise to clarify or amend administrative details of substantial importance to specific groups.

The activities of pressure groups need not be confined within national boundaries. When the British government had worldwide influence, its citizens often lobbied Westminster to advance claims for natives or settlers of a colony on a distant continent. Foreigners came to London to lobby too. For instance, Britain's responsibility for the government of Palestine between the wars made Westminster a center of interest for both Zionist and Arab organizations. Today, public-relations firms operating on behalf of foreign governments sometimes solicit MPs to act as their spokesmen. British pressure groups

[21] For a study of politicians' reactions to being lobbied, see John Dearlove, "Councillors and Interest Groups in Kensington and Chelsea," *British Journal of Political Science*, I:2 (1971).

[22] See, e.g., Peter Self and Herbert Storing, *The State and the Farmer*.

are also interested in having a voice outside Britain, when decisions affecting them are made. For example, the British Trawlers' Federation, representing deep-water fishermen operating in international waters, lobbies at the United Nations as well as in London.[23] The growth of multinational firms and British entry to the European Common Market gives British unions an interest in the efforts of continental unions to raise wages and in wage and social-service differentials among nations, as well as among British workers.

Competing group demands constitute a major constraint upon the claims of any single pressure group. Government officials are particularly sensitive to conflicting claims because they must listen to a wide variety of spokesmen, some advocating a case for reforming existing policy and others defending the status quo. The system of checks and balances is most notable in economic affairs, in which the largest number of pressure groups operate. The claims of finance, industry, and commerce are often opposed to those of trade unions. The claims of the commercial broadcasting industry for more generous provision of commercial broadcasting facilities are opposed by the newspaper proprietors association, fearful of loss of advertising revenue. The demands of Scottish-based trade unions for a movement of government offices north from London may be opposed by unions of civil servants with members opposed to uprooting homes and families. Members of pressure groups are themselves subject to conflicting claims upon their individual loyalties. For example, a businessman who wishes taxes lowered may, as a parent and motorist, wish more public money spent on education and roads. Socialist proponents of greater state spending on such welfare services as education, health, pensions, and housing face the prospect that public resources are inadequate to meet all their claims: Increased spending in one area may mean no change in another.[24]

[23] Morris Davis, "British Public Relations: a Case Study," *Journal of Politics*, XXIV:1 (1962); and the same author's "Some Neglected Aspects of British Pressure Groups," *Midwest Journal of Political Science*, VII:1 (1963).

[24] See William A. Robson and Bernard Crick, editors, *The Future of the Social Services* (Harmondsworth: Penguin, 1970).

When a Whitehall department reaches agreement with pressure groups on an issue of joint concern, whether this then becomes government policy depends upon the scope and scale of the decision. The greater the importance of a question, the greater the likelihood that the Cabinet must be consulted, because its members will be collectively responsible for what is agreed. The greater the scope of an issue, the greater the probability that other departments will also have their interests affected. For example, a decision to resolve a housing problem by building a new town will have consequential effects for departments concerned with industrial location, employment, transport, education, and hospitals. In such circumstances, a government department must engage in negotiation across a range of Whitehall departments, as well as negotiating with pressure groups. All departmental decisions requiring public expenditure must be examined and approved by the Treasury before they become binding government commitments. Once a matter requires interdepartmental negotiations, especially at Cabinet committee level, then the department initiating proceedings becomes another interest seeking to advance claims on behalf of its own preferred policy. Once the Cabinet has taken a decision, then the department, like the pressure groups associated with it, will find that it can obstruct but not reverse policy, because of the convention binding all departments to accept collectively made decisions.

Party also limits the influence of pressure groups within government. The governing party's policy in a given area will exclude many policies as politically unacceptable. In positive terms, a party enters office with some long-term policy commitments. For example, the 1945 Labour government entered office committed to nationalize a number of industries. It was not concerned with negotiating the question of principle – whether the mines or the railways should be nationalized – but only with negotiating how the event should take place. A commitment to socialized medical care similarly constrained the number of questions that were open to negotiation with the doctors' representatives in the British Medical Association. Conversely, where the governing party's commitments are less strongly held, the scope for negotiation is wider. This was demonstrated in the prolonged negotiation with steel industry representatives in the 1945–51 Labour government, for steel, unlike coal and the railways, was not an established object of nationalization policy.[25] The Conservatives too have made party policy a basis for rejecting demands to negotiate actions. For instance, the Heath government, elected in 1970, promptly enacted an Industrial Relations Act against the vocal opposition of trade unions, because this was a major policy in the party's preelection program.

The fortunes of every pressure group are much affected by whether or not its claims are considered partisan. A pressure group perceived as partisan will be advantaged or handicapped by this association, according to which party is in power. Spokesmen for organizations that wish to maintain a nonparty status must be very circumspect in their comments on public affairs outside their immediate field of interest. The Bishop of Leicester, in a debate on the economic situation in the House of Lords in 1968, explained:

> There are many inhibitions which might operate to prevent those of us who sit on the episcopal benches from taking any part in a debate of this kind. There is the obvious inhibition of ignorance. Most of us lay no claim to a detailed knowledge of the financial and economic matters which are being debated. And there is the inhibition of discretion, for it is a matter on which it is difficult to speak without betraying in one way or another some political bias and that is something which in the modern situation Bishops, on these benches at least, strive strenuously to avoid.[26]

A pressure group that is granted nonpartisan status, such as the RSPCA, can deal with the government of the day without fear of a party veto of its proposals. In exceptional cases, a pressure group may enjoy bipartisan support. For decades the National Farmers Union found its claims for agricultural price supports endorsed by both the Conservative and Labour

[25] Cf. Harry Eckstein, *Pressure Group Politics;* and George W. Ross, *The Nationalization of Steel* (London: MacGibbon & Kee, 1965).

[26] Quoted in Gavin Drewry and Jenny Brock, "Prelates in Parliament," *Parliamentary Affairs,* XXIV:3 (1971), p. 237.

parties. The NFU learned, however, that this support was not inevitable, for the Conservative government of Edward Heath put British entry into the Common Market ahead of protectionist agricultural demands.[27]

It is up to the parties to decide whether or not a pressure group is allowed nonpartisan status. By making a political issue of any social activity, it can deprive an organization of its claim to nonpartisan status. For example, the Labour Party's move to support comprehensive education made it necessary for many teachers and educational groups to decide whether to oppose the change and become involved in party political controversy or retain their nonpolitical status, at the price of remaining on the sidelines when major decisions about their future were taken.[28]

THE EXCHANGE OF INFLUENCE

In contacts between pressure groups and government, influence moves in two directions. Governments seek to influence pressure groups, just as groups press claims on governments. An exchange of influence occurs because each has things that the other wants, and each can offer things that the other needs.

Pressure groups seek four things from government. First, they seek information about government attitudes so that they can inform their members of likely shifts in policies affecting them. Second, groups seek the goodwill of Whitehall administrators who carry out established government policies. Administrative officials have discretionary powers in ruling whether or not a host of actions are allowable under established laws and regulations. The questions can range from the construction of a large new factory to the export of a work of art. The greater the amount of government supervision of a particular field, the greater the importance a pressure group

27 Cf. J. Roland Pennock, "Agricultural Subsidies in England and the United States," *American Political Science Review,* LVI:3 (1962); and Robert J. Lieber, "Interest Groups and Political Integration: British Entry into Europe," *ibid.*, LXVI:1 (1972).

28 See Paul E. Peterson, "British Interest Group Theory Re-examined," *Comparative Politics,* III:3 (1971).

places upon frequent and friendly contacts in Whitehall. Third, pressure groups seek to influence government policy. The most dramatic examples of influence are the introduction of legislation, such as the bill establishing commercial television.[29] Often pressure groups seek to influence one part of a general government decision. For example, when a new tax is imposed, pressure groups will clamor to have their own products exempt from its provision. Fourth, pressure groups seek status. This may be given symbolically, by allowing an organization to add the prefix Royal to its title, or by the award of a knighthood to its general secretary. A group's status may rise by virtue of its consultations with government and membership in official committees, even if its actual influence does not change.[30]

Government seeks four things from pressure groups. Information is the simplest of its needs. By virtue of their contacts with members, pressure groups accumulate much information about society that does not otherwise come to the attention of Whitehall. Information may come from organizations lobbying on behalf of unwed mothers or narcotics addicts, or it may come from spokesmen for major unions or trade associations. When a department reviews a policy, it wants to collect information from as many different interested parties as possible. The solicitation of information leads to the solicitation of advice. Government departments want to know what pressure groups think ought to be done and how they would react to various policies being canvassed within the department. Once a decision is taken, a department expects those pressure groups that are likely to benefit from the measure (and those that wish to retain its long-term goodwill) to support the official proposal. When a policy has been made formally binding, government looks to pressure groups to cooperate in administering the law. In important fields of economic affairs, for instance, policies to hold down prices or wage increases, cooperation is a prerequisite for success. In extreme instances, a government may look to an interested

[29] H. H. Wilson, *Pressure Group* (London: Secker & Warburg, 1961).
[30] The point is discussed interestingly by J. P. Nettl, "Consensus or Elite Domination: the Case of Business", *Political Studies,* XIII:1 (1965).

group to carry out policies on its behalf. For example, the Marriage Guidance Council receives an annual government grant to carry out work in a field which the government considers in the national interest but not suited to civil service procedures.

Because of the complementary nature of most of these needs, pressure groups and government find it easy to negotiate. They can exchange information and discuss the administrative cooperation that each would like from the other. Pressure groups can offer advice on pending decisions, and government officials can request support for decisions already taken. The negotiations can proceed without threats of coercion or bribery because each needs the other. The interdependence of organized groups and government often results in an exchange of influence in which policies are the product of the dialectic and not specifically the product of one or the other group.

The object of negotiations is agreement. Public officials and group spokesmen know it is a matter of great convenience, if there are many interests and points of view, for compromises to be reached or a general consensus achieved by extragovernmental groups themselves. Agreement is convenient for participants because it avoids decisions being taken by remote "outsiders," who know and care less about details than do those most involved. Agreement may not be in everyone's interest. It might be agreement by producers and government to practices mutually convenient to themselves but not necessarily to consumers, as in the reluctant partnership between government, industry, and affected unions, which arose from Whitehall efforts to "restructure" the British economy.[31]

The amicable relations that often exist between pressure-group leaders and public officials can lead to allegations that one side has been "captured" or "tamed" by the other. Sometimes cabinet ministers are accused of becoming captives of pressure groups when they advance as departmental policies various claims that the groups endorse. Conversely, pressure-group officials can be accused of becoming "tamed" by contact

31 See Eric Moonman, *Reluctant Partnership* (London: Gollancz, 1971).

with government, when they defend government policies in discussions with their own members. Suspicions arise because those not involved in negotiations tend to see only their own side of the problem. If their own claims are not met completely, they may believe this is because their leaders have sold them out. Those not involved in negotiations are not confronted by the opposing arguments and demands that prevent any organization from getting all that it wishes in a typical pressure-group negotiation. Each spokesman is likely to trade a few of his demands in order to gain other negotiating points. In such circumstances, the most meaningful evaluation of a political agreement is not an assessment of what was yielded or what was gained, but rather, a total appraisal of what both sides exchanged.

There is no single or clear set of criteria by which the pressure exerted by groups can be measured. The element of uncertainty involved in estimating the weight of pressure groups prevents a British government from making policy mechanically by weighing pressures for and against courses of action. At a minimum, government influences policy by deciding what the balancing point is. At a maximum, government's power to strike the balance can change the "weight" of pressure groups concerned with a policy, or even destroy them. For instance, the decision of the Attlee government to establish a free National Health Service not only affected the medical care of millions of Englishmen, but also created a new situation within which medical pressure groups have since had to operate. Consultation has an element of sham if the government has made up its mind before talks begin. Harold Wilson unintentionally called attention to this point when he prefaced an offer by the Labour government to discuss a controversial measure by saying, "The consultations will be real consultations." [32]

The complexity of the political system constrains all participants in pressure-group activity. Pressure groups can rely upon cultural norms for legitimating their claim to have some share in the benefits of government. But the relative cohesive-

[32] House of Commons *Debates,* Vol. 753, Cols. 29 ff (October 31, 1967).

ness of its machinery strengthens government's ability to resist permeation by group spokesmen. Furthermore, the leaders of government know that in any major clash of wills with a pressure group, they can claim superiority within their limited scope for action. The balance has been aptly described by a director-general of the Confederation of British Industries:

> Industry may or may not like the policy; and the C.B.I. will say so on its behalf. But when the issue is decided, it may make a world of difference to industry how the policy is implemented and translated through administration into action.[33]

[33] *American Political Science Review,* L:1 (1956), p. 8. The F.B.I. (Federation of British Industries) was the predecessor of the C.B.I. (Confederation of British Industries).

CHAPTER IX

The Choice of Parties

Party organization is the vital principle of representative government, but that organization is permanently efficient because it is not composed of warm partisans. The body is eager; but the atoms are cool.

BRITISH GOVERNMENT is party government. At a general election Englishmen must choose among candidates who represent parties aggregating the interests and values of millions of citizens. The counting of votes does not determine who shall govern, but which party shall name the governors. Once placed in office, the governors use their position as party leaders to maintain support in Parliament for their policies. Parties are the means by which government is constituted; the men in charge of the executive are chosen first and foremost to maintain the confidence of the majority in the Commons. To note this is not to make any claim about the significance or inevitability of party government. The King, Lords, and Commons governed England for centuries without parties; the institutions that we know today are only a century old.[1]

Political parties are complex organizations. Their members

[1] For historical evolution, see e.g., I. Bulmer-Thomas, *The Growth of the British Party System* (London: John Baker, 1965, 2 volumes); and A. J. Beattie, editor, *English Party Politics* (London: Weidenfeld & Nicolson, 1970).

can be concerned with everything from majorities in the House of Commons to fund-raising cake sales for a local ward branch. Because parties are complex organizations, the motives that lead people into party politics are several. Making policy is but one of many things that can bring satisfaction to a party member. Making a career is another. The intensity of personal contacts among full-time politicians can make party life dominate a person's social life too.

In order to understand the significance of parties in the political system, one must first consider in what way elections give voters a choice, and the organizations among which the voters can choose. One must also consider the extent to which parties offer a choice of different measures as well as different men, and the extent of competition and coalition within and between the parties.

ELECTORAL ALTERNATIVES

A voter's choice does not take place in a world of infinite alternatives. The mechanics of aggregating individual preferences limit the possibilities of individual choice. The mechanics of the electoral system determine how a person's vote is counted; social characteristics affect how his vote is cast; decisions by those who run the parties determine the candidates for whom he can vote. The decision of one man – the Prime Minister – determines the date on which an election is held. An Act of Parliament states an election must occur at least once in every five years. Political conventions give the head of government, the man with the most to win or lose by picking the right date for his party, the power to call a general election. Notwithstanding the efforts of some Prime Ministers to arrange political events to produce popularity when time for another election is approaching, the governing party has been defeated in four of the eight postwar elections.

The ballot is very simple.[2] A voter is presented with a single sheet of paper containing the name, address, and occupation of the several persons who seek the single seat of each

[2] For a general description of the mechanics of the electoral system, see R. L. Leonard, *Elections in Britain* (London: Van Nostrand, 1968).

constituency. Until 1970, no reference to party affiliation could appear on the ballot paper. While nomination requires only the written endorsement of ten of the constituency's electors, each candidate is required to post a deposit of £150 with his nomination papers. The deposit is forfeited if the candidate does not secure at least one-eighth of the vote in the constituency. In 1970, a total of 408 candidates forfeited deposits: The two major parties in sum lost 16 deposits, the Liberals lost 184 deposits and nationalist candidates fighting outside England lost 74 deposits.

The logic of the electoral system favors the single strongest party. To win election to Parliament, a candidate need not gain an absolute majority of the votes; the "first-past-the-post" system gives victory to the candidate with a plurality of votes, as in an American Congressional election. In 1970, 80 per cent of MPs were returned with an absolute majority of the vote. Mechanical properties of the electoral system result in the single strongest party winning a disproportionately greater share of seats than of votes. In the eight general elections since 1945, the winning party has on average gained 47.5 per cent of the vote and 54.6 per cent of the seats.[3] The second party has, on average, received 43.4 per cent of the seats in the Commons, with 43.8 per cent of the vote. At only two elections since 1918 has a single party succeeded in winning an absolute majority of the votes, the 1931 poll held in the midst of economic crisis and party chaos, and 1935. Since 1945, the victor's vote has varied from a high of 49.7 per cent for the Conservatives in 1955 to a low of 44.1 per cent for Labour in 1964.

Whether Britain has a two-party system is a matter of definition; by some standards it does and by others it does not.

1. By any measure, the statement is more nearly true of England than of non-English parts of the United Kingdom (Table I.3, p. 23). Yet the generalization cannot be confined to England because an election concerns the whole of the United Kingdom.

[3] All calculations from election results are based upon the definitive text of F. W. S. Craig, *British Parliamentary Election Statistics, 1918–1970* (Chichester; Political Reference Publications, 1971).

2. Since 1945 every election has given an absolute majority in the House of Commons to one of two parties, the Conservatives or Labour. But between the wars, three elections resulted in government by a Conservative parliamentary majority, two in a Labour minority government, and two in coalition government.

3. Two parties – the Conservatives and Labour – have together won an average of 97.8 per cent of all seats contested; only in 1945 did the two parties together take less than 95 per cent of all seats.

4. The Conservative and Labour parties do not enjoy a similar duopoly of votes. Their collective share of the poll has ranged from a high of 96.8 per cent in 1951 to a low of 87.5 per cent in 1964.

5. If a two-party system is defined as one in which only two parties nominate candidates to contest elections, then Britain has never had a two-party system. In five of the eight contests since 1945, a majority of seats have had three or more candidates. In 1970, less than one-third had a straight fight between Conservatives and Labour.

Because there is no simple formula for identifying which is the "third" party, or whether there are only three parties, it might be argued that Britain has a two-party system by default. Among the lesser parties, the Liberals have the most substantial claim to the title of third party. The Liberals are third in votes in England, but take fourth place to nationalist parties elsewhere in the United Kingdom (Table I.3). Since 1945 the Liberal party has polled an average of 7.1 per cent of the United Kingdom vote. Its total share of the vote is diminished by the fact that it does not contest every seat; in five of the eight postwar elections the Liberal Party has fought less than half the seats in the Commons. Where it stands, its candidates usually take between 15 and 20 per cent of the poll. The Liberals have not won a majority of seats in the Commons since 1906, nor has the party formed a government on its own since World War I. It has won an average of eight seats in elections since 1945; its best postwar parliamentary showings were in 1945 and 1964, when twelve Liberals won seats. The chief claim of the Liberal Party to recognition, besides persistence, is that it is a national party, contesting seats in all parts of the United Kingdom. One might say that Britain has a two-plus party system; the number and names of the "plus" parties differ in different parts of the kingdom. There is always a third choice even in a two-party ballot: abstention. The level of voluntary or involuntary abstention is relatively low by comparison with the United States, but relatively high by European standards. Non-political reasons appear to explain why some individuals do not vote at a general election. It is nonetheless noteworthy that the proportion of the able electorate not voting at a general election has risen from 11.6 per cent in 1951 to 24.9 per cent in 1970.[4]

The Conservative and Labour parties benefit because the electorate believes that they are the only parties with a chance of gaining office. Gallup Poll surveys consistently find that people say they would be much readier to vote Liberal if they thought the party had a reasonable chance of gaining political power, or winning their constituency.[5] The Liberals are weakened by the fact that their support is national, that is, dispersed more or less evenly throughout the country. Under the single-seat simple plurality system, a weaker party benefits electorally only if it can bunch its votes in a few constituencies. Irish Republicans have always had a localized appeal and achieved greater success than other third parties. For example in 1970, three Irish unity candidates were returned to Westminster from Northern Ireland, giving a ratio of one MP for every 63,821 votes cast for candidates in 11 Ulster constituencies. By contrast, the Liberal Party gained one MP for every 352,833 votes cast for it in Britain. A lesser party seeking major status cannot exploit this feature of the electoral system because, by definition, a national party must seek its votes nationwide.

It is sometimes argued that the two-party system results

[4] For calculations of voting as a proportion of the able-bodied electorate, in a more accurate formula than conventional turn-out figures, see Richard Rose, "Britain: Simple Abstractions and Complex Realities," Table 5.

[5] See *Gallup Political Index,* No. 150 (January 1973), p. 8. Note also, David Butler and Donald Stokes, *Political Change in Britain,* Ch. 14.

from a conscious electoral desire for two – and the two existing – party alternatives. But this is to confuse individual decisions with collective outcomes. A single individual votes for only one party. He cannot know in advance how to vote to prevent a two-party system from turning into a three-party or a one-party system. Insofar as he can calculate outcomes, he is most likely to be affected by a recognition that only two parties have a chance of forming a government. Moreover, every election, however many the candidates, can be seen as a contest between two parties, the Ins and the Outs. A voter may therefore favor a party as the lesser evil or regard either alternative as suitable to govern.

While the consequence of an individual's vote reflects the mechanics of the electoral system, the direction of his vote reflects party characteristics and social influences, as well as preferences for individual issues. The images of the parties that persist in the minds of voters are relatively stable, for they are derived from the past achievements of the parties and the past experiences of the voters. The statements that voters make when asked what they like or dislike about the Conservative and Labour parties rarely contain explicit references to past events. But the statements most often cited, "Know how to run the country" or "Don't know how to run the country," "Good for the working class" or "Bad for the working class," or "They have the right ideas and goals," imply a judgment that past performance will persist in the future; they are not divorced from historic achievements.

By comparison with party images, the images of individual leaders are relatively ephemeral and volatile. Not only are party leaders changed from time to time, but also esteem for an individual fluctuates during his period of party leadership, and, even more, if he becomes Prime Minister. While the man remains the same personality, voters' opinions of him change more or less in tandem with the evaluation that they put on his government's record. The influence of a leader's personality upon the electorate is much less than it is in America, where the less well-defined image of American parties and the freedom from party discipline of elected officials make personal considerations more important. Moreover, neither party has a consistent advantage in the personality of leaders. In the last three general elections, a majority of Conservative and Labour candidates did not mention their party's leader in their election address; in 1970, only one-fifth of the candidates gave their leader specific mention.[6]

Insofar as the parties are perceived as standing for classes, an individual's party choice is usually influenced by his own position in society. The Labour party is most often perceived as a party standing for class interests. The Conservatives would rather see themselves as a "national" party than as the party of one section of society. Their opponents like to attack them as the party of the wealthy or upper class. The Liberals can be accommodated within this frame of reference as a party rejecting a class-based appeal or as standing for a class in between the wealthy and the lowest class.[7] In 1970, 55 per cent of the electorate voted for the party whose class image was consistent with the voters' own class, and 35 per cent voted for the party that social scientists would associate with the class to which the voters did not belong. This degree of difference between sociological expectations and individual behavior indicates the scope for choice free from crude social determinism.

In aggregate, the differences in class size and electoral cohesiveness result in an asymmetrical profile of party supporters. In terms of its vote, the Labour party is a class party; 75 per cent of its vote comes from working-class electors. By contrast, the Conservative party draws 48 per cent of its vote from the middle class, and 52 per cent from the working class. The greater social cohesion of the Labour vote gives that party's leaders a relatively clear indication of issues and interests that concern its supporters. The existence of trade unions and Co-operative societies creates a labor movement, of which party politics is but one aspect. There is the risk that the labor

[6] For a summary table, see Monica Charlot, *La Démocratie a l'Anglaise* (Paris: Armand Colin, 1972), p. 378. More generally, see David Butler and Donald Stokes, *Political Change in Britain,* pp. 387–88.

[7] Cf. David Butler and Donald Stokes, *Political Change in Britain,* pp. 318 ff; Arthur Cyr, "Class in Britain through Liberal Eyes," *Comparative Politics,* V:1 (1972); and Jorgen Rasmussen, "The Implications of Safe Seats for British Democracy."

movement, because of its size, can become a world unto itself with party activities judged by criteria of the movement and not of the whole electorate. By contrast, the Conservatives lack a single social constituency and must maintain the confidence of a more heterogeneous group of voters. The party's leaders must consider the implications of their policies for working-class voters, as well as for their well-defined middle-class constituency.

The extent to which voters can be considered floating voters rather than persistently loyal partisans depends upon the definition given persistence and change. A politically significant portion of the change in vote at each national election can be accounted for by demographic change in the electorate. The coming of age of young voters and the dying off of the elderly, if combined with differing profiles of party preference by age groups, could by itself create a change in the party controlling government. Differential rates of abstention or shifts into and out of the Liberal ranks could also affect outcomes. Between 1959 and 1964, for example, a period that saw a shift in votes that was large by British standards, 54.8 per cent of the electorate acted exactly the same at both elections. Only 3.9 per cent made a direct switch between the two major parties. Five-sixths of the net gain by Labour, which was sufficient to take control of government from the Conservatives, was accounted for by partisan differences in turnout, the movement in and out of the Liberal ranks, and changes in the electorate due to the coming-of-age of new voters and the deaths of old ones.[8]

Because many movements of voters tend to offset each other, the net fluctuation in the vote for the two major parties is small by absolute or comparative standards. Since 1945 the Conservative share of the national vote has varied by 10.3 per cent between its high and low, and the Labour share by 5.7 per cent. For comparison, in America the Republicans' share of the total vote had varied by 22.2 per cent between its peak and trough, and the Democratic Party's share by 23.6 per cent.

[8] See David Butler and Donald Stokes, *Political Change in Britain*, pp. 288 ff; and W. L. Miller "Measures of Electoral Change Using Aggregate Data," *Journal of the Royal Statistical Society*, Series A, CXXXV:1 (1972).

A comparative study of postwar voting trends in nineteen Western nations found Britain the most static system, because of the lack of long-term change in party support since 1945 and because of the low fluctuations in party votes between elections.[9] Election results look as if big changes are taking place in the nation, because a swing of one per cent of the vote between the two major parties will change control of approximately fifteen seats; this in turn will alter a party's majority in the Commons by thirty. A shift of this size can sometimes be sufficient to change control of the Commons and the government for up to five years.

The two major parties are very evenly matched in their national electoral appeal. The mean Conservative vote at eight elections since 1945 is 45.2 per cent; the mean vote for Labour, 46.6 per cent. They are also evenly matched in terms of electoral success. Each party has won four of the eight postwar elections. The margin of votes between the two parties is usually small. The biggest gap occurred in the 1945 election, when Labour led the Conservatives by 8.4 per cent; the closest race occurred in 1951, when Labour secured 0.8 per cent more of the popular vote, but the Conservatives won a majority of seats in the Commons. The average margin of victory has been 3.6 per cent. The evenness of the national strength of the parties is not, however, matched by competition at the constituency level. The evenness, nationally, is an accidental consequence of large local majorities for each party, which tend to cancel each other out on the national scale. At a general election less than one-tenth of all seats in the Commons are likely to change hands.

In such circumstances, nomination is usually tantamount to election. But nominations are not the concern of the whole electorate, nor are they even the subject of a public ballot as occurs in American primary elections, when each party's candidates are chosen by a vote open to all who identify with the party. In England, nomination is the prerogative of those ac-

[9] See Richard Rose and Derek W. Urwin, "Persistence and Change in Western Party Systems since 1945," *Political Studies*, XVIII:3 (1970), p. 306.

tive in the party organization. If a voter does not like the nominee chosen by his local constituency party, he can abstain, vote for him nonetheless on party lines, or vote against his party's man. Overwhelmingly, voters faced with a conflict between their allegiance to a party and their dislike of the local parliamentary candidate resolve it by casting their ballot along party lines.[10]

CONTROL OF ORGANIZATION

The familiar terms "Conservative Party" and "Labour Party" refer to a complex set of institutions and activities. Institutionally, one must distinguish the party in Parliament, the party headquarters, the party in the constituency, and the party in the electorate. Each of these institutions is concerned with several of the party's activities.

The party in Parliament enunciates and applies party policy in everyday and crisis situations. Events come so fast that the party in Parliament must often take a position without having time for detailed consultation with party members outside Parliament. Commitments once taken become important political facts. Commitments are most consequential for the governing party; questions of speed and constitutional conventions greatly limit consultation by the party leadership and sometimes exclude prior consultation with back-benchers in the parliamentary party.

The organization of a party in Parliament varies with its electoral fortunes. The leader of the majority party automatically becomes Prime Minister and forms a Cabinet that constitutes the "front bench" or leadership stratum in Parliament. When out of office, the Parliamentary Labour Party elects a Parliamentary Committee of twelve to act as its executive committee. The party leader allots "shadow" ministerial posts to the Committee members, as well as to those not elected to it. In the Conservative Party, the party leader distributes "shadow" posts as he thinks best; the back-benchers elect a chairman of their own group, the 1922 Committee.

[10] See Philip M. Williams, "Two Notes on the British Electoral System," *Parliamentary Affairs,* XX:1, (1964).

TABLE IX.1 *Full-time Party Staff by Activity, 1973*[a]

	Con.	*Lab.*	*Lib.*
Organization			
National headquarters	10	9	3
Regional offices	41	38	6
Constituencies	390	125	16
Research	31	19	4
Publicity	12	15	6
Finance	15	3	1
General administration	24	12	2
Total	523	221	38

[a]Labour figures for Great Britain; Conservative and Liberal for England and Wales only. Clerical and ancillary staff excluded.

The party headquarters of both major parties are symbolically opposite each other in Smith Square, slightly removed from the central axis of Whitehall and the Palace of Westminster.[11] The size of the staff working for each party differs substantially (Table IX.1). The Conservatives have more than twice the staff of Labour, and Labour almost six times that of the Liberal party. Only the Conservative Party has a full-time official in a majority of constituencies. The Labour Party maintains a full-time worker in less than half the constituencies from which it returns MPs. In all three parties, the bulk of officials are agents, specialists in organization. The job of the agent is to maintain the institutions of the party locally so that when an election is held, the party's candidates will have a maximum of voluntary assistance in canvassing for votes. The influence of agents is limited by their dispersion throughout the country; they represent a relatively small proportion of staff at party headquarters. At headquarters, the research staff is the largest single group. The research departments of the parties are concerned with policy rather than organization; their staff usually consists of university graduates. The research department is not only concerned with long-term policy analysis but also with briefing MPs and front-

[11] For a structural analysis, see Richard Rose, "The Professionals of Politics," *New Society*, August 8, 1963.

bench spokesmen and serving as staff for party policy committees. The briefing work overlaps the efforts of the publicity department, concerned with press releases, advertising, and television. The Conservatives maintain a regional as well as headquarters staff for their Central Board of Finance.

The Conservative Party has a dual structure; two organizations share common facilities in Smith Square.[12] One organization is the Conservative Central Office, which provides the full-time headquarters staff as well as servicing the Conservative Party in Parliament. The chairman of Central Office is appointed by the leader of the party in Parliament. He is usually a front-bench MP, and, when the party is in government, in the Cabinet. Much responsibility devolves upon the senior full-time official at Central Office, Sir Michael Fraser, the deputy chairman. The second organization is the National Union of Conservative and Unionist Associations, which brings together the parties in each constituency. At the Annual Conference of the National Union or between conferences, individual constituency associations may express views at variance with a majority of the parliamentary leaders. The votes at the Annual Conference are allotted in equal numbers to each constituency association. The leaders in Parliament have no voting rights; the gathering is technically not "their" conference. The parliamentary leadership exercises influence informally, by the exclusion of resolutions that could embarrass the leadership and by speaking frequently in Conference debates. Because resolutions are usually not phrased to reflect splits within the party, nor are many delegates anxious to vote against their leadership in Parliament, it is rare for a Conference debate to conclude with a vote. Between 1950 and 1964, no ballot was held.

The Labour Party organization is federal in theory and in practice. It incorporates independent centers of power in one body, thus institutionalizing a potential for disagreement that is averted by the dualistic Conservative structure. The constitution of the Labour Party states, "The work of the party shall

12 See Michael Pinto-Duschinsky, "Central Office and 'Power' in the Conservative Party," *Political Studies,* XX:1 (1972).

be under the direction and control of the Party Conference." The five-day meeting of the party's Annual Conference is primarily concerned with debating policy resolutions. It thus differs in purpose and tone from an American presidential nominating convention. As in the Conservative Conference, the parliamentary leadership assumes a prominent role in debates. But the Labour Conference differs, in that resolutions and amendments are not fixed by the platform, and controversial resolutions are usually pressed to a vote. Votes are distributed according to theoretical figures of membership. Approximately five-sixths of the Conference vote is in the hands of trade unions, distributed in proportion to the money that each union pays annually as a per capita affiliation fee for membership. The vote of each union is cast as a single unit, even though the union's membership and delegation may be divided almost evenly about how to cast its bloc vote. The five largest unions – the Transport and General Workers, the Amalgamated Union of Engineering and Foundry Workers, the General and Municipal Workers, the Electrical and Plumbing Trades Union, and the Shop, Distributive & Allied Workers – together have an absolute majority of the Conference vote. This concentrates far more power in the hands of a few political caucuses than is done in an American presidential nomination convention. For example, at the Democratic National Convention in 1972, the vote of the nine largest states would have been required to carry a measure, if each state delegation voted unanimously. But the abolition of the bloc vote in the convention meant that power was not thus concentrated; differences within delegations could be expressed as well as differences among delegations. This does not happen at a Labour Party Conference.[13]

Between Annual Conferences, the National Executive Committee acts on the Labour Party's behalf. Its membership is also dominated by trade-union votes. The unions elect twelve of the committee's twenty-eight members in their own name, and their votes dominate the selection of the five women's representatives and the party's treasurer. The constituency parties

[13] See Richard Rose, "Between Miami Beach and Blackpool," *Political Quarterly,* XLIII:4 (1972), p. 420.

elect seven representatives, often back-bench MPs, and the Co-operatives, one. Seats are also reserved for the leader and deputy leader of the Parliamentary Labour Party, and for the treasurer. The full-time headquarters staff at Transport House works under the direction of the National Executive Committee and its subcommittees. The party chairmanship rotates annually by seniority; this limits its political importance and adds to the stature of the party's general secretary, the senior full-time staff official. The leader of the Parliamentary Labour Party remains the chief spokesman for the party as a whole. But he does not have the formal authority to issue directives to Transport House staff or to countermand decisions of the National Executive Committee. The activities of Transport House are similar in intent to those of Conservative Central Office except that the Labour Party has historically given greater emphasis to international affairs, including Afro-Asian countries as well as Europe.

The headquarters staff in each party must try to satisfy two distinct groups: the party in Parliament and the party in the constituencies. In addition, the Transport House staff must consider the views of trade unions affiliated to the party. To keep headquarters and constituency groups in contact, the parties maintain regional offices. Regional offices are directed by headquarters and do not control constituency parties. They can act as observers and advisers to constituency associations but cannot issue orders, nor are their staffs sufficiently large to provide organizational assistance to constituencies where the party is weak.[14] Illustrative of the limited contact between local parties and national headquarters is the inability of each party headquarters to estimate accurately how many individuals have joined their party at the local level.

The local organizations of the parties are based upon the boundaries of parliamentary constituencies. Often these boundaries do not encompass a natural geographical entity. The constituencies are larger than wards comprising urban neigh-

[14] Cf. David J. Wilson, "Party Bureaucracy in Britain: Regional and Area Organization," *British Journal of Political Science,* II:3 (1972); and contributors to Inigo Bing, editor, *The Labour Party: an Organisational Study* (London: Fabian Tract 407, 1971).

borhoods, yet are not the same in size as a city or county. The ward divisions within the constituencies are often the boundaries for local government elections. Where the party controls local government, there are immediate incentives for members to give priority to affairs within their own community. The interest of headquarters in developing a mass-membership organization in every constituency need not be matched by their constituents. In the extreme instance of Glasgow, the fifteen constituency parties there (thirteen of them with Labour MPs) had an average of 119 members each before the National Executive Committee intervened in an attempt to improve operations.[15] A high level of membership does not necessarily indicate great interest in parliamentary politics. It may indicate that the local party provides a good social club, can organize garden fetes and bazaars, or runs a well-organized lottery on football results.

The emphasis that students of politics give to the constituency association's nomination of a parliamentary candidate can distort the significance of this event for constituency party members. In many seats, constituency activists can have no hope that their choice will become an MP. Where the seat is safe for their party, they will have many chances to influence the views of an MP, but not to contest his renomination. The formal rules and informal conventions of party politics give the sitting MP an almost certain claim on renomination. The winnowing of prospective candidates is usually undertaken privately by a specially constituted nomination committee of the constituency party; the final choice is usually made by a committee of about 100. Decentralization of choice in more than 1200 constituency associations gives many different kinds of people the chance to enter the Commons; a person unsuccessful in one place can try his luck in dozens of selection conferences or several general elections, if he has the time and ambition.[16]

To ask who controls the party organizations is to assume

[15] See David Butler and Michael Pinto-Duschinsky, *The British General Election of 1970,* p. 265, 276n.

[16] See Edward G. Janosik, *Constituency Labour Parties in Britain* (London: Pall Mall, 1968), Ch. 5; Michael Rush, *The Selection of Parliamentary Candidates;* and Austin Ranney, *Pathways to Parliament* (London: Macmillan, 1965).

that someone must be in effective charge. Yet it is logically possible that no one official or committee controls all of the disparate institutions described above.[17] The most obvious claimant to control is the party leader in Parliament. In both parties, the position of the leader is strongest when he is also Prime Minister. Constitutional conventions and Cabinet patronage give him positive claims for support. Moreover, an open attack upon his position threatens the party with loss of office through internecine conflict. By definition, only one party leader can enjoy the status of Prime Minister at any one time. The opposition leader has no powers of patronage, and his influence will vary with the expectation of his followers that he will be Prime Minister after the next election. The dynamics of electoral competition alter the status of the leader during the lifetime of a Parliament. The leader of a newly elected government can claim popular justification for his authority. Conversely, the leader of the opposition has just had his efforts repudiated, with disastrous effects on the ministerial ambitions of his colleagues and a wait of four or five years before he can try to reverse the defeat. Midway in the life of a Parliament the positions usually reverse, as the governing party becomes unpopular. The Prime Minister is no longer the man who led the party to victory; he may appear as the man who will lead it to defeat if he is not replaced before the next election. His influence is discounted appropriately. At the same time, the leader of the opposition becomes the "next" Prime Minister, and the value of his shadow patronage appreciates. As another general election approaches, the need to unite a party – whether in government or opposition – increases the leader's influence, as he claims the position around which others must rally.[18]

The influence of the party leader is a variable, not a con-

[17] For a discussion of theoretical criteria, see W. J. M. Mackenzie, "Mr. McKenzie on the British Parties," *Political Studies,* III:2 (1955); and Richard Rose, "Complexities of Party Leadership," *Parliamentary Affairs,* XVI:3 (1963). For a conflicting interpretation, see R. T. McKenzie, *British Political Parties* (London: Heinemann, 2nd edition 1963).

[18] Cf. R. M. Punnett, *Front-Bench Opposition* (London: Heinemann, 1973); and W. L. Miller and M. Mackie, "The Electoral Cycle and the Asymmetry of Government and Opposition Popularity," *Political Studies,* XXI:3 (1973).

stant. It may vary according to the personality of the individual. For example, at the height of his wartime success, Winston Churchill had greater influence upon Conservatives than did Sir Alec Douglas-Home. But influence varies even more during one man's tenure of office. For example, after his stroke in 1953, Churchill passed the last eighteen months of his Prime Ministership without the physical ability to exert such influence as he retained. An individual party leader is likely to reach the apogee of influence midway in his tenure of office, for instance, Harold Wilson in 1966 or Harold Macmillan in 1959. At this stage, he will have had the opportunity to achieve electoral success and to establish his personality and preferences among the party followers. In theory, a party leader could retire at the height of his influence. Stanley Baldwin, who left office voluntarily in 1937, was the last party leader to do so. Every leader since has retired after ill health had visibly reduced his influence, after political failures had reduced his followers' confidence, or after his standing had diminished on both counts.[19]

The influence of the Labour Party leader is complicated by the status accorded the party's Annual Conference. R. T. McKenzie has argued that the party's constitution is at variance with the British constitution. A nonelected party conference has no right to dictate to an elected Parliamentary Labour Party, whether it is in office or the alternative government in opposition. The party's constitution recognizes that in practice the Annual Conference cannot bind MPs dealing with complex and changing events; they are expected "to give effect as far as may be practicable to the principles from time to time approved by the Party Conference" (Clause IV.3). Because the National Executive Committee is dominated by the same extraparliamentary constituency that dominates Annual Conference, there are continuing opportunities for the extraparliamentary organization to influence the Parliamentary Labour Party. In turn, the actions of the party in Parliament

[19] Hugh Gaitskell is exceptional in that he died unexpectedly in 1963 at the age of 56, when his popularity was rising as leader of the Labour Party in opposition.

affect the views of the party rank and file. The two can take policy positions that differ significantly, and controversy can ramify throughout all the institutions of the Labour movement. In 1960 the Annual Conference endorsed unilateral nuclear disarmament, overriding the wishes of Hugh Gaitskell, then opposition leader. Gaitskell denied the right of the Annual Conference to dictate to popularly elected MPs. But he and his friends also paid silent respect to the Annual Conference, by organizing support within the extraparliamentary party so that the decision was reversed by the Annual Conference the following year. At the height of the dispute, the party's general secretary summarized the practical political moral:

> Within the party there are three centres of decision making: the Annual Conference, the National Executive Committee and the Parliamentary Labour Party . . . None of these elements can dominate the others. Policy cannot be laid down: it must be agreed.[20]

The problem does not arise in the Conservative party because of the absence of formal accountability of the party leader to the Conference of the National Union. Moreover, Central Office does not issue policy statements in the manner of Labour's National Executive Committee.

The autonomy of different parts of the two major parties is most clearly demonstrated by an analysis of party finance. Of all commodities, money is in principle among the easiest to transfer.[21] Yet neither the Conservative nor the Labour party has any institutional mechanism by which money can be centrally allocated. The problem of finance affects both the relatively affluent Conservatives and the Labour Party which operates in a chronic state of financial difficulty while individual

20 Morgan Phillips, *Constitution of the Labour Party* (London: Labour Party, 1960), p. 4. See also, Lord Windlesham, *Communication and Political Power,* Ch. 4; and Stephen Haseler, *The Gaitskellites* (London: Macmillan, 1969).

21 See Richard Rose, *Influencing Voters,* Appendix: "Financing Party Politics," and the discussion by Michael Pinto-Duschinsky, and Uwe Schleth in Arnold Heidenheimer, editor, *Comparative Political Finance* (Lexington, Mass.: D. C. Heath, 1970).

trade unions simultaneously accumulate large reserves in their own political funds. For example, after the 1964 election the unions held an aggregate of £1,440,000 in their separate political funds, equivalent to three years' revenue for an underfinanced Transport House. Of the total revenue the unions raised from members by an automatic levy paid with their dues, only 31 per cent was contributed to annual expenses of Transport House; another 14 per cent was given in advance of the 1964 election. In the Conservative Party, constituency associations make contributions to Central Office totaling more than one-fifth of its income. But they retain the great bulk of funds raised locally to spend on local activities, no matter how safe the seat. Similarly, Central Office spends centrally money raised in large contributions from industry. Neither party headquarters can gain extraparliamentary authority by the promise of public jobs. The honors list is the chief form of patronage of the governing party; by definition, the number of honors must be kept low, in order to maintain their prestige. Once awarded, a knighthood cannot be withdrawn, as a contract or public appointment might be canceled.

Party organizations are often referred to as machines, but the term is a misnomer. The parties do not use their "machine" to manufacture votes at election time, nor can a party headquarters necessarily manufacture support for the party's leader when he is under criticism. It must be recognized that party organization is not designed to convert the preferences of voters into government policy by any process recognizable as mechanical even in a metaphorical sense. By the standards of American political parties, British parties are organizations, that is, they have formal institutions and offices, established by a written constitution and staffed by long-service bureaucrats whose careers depend upon organizational loyalty rather than loyalty to an individual politician or to a financial supporter of the party. But judged in terms of concepts, a British party is best described as a "stratarchy," rather than an imperatively coordinated organizational "weapon." [22] A stratarchy is char-

[22] See Samuel J. Eldersveld, *Political Parties: a Behavioral Analysis* (Chicago: Rand, McNally, 1964).

acterized by different groups ruling at different levels of organization. Local councillors can run their local constituency party as an adjunct of local concerns; the party's chief full-time officer in Smith Square can be primarily concerned with bureaucratic problems of coordination; and the parliamentary leader can run the party in the Commons in the way he deems best suited to that environment.

POLICY PREFERENCES

Whether and to what extent parties stand for different policies is a matter of theoretical and practical controversy.[23] To deny differences of opinion among parties and partisans is to deny that parties are concerned with politics, that is, the regulation of disagreements about matters of public choice. But it is often argued that foreign policy should be above party dispute; all Englishmen are said to have a common interest *vis à vis* other nations. In domestic affairs, differences may be matters of degree. Even a seemingly clear-cut ideological issue such as nationalization can become a matter of degree: How many industries should be nationalized? Parties can also differ on matters of timing. Typically, Conservatives are inclined to argue that the time is not yet right for change, whereas Labour MPs may argue change is overdue. Parties may agree about means and ends, but disagree about which group of MPs is best qualified to carry through policies in the "national" interest.

At a very high level of abstraction, parties may differ about their vision of an ideal society. But none of the parties is so explicitly ideological that it presents an election manifesto as a logical conclusion deduced from a theory of society. The Conservative Party does not even offer a statement of goals in the constitution of its National Union, as the Labour and Liberal parties do.[24] Many of the goals enunciated are not

[23] For example, in the second sentence of the preface to *British Political Parties,* R. T. McKenzie rules out concern with "party ideologies or programmes"; he assumes power can be studied independently of these considerations.

[24] See John D. Lees and Richard Kimber, editors, *Political Parties in Modern Britain* (London: Routledge, 1972), pp. 14 ff.

specific to a single party. For instance, the Liberals' endorsement of peace, prosperity, and liberty and denunciation of poverty and ignorance could be echoed by almost any party anywhere. Statements of principle must inevitably be general, if they are to be of enduring significance. But their generality reduces their utility in application to day-to-day politics. The gap between idealized goals and everyday reality is such that goals may best be considered symbols to inspire partisans to battle. Harold Wilson aptly caught the theological flavor of much debate about party principles when he said, concerning efforts to abandon Labour's symbolic commitment to total nationalization:

> We were being asked to take Genesis out of the Bible. You don't have to be a fundamentalist in your religious approach to say that Genesis is part of the Bible.[25]

If contrasting political philosophies affect everyday politics, then the policy preferences of partisans should differ at least as much as the outlooks of conservative, liberal, and socialist philosophers. These differences can appear among voters, party activists, or among MPs. To conclude that parties differ in their policy preferences, a majority of one party should endorse a view in opposition to a majority of the other. Insofar as profiles of opinions resemble each other within each party, then the area of agreement is widened, and the distance between policies narrowed on this issue.

A review of popular attitudes on a variety of political issues – economic, social, and moral – shows that a majority of Conservatives and a majority of Labour voters hold the same views on six of eighteen issues, and a plurality agree on four issues (Table IX.2). Many issues on which partisans are in agreement have moral overtones: treatment of immigrants, capital punishment, control of political demonstrations, and abortion. Even the judgment that farmers are paid too little might be considered altruistic, coming from a heavily urban electorate. Agreement usually involves endorsing the more conservative of the two policy alternatives. It is also noteworthy

[25] In a radio interview reprinted in *The Listener,* October 29, 1964.

that in five of the six issues on which the voters expressed agreement, they were collectively disagreeing with government policy of the day.

Only three issues show a majority of Conservative voters disagreeing with a majority of Labour voters: the Common Market, pensions, and comprehensive schools. On three other issues a majority in one party disagrees with a plurality in the other: steel nationalization, housing, and taxes. Levels of disagreement are highest on issues with economic overtones; this pattern has persisted for decades. Differences in economic views can be interpreted as differences of interest rather than principle; this interpretation is reinforced by the fact that partisan differences do not extend to moral questions, where outlooks on life rather than economic interests are likely to determine attitudes. It is especially noteworthy that the two issues showing the highest measure of interparty difference – steel nationalization and the power of trade unions – do *not* reflect sharply conflicting preferences among partisans. In both instances the interparty difference appears high because of the virtual unanimity of Conservatives, as against a major division of opinion among Labour voters.

Conservatives are more likely to agree among themselves than are Labour voters. Their average score on an index of intraparty cohesion is 41 per cent; within the Labour Party, the index of cohesion is 25 per cent. The greater extent of disagreement among Labour voters is shown by the fact that on eight issues – steel nationalization, the power of the unions, internment in Ulster, housing, taxation, Britain's world role, abortion, and commercial radio – there is no majority opinion within the party. On ten of the eighteen issues, the index of intraparty cohesion falls below 20 per cent, thus indicating Labour voters divide by a margin of closer than six to four. By contrast, the cohesion index falls below 20 per cent three times among Conservatives, and an absolute majority endorses a position on fourteen of the eighteen issues listed in Table IX.2. These findings suggest that one reason the Conservative Party draws support across class lines is because its supporters tend to agree on issues; Labour maintains support within the working class because of social solidarity more than issue soli-

TABLE IX.2 *Policy Preferences of Voters by Party (in percentages)*

	Policy	*Inter-party difference*[a]	*Conservative Pro*	*Conservative Con*	*Conservative Intra-party cohesion*[b]	*Labour Pro*	*Labour Con*	*Labour Intra-party cohesion*[b]	*Source*
	Steel nationalization	42	4	89	85	46	31	15	Mar. '66 survey
	Unions have too much power	39	87	9	78	48	43	5	Mar. '71:14
D[c]	Joining Common Market	36	60	28	32	24	60	36	Oct. '72:16
D	Comprehensive schools	29	32	51	19	61	25	36	Apr. '70 survey
D	Earnings-related state pension	28	31	51	20	59	26	33	Feb. '69:Supp. 2
	Internment in Ulster	22	67	24	43	45	42	3	Apr. '72:9
	More council than private houses	19	23	46	23	42	25	17	Mar. '70:14
A[d]	Farmers paid too little	16	66	22	44	50	36	14	Feb. '70:11
	Higher income tax rather than higher purchase tax	14	28	60	32	42	41	1	Mar. '71:12
A	No Rhodesian independence before majority rule	12	57	27	30	69	17	52	Nov. '68:11

A	Encourage colored immigrants to go	11	67	26	41	56	36	20	May '68:11
	Britain should remain world power	10	45	35	10	35	40	5	G Nov. '71:205
A	Hanging to punish murder	9	89	11	78	80	20	60	Mar. '70
A	Cuts in government spending	7	80	12	68	73	15	58	Aug. '70:13
A	Welfare services free to all	7	36	60	24	44	53	9	Mar. '68:9
A	More controls of political demonstrations	4	85	13	72	81	16	65	Feb. '70:13
	1967 Abortion Act	1	48	44	4	47	44	3	May '72:19
	Favor commercial radio	1	41	43	2	40	43	3	G Je-Jy '70:95
	Average score	17			41			25	

Sources: National Opinion Polls Surveys, *Monthly Bulletin*. Two entries preceded by "G" are from *Gallup Political Index*. Column gives month, year, page. Reprinted by permission.

[a]Interparty difference = gap between pro answers of two groups of partisans.

[b]Intraparty cohesion = gap between the pro and con groups within each party.

[c]D = disagree: at least 50% in one party disagree with 50% in the other.

[d]A = agree: at least 50% in each party give the same answer.

darity. Party leaders, faced with a division of opinion on issues listed here, have little hope of winning over the don't knows; the average of don't knows among Conservative respondents is 11 per cent, and among Labour respondents 14 per cent.

When voters choose between the parties at election time, they believe that the parties differ in their ability to handle major issues facing the country. A survey by National Opinion Polls shortly before the 1970 election found that when questioned about 10 major issues, only 10 per cent on average said they saw no difference in the relative competence of the parties.[26] The Conservatives, the winners in the 1970 election, were thought better able to handle seven of the ten issues examined. The Labour Party was thought better able to handle pensions, the problems of the poor, and repaying Britain's overseas debts.

While voters decide which party shall govern, they do not determine what policies the winning party will adopt. Political scientists have argued that active party workers tend to distort the policy preferences of the parties, on the assumption that only persons holding extremist views would undertake the unpaid volunteer work required by constituency party organization. (The absence in England of "jobs for the boys," as in a patronage party system, is assumed to intensify extremist tendencies.) In fact, analysis of the resolutions submitted by constituency parties to Annual Conferences found in a six-year period that 46 per cent of all resolutions were nonpartisan. They concerned matters agreed across party lines, such as the reduction of road accidents, or pressure-group views that would be advanced within both parties, such as a demand for more teachers in schools. Among those advocating partisan views, 13 per cent endorsed policies agreed among most Labour supporters, and 17 per cent positions sufficiently on the left to be controversial within the Labour Party. In a similar fashion, 11 per cent of all resolutions were acceptable to nearly all Conservatives, and 13 per cent were so right-wing as to be

[26] See National Opinion Polls, *Monthly Bulletin* (April 1970), pp. 12 f; and John D. Lees and Richard Kimber, *Political Parties in Modern Britain*, pp. 174–75.

controversial within the party. The aggregate profile shows how moderate and nonpartisan views co-exist with distinctly partisan and extremist views within each party.[27]

The policy preferences of MPs cannot readily be inferred from their voting records, because party discipline is such that MPs rarely vote against the party whip. A content analysis of constituency election addresses circulated by each Conservative and Labour parliamentary candidate before the 1970 election found that of the top ten issues mentioned by the candidates, only one issue – housing – appeared on the lists of both parties. The candidates tended to stress the issues on which they felt their party was popular, for instance, inflation and union reform on the Conservative side, and education and the health service on the Labour side. The candidates were not so much advocating different policies for the same problems as describing the country's problems in ways that made their respective party policies seem most attractive. The emphasis upon tactical differentiation rather than alternative strategies for governing was also clear in the speeches of the two party leaders. Harold Wilson devoted 75 per cent of his major speeches and broadcasts to attacks on the Conservatives opposition. In turn, Edward Heath devoted 70 per cent of his major speeches to attacks upon the Labour government.[28] The choice that the party leaders stressed was negative: Reject my opponent.

The views of successful parliamentary candidates can be analyzed by looking at their private responses to survey questions on issues and by looking at votes on conscience questions when the party whip is not invoked. A sample survey by Allen Kornberg and Robert Frasure provides evidence of MPs' attitudes on ten foreign and domestic policy issues in 1969; free votes on five moral issues during the 1964–70 Labour government afford additional evidence about MPs' policy preferences.

[27] See Richard Rose, "The Policy Ideas of English Party Activists," Tables la–c. Note also, Edward G. Janosik, *Constituency Labour Parties in Britain,* pp. 29; and Henry Steck, "Grassroots, Militants and Ideology," *Polity,* II:4 (1970).

[28] See David Robertson, Appendix IV in David Butler and Michael Pinto-Duschinsky, *The British General Election of 1970.*

While the style of politics in England deemphasizes extreme conflicts of ideology, the substance of politics reflects contrasting value preferences among leading party politicians. A majority of Conservative MPs disagree with a majority of Labour MPs on ten of fifteen issues (Table IX.3). The MPs disagree on party lines on all five of the conscience issues, even though a free vote does not require members of a party to vote together. Labour MPs show a higher degree of intraparty cohesion (73 per cent) in their votes on conscience issues than they do in their private attitudes on ten issues on which party whips defined a party line (53 per cent). A majority of MPs in both parties agree on five of ten opinion questions. The Labour MPs show an 8 per cent lower degree of cohesion than do the Conservatives.

The attitudes of MPs in opinion surveys have not always determined behavior since the Conservatives replaced the Labour government in June, 1970. A majority of Labour MPs have voted against entry to the Common Market, against a Conservative prices-and-incomes policy, and against an Industrial Relations Act, even though they had supported such policies while their party was in office. Similarly, the Heath government abandoned opposition to a prices-and-incomes policy, accepted the withdrawal of British troops from East of Suez, and refused a compromise Rhodesian settlement, going against views previously held by a majority of Conservative MPs.

The policy preferences of MPs and voters differ substantially. MPs are much more likely than voters to differ along party lines. In the Commons, the two groups oppose each other on ten of fifteen issues, but in the electorate the proportion is only three of eighteen issues; the average index of difference is 46 per cent for MPs and 17 per cent for voters. Labour MPs (cohesion: 60 per cent) are much more likely to agree among themselves than are Labour voters (25 per cent). Conservative MPs (cohesion:51 per cent) are a little more in agreement than Conservative voters (41 per cent). The greater involvement of MPs in politics gives them a higher degree of commitment to party policies than is found among the electorate as a whole.

An incidental effect of this higher commitment of MPs is

that their policy preferences differ to this extent from those of the electorate. This can be demonstrated by comparing attitudes of voters and MPs on seven issues common to the studies of both groups (Table IX.4). Conservative and Labour voters tend to show the highest profile of agreement; the difference between them on the seven policies averages 16 per cent. Conservative MPs and Conservative voters are next in their tendency to agree; the average difference between these two groups is 27 per cent. By contrast, the average difference between Labour MPs and their voters, 38 per cent, is 4 per cent higher than the average difference between Labour voters and Conservative MPs.

The contrast between MPs and voters can be further explored by comparing the proportions in each of the four groups that are "reformist" oriented. (Because of the wording of the questions, persons giving a negative answer to the first two questions in Table IX.4 and a positive answer to the following five questions are here classified as reformist).

Labour MPs – 83% reformist
Labour voters – 46% reformist
Conservative MPs – 43% reformist
Conservative voters – 41% reformist

This comparison brings out the isolation of Labour MPs from Labour voters. The Labour Party shows a gap of 37 per cent between its MPs and voters, compared with a difference of 2 per cent between MPs and voters on the Conservative side, and a difference of 3 per cent between Conservative MPs and Labour voters.

The mechanics of the electoral and party system do not allow voters to ballot on single issues; instead Englishmen must vote for or against the party that offers the most appealing package of policies. For a vote to be meaningful, the two parties must offer a voter contrasting policies on a number of issues. Insofar as the outcome is to resemble a mandate, a majority of those who vote for a party should also agree with the policies it propounds. The extent to which this occurs can be examined by comparing the preferences of partisans with the statements that the Conservative and Labour parties make

TABLE IX.3 *Policy Preferences of MPs by Party (in percentages)*

Policy	Interparty difference	Conservative			Labour		
		Pro	Con	Intraparty cohesion	Pro	Con	Intraparty cohesion
Opinion Survey							
D[a] Comprehensive schools	84	8	91	83	92	4	88
D Military presence East of Suez	75	83	12	71	8	91	83
D No Rhodesian independence before majority rule	70	4	91	87	74	21	53
D Compromise Rhodesian settlement	50	81	13	68	31	66	35
D Legally enforced prices and incomes policy	43	8	90	82	51	45	6
A[b] Encourage colored immigrants to go	32	38	57	19	6	92	86
A Reform parliamentary committees	21	56	43	13	77	19	58

A	Reform trade unions	16	97	3	94	81	13	68
A	Maintain special relationship with USA	15	78	22	56	63	34	29
A	Joining Common Market	6	66	27	39	60	38	22
	Free Votes in Commons							
D	Hanging to punish murder	68	68	32	36	0.4	99.6	99
D	Divorce Law reform	66	22	78	56	88	12	76
D	Allow more Sunday entertainments	34	42	58	16	76	24	52
D	1967 Abortion Act	51	34	66	32	85	15	70
D	Legalize homosexuality	43	42	58	16	85	15	70
	Average score	46			51			60

Sources: Opinion Survey: Allan Kornberg and Robert C. Frasure, "Policy Differences in British Parliamentary Parties," *American Political Science Review*, LXV:3 (1971). Free Votes: Reported in P.G. Richards, *Parliament and Conscience*, p. 180. Because of abstentions, figures have been recomputed to show differences among MPs present and MPs voting.

[a]D = disagree: at least 50% in one party disagree with 50% in the other.

[b]A = agree: at least 50% in each party give the same answer.

TABLE IX.4 *Differences in Policy Preferences, MPs and Voters (in percentages)*

	Conservative			*Labour*		
Policy favored	*MPs*	*Voters*	*Difference*	*MPs*	*Voters*	*Difference*
Hanging to punish murder	68	89	21 A[a]	½	80	79 D[b]
Colored immigrants to go	38	67	29 D	6	56	50 D
1967 Abortion Act	34	48	14 D	85	47	38 A
Comprehensive schools	8	32	24 A	92	61	31 A
Trade union reform	97	87	10 A	81	48	33 D
Join Common Market	66	28[c]	38 D	60	42[c]	18 D
No Rhodesian independence before majority rule	4	57	53 D	74	69	15 A
Average difference			27			38

Sources: See Tables IX.2–3
[a]A = a plurality of MPs and voters in a party agree.
[b]D = a plurality of MPs disagree with a plurality of their voters
[c]Voters opinions taken from NOP July 1969 *Bulletin*, p. 7, to match date of MPs' survey.

in their election manifestos. Comparison does not imply that voters necessarily read party manifestos. It shows to what extent those who write the manifestos propound policies consistent with the views of most of their supporters on the wide range of issues analyzed above.

Table IX.5 shows that the two parties offer contrasting policies on a wide variety of issues. Moreover, both parties propose policies sufficiently specific to show an interested voter how they would handle major questions. They rarely take refuge in evasion. The Conservative manifesto is very consistent with the views of Conservative voters. In twelve of the fifteen instances in which comparisons can be made between voters' opinions and the party's manifesto, a manifesto declaration is in agreement with the views of the majority of Con-

TABLE IX.5 *Policy Preferences of Parties and Partisans*

	Conservative manifesto, 1970[a]		*Labour manifesto, 1970*[a]
MAJ[b]	No more nationalization	PLUR[b]	Extension of government investment and controls
MAJ	New law stating rights and obligations for unions and employers	MIN	New law to increase union rights; labor contracts need not be legally binding
MAJ	Favors entry to Common Market	MIN	Favors entry to Common Market, provided Commonwealth safeguarded
MAJ	Local option for secondary schools	MAJ	Law to require all schools be comprehensive
MAJ	Occupationally based pension plans	MAJ	Earnings-related state pensions
MAJ	Support reformed Stormont government	(NJ)	Support reform in Northern Ireland
PLUR	Encourage private house building	(NJ)	Encourage council and private housing
(NJ)	Reform agricultural subsidy system	MAJ	Increase farm production, subsidies
MAJ	Cut income tax	MIN	No tax cuts promised
MAJ	No Rhodesian independence before majority rule	MAJ	No Rhodesian independence before majority rule
MAJ	No further permanent large immigration	MIN	Control immigration; strengthen antidiscrimination legislation
PLUR	Strengthen Britain's world role	PLUR	Promote disarmament and reduce world role to "more credible" level
MAJ	Restrain public expenditure	MIN	Increase in public expenditure implicit in manifesto
MAJ	More welfare benefits based on economic need	MIN	More welfare benefits for all
MAJ	Strengthen police force; more constraints on criminals	MIN	Reform treatment of criminals
MIN	Introduce commercial local radio	PLUR	Reject commercial radio

Sources: *A Better Tomorrow* (London: Conservative Central Office, 1970) and *Now Britain is Strong—Let's make it Great to Live In* (London: Labour Party, 1970).

[a]No mention in either manifesto of hanging or Abortion Act.

[b]The abbreviation before a policy indicates whether a Majority (MAJ), Plurality (PLUR), or Minority(MIN) of a party's voters are in general agreement with the promised action. (NJ) indicates no judgment practicable.

servative voters; commercial radio was the only issue with a manifesto pledge aligned with a minority of the party's voters. By contrast, the Labour manifesto contained statements consistent with a majority of its partisans on only four issues: foreign affairs, comprehensive schools, farm incomes, and pensions. The manifesto's policies were inconsistent with the preferences of a majority of Labour voters on seven issues, ranging over economic affairs, welfare measures, and humanitarian policies. The gap between the party manifesto and Labour voters is greater than that between Labour MPs and Labour voters (Table IX.4).

In aggregate, the party manifestos provide voters with a clear-cut choice between teams of politicians with differing intentions about what government should do. Of the eighteen issues reviewed here, the Conservative and Labour parties agreed in their 1970 manifesto statements on only one issue: no independence before majority rule in Rhodesia. On most of the issues, differences were unambiguous, whether cast in the form of mutually exclusive pension schemes or attitudes to commercial radio or as alternative responses to meet a problem, for instance, a Conservative wish to stop immigration, as against a Labour emphasis on better race relations. The contrast is even more striking when one notes that the issues were not selected because the parties differed but by an independent criterion: the availability of survey evidence.[29]

Voters and leaders of each party agree with each other and disagree with party opponents on three issues: income tax, comprehensive schools, and pensions. Because a majority of voters in both parties agree on seven issues analyzed here, the Labour Party's official position is often opposed to the views of a majority of Labour voters as well as Conservative voters. The party leaders, speaking through manifestos, offered a wider choice in policy preferences in 1970 than the electorate desired.

[29] The choice of issues commenced with a systematic analysis of NOP and Gallup monthly bulletins for the years before and after the 1970 election, abstracting those questions reporting voters' policy preferences by party. The use of another method of sampling manifestos is not likely to alter the general pattern of results reported in Table IX.5 or XI.1.

COALITION AND COMPETITION

Coalition is the opposite of competition; the two coexist within the British party system. Competition and coalition occur first within each party. Before a parliamentary party asserts apparent agreement in a whipped division (party whips issue instructions that MP's who belong to the party are expected to follow) on a major issue, groups within the party compete to determine the line around which they are to coalesce. Parliamentary parties can be divided into factions, tendencies, and nonaligned partisans.[30] Factions are self-consciously organized groups persisting as time passes and collectively advancing a program for government and a leader to govern. Factionalism gives stability to intraparty disputes and may even stimulate controversy, insofar as old factional enemies transfer their enmities to new issues to continue conflict. The left-wing Bevanite faction in the Labour Party in the 1950s, often called "a party within a party," is the outstanding postwar example of a faction. A tendency is a stable set of attitudes rather than a stable collection of politicians. The names and numbers of MPs adhering to right-wing or left-wing tendencies within a party can vary greatly from issue to issue. Some politicians, on grounds of tactics or principles, identify with contrasting tendencies on different issues: This makes for instability. Nonaligned MPs ignore intraparty differences on policy, emphasizing differences between parties. A Conservative who concentrates on attacking Socialism aligns himself against one party but does not align himself within his party. When factions or followers of tendencies dispute, they make special efforts to convince nonaligned partisans that their own position is most nearly in accord with the "real" principles and interests of the party.

The Conservatives are preeminently a party of tendencies. An analysis of resolutions signed by back-bench Conservatives found that "such disagreements as arise are struggles between ad hoc groups of members who may be left or right on specific questions: but as new controversies break out, the coherence

[30] The paragraphs that follow summarize briefly Richard Rose, "Parties, Factions and Tendencies in Britain," *Political Studies,* XII:1 (1964).

of the former groups dissolves, and new alignments appear, uniting former enemies and separating old allies." [31] The chief tendencies within the party are to favor reaction, defense of the status quo, and gradual reform. Factionalism rarely occurs within the party. The leaders of the Bow Group, youthful Conservatives of potential front-bench stature, have carefully refrained from becoming a faction promoting specific causes and personalities. Enoch Powell has never hesitated to offer policies in competition with his own party leadership, but he has not consistently taken a reactionary line; for example, he has consistently opposed capital punishment and favored homosexual law reform. The members of the Monday Club have sought to change the party's policy in right-wing directions – but they have not become a full-fledged faction, for lack of a leading figure in Parliament. Enoch Powell, a potential factional leader, has not cultivated a following among Conservatives in the Commons; in the 1965 ballot for the leadership, he received 15 out of 298 votes. Conservative MPs find it easy to agree on an ad hoc basis on many issues, because they are not constricted by factional allegiances. But because intraparty opposition is not stabilized, it is more difficult for party leaders to anticipate how much disagreement will arise within the party on controversial issues.[32]

The Labour Party has almost always had competing views put forward within its ranks by politicians grouping themselves into identifiable factions. Labour politicians differ about immediate priorities as well as about the nature of the party's ultimate goal, a socialist society. The persistence of controversy illustrates the truth of the late Lord Samuel's remark, "There is only one way to sit still, but there are many ways to go forward." From 1951 until the return of a Labour government in 1964, factions remained stable, whether the issue was the

[31] S. E. Finer, Hugh Berrington, and D. J. Bartholomew, *Backbench Opinion in the House of Commons, 1955–59,* p. 106. See also, Robert C. Frasure, "Backbench Opinion Revisited," *Political Studies,* XX:3 (1972).

[32] Cf. Richard Rose, "The Bow Group's Role in British Politics," *Western Political Quarterly,* XIV:4 (1961); Patrick Seyd, "Factionalism within the Conservative Party: the Monday Club," *Government and Opposition,* VII:4 (1972); and T. E. Utley, *Enoch Powell, the Man and his Thinking* (London: Kimber, 1968).

H-bomb or nationalization. Clement Attlee led the party for the first part of the period by reserving his personal position until it was clear which faction would dominate. Hugh Gaitskell was the leader of the right-wing faction as well as of the party. Harold Wilson, by temperament and on tactical grounds, has sought to be a nonaligned partisan, straddling differences or shifting from side to side according to the issue. As Prime Minister, however, he could not avoid taking responsibility for major decisions. This fixity of commitment has proven an embarrassment to him subsequently, when he was trying to remain unaligned in the debate about the Common Market within the Labour Party.

Reform, a doctrine of change for the sake of improving society, is a tendency with a great historical tradition in England from the time of Jeremy Bentham to the present. It antedates reform in accord with socialist ideas and at times may be in conflict with received ideas of socialism. On specific issues, reform can create ad hoc alliances across party lines. This is illustrated by the coalition of a minority of Conservative MPs with a majority of Labour MPs on a variety of conscience issues; the proreform tendency of the Conservatives has ranged from 22 to 42 per cent of MPs voting (Table IX.3). Coalition is made easier by the fact that reform often concerns issues excluded from party manifestos. Ad hoc groups find it difficult to operate across party lines when they are expected to vote as a single disciplined bloc. On very important issues cross-party alignment can occasionally occur. Entry to the Common Market (progress to some, disaster to others) was carried by a cross-party coalition consisting of 282 Conservative MPs and 69 Labour MPs; 39 Conservatives and 198 Labour MPs voted against entry.

The Liberal Party, although small in size, is complex in its relations with other parties, factions, and tendencies. Under Jo Grimond, the Liberals sought to make common cause with Labour on many issues before and immediately after the 1964 general election. Subsequently, the party moved away from Labour under the leadership of Jeremy Thorpe. Its MPs are not constant in their parliamentary alignment. In the 1951–55 Parliament, Liberals usually voted with the Conservative government, but from 1959 to 1964 they voted increasingly often against the Conservative government;[33] from 1964 to 1970 Liberal MPs usually voted against the Labour government.

Individuals as well as parties find competing claims for allegiance pressing upon them, because the coalition of policies that each party represents does not match exactly their personal combination of preferences. For example, one person might favor reformist moral policies usually advocated within the Labour Party but liberal economic doctrines usually advocated within the Conservative Party. Conversely, another voter might favor government intervention in the economy, a Labour tendency, yet also favor "tough" policies on moral issues. In such circumstances, an individual must abstain from voting or choose one party while finding himself in agreement with its competitors on some issues. In theory, the even balance of popular support for the two major parties could arise from the averaging out of conflicts between voters at each extreme. In fact, the opposite is the case. The largest single group of voters is "in the middle" on a scale measuring attitudes toward the two parties. This is because individual respondents tend to find some things that they like and dislike about each of the parties.[34]

The competing attractions of major parties are felt by political leaders as well as political followers. A list of party leaders who have switched from one party to another includes such men of stature as Sir Robert Peel, William Gladstone, Joseph Chamberlain, David Lloyd George, Ramsay MacDonald, Winston Churchill, and the youthful Harold Wilson, a Liberal as an undergraduate but Labour when he stood for Parliament a decade later.

The tensions within individuals and within parties have resulted in the rejection of party competition along established

[33] For a handy tabulation of the division patterns of Liberal MPs, see appropriate sections of *The Campaign Guide* (London: Conservative Central Office, 1959, 1964, 1966, 1970).

[34] The distribution of popular opinion is subject to change. See Samuel Brittan, *Left or Right: The Bogus Dilemma* (London: Secker & Warburg, 1968); and David Butler, "The Paradox of Party Difference," in Richard Rose, editor, *Studies in British Politics*.

lines and the creation of coalition governments and fundamental changes in the dimensions of competition within the party system. In a sense, all British Cabinets are coalitions, because of the existence of so many differing groups within an electoral party, most of which must be represented in the Cabinet. In the formal sense of a government's depending upon a second party to secure a parliamentary majority or making a Cabinet with leaders of more than one party, the two-party system is an ideal, not an accurate generalization about English history. Since 1885 seven parties have shared in the making of government majorities: Conservatives, Liberals, Liberal Unionists, Irish Nationalists, Labour, National Labour and National Liberal. Three historical periods are fairly clearly defined: 1885–1914, a period of four-party politics – Conservative, Liberal, Liberal Unionist, and Irish Nationalist – with Labour as a fifth wheel in the latter half; 1914–45, a time of coalition and minority governments, twice interrupted by Conservative majority governments; and 1945–70, a time of two-party electoral competition, with smaller parties preventing either major party from securing a majority of popular votes, but not preventing a single-party parliamentary majority.[35] The persistence of the present system is contingent upon events and individual attitudes; it is not a necessary feature of the electoral system.

The postwar concentration of electoral competition between the Conservative and Labour parties has occurred along with a reduction in the distance between the two parties on policy issues. At each general election for the past two decades, voters have been asked by the Gallup Poll whether they think there are or are not important differences between the parties; the proportion stating that there are important differences declined from 74 per cent in 1955 to 54 per cent in 1970. Parties have also been modifying their manifestos to reduce differences between them. A content analysis of party manifestos found that the distance between the two parties on economic plan-

[35] For an interpretation of party politics in terms of shifting coalitions, see R. Bassett, *The Essentials of Parliamentary Democracy* (London: Frank Cass, 1964 edition). Note also Alan Beattie "British Coalition Government Revisited," *Government and Opposition*, II:1 (1966).

ning versus free-market measures dropped by half from its prewar level in the period from 1955 to 1966; the distance also dropped by more than two-thirds on issues concerning welfare policies. The greatest change in each dimension resulted from Conservative shifts in policies. In the 1960s each party showed a movement toward the other during the period known as the "Butskellite era," because of the coalition in outlooks on some issues between R. A. Butler, a leading Conservative reformer, and Hugh Gaitskell, the revisionist leader of the Labour Party.[36] The Conservative reformers are proud of the adaptiveness of their party, arguing that it is an old party tactic to campaign for "Tory men and Whig measures." The economic policy of the 1964–70 Labour government showed that it is also possible to have a government with "Labour men and Tory measures." The harmony has diminished since then. At the 1970 election Edward Heath spoke of "a great divide" between the parties.

The extent of coalition and competition between the parties can be measured by voting in the House of Commons.[37] While the convention of party discipline requires that MPs of a party vote together, it does not require that opposition MPs vote against all measures of the governing party. A vote takes place in the Commons only if there is an explicit request to divide the House. When the object of legislation is likely to be popular, for instance, the provision of greater welfare benefits, the opposition party will hesitate before going on record against a benefit. It will confine criticism to amendments challenging the operation of a bill, but not its principles. Refusing to request a division, in effect, gives tacit consent to the government's legislation.

Many measures coming before the Commons are of a procedural or administrative kind. In a detailed analysis of par-

[36] See *The Economist*, February, 13, 1954, p. 440; David Robertson, "Dimensional Analysis and the Study of Party Competition," (Birmingham: Political Studies Association Conference, 1971) ; and Monica Charlot, *La Démocratie a l'Anglaise*, pp. 166 ff.

[37] For a useful analysis of different forms of cross-party voting in an era when this still occurred, see Hugh Berrington, "Partisanship and Dissidence in the 19th century House of Commons," *Parliamentary Affairs*, XXI:4 (1968).

liamentary legislation, Ivor Burton and Gavin Drewry have identified approximately two dozen bills in each annual session that are policy bills, that is, they introduce a new line of action.[38] In the 1969–70 session, the last of the Wilson government, Labour introduced twenty-three such bills and they received a second reading in the Commons. The Conservatives gave tacit support to eighteen measures; only five were the subject of a second-reading division, measures dealing with manpower and industry, electricity, pensions, ports, and hare coursing. In the next session of the House, 1970–71, the Conservatives introduced twenty-six policy bills. The Labour opposition allowed twelve to pass with its tacit consent and requested a division on fourteen measures. The greater number of divisions reflected a change in the balance of agreement and disagreement between the parties, resulting from Edward Heath's desire to alter the course that the Labour government had set. But the twelve bills that passed without division also reflected the fact that, of twenty-four Labour measures pending in Parliament when the 1970 election was held, fourteen were reintroduced in the following session by the new Conservative government. Of these, ten were virtually identical with the measures that their Labour opponents had previously been sponsoring.

The character of the parties and party system is emphasized by comparison with party politics in other member countries of the European Common Market. The most obvious difference is the greater number of parties in almost every European country. This is not only the consequence of a proportional representation system, which encourages more representation for less strong parties, but also results from the more intense religious, class, and language differences within continental European societies. A second point to note is the greater political distance between the European parties. France and Italy both have strong Communist parties, and in most European countries the Communists (sometimes abetted

[38] See Ivor F. Burton and Gavin Drewry, "Public Legislation: a Survey of the Session 1969–70," *Parliamentary Affairs,* XXIII:4 (1970); and "1970/1"; *Ibid,* XXV:2 (1972).

by breakaway left-wing Socialist parties) achieve more parliamentary representation than in England. The British Labour Party, notwithstanding its internal factionalism, has not had to split working-class votes with a Communist competitor. The Conservatives differ from their European counterparts in not being an explicitly religious party, as are the Christian Democrats in Germany or Italy, and also in not being based upon doctrinaire expressions of free enterprise. Because of this, the Conservatives cannot join a major grouping of parties in the Parliament of the European Community; the only other party that aligns itself with British Conservatives is the Danish Conservative group.[39]

By comparison with America, British parties cover a different and perhaps narrower ideological spectrum. American parties include a larger right-wing element, whether this is defined in political, economic, or cultural terms. There is, for example, no British electoral equivalent for the relative success of George Wallace in presidential and primary contests in 1968 and 1972. The British Labour Party represents a larger left-wing element on economic issues than would be found in the Democratic Party in America. The absence of a strong Goldwater wing among the Conservatives makes the relative distance between the two parties in Britain less. The most persisting distinction between the parties of the two nations is the greater cohesion – both organizationally and in policy terms – of the two largest British parties. The Conservative and Labour parties, notwithstanding their coalition attributes, do not seek to cover as wide a spectrum of political views, with as many different and even competing organizations, as do the two American political parties. In England, the voter chooses *between* the parties. In America, at primary and at state and federal elections, he chooses *within* as well as between the parties.

[39] Cf. Charles R. Dechert, "The Christian Democratic International," *Orbis*, XI:1 (1967); J. H. MacCallum Scott, *Experiment in Internationalism* (London: Allen & Unwin, 1967); and Murray Forsyth, "European Assemblies," in P.E.P. *European Political Parties* (London: Allen & Unwin, 1969).

CHAPTER X

Making Policy

If we think what a vast information, what a nice discretion, what a consistent will ought to mark the rulers of that empire, we shall be surprised when we see them. We see a changing body of miscellaneous persons, sometimes few, sometimes many, never the same for an hour.

When a government has more than two million employees and spends thousands of millions of pounds annually, it can appear united only if seen from afar. Any examination of what this familiar abstraction does in a particular instance will show that much of the stuff of politics occurs within the black box of government. In order to understand how a British government policy comes about, one must first understand how the many different agencies of government are more or less related.[1] In a federal government like the United States, one expects to find the parts of government less related; in the formally unitary government of England, one expects to find the parts more integrated.

Many different theories of power in Britain share one assumption: There is a single, central place of power. Yet there is no logical necessity that political activity be neatly and hier-

[1] For a variety of views, see Richard Rose, *Policy-Making in Britain.* More generally, see Richard Rose, "Models of Governing," *Comparative Politics,* V:3 (1973).

archically centralized. The unity seen from afar may be no more than a framework imposed by an observer. Unity in the abstract is not necessarily matched in life. Even the Official Secrets Act cannot prevent politicians and civil servants from disclosing in their memoirs the difficulties of securing coordination, if not control, behind the formally ordered facades of Whitehall.

In order to carry out any policy requiring positive action by government, those concerned must command sufficient resources to win what a minister once described as "the Whitehall obstacle race,"[2] as well as emerging victorious from intraparty and interparty struggles elsewhere. Within Whitehall, a determined minister must secure departmental agreement that a proposal is administratively practicable and gain consent from other departments that are affected by the policy. The Treasury must give positive consent if money is to be spent. The Cabinet will be asked to give formal approval and to find room in a crowded parliamentary timetable for a bill if legislation is required. To mobilize all these institutions to support a specific measure is no simple task; reciprocally, once the inertia of Whitehall is behind a policy, it is difficult to stop it. The effort required to mobilize support can be so great that politicians come to regard the mere means of policy, for instance, an Act of Parliament or a new Treasury grant, as a veritable end in itself, without regard to the impact of a policy once implemented.

THE LIMITS OF CENTRAL CONTROL

In theory, party is the great institution that unites disparate groups of citizens into a governing force. Two disciplined parties provide voters with a choice between alternative teams of governors. The common bond of party loyalty holds Parliament and Cabinet together and strengthens the claim of collective Cabinet responsibility. But to be the ex officio governor is not necessarily to be the de facto governor. "Parties live in a house of power," Max Weber wrote in one of his most gnomic sentences; he did not say whether they resided as

[2] Hugh Dalton, *Call Back Yesterday* (London: Muller, 1953), p. 237.

masters, prisoners, or spectators.[3] To consider whether party provides a means of central control, one must first examine what a party must do if it is to direct as well as answer for what government does. The basic requirements are as follows:

1. *Partisans must formulate policy intentions.* The burden of formulating policies in advance of gaining office is greatest for the Labour Party, because of the activist and change-oriented outlook of its leadership. The Conservative Party in opposition may simply abandon old commitments and assimilate Labour government measures as its new program. The conventions of British politics anticipate that each party will offer the electors a manifesto containing a substantial number of statements of intent. In debates and divisions in the Commons, the opposition as well as the governing party can establish what it would like to have happen.

2. *Intentions must state means to ends.* A statement of intent without reference to means – for instance, a pledge of peace and prosperity – is not a basis for action but a vague and perhaps vain hope. The conventions of British government work against the opposition's preparing detailed policy plans. An opposition can enjoy the luxury of simply criticizing the government of the day. The more unpopular the government and the more likely the opposition's electoral victory, the greater the incentive to assert as policy, "throw the rascals out." The opposition has no chance of its parliamentary motions becoming law; hence it may be negative rather than constructive. This is also convenient, should the leader of the opposition party find that his colleagues disagree about the specific alternatives the party should adopt, while he lacks authority to compel agreement.

MPs do not have the staff to aid them in drawing up draft bills; the flow of information from Whitehall to the Commons does not usually provide MPs with sufficient knowledge of administration to enable them to work out the details of policies. Moreover, Parliament places emphasis upon fluency in

[3] For an elaboration and documentation of the argument that follows, with American and Russian comparisons, see Richard Rose, "The Variability of Party Government," *Political Studies,* XVII:4 (1969).

oral discussion and not upon the skills important in drafting legislation and administrative orders. Party headquarters have research departments, but these are overworked and understaffed in relation to their tasks. The research department of the governing party will find the civil service interposed between itself and the party's leaders, thus reducing its immediate influence.

The practical problems of implementing policies may not be noticed by MPs until they are installed in office. Emanuel Shinwell, a Labour MP placed in charge of nationalizing the mines in 1945, recalled:

> We are about to take over the mining industry. That is not as easy as it looks. I have been talking of nationalization for forty years, but the complications of the transfer of property had never occurred to me.[4]

The 1964–70 Labour government showed such lack of preparation – not least, on economic matters in which the party had claimed special competence when it was in opposition – that the Conservative opposition, as well as Fabian Socialists, concluded that such lack of preparation should not happen again.[5]

3. *Partisans must occupy important positions.* This condition is met. The Queen's formal position as head of state does not detract from the importance of the offices assigned the Prime Minister and his Cabinet.

4. *The number of partisans in office must be sufficient to involve partisans in all policy areas of government.* The number of party politicians who receive jobs when a government changes hands in Britain is less than one hundred, including many MPs in junior ministerial posts. Given the need to staff about two dozen complex government departments, as well as

[4] Quoted in Alan Watkins, "Labour in Power" in Gerald Kaufman, editor, *The Left* (London: Blond, 1966), p. 173.

[5] See e.g., Wilfred Beckerman, editor, *The Labour Government's Economic Record, 1964–1970* (London: Duckworth, 1972); and Peter Townsend and Nicholas Bosanquet, editors, *Labour and Inequality* (London: Fabian Society, 1972).

the many extradepartmental demands upon ministers, the ratio of partisans to administrative tasks is very low, by comparison with the number of partisans in government in Washington or Moscow.

5. *Sufficient number of partisans in office must have the managerial skills needed to control large bureaucratic organizations.* The skill that a minister is most likely to have is skill in the persuasion of Parliament. The ability to argue for a policy in the Commons is not the same as the ability to formulate the policy initially. The conventions of British government make it difficult for Conservative or Labour ministers to acquire experience of decision making in large organizations before becoming a minister.

6. *Partisans in office must give priority to implementing party policies.* In office a minister must consider administrative means, counterpressures from ministers in other departments and the reactions of Parliament and pressure groups, as well as policy intentions laid down in his party's manifesto. Many issues of importance within a department are unlikely to be mentioned or anticipated in the manifesto. Extradepartmental claims upon a minister's time require much attention during a working week. In his study of the job of Cabinet ministers, Bruce Headey found that a majority entered office with no specific policy intentions. Moreover, as ministers are reshuffled during the lifetime of a government, the likelihood increases that the incoming minister will have no clear idea about what policies he is meant to carry out in the name of the party that is said to govern. Once established in office, only half the ministers see their role as initiating policy. Virtually as many see their role as selecting policies from among the alternatives put before them by the consultations and deliberations of civil servants within the department.

The permanent head of the civil service, Sir William Armstrong, has stated that the process results in the ministers' entering office with a vain optimism about the ease with which their intentions can be translated into achieved policies. The civil servants then call the minister's attention to "ongoing reality," that is, circumstances that the civil servants regard as inhibiting or dooming the realization of ministerial intentions.[6] In such circumstances, a minister requires a strong commitment to partisan goals if he is not to be merely a department manager seeking to satisfy the strongest pressures inside and outside his department, especially the pressure to confine his policy directives to alternatives that civil servants have preselected as administratively practicable.

7. *Civil servants must co-operate in implementing party policies.* Civil service advisors of ministers are far more numerous and important than are partisan advisors. In Sir Kenneth Wheare's phrase, a civil servant "is not a one-party man. He is a government party man." Sir Kenneth added, "He offers his best services to the party in power, to the government of any party." [7] After retirement, ministers usually praise their civil servants for their loyal service and capabilities. Civil servants speak well of ministers who give clear and consistent directions. It is part of the professional ethos of senior civil servants to be clear and consistent in instructing their political superiors, whatever their party. Sir William Armstrong emphasized that there is "a great deal of common ground – what I have called ongoing reality – which is properly, necessarily and desirably the concern of a permanent civil service." [8] In the circumstances, it is hardly surprising that there is much continuity in policies between a Conservative and Labour government. Immediately after the 1964 general election, Reginald Maudling, the former Conservative Chancellor of the Exchequer, said the Labour government had inherited "our problems and our remedies." [9]

Accession to office offers great advantages to the leaders of the winning party. The doctrine of collective responsibility imposes a formal unity upon what the party leaders do as Cabinet ministers. Powers of patronage, reinforced by the status

[6] "The Role and Character of the Civil Service" (Text of a talk to the British Academy, London, June 24, 1970), p. 21. Cf. Bruce W. Headey, *The Job of Cabinet Minister.*

[7] K. C. Wheare, *Government by Committee,* p. 27.

[8] Sir William Armstrong, "The Role and Character of the Civil Service."

[9] David Butler and Michael Pinto-Duschinsky, *The British General Election of 1970,* p. 62.

of government, make ministers preeminent in the conclaves of the party in Parliament and elsewhere. If a minister can get on top of his department, he has the whole weight of the Whitehall machine behind him to lend its authority to what is done in the name of the party. What is advantageous for individual ministers is most of all advantageous for the party leader, who becomes Prime Minister as well. While MPs may not dominate as partisans, they may nonetheless dominate by their status as chief officers of the executive branch of government.

The prerogatives and responsibilities of the Prime Minister are formidable. He is party leader, dispenser of Cabinet patronage, chairman of Cabinet discussions, and chief spokesman for the government in the Commons, in the mass media, and in world politics. Because of this eminence, a variety of writers have argued that Britain now has Prime Ministerial government. While often invoked, the phrase is rarely defined. R. H. S. Crossman argues that "primary decisions" are taken by the Prime Minister and "secondary decisions" by departmental ministers in consultation with the Cabinet; any decision taken solely by a minister becomes by definition "not at all important." John P. Mackintosh, a professor turned back-bench Labour MP, asserts, "Now the country is governed by the Prime Minister, who leads, coordinates and maintains a series of ministers." [10] But Mackintosh immediately retracts the full force of this statement by noting that some decisions are taken by the Prime Minister alone, others in consultation with senior ministers, while others still are taken by Cabinet, Cabinet committees, ministers, or senior civil servants. Thus, even proponents of a theory of centralized power in Downing Street hedge their generalizations with statements about the limits of the Prime Minister's authority.

The weaknesses of the theory of Prime Ministerial government are several. The first is vagueness. The distinction between important and unimportant decisions is never clearly

[10] Cf. John P. Mackintosh, *The British Cabinet,* 2nd edition, p. 529; and R. H. S. Crossman, "Introduction" to an edition of Bagehot's *The English Constitution* (London: Fontana, 1963), pp. 51 ff.

defined. Yet, without knowing this in advance, there is the tautological implication that important decisions are those taken by the Prime Minister and unimportant decisions those taken by others. While individual decisions in crises of greatest importance are usually reserved for the Prime Minister, the decisions in which he does not involve himself can be *collectively* more important than the dramatic but occasional crisis. Second, writers such as Mackintosh attend less to the decision-making activities of the Prime Minister than to his longevity in office.[11] To argue that the Prime Minister's significance arises from his ability to maintain himself in office is to apply a criterion that treats him as a constitutional monarch – but for the fact that today the monarch is more secure than is a Prime Minister. There can be times when the price of a Prime Minister's retaining office is that he gives way on a policy matter to Cabinet colleagues, reinforced by extra Cabinet pressures. The point is aptly summed up in Peter Jenkins's account of Harold Wilson's position in 1969, after the Prime Minister abandoned his much resisted proposal for a major industrial relations bill.

> The power of the Prime Minister was thus sufficient for him to remain in office, but insufficient for him to remain in office *and* have his way.[12]

The literature on Prime Ministerial power rarely considers the problem of Prime Ministerial overload. Overload results from the expansion of responsibilities without a comparable expansion of capabilities. The greatest of all limitations upon a Prime Minister is the clock. He has only a finite number of hours in the week in which to discharge all his responsibilities, including many only remotely connected with executive decision making. Mackintosh portrays the Prime Minister as "at the apex supported by and giving point to a widening series of rings of senior ministers, the Cabinet, its committees, non-Cabinet ministers and departments." [13] This description can be interpreted as showing the remoteness of

[11] The same mistake is made by R. T. McKenzie in his analogous discussion of party leadership in *British Political Parties.*

[12] Peter Jenkins, *The Battle of Downing Street,* p. 163.

[13] John P. Mackintosh, *The British Cabinet,* p. 531.

the Prime Minister from everyday acts of government. The volume of things happening beneath him means that only a small portion can filter through to the top. One might equally interpret the pyramid description as showing that the departments are the basis of government and that the Prime Minister has a lonely eminence in the superstructure.

Because he has the opportunity to intervene in so many affairs of government, the Prime Minister pays a very high opportunity cost for any action that he takes. His time is scarce, and it is exhaustible. To participate in negotiations about an industrial dispute is to forgo the opportunity of discussing other issues with other ministers. One man cannot keep abreast of the complexities of foreign affairs, defense, internal security, economic policy, industrial relations, the environment and housing, education, health and social security, and public order – especially when he has other tasks besides. For every Cabinet minister whom the Prime Minister sees often, there will be many more whom he will see infrequently or not at all about matters of government policy.

Many writers – including retired Prime Ministers in their memoirs – emphasize the time spent on foreign affairs.[14] The choice is understandable, inasmuch as a chief executive is often expected to speak for his country in international affairs. The Prime Minister receives Foreign Office papers as a matter of course; he does not similarly receive papers from domestic departments. By appointing a relatively weak Foreign Secretary, a Prime Minister can easily give directives to Foreign Office officials. Because foreign policy rarely impinges directly on domestic policy and often requires quick decisions at short notice, it is unsuited for discussion in Cabinet. Yet as long ago as 1900, Sir Henry Campbell-Bannerman commented, "It is absolutely impossible for any man who conducts the foreign affairs of the country at the same time to supervise and take charge of the general action of the government."[15] When Britain no longer has as much influence internationally as it did in Queen Victoria's time, the Prime Minister's continuing

[14] See, e.g., A. H. Brown, "Prime Ministerial Power."

[15] Quoted in H. J. Hanham, editor, *The Nineteenth Century Constitution,* p. 69.

involvement in matters which he or his government can little affect may be a token of weakness, rather than of power.

The Prime Minister's ability to extend his influence is further limited by the small size of his personal staff and by it being composed of civil servants, rather than political lieutenants acting as surrogates on policy questions. The Prime Minister's own private office consisted of seven men in the early 1960s and eight in 1970. These men are primarily concerned with the Prime Minister's personal responsibilities. Their work is supplemented by civil servants in the Cabinet Office, which is responsible for managing a multitude of Cabinet committees, as well as coordinating civil service work. The Cabinet Office staff numbers in the dozens, by contrast to the hundreds on the White House staff of an American president.[16] The preeminence of the departments *vis à vis* Downing Street led an adviser of Harold Macmillan to comment that a Prime Minister "may well ache to collar a department for himself." [17]

In such circumstances one must conclude that the Prime Minister, while usually the most important single person in government, cannot be the central figure in government. He lacks the time and staff to claim so large a role. Describing the Prime Minister as at the apex of government aptly symbolizes the smallness of the space that he can occupy. If success is defined in terms of achieving one's intended aims, then paradoxically, a Prime Minister may be most successful when he defines his role as doing only those things within his immediate competence. There is no evidence that post-1945 Prime Ministers have been any more successful in centralizing authority than have such predecessors as David Lloyd George or Neville Chamberlain or such nineteenth-century leaders as Gladstone, Disraeli, Peel, and Palmerston.

The Cabinet is constitutionally the chief mechanism for coordinating government policy. It is large enough to include men with day-to-day executive responsibilities for major areas of public policy, such as education, agriculture, and the social

[16] R. K. Mosley, *The Story of the Cabinet Office* (London: Routledge, 1969), especially pp. 75 ff.

[17] Lord Egremont in Anthony King, editor, *The British Prime Minister,* p. xii.

services, yet small enough so that every member can sit around a table and participate, if he wishes, in its deliberations. In theory, the most important men in government can deliberate in Cabinet upon the general wisdom of particular measures, and consider priorities among policies, for instance, promoting economic growth or price stability. Once a Cabinet decision is minuted, ministers are expected to give public support to what is collectively their responsibility.

There are many grounds for differences between Cabinet ministers. Disagreements may arise from overlapping areas of responsibility, for instance, the Department of Education & Science, the Home Office, and the Department of Health & Social Security each have some responsibilities for children. Or they may arise from the efforts of one department to encroach upon the authority of another; for instance, the Welsh Office might seek to take over powers currently exercised in Wales by another department. At times ministries may be competing for scarce resources, such as money, skilled manpower, or parliamentary time for legislation. The expanding activities of government multiply problems of interdepartmental coordination and conflict.

The chief formal mechanisms for resolving interdepartmental differences are Cabinet committees consisting of ministers, and counterpart committees consisting of departmental civil servants. Before 1914, there was only one Cabinet committee, Defense. The 1964 Labour government established fourteen Cabinet committees on subjects ranging from nuclear defense to agricultural policy. Ministers may also privately meet each other or the Prime Minister, seeking to gain wider support for departmental policies or to resolve disputes by unofficial negotiation, in order to avoid the risks and potential opposition of formal committee deliberations. The existence of formal coordinating committees acts as a check upon private bargains between ministers or bilateral bargaining between a Prime Minister and a favored departmental colleague.[18]

[18] See Patrick Gordon Walker, *The Cabinet,* pp. 46, 176–77. Note also G. W. Jones, "Prime Ministers and Cabinets," *Political Studies,* XX:2 (1972), p. 218.

Before a matter can be placed upon the Cabinet agenda, the Cabinet Office must be satisfied that it is sufficiently important to merit discussion there and that the necessary preparatory work for discussion has been undertaken in committees. Strict control of the agenda is necessary because of the scarcity of time for discussion. Meetings of Cabinet occupy about six hours a week. By convention, the agenda regularly includes discussion of foreign affairs and of parliamentary business. It must also allow time for issues that involve great political controversy, however limited their policy impact or transitory their significance. So heavy was the overload of business in the 1964 Labour government that the Prime Minister at one time decreed that decisions of Cabinet committees were to be final, without appeal to the full Cabinet, unless the committee chairman agreed to reconsideration there.

If affected ministers can agree among themselves about an issue before it goes to Cabinet, it is likely that the matter will be presented, as it were, for information only. The very fullness of the files accompanying Cabinet business is a sign that there is little for an uninvolved minister to contribute that has not already been debated prior to reaching Cabinet. Moreover, if every minister sought to speak on each item on the agenda, there would be time to discuss only two or three items per meeting. In such circumstances, there are many incentives for individual Cabinet ministers to engage in tacit logrolling, remaining silent on matters outside their field of responsibility in the expectation that other ministers will be quiescent when they themselves put forward proposals. At most, the Cabinet can have only a collective view about the political acceptability of a measure. When action is not demanded by a crisis, the Cabinet can veto or delay a minister's policy that it finds politically undesirable. But when crisis requires prompt action, it cannot veto a policy unless an alternative can be found. Often there is not time for nonexpert ministers to second-guess a departmental minister involved in a crisis negotiation. There may not even be time for the Cabinet to be told about decisions until they are a *fait accompli*.

In Cabinet deliberations, according to a former minister, "The one thing that is hardly ever discussed is general policy," that is, questions of underlying priorities and objectives. He continued, "Nothing, indeed is more calculated to make a Cabinet Minister unpopular with his colleagues, to cause him to be regarded by them as 'Public Enemy No. 1,' than a tiresome insistence on discussing general issues."[19] The Cabinet is not an institution for coordinating policies; it enforces collective responsibility but not collective decision making. In the words of Colin Seymour-Ure:

> The Cabinet seems to have disintegrated in the literal sense of that word. Every member of the Cabinet is important, but his importance depends on functions that are performed almost entirely *outside* the Cabinet.[20]

The limits of centralization thus become the limits on the range of activities for which a single minister may be responsible. The growth in government activity since 1914 has not been matched by a growth in the number of government departments, but by a growth in the variety and volume of departmental activities. Edward Heath has shown a preference for creating "superdepartments," in which a single senior minister, for instance, Environment, is responsible for housing, building, local government, and transportation problems, previously divided among three different ministries. Sir Richard Clarke has argued that the creation of superdepartments can often lead to the better coordination of major policy decisions, because a single minister can see within one large department the interrelatedness of policies, such as housing, roads, and planning decisions. Moreover, within a superdepartment a minister will have to rank policies in terms of their importance; only one issue can come first at a time. By contrast, when problems are dispersed among three ministers, each can seek to make one issue a first claim upon government resources.[21] But changing the names of departments and adding another layer to an enlarged pyramidal organization does not, of itself, centralize decision making. There still remains only

[19] L. S. Amery, *Thoughts on the Constitution,* p. 87.
[20] "The 'Disintegration' of the Cabinet," p. 196.
[21] See Sir Richard Clarke, "The Number and Size of Government Departments," and his *New Trends in Government.*

a limited amount of time in which one minister can become aware of the multitude of problems arising beneath him. The resolution of disputes within the walls of a superdepartment makes it more difficult, too, for Cabinet ministers to perceive and correct in advance the mistakes that individual ministers inevitably make.

Every Cabinet minister has great incentives to deemphasize his collective Cabinet role and bury himself in his department.[22] Within the department, he is the chief personage; the limits upon his influence in other departments also defend him from interference by his colleagues. In a group of Cabinet ministers studied by Bruce Headey, half made no mention of their Cabinet role. Only one in ten saw himself as in any way a *Cabinet* minister. Headey comments, "Insofar as the Cabinet is important to ministers, it is seen as an interdepartmental battleground rather than as a forum for collective deliberation on policy." [23] Government policy can come to mean no more than the sum of what individual ministers will defend departmentally.

Within a department, a minister is limited in his impact by a shortage of time and competence. A minister can initiate, veto, or suggest revisions in specific policies. But he cannot himself coordinate the work of his department, because he cannot continually and intelligently monitor the variety of things done in his name. At most, he can communicate a point of view that is sufficiently general so that civil servants can see its applicability to many problems and yet is sufficiently specific so that civil servants can agree about the conclusions that should be drawn — and have these conclusions agree with what the minister himself would wish. In default of a ministerial view, civil servants may fall back upon the departmental point of view.

Civil servants rather than ministers provide the most important personnel for cooperation between Whitehall departments. Every Cabinet committee is "shadowed" by another committee of civil servants from the same departments. The

[22] For illustrations, see Maurice Kogan, *The Politics of Education*.
[23] See Bruce W. Headey, *The Job of Cabinet Minister*, pp. 67, 230 ff.

shadowing occurs at the highest level too. Because civil servants are more numerous than ministers and have fewer demands on their time outside Whitehall, they have far more time to invest in interdepartmental contacts. As permanent officials, civil servants will accumulate more knowledge of Whitehall than ministers who come and go with electoral tides. They will have less incentive to press short-term departmental views, because of the likelihood that the rotation of jobs will sometimes reverse their positions around a negotiating table. As administrators, they will also be concerned with making sure that any government policy is workable in interdepartmental terms, as well as departmentally. Not least of their characteristics in negotiation is that civil servants have a "disposition to seek agreement." [24]

Insofar as money is required to further policies, the Treasury is potentially the means to coordinate government policies. It can do this first by its continuing involvement in expenditure questions. Before a new measure is put to Cabinet, the Treasury must be consulted about its cost. No measure can be put before Parliament requiring additional expenditure without Treasury approval. Even when it considers a proposal niggardly, the opposition must express disapproval by moving a token reduction in the estimates rather than a politically more popular increase in spending. The annual budget cycle provides a second point for departmental policies to come under review, especially if they involve a noteworthy increase in expenditure. The long-term aggregate implications of spending policies are reviewed in the five-year forward look of the Public Expenditure Survey Committee. Third, the Treasury's responsibilities for national economic policy at irregular intervals lead it to issue directives requesting departments to cut or increase public spending, depending upon whether the macroeconomic policy of the moment is deflation or reflation. Treasury directives on spending not only affect central government departments, but also local authorities and nationalized industries. Until the establishment of the Civil Service

[24] Sir Burke Trend, "Great Britain," *International Bulletin of Social Sciences,* VIII:2 (1955), p. 242.

Department in 1968, the Treasury was also responsible for all personnel matters, including promotion of senior civil servants. The prestige and power of the Treasury attract civil servants of very high calibre. Treasury officials are usually not economists by profession, but rather professional experts in wielding political influence.

While the organizational structure of the Treasury is subject to recurring change, its problems remain constant. The changes reflect an "insoluble problem of organization . . . all areas of economic policy are, or ought to be, interrelated. But the number of tasks involved, even of a central coordinating kind, are more than one minister can handle." [25] Three activities of utmost importance are interrelated, yet each is so substantial that they are separately managed – and at times can be in conflict.

First, the Treasury is manager of the domestic economy. Economic indicators provide it with much information about the state of the economy. Theories about the interrelationship of public and private spending, domestic and overseas trends, and factors that may stimulate or depress economic growth, employment, wage increases, or price inflation offer guides to alternative policies. The Treasury makes major decisions concerning economic conditions in the private as well as the public sector. The decisions reflect trend forecasts and political judgments about what the economy ought to be like. Treasury officials have learned from experience that many of their goals may be in conflict. For example, measures taken to reduce price inflation may also reduce economic growth and increase unemployment. Measures taken to increase growth may also increase price inflation. In such circumstances, coordination does not involve planning how all desirable targets can be achieved, but rather "trading off" disadvantageous consequences in some parts of the economy in the hope of benefits in others.

Second, the Treasury is responsible for the balance of payments. Measures taken to stimulate economic growth tend to

[25] Samuel Brittan, *Steering the Economy,* p. 40. This book provides a good general description of the Treasury.

increase imports and decrease exports, as well as reducing foreign confidence in the value of the pound. This reduction of confidence in the pound depresses its value in relation to other currencies and encourages the movement of capital and cash balances out of England. Measures taken to improve the balance of payments are likely to reverse such trends – but they also tend to reduce growth and increase unemployment. Here again, coordination involves choices between policies involving a mixture of advantages and disadvantages.

The third Treasury activity – budgeting – is no longer primarily concerned with "saving candle ends," to use Mr. Gladstone's picturesque phrase equating economics with economy. Nor is it to make public expenditure and public revenues balance. For the Treasury, budgets are now a major device to manage the economy and regulate the balance of payments. Public expenditure, including capital and current expenditure by nationalized industries and local government, accounts for upwards of half the gross national product; [26] taxation has a similarly important effect. By creating a budget surplus, whether by raising taxes or cutting public expenditure, the Treasury can use the budget for deflationary objectives. By creating a budget deficit, whether by cutting taxes or raising public expenditure or both, it can reflate the economy, stimulating growth. Insofar as real resources increase through greater productivity and beneficial investment decisions, there is more money for the Treasury to allocate for public expenditure and for tax cuts.

Given the importance of economic issues in Britain, there is no doubting the impact of such decisions. It does not follow, however, that these decisions are (or can be) taken by a single economic ministry. Their very political significance makes them questions of public choice. The balance of payments is least subject to Treasury control in the short term, because of the effect that international economic conditions have upon the payments position. In the long run, Treasury measures can eliminate deficits in the balance of payments. But the more successful the Treasury is in creating a budget surplus,

[26] *Ibid.*, pp. 90 ff.

the stronger the political disadvantages become, and the greater the pressure within the Cabinet and the majority party to abandon deflationary policies adopted for external considerations, and reflate to meet domestic political aims. In managing the domestic economy, the Treasury is subject to pressures from industry and from trade unions, as well as being forced to react to their independent market behavior. The strength of these extragovernmental forces makes it difficult for government to regulate wages or prices, notwithstanding their significance for the economy. In framing monetary policies, the Treasury must consult with the Bank of England, a nationalized central bank but organizationally separate from Whitehall. Within the field of public expenditure, the Treasury is subject to pressures from spending departments to increase resources, whether to meet higher levels of demand for existing services (e.g., more roads, more university places, and more houses) or new services (e.g., antipollution policies or nursery schools). In contests between the Treasury and the spending departments, the Chancellor's influence is not constant but depends upon circumstances. The political climate may make a rise in public spending necessary as part of a "preelection boom" intended to make voters feel prosperous. In between elections, reflation may become the priority in order to arrest popular decline in the governing party. When emergencies arise, as in wartime, the influence of the Treasury falls, as economic considerations are subordinated to an overriding political objective.

Government concern with the inconsistencies between its several economic objectives and the undesirable "spillover" effects of one policy upon another results in periodic efforts to introduce economic planning to Whitehall. Few assume that economic planning will of itself eliminate disparate and conflicting consequences of government economic measures. But there is a persisting demand to improve the government's machinery for coping with recurring economic problems. Planning is considered desirable, because it may reduce the disturbance caused by abrupt shifts in policy, for instance, the "stop-go" management of the economy by abrupt moves from deflation to reflation. Planning is also seen as a prospective means of improving the allocation of resources within the public sector, between public and private sectors, and within the private sector.

The history of Whitehall's efforts to undertake economic planning shows a slow but gradual increase in the Treasury's economic sophistication, as it alternates cycles of new forms of planning and abolishing of planning machinery. The Treasury began to experiment with economic planning during World War I. These efforts were abandoned between the wars, only to reappear during World War II. Planning remained popular in the first two years of the 1945–50 Labour government, but became discredited by that government's recurring economic difficulties. In the 1950s Conservative governments reacted against planning, only to have a Conservative Prime Minister, Harold Macmillan, reintroduce the idea of planning in 1961, with a National Economic Development Council. This was given expanded significance by the subsequent Labour Government, which also established in 1964 a Department of Economic Affairs, to plan the development of new industries and exports to replace declining sectors of trade. After the 1966–67 economic crisis brought about devaluation, economic planning once again became unfashionable. The Department of Economic Affairs was abolished in 1969. A year later a new Conservative government announced that it favored greater reliance upon market mechanisms than upon central coordination of the economy through economic planning. Two years later it adopted a strongly interventionist policy on prices and wages.

Each planning initiative has been marked by efforts to divide economic responsibilities within Whitehall, rather than concentrate greater power in the Treasury. The Treasury's concern with short-term fiscal policy is regarded as inimical to the long-term development of productive resources. The creation of the Department of Economic Affairs was a conscious attempt to play off a "growth-oriented" planning ministry against a Treasury seen as inevitably biased toward deflationary policies. The creation of the National Economic Development Council brought in representatives of industry, the trade unions, and nationalized industries, in an effort to close the gap between plans and achievements.

The problems of coordinating public policy led Edward

Heath to establish a Central Policy Review Staff (CPRS) within the Cabinet Office. The unit is intended to maintain a comprehensive review of government strategy, evaluating alternative policy options and priorities open to the government, and considering how policies of different departments relate to more general objectives of the governing party. Lord Rothschild, a scientist and science administrator, was appointed its head. With a staff of fifteen, less than one man for each government department, the CPRS cannot be compared with the United States Office of Management and Budget. Its creation is evidence of perceived weaknesses within Downing Street, rather than a surety that the problems identified have been removed. When asked to name the new group's major achievement, Lord Rothschild said:

> I don't know that the government is better run as a result of our work. I think the highest compliment I ever got paid was from a Cabinet minister who said: "You make us think from time to time." I thought that was a great achievement, considering how much ministers have to do. They don't have much time to think.[27]

THE LIMITS OF DECENTRALIZATION

The tasks of government today are so great that the powers of the center can only be exercised by decentralization. Delegating duties gives Cabinet ministers more time to attend to activities that cannot be delegated because of their importance for the political success or failure of the government.

Many different motives can lead ministers to decide that they do not wish to be directly responsible for policies that carry statutory sanction, affect the public, and spend public monies.[28] Ministers may wish to insulate activities from charges of political interference (e.g., the National Theatre),

[27] "Thinking about the Think Tank," *The Listener,* December 28, 1972. See also *The Reorganisation of Central Government* (HMSO, Cmnd. 4506, 1970), p. 13; and W. J. L. Plowden, "The Central Policy Review Staff: the first two years" (Reading: Political Studies Association Conference, 1973).

[28] See Bruce L. R. Smith and D. C. Hague, editors, *The Dilemma of Accountability in Modern Government* (London: Macmillan, 1971).

to provide flexibility in commercial operations (the Gas Board), to give an aura of impartiality to quasi-judicial activities (the Monopolies Commission), to respect the extragovernmental origins of an agency (the British Standards Institution), to allow qualified professionals to regulate technical matters (the Royal College of Physicians and Surgeons), to remove controversial matters from Whitehall (Family Planning Association), or to concentrate efforts for a special purpose (a fund for disaster relief).

Decentralization can be functional or spatial. Functional decentralization gives a special-purpose agency responsibilities covering the whole country, for example, the National Coal Board or the Arts Council. Spatial decentralization gives multiple powers to agencies operating within restricted areas, such as local government authorities or the Scottish Office. Some agencies may combine both attributes; for example the BBC is divided into regional units for some program purposes, just as New Town Corporations are multipurpose bodies operating within a limited geographical area.

A great variety of bodies operate with government authorization, yet remain outside the framework of governing departments. *Whitaker's Almanack, 1973,* a standard reference book, requires seventy-seven double-column pages to list government and public offices. In addition, it separately catalogues commissions, banks, the armed services, churches, universities and schools, nationalized industries, museums and art galleries, local government bodies, etc. Any classification of agencies affecting the public interest can only be illustrative. The following list ranges from those most subject to explicit direction by government to those least subject.

Executive agencies not directly under ministerial supervision. The Board of Inland Revenue and the Royal Mint are formally independent of departments, because of the desire to retain operational flexibility and freedom from political intervention. Yet both agencies are solely concerned with applying policies that are decided elsewhere. The Mint cannot coin money independently of Cabinet authority, nor can the Inland Revenue alter tax laws of its own accord.

Nationalized industries. The government not only owns the corporations that operate nationalized industries, but also appoints the boards that direct them, provides investment capital, and underwrites financial losses. Yet each industry is formally independent of Whitehall, and its employees are not civil servants. This is intended to increase the freedom of action of the industries. Coal, electricity, gas, and the railways are constantly in contact with millions of consumers. Nationalized industries that have fewer consumers, like the British Steel Corporation, are no less affected by market pressures, for the demand for steel is variable, not a constant. Because nationalized industries have about two million employees and net assets of £13,700 million, ministers cannot be unconcerned about their economic activities. Yet having created boards to run the industries, they cannot ignore the views of their appointees. The relationship between ministers and leaders of nationalized industries is further confused by the coexistence of multiple and sometimes conflicting objectives: profitability, a "fair" rate of return on investment, the provision of services for consumers, and the protection of jobs of those employed in the industry.

Sponsored companies. The Crown does not need to own all a company's shares in order to affect its policies. If it is the sole or primary purchaser of its products, it exerts influence as a consumer. This is intensified if government regulations greatly influence price competition between British manufacturers and those elsewhere. On their part, the success of privately owned companies in growth industries affects the nation's total exports, just as the failings of companies in declining industries affect national (and even more, regional) unemployment figures. The result is that in areas as different as shipbuilding and computers, the government has given massive financial subsidies to companies without assuming full ownership.

Publicly maintained regulatory or administrative agencies. A regulatory agency such as the Independent Broadcasting Authority grants licenses to commercial television companies, and monitors the program content of the companies it licenses. An administrative agency, such as the Social Science

Research Council, draws funds from the Treasury and has its Council appointed by government. Its activities are primarily administered by staff working in accordance with policies laid down and monitored by part-time academic members of SSRC committees.

Publicly assisted agencies. These bodies owe their origins or continuance to support outside of government, yet receive government aid. For example, direct-grant schools are usually private foundations with independent boards of governors. But they are substantially assisted by grants from public funds.

The many kinds of "paragovernmental" institutions affecting public policy are distinguishable in important respects by their origins. Institutions that grow from the top down, created by the initiative of central government, are most likely to be subject to Whitehall influence. For example, the new universities founded in the early 1960s in consequence of a government decision to expand higher education are immediately sensitive to government policies. By contrast, an institution originating outside the public sector grows from the bottom up; its leaders are likely to be less ready to accept uncritically changes in government policy. For example, in a self-regulating profession such as medicine, doctors think of themselves as free professionals and not as civil servants. The creation of the National Health Service has not altered the doctor's insistence upon autonomy, even though his income is almost wholly derived from public funds. In a few instances, there is a symbiotic closeness between government and those it seeks to regulate; this relationship has existed in the steel industry under public or private ownership. In such circumstances, nationalization of a company does not reverse previous roles, but rather is a "sidewise" change in working relationships.

In form, English local government today reflects a "from-the-top-down" concept of authority. All local authorities operate on the sufferance of central government, which determines their boundaries and powers. It can transform both by a single Act of Parliament. This was done in Local Government Acts of 1888 and 1894, and again in the Local Government Act of 1972. Central government can also withdraw powers devolved to authorities outside England, as shown by the suspension of the Northern Ireland Constitution in 1972. Yet, historically English government is the result of a "from-the-bottom-up" agglomeration of power in medieval and postmedieval times, as local territorial magnates were gradually brought under the control of a centralizing monarchy. The resistance to monarchical absolutism, which came to a climax in the seventeenth-century civil war, made local authority, in the eyes of many, a bulwark of individual liberty. The independent role of local government reached its height in the nineteenth century, when local authorities helped in the early development of the welfare state.[29]

London has always been governed by special institutions. The Greater London Council, which came into effect with a 1963 reorganization act dividing powers between the Council and the thirty-two boroughs into which its area is partitioned, covers more than seven million people. The new structure divides England and Wales into forty-four two-tier authorities, except for six major metropolitan areas that, like London, have broad powers as metropolitan counties. The new county councils have responsibility for education, personal social services, highways, and strategic planning powers. Other powers are shared or granted to the districts beneath them: Housing and recreation are the principle district responsibilities. The intent of the change is to increase efficiency by creating larger units with greater aggregate revenues and to reduce problems of coordination by reducing the number of smaller governmental units. The two-tier structure is retained to provide some services by officials not "too distant" from those affected.

Within each local authority, control is formally vested in the hands of an elected council. The effectiveness of councillors is limited by the fact that these men hold office as unpaid representatives. This limits the time they can give to local politics and the kinds of people who can afford to participate. Low

[29] For documents on the evolution of local government, see W. Thornhill, editor, *The Growth and Reform of English Local Government* (London: Weidenfeld & Nicholson, 1971). Note also H. J. Hanham, *The Nineteenth Century Constitution,* pp. 372 ff.

levels of turnout at local elections – often half the turnout at a parliamentary election – indicate the limited interest of the public in participation in local government.[30] The presence of disciplined parties in most local authorities provides a means of organizing council activities and guidelines for policy. While local parties are not amenable to discipline from national headquarters, councillors tend to voice views that are in harmony with the views of their parliamentary parties on such contentious matters as housing and education. In larger cities, Labour has had long periods of uninterrupted control. The county councils have usually been in the hands of pro-Conservative groups. Hence, a substantial portion of local government will always be run by a party opposed to the central government of the day.

Unlike central government, local government is organized along committee lines. Council committees include members of both parties, but the dominant party normally takes the chairmanship of all important committees. This practice further decentralizes authority, inasmuch as there is nothing equivalent to the Cabinet in local government, trying to relate and review decisions taken within committee.[31] The meetings of the majority party on the council mix "front-bench" chairmen and "back-bench" councillors for discussions of politically controversial issues. Within each committee the chief local officer, a full-time council official appointed on grounds of merit and seniority, is likely to exercise great influence because of his technical knowledge, involvement in the job, and by default of competition from individual councillors. The influence of local officials is further strengthened by the ability of their national professional associations to make representations to central government departments.[32] The differing professional outlooks of solicitors, educationists, architects, and

[30] See, e.g., J. G. Bulpitt, *Party Politics in English Local Government* (London: Longmans, 1967); cf. L. J. Sharpe, "Theories and Values of Local Government."

[31] See R. Greenwood, J. D. Stewart and A. D. Smith, "The Policy Committee in English Local Government," *Public Administration,* L (Summer 1972).

[32] See, e.g. Howard Scarrow, "Policy Pressures by British Local Government," *Comparative Politics,* IV:1 (1971), p. 18.

planners lead each to give priority to differing policy concerns, decentralizing influence within each local authority.

Because decentralization is an inevitable feature of large-scale administration, the question becomes: What are the terms on which powers are decanted? The formal position emphasizes central government as the source of authority, as the supervisor of administration, and as the place of appeal against local authority decisions. The most obvious example of the power of central government is the *ultra vires* rule.[33] This doctrine prohibits local authorities from doing anything that is not authorized by Act of Parliament. Given the distance between local concerns and parliamentary legislation, it has been an important constraint upon local government initiative, both legally and psychologically. By contrast, in the United States the constitution leaves states with the residual power to do anything not exclusively granted to the federal government.

The financial powers of local authorities are very much affected by central government, both positively and negatively. The current and capital expenditure of all local authorities is in total a little less than half that of central government. More local revenue comes from central government grants than from local authority rates (i.e., taxes on real estate). Some central government grants are made for specified services, thus enabling Whitehall to lay down minimum or maximum standards for services. Poorer local authorities benefit from special central government grants made to areas with relatively low revenue from local tax rates. The new local authorities have only the power to levy a tax rate of twopence for services that they deem desirable, but are otherwise *ultra vires* — further taxation is beyond their authority. Whitehall has resisted any change in local government finance (e.g., a local sales or earnings tax), because existing arrangements strengthen its supervisory role and make the regulation of local authority expenditure a means of regulating national economic conditions.

[33] See D. N. Chester, "Restoring Power to the People," *The Times*, February 14, 1972. Note also, G. W. Jones, "The Local Government Act 1972 and the Redcliffe-Maud Commission," *Political Quarterly*, XLIV:2 (1973).

Central government departments also exercise a variety of supervisory powers over local government. Inspectors examine schools, police, and fire service. Auditors examine both small and large items of expenditure to ensure that they are sanctioned by statute. The salaries and terms of appointment of many local authority employees are affected by central government decisions. Circulars from Whitehall can "request" local authorities to review or revise their practices; A request carries the threat that compulsion may follow. The land-use planning decisions of local authorities are subject to appeal to central government, even when the dispute lies within a single local authority area. In extreme cases, a minister can exercise default powers, overriding decisions taken by elected local councils, suspending councillors, and assuming administrative powers directly.[34]

Studies of local authority expenditure show that several influences affect the level of financial provision made. First, there is the level of local need as defined by central government statutes and local social conditions. For example, there is a high correlation (0.72) between the proportion of children in an area and spending on schools. A second influence is party control. Local Labour authorities make greater use of discretionary powers to spend money on council housing than do Conservative authorities. A third influence is local discretion. Local councils retain substantial areas of autonomy in administering public services and in deciding when, whether, and how to cooperate with central government directives. The discretion of local authority, intervening between central government and individual citizens, thus results in noteworthy variations in the degree and character of local authority services.[35]

[34] For the most thorough study of the subject, see J. A. G. Griffith, *Central Departments and Local Authorities* (London: Allen & Unwin, 1966). Note also, Owen A. Hartley, "Inspectorates in British Central Government," *Public Administration,* L (Winter 1972).

[35] See Bleddyn Davies, *Social Needs and Resources in Local Services* (London: Michael Joseph, 1968); James E. Alt, "Some Social and Political Correlates of County Borough Expenditures," *British Journal of Political Science,* I:1 (1971); and Noel Boaden, *Urban Policy-Making* (Cambridge: University Press, 1971).

Notwithstanding its formal powers, central government has consistently rejected responsibility for the administration of most major services of the welfare state. Education is a local authority responsibility, as is the provision of a wide variety of social work services. Local authorities build and manage housing. Planning, road, and environmental services are also locally administered, as are police and fire services. The resistance of medical doctors to control by local authority led to the establishment of regional hospital boards outside the control of local authorities, but outside the immediate control of Whitehall departments too. Among the chief activities of the welfare state, only employment services and the payment of pensions and similar money benefits to individuals are administered by central government through its own field service.

The paradox of central authority and administrative devolution is aptly summed up by John P. Mackintosh:

> Central government can plan, control, guide, review, audit and so on, but never actually execute. Foreign students find it scarcely credible that in Britain ministries of housing have never built a single house and ministries of education have never run a single school.[36]

The lack of direct control by nationalized industries and other functional bodies, as well as by local authorities, forces central government to spend much effort issuing instructions, requests, or advice to other parts of government. The center's power of authorization is balanced by the decentralized bodies' powers of execution. While local government officials complain about the restrictiveness of central government, ministers complain about their own lack of influence. Lord Hailsham, a minister with experience in many departments, has aptly summarized the contrast between being a defense minister, with the armed forces exclusively under central government control, and minister in a department whose program is administered by local authorities.

[36] "The Report of the Review Body on Local Government in Northern Ireland 1970," *Public Administration,* XLIX (Spring 1971), p. 20.

> In the Admiralty you are a person having authority. You say to one person "come" and he cometh, and another "go" and he goeth. It is not so in the Ministry of Education. You suggest rather than direct. You say to one man "come" and he cometh not, and to another "go" and he stays were he is.[37]

Decentralization exists, even within a unitary state, because central government cannot administer all its services in all parts of the kingdom without creating a great "overload" of responsibilities at the center. The desire to push administration out of Whitehall – whether by functional or spatial decentralization – has become a prominent feature of administrative reorganization. It is justified as necessary in order to allow government departments to concentrate upon responsibilities uniquely their own. Yet central government does not wish to let go of its power to constrain the authorities that it has created. The positive argument is that only Whitehall supervision can ensure "territorial justice" to its subjects, that is, an equality of services and opportunities for individuals, wherever they live within England, subject only to the limits of human mismanagement and extremes of population dispersion.[38] The negative argument is that only Whitehall supervision can prevent a local authority from carrying out policies or doing things that it ought not to do in the eyes of the government of the day. The critics of central direction argue that local discretion ought to be greater; local decision making is assumed to be morally superior, and local authorities are expected to know and care more about local concerns. But no proponent of decentralization wishes to do without central government financial subsidies.

The dilemma of centralization and decentralization is illustrated most clearly in land-use planning disputes between a nationalized industry and a local authority. The two types of agencies that central government has given powers in the public interest meet and clash. The nationalized industry

37 Quoted in Maurice Kogan, *The Policies of Education,* p. 31.

38 See Bleddyn Davies, *Social Needs and Resources in Local Services,* pp. 16, 289 ff.

claims it needs to turn land to industrial use for the common good, and the local authority may wish to keep land free from industry because it views green spaces as even more important for the common good. Central government cannot eliminate disagreement; it can but exercise its superior status to hear appeals and determine which of its creatures is most in accord with its own notion of the public interest.[39]

RULING CLIQUE OR WINNING GROUPS?

Some theories of governing postulate the centralization of power through the actions of a single ruling clique.[40] The ruling clique can coordinate actions within government as well as between government and other institutions in society. By contrast, other theorists postulate the fragmentation of power among a plurality of winning groups, each of which is victorious in some struggles to control government policy. Their actions are not integrated, and winners on one issue may be losers on another. To speak of a ruling clique is much more precise than reference to a "ruling class," for the latter term can be used to describe a heterogeneous category of people who have nothing in common except that at some time each has successfully influenced government. The term "Establishment" is also vague insofar as it may not specify whether the reputation of "established" persons for political influence accords with observable events or is simply a belief used to bolster the self-esteem of the so-called Establishment and the polemics of their critics. To describe the pattern of power as pluralist means only that it is not perfectly integrated; it leaves open how many and what kind of groups compete for influence and which ones are most often successful. In a pluralistic situation with dispersed inequalities, one observer can emphasize dispersion and the other, inequalities.[41]

The struggle of groups to determine the actions of government is continuous, and the areas of contest are multiple. A

[39] See Roy Gregory, *The Price of Amenity* (London: Macmillan, 1971).

[40] For a more general discussion and references to the literature, see Richard Rose, *People in Politics,* Chs. 6–7.

[41] Cf. Robert A. Dahl, *Who Governs?* (New Haven: Yale, 1961), p. 228.

group successful in one policy area will not necessarily be successful in another. In theory, any of at least seven different patterns of power could characterize policymaking in England.[42] These seven patterns of power are:

Ruling clique: A single group coordinates and controls decisions across a range of policy areas.

Coordinated cliques: A few groups, each preeminent in a policy area, consciously coordinate their actions across areas.

Balance-of-power pluralism: A few stable groups compete across a range of policy areas, each winning some of the time.

Segmented pluralism: Different groups consistently compete within a policy area, each winning some of the time; the groups are not related from policy area to area.

Amorphous pluralism: No consistent pattern of group competition or success exists within a policy area or between areas.

Populism: The mass of the electorate controls the resolution of an issue within a policy area or areas.

Veto power: A group consistently prevents the discussion or resolution of problems within one or more policy areas.

Power cannot be studied in isolation from the actions of government. In this book there is not space to present a comprehensive review of the conditions characterizing the exercise of power in Britain today. But one can see whether instances can be found to fit each of the above models. If there is some substance in each, then two very familiar models of power – the ruling clique and populism – cannot claim universality. The policies cited in the illustrations are heterogeneous, but each affects a large portion of the population, and/or affects some people intensely or for long periods of time.[43]

The *Ruling-clique* model is most appropriate to describe foreign policy making in Britain. Major decisions about diplomacy and defense are consistently made by a single group of people. The group consists of public officials: those around

42 These categories are developed from those initially proposed in C. J. Hewitt, *The Power Structure of Britain* (Providence, R.I: Ph.D. thesis, Sociology Department, Brown University, 1970), Ch. 2. The present author is responsible for interpretation.

43 See Richard Rose, *People in Politics,* pp. 200 ff.

the Prime Minister, the Foreign Office, the Ministry of Defense, and, when financial implications are significant, the Treasury. To describe these persons as a single group is not to impute agreement among everyone involved, but rather to note their relative isolation from influences outside Whitehall. Concerning very important measures, like the decision to manufacture British nuclear weapons or the decision to enter the Suez War, it is uncertain whether even the Cabinet was asked to approve the policy. A large measure of bipartisan agreement – especially among those on the front benches of the two parties – has made party of little importance in foreign affairs since 1945. One constraint upon the ruling clique in foreign affairs is the dependence of foreign policy upon domestic resources. The limit on manpower and public money (especially foreign exchange for supporting overseas bases) has caused a gradual contraction in the scope of British foreign policy since the last major rearmament effort of the early 1950s ran out of resources. This diminished scope calls attention to the importance of a second constraint: the power of other nations.

The *Coordinated-clique* model provides an idealized description of the two wings of the labor movement, parliamentary and industrial. Trade-union leaders expect to manage industrial relations without interference by Labour MPs or Labour governments, and Labour MPs expect to retain their freedom of action on measures not directly affecting trade-union rights. The experience of the 1964–70 Labour government shows how each side can assert its autonomy. The model would seem generally unsuited for British politics because it assumes that parties and pressure groups are sufficiently cohesive to engage in formal coordination with each other.

Balance-of-power pluralism characterizes economic policy. Typically, business and financial interests are arrayed on one side, and unions on the other, with the government's senior economic officials more than merely disinterested brokers. The weight of each side in the balance is not fixed. It can vary as changing economic circumstances make it more important for the government of the day to conciliate industry or unions. It can also vary with political circumstances. For example, the steel industry was nationalized, denationalized and renationalized in a space of fifteen years, as a consequence of changes in the balance of party politics.

Social welfare policies show *Segmented pluralism*. The cluster of groups concerned with education policy are few and stable, as in the balance-of-power model. But they differ from the cluster of groups involved with medical policies. In turn, these differ from the groups involved in the administration of social services for the poor and the handicapped. The relative narrowness of each group's concern – for instance, teachers have different professional associations or unions for different levels of education – makes it apt to speak of segmented politics. Within a well-defined area, policies are typically made by a complex of Whitehall officials, local authority officials or their spokesmen, leaders of affected professional groups, university-based experts on the subject, and representatives of the clients of a particular welfare service. Because segmentation between policy areas reflects a high degree of institutional organization within policy areas, the policy-making process requires lengthy negotiations. Welfare policies are more slowly changed than economic policies.

Amorphous pluralism describes a policy area in which participants change from issue to issue. Political controversies about land use concern particular plots of land. While government and professional planners are concerned with the consistency of principles from case to case, nearly all the other participants are concerned with who wins a particular battle in what may literally be their own back yard. The groups that come forward in a planning controversy usually live near the disputed land. Thus they are ad hoc and transitory in nature. Amorphous pluralism also characterizes the policy process in the field of minority rights, for instance, capital punishment and homosexual law reform. Issues are raised and contested by ad hoc combinations of people whose organization may not persist beyond the point of legislative success.[44]

Policy making is *Populist* when the mass of the electorate is

[44] See Roy Gregory, *The Price of Amenity,* and C. J. Hewitt, *The Power Structure of Britain,* pp. 81 ff.

directly involved in determining the outcome. In areas where government policy depends upon consumer response, for instance, encouraging people to save money by the purchase of government savings certificates, popular response determines success or failure. Sometimes the decisions of masses of consumers can be crucial in creating an issue and determining the outcome. For example, the independent decision of many Englishmen to buy automobiles and rely less upon railways and busses has greatly influenced government transport policy. Law enforcement, too, depends upon how the masses of the populace voluntarily comply with government decrees. The police and courts can only operate effectively if their attention can be concentrated upon a small part of society. In race relations, popular opinion has increasingly been used to justify laws intended to restrict entry to England of colored Commonwealth citizens.

In one sense, every political deliberation accepts limits determined by the "nonnegotiable" rights of participant groups. A *Veto* model describes activities that are not canvassed as issues, because of the known opposition of one or more groups or because a claim to nonnegotiable rights is accepted as forestalling action by government. For example, the Trades Union Congress long sought to veto the discussion of a new industrial relations law, because it is against *any* Act of Parliament in this field. Reciprocally, wealthy Englishmen do not debate the merits of different forms of capital levy, because they oppose the very principle of *any* wealth tax. In neither instance has the intended veto prevented discussion of such major policy changes. Today, the Veto model best fits the position of the churches, especially the established Church of England. No government has sought to introduce major legislation since the House of Commons defeated a proposal to amend the Prayer Book in 1927. The absence of discussion about the position of the State Church reflects the fear of sectarian controversy that would result from broaching the matter. It also reflects the slight political importance of religion in England today.[45]

[45] See E. J. Heubel, "Church and State in England: the Price of Establishment," *Western Political Quarterly*, XVIII:3 (1965).

The wide spectrum of opinions within political parties and the freedom of speech of the media provide many opportunities to raise issues of all kinds, from the nationalization of major industries to the repeal of major legislation of the welfare state. The tradition of free speech, far older than that of universal suffrage, makes silencing deviant opinions even less acceptable than the utterance of them. To note that many voices proliferate in policy discussions is not to assert that all are equally significant in policy making. Political controversy not only gives all sides a chance to advance their views but also results in the defeat of some as a condition of the success of others.

Every model of the policy process is conditional: it will fit some problems but be inappropriate to others. The political influence of a group is not only a function of its own resources but also a function of the policy area. The resources of bankers, trade unions, prelates, or motorists cannot be generalized across all policy areas, though they may be specially salient in some. The influence of Whitehall is a variable too; it is not constant in education, economics, and environmental planning.

An elaborate secondary analysis by C. J. Hewitt of twenty major political issues in postwar Britain provides data for generalizing about policy making. These are four of the generalizations:

1. The policy-making process is relatively segmented, because few groups are consistently involved in a wide range of policy areas. Of 339 extragovernmental organizations identified as active in at least one of the twenty issues, more than five-sixths were concerned with only one issue, and only 6 per cent with three or more issues.

2. The policy-making process is more often amorphous than a stable balance of power, because the groups opposing each other tend to change from issue to issue. The stable balance-of-power model only applies to economic concerns.

3. All groups recurringly involved in the policy process enjoy some victories and some defeats. The most consistently involved groups – business and labor – tend to have their victories offset by their defeats. By contrast, where opinion-poll

data indicated a clear popular preference, government policy was consistent with popular preferences in eight of nine cases.

4. The successful groups are greater in number than the unsuccessful groups.

The intermittent and limited involvement of many groups gives special advantage to those most consistently involved in making policy: public officials in government. Ministers and civil servants must be involved in policies that require positive state action. They are not only participants, but also the men who decide on what terms the government defines public policy. Ministers do not dominate in all policy areas, for extra-governmental groups often have strong market powers. But governors can extract advantage from whatever room for maneuver there is within a situation, and set terms to which others can only react. They are not only experienced players but also umpires, who at the end of the day arbitrate between group demands.

DYNAMIC COMPLEXITIES

To concentrate attention upon decisions is to limit attention to one point in a complex process. The word "outcome" more aptly emphasizes how policy making involves a multiplicity of prior and current conditions, of which conscious decisions are only one part. To think of an outcome as something separate from a decision is to recognize that a decision is but an intention. The outcome may be very different from – or even the opposite of – what governors intend. To approach policy making in dynamic terms is to recognize that the results of a policy may subsequently be a stimulus for changing policy.

The dynamic nature of policy making can best be emphasized by illustration. What is lost by condensing a long and complex history is offset by a better understanding of the gradual and cumulative nature of policy making. The two policies chosen to illustrate the dynamics of policy – the introduction of comprehensive schools and house building – concern policy areas common to all Western governments. The two cases illustrate how the role of government differs between policy areas. Education is primarily a state service and is compulsory by law. The Department of Education and Science sets expenditure standards for secondary schools operated by local authorities with central government finance. By contrast, the majority of houses are privately owned. Whitehall neither builds nor rents houses. It seeks to influence policy by affecting the market in which the housing industry operates.[46]

THE PREEXISTING ROUTINE

The exigencies of time and individual competence limit what any minister or Whitehall department can do. Ministers "govern by exception";[47] what they ignore becomes administratively routine.

Education. The 1944 Education Act introduced free compulsory secondary education. The measure was supported by all parties; subsequently, both Labour and Conservative governments sought to implement the scheme by building new grammar and secondary modern schools.

Housing. There is no single starting point for the study of housing, for Englishmen have been building shelter for themselves from time immemorial. The end of World War II is an appropriate point to enter the policy process, because of the virtual cessation of house building during the war.[48]

THE RECOGNITION OF NEED

To note a condition is not necessarily to define it as evidence of need. The same data may be interpreted as evidence of satisfaction.

[46] For a fuller outline model of policy making, see Richard Rose, "Comparing Public Policy," *European Journal of Political Research,* I:1 (1973).

[47] Maurice Kogan, *The Politics of Education,* p. 48. See also Michael Parkinson, *The Labour Party and the Organization of Secondary Education, 1918–1965.*

[48] For a general review of housing policy since the war, see David Donnison, *The Government of Housing* (Harmondsworth: Penguin, 1967).

Education. The implementation of the 1944 Education Act caused the conventional indicators of "good" policy to rise: More children stayed in school longer, more money was spent on education, and more children secured academic credentials. A change in secondary school policy required a new criterion for evaluating secondary schools. During the 1950s, educational sociologists began criticizing the predictive value of tests used to separate children at the age of eleven into academic and nonacademic secondary schools. They also began evaluating secondary schools in terms of the distribution of benefits; the divided structure (academic and nonacademic) was criticized as conferring disproportionate academic benefits upon children from middle-class homes.

Housing. In 1945 policy makers agreed on the need for more new houses. The demand was intense because of the loss of houses through bombing, the inability to build new houses during six years of war, and because many nineteenth-century houses did not meet mid-twentieth-century minimum standards, lacking a fixed bath, an indoor toilet, or other basic amenities.

THE DEVELOPMENT OF DEMAND

Policy makers may perceive a need, but there is no requirement for them to act until political pressures compel them to change an "intolerable" situation, or alternatively, to secure an improvement in the status quo.

Education. The critics of divided secondary schools (most of whom were Socialists) spent much of the 1950s lobbying within the Labour Party for a reform of secondary education. Out-of-office Labour politicians had no vested interest in established government policy. Moreover, evidence that selection at the age of eleven tended to favor middle-class children produced a negative reaction among MPs dependent primarily upon working-class votes. In the 1955 Labour manifesto the party stated it would "encourage" comprehensive schools; by 1964 the manifesto stated that "secondary education will be reorganized on comprehensive lines."

Housing. While everyone favored house building in principle, the articulation of demand was weak. In the 1945–50 Labour government, Aneurin Bevan, the responsible minister, devoted nearly all his time to establishing the National Health Services. In the first five years after the war, 118,000 new houses per annum were being built, barely one-third the annual rate of the five years immediately before the war. In the 1950 general election, more than nine-tenths of Conservative candidates attacked this record. Labour candidates answered defensively, stressing achievements in other areas. At the October, 1950, Conservative Party conference, an atypical display of militancy by delegates resulted in the party's pledging to raise building to 300,000 houses a year.

PUBLIC CHOICE

Secondary school and housing policies reflect contrasting patterns of choice. The government could and did make explicit and specific decisions about schools. In housing, successive governments have made a series of attempts to increase house building without expecting that the housing problem would necessarily be abolished, as the separation of children into two types of school might be abolished.

Education. The first effective choice of comprehensive schools was taken by a small number of local authorities in the late 1940s and 1950s. The Conservative government of the day restricted local plans to build comprehensive secondary schools. After the return of the 1964 Labour government, the question facing the minister was how to carry out the pledge to introduce comprehensive education nationally. In October, 1965, Anthony Crosland issued a circular requesting all local authorities to submit plans for reforming secondary education along comprehensive lines.

Housing. After the return of a Conservative government in 1951, a new minister of Housing, Harold Macmillan, was appointed. By his own admission, Macmillan "knew nothing whatever about the housing problem." The new Conservative Prime Minister, Churchill, told him that he had no idea about the subject either, but that the civil servants would know.[49] Macmillan sought to fulfill the Conservative pledge rather than justify a lower housing target. The ministry produced a variety of measures, such as the abolition of controls upon the private house-building industry and newer, simpler, and less solid forms of construction. The Conservative government also decided not to restrict council house building, even though the Conservatives were ideologically committed to a property-owning democracy, with homeownership central to that philosophy.

IMPLEMENTATION

Few government choices – except a decision to repeal a bill – can be put into effect solely by legislation. In education and in housing, central government is dependent for success upon the actions of those outside Whitehall.

Education. Implementation required changes in more than two hundred education authorities. The preexisting complement of secondary schools varied substantially from authority to authority. Most had built a substantial number of secondary modern and grammar schools in the 1950s; many of these buildings could not be adapted to meet the ideal requirements of a comprehensive school. In an effort to minimize detailed central government involvement and encourage local authority cooperation, Crosland's circular requested rather than compelled local authorities to put forward reorganization schemes. Moreover, it ostentatiously called attention to six different ways in which secondary schools might be reorganized to become comprehensive.

Housing. To implement the 1950 Conservative pledge to build 300,000 houses annually, the government relied in the first instance upon an increase in the building of council houses, because only local authorities were organized to accelerate building at the speed required. The target was reached

[49] Harold Macmillan, *Tides of Fortune, 1945–55* (London: Macmillan, 1969), p. 363.

in 1953, with building up from 239,000 houses to 318,000 houses; four-fifths of the new houses were council houses.[50] As private builders began to expand, the government discouraged council house building. The number of council houses built each year reached a peak in 1954, then fell sharply to a low of two-fifths of total new housing in 1961. The Conservatives also sought to encourage the building of rental property and to increase demand for private housing by greatly reducing rent restrictions in the 1957 Rent Act.[51]

ROUTINIZING POLICY

Because paying close attention to policies is costly in terms of time, every minister welcomes the moment when a policy can be looked after routinely by civil servants.

Education. The task of reviewing local authority proposals involved three stages. The first required decisions of principle, as well as establishing procedures concerning how much (or how little) the minister wished to know about what was done in his name. A large number of proposals could then be reviewed routinely. A minister could readily monitor two indicators of administrative achievement: the number of local authorities that had abolished the segregation by ability in secondary schooling and the proportion of young people in comprehensive secondary schools. The third stage – departmental reaction to recalcitrant local authorities that did not wish to reorganize schools in accord with the minister's request – required ministerial decision.

Housing. Reliance upon the private housing market to produce new houses abolished the heavy load of routine work required by the Labour government's licensing scheme. By 1956, 300,600 new houses were built, declining from the "overachievement" of 1954, when 347,000 houses were completed.

50 On housing statistics generally, see *Social Trends* and Constance Rollett, "Housing," in A. H. Halsey, editor, *Trends in British Society since 1900* (London: Macmillan, 1972).

51 See Malcolm Joel Barnett, *The Politics of Legislation: the Rent Act, 1957* (London: Weidenfeld & Nicolson, 1969).

The government could then maintain house building near the 300,000 target, by restricting council house starts as private housing increased. In six of the eight years, 1956–1963, the total of new houses completed was within 5,000 of the 300,000 target. As early as 1953, Aneurin Bevan could pronounce that housing needs were "not very far away" from being met, a comment echoed in 1956 by Enoch Powell, then a junior housing minister.[52]

DEROUTINIZING POLICY

Just as the sixth or "routinizing" stage in one cycle of policy making is also the first or "preexisting" stage in a succeeding cycle, so deroutinizing policy is analogous to recognizing a new need in the earlier cycle. At this point the new need involves altering or reversing (deroutinizing) policies previously treated as successfully routinized.

Education. The unwillingness of some education authorities to conform to government policy was creating a need for additional ministerial action at the time of the 1970 general election. But the return of a Conservative government created pressures in the opposite direction. A majority of Conservative voters disapproved of comprehensive schools (Table IX.2), and Conservative-controlled local authorities did not expect their government to compel them to implement Labour policies. The change of government was quickly expressed by the new minister, Mrs. Margaret Thatcher, in Circular 10/70. It rescinded the central government directive to reorganize secondary schools and left local authorities to decide whether to proceed with reorganization schemes. The Conservative government did not, however, recommend or require the reintroduction of the selective secondary school examination. The proportion of pupils in comprehensive secondary schools has continued to rise since, demonstrating the extent to which the Labour reform had become routinized. The Conservative shift

[52] Bevan, House of Commons, *Debates,* Vol. 521 Col. 826 (November 30, 1953); Powell, *ibid.,* Vol. 560 Col. 1759 ff (November 21, 1956).

in policy has resulted in slowing the rate of change, rather than reversing the direction of educational trends.[53]

Housing. An unanticipated consequence of the 1957 Rent Act was to increase the demand for new houses, as tenants of private landlords sought to buy houses or secure council houses. New flats were not built for moderate rental, as had been expected by the government. Treasury fiscal policy trebled interest rates between 1951 and 1960; this forced up housing costs, because of the importance of loan charges in the prices of council and private housing. Housing became a major political issue in the early 1960s, with the Labour opposition criticizing 300,000 houses a year as "not enough." In autumn, 1963, the Conservative Prime Minister announced a target of 400,000 houses. The opposition welcomed an increase, but showed caution about the ease with which the target could be reached. In the election year of 1964, the Conservative government increased house building by 75,000 to 373,000; once again, council housing expanded more rapidly than private housing. The target of 400,000 houses was achieved in 1967. In the 1966 election manifesto, the Labour government pledged to build 500,000 houses annually by 1970. Because of the government's economic difficulties the total fell to 362,000 houses in 1970.

In both policy areas, the measurable consequences of new policies have been incremental. But the increments are very large. By 1971, 40 per cent of all houses in Britain were of postwar construction; building programs are increasing this proportion by about 2 per cent per annum. Similarly, the proportion of adolescents in comprehensive secondary schools increased from 4 per cent in 1961 to 10 per cent in 1966, and under the impetus of policy changes, to 41 per cent in 1972.

Brief as the above accounts are, they clearly illustrate the dynamic nature of policy making. Statements of policy intent

[53] For up-to-date figures of proportions in comprehensive schools, see *Social Trends.*

are not carried out overnight. Sometimes goals are achieved, as in the Conservative housing pledge of 1950; sometimes they are not, as in the Labour housing pledge of 1966. Yet even when intentions are realized, subsequent events may lead to new policy demands. Ten years after a Conservative government achieved its target of building 300,000 houses a year, its Conservative successor regarded the figure as 100,000 houses too few. The Labour record on housing, 1945–51, and the Conservative circular on secondary schools of 1970, emphasize the importance of "non decisions" as well as of positive actions. In education, changes in policy appear more secular than cyclical. Whereas house-building figures rise and fall, there is no expectation that pupils will shuttle back and forth between different types of secondary schools. The expansion of comprehensive secondary schools appears a trend that can be slowed, delayed, or halted, but not reversed – at least in the foreseeable future. As the pupils of the new secondary schools move toward the tertiary section of further education, the trend will have further consequences. In both policy areas it is much more easy to speak of problems than solutions.

DILEMMAS OF POLICY MAKING

The central dilemma of government in Britain arises from the dignified constitutional convention that the Cabinet is responsible for every act of public policy and the efficient limits upon the activities that any man or committee of men can direct. Mechanical and organizational developments have given governors greater capabilities than their early nineteenth-century predecessors for whom the doctrine of ministerial responsibility was framed. But the growing demands upon government have concurrently increased the range and detail of their responsibilities.

The dilemma becomes most apparent in such fields as economic planning, where the importance of success is great, yet the complexity of the subject is also great. In a review of British economic planning in wartime, Ely Devons noted the tension between "the need to split up the field to be covered so that each administrative unit can deal efficiently with its own sector," and "the need to secure that the actions of these separate units all fit into the general plan."[54] In such circumstances, busy policy makers must either emphasize details or generalities. In the former instance, the danger at the extreme is that the literary style of a policy statement may take precedence over consideration of the aims and realism of the plan. Alternatively, there is the risk that planners will become addicted to what Anthony Downs has described as "Superman" planning, ignoring detailed practical constraints as if they could be vaulted over Superman-fashion.[55] Even if policy makers link details and general goals, they still suffer from a lack of prevision.

Any plan for the future inevitably includes an "other-things-being-equal" clause. But the assumption that all other conditions remain equal (or "errors cancel out") is not always met. While unanticipated or unforeseeable developments may sometimes assist a government, at other times they will frustrate aims. In such circumstances, policy makers face another dilemma. Plans made with sufficient clarity to serve as meaningful targets can become post hoc evidence of failure if things go astray. Alternatively, plans can be stated in terms so general and vague that whatever happens, success can be claimed on the grounds that "Whatever is, is right." The former alternative is preferable for those who regard the aim of government as doing things; the latter makes greater appeal to those who believe government should react to events rather than seek to cause them.

Because policy making involves choice, there is more than one course that governors can take. Moreover, it is in the nature of dilemmas that there is much to be said for each competing alternative. Usually policy makers are not required to make "all-or-nothing" choices between complete centralization and the complete abdication of influence. Choice is likely to involve trading off some of the benefits of decentralization against some losses of central coordination — or vice versa. Choices also involve matching the intentions of government to

[54] See Ely Devons, *Planning in Practice* (Cambridge: University Press, 1950), especially Ch. 8.

[55] See Anthony Downs, *Inside Bureaucracy* (Boston: Little, Brown, 1967), pp. 216 ff.

limits upon its power. Insofar as success arises from getting the ratio right, then busy men can try more than one alternative. Because success is measured in ratio terms, it could be hypothesized that all the changes in the organizational capabilities of government since the mid-nineteenth century, when viewed in relation to the rising demands made upon government, have left unaltered the *relative* policy-making capability of British government.

CHAPTER XI

The Impact of Policy

What grows upon the world is a certain matter-of-factness. The test of each century, more than of the century before, is the test of results.

THE IMPACT OF POLICY is not necessarily what governors intend. Measures adopted to secure peace and prosperity may be followed by war or depression. Moreover, in a world of complex causation, many conditions of society change independently of or in spite of actions of governors. Hence, in order to review the effects of government policies upon society in England, one must examine what governments intend, what they do, and what happens afterwards.

Examining the impact of public policy upon society shifts attention from government as a reactive force, responding to popular demands, to government as an active force, positively trying to influence the conditions of society. The reactive model reflects liberal values. The model of the positive state is especially consonant with a set of collectivistic values, whether a paternalistic Tory philosophy or a Socialist outlook. The dominant political philosophies in England today stress positive action by the state, albeit in ways responsive to popular reactions.[1]

[1] For a detailed discussion of points raised here, see Richard Rose, "Models of Governing." For historical background, see Samuel H. Beer, *Modern British Politics.*

Analyzing the impact of policies directs attention to considerations beyond the articulation of popular demands and the policy-making machinery of government. A Cabinet decision, an Act of Parliament, or public expenditure figures are no longer viewed as the final output of a process whereby popular demands are converted into authoritative decisions by the "black box" of government. When studying the impact of policies, one now sees the actions of government as inputs to society, which then converts these (and other) inputs to affect social conditions. The ultimate output in this extended framework is a set of social conditions. The policies of government are here seen as means to a social end, rather than as ends in themselves. Actions of policy makers need not be taken with social ends in mind. Policy makers may be thinking of economic, electoral, or administrative ends, or of personal careers. Figure XI.1 makes explicit a framework in which policy consequences can be considered, whether intended or not by policy makers.

The policy inputs described in Figure XI.1 emphasize, first, that government policies are not the only inputs affecting social conditions. Social and economic activities, both domestic and international, directly influence social conditions or are indirectly important as influences upon the policy inputs of government. The policy inputs of government are multiple and come from a variety of organs of government. The simultaneity of actions does not mean that they are purposefully coordinated; one policy may even cancel out another.

The subdivision of the box representing society in Figure XI.1 emphasizes that many policies of the modern welfare state are selective in intent. Some policies are intended to benefit people at different phases of the life cycle, for instance, elementary education, industrial injury compensation plans, and old age pensions. Others are intended to affect people according to their economic standing, whether at the extremes of the very poor or the very wealthy, or middle class and working class. Today many of the debates about policies go beyond simple measures of aggregate effects. People debate the distribution of impact: Who benefits at whose cost?

The lines indicating policy consequences are multiple be-

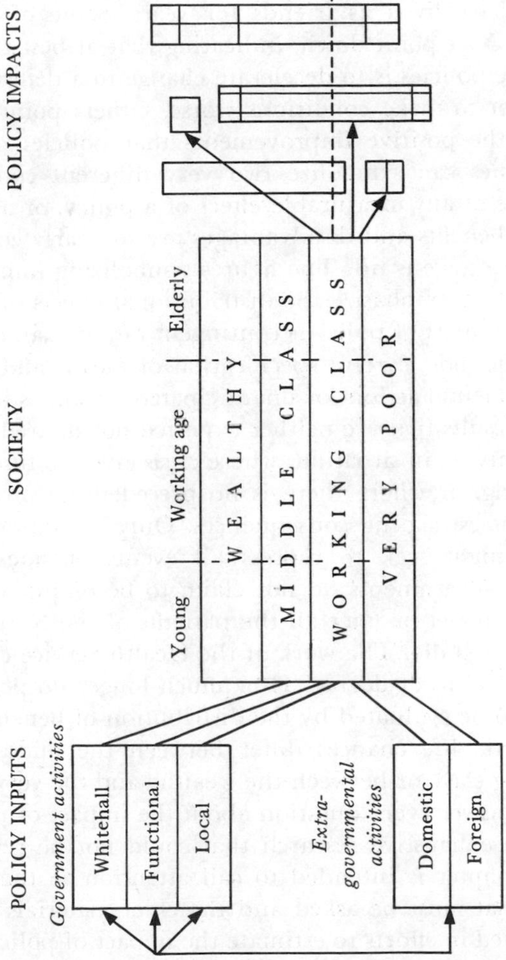

FIGURE XI.1 *The Impact of Public Policy on Society*

POLICY INPUTS

Government activities

Whitehall

Functional

Local

Extra-governmental activities

Domestic

Foreign

SOCIETY

Young | Working age | Elderly

WEALTHY

MIDDLE CLASS

WORKING CLASS

VERY POOR

POLICY IMPACTS

Desirable

Undesirable

cause many policies have multiple effects; for example, the National Health Service is not only intended to be good for physical and mental well-being but also good for the economy, preventing workers from losing days at work. Some consequences are not necessarily perceived as benefits. For example, slum clearance schemes not only remove physically insanitary buildings, but may also destroy neighborhoods where residents have lived as friends for years. Some of the lines in Figure XI.1 point down, indicating that at best the net result of some policies is to decelerate change in a deteriorating situation or to make conditions worse. Others point up, emphasizing the positive improvements that policies can produce. Flat lines can symbolize two very different conditions: the absence of any measurable effect of a policy, or a situation in which benefits and disadvantages are so nearly equal that the net advantage is nil. The figures symbolizing impacts are subdivided, to emphasize the distributional effects of policies.

The impact of policy is contingent rather than certain. Even with the most careful specification of means and ends, extragovernmental actions or unanticipated responses in society can cause results that are neither expected nor desired. Often, governments act in situations where crisis gives no time for careful planning, or where there is no precedent to provide experience for estimating consequences. Only a totalitarian government might seek to repress all events outside its control. British governments do not claim to be omnipotent. For example, sooner or later all the patients of the National Health Service will die. The work of the Health Service can be evaluated in terms of degree: How much longer do people live? It can also be evaluated by the distribution of benefits: To what extent do life chances differ between the middle class and working class, or between the wealthy and the very poor?

To answer every question about the impact of policy would require exhaustive research that could not be reported here. This chapter is intended to call attention to the main questions that must be asked and the chief materials that can be examined in efforts to estimate the impact of policy. One must consider the resources available to government, the intentions of governors, what resources are committed, and to what effect.

It is also desirable to consider the evaluation of results, not only in terms of technical efficiency but also in terms of alternative concepts of the good society.

THE RESOURCES OF GOVERNMENT

The raw materials of government are few but potentially powerful. Yet none of these resources is of itself effective. Laws represent an attempt to alter social actions, but classifying speeding or drug taking as illegal does not, by itself, prevent these offenses from occurring. Money too is but a means to a social end. Giving cash benefits to persons in need is intended to improve their condition, but if an individual's problems are psychological rather than financial, it may not help. Skilled manpower may be frustrated; the assignment of civil servants to devise a solution to the nation's economic problems does not guarantee that they will find one.

The foremost resource of any government is its ability to make binding rules. Whether rules are stated as Acts of Parliament or in some other form, they guide actions by governors, and legitimate the demand for compliance from subjects. British policy makers are fortunate in that the endorsement of political authority in the political culture makes popular compliance virtually certain for laws of political significance.

The most familiar rules are those contained in Acts of Parliament. The continuity of government from medieval times results in a vast accumulation of legislation from many different ages, even though few laws from preindustrial England are today significant. More important is the legislation of a century of modern government, which has never been codified. The government's policies in any area are derived from legislation, some of it enacted at points distant in time, and all of it without logical and comprehensive analysis of cumulative effects. In 1965, the English Law Commission was established to review continuously the laws of the land, and suggest reforms and codification where necessary. The backlog of work is such that the Commission moves slowly; meanwhile, new legislation is added to the existing corpus of law. The official *Chronological Table of the Statutes,* giving the title of each Act of Parliament, runs to more than 1300 pages. The earliest statute still in force dates from 1235; nearly one-quarter date from before the accession of Queen Victoria in 1837.

In the course of a year the majority party in Parliament has the opportunity to pass twenty to thirty bills with significance for some field of public policy. The number of bills passed each year has altered little in the last half-century.[2] Because the government can be nearly certain of success for almost any bill it cares to introduce, its relative efficiency in legislating – the ratio of bills proposed to laws enacted – is very high. But it is still greatly constrained by a short supply of parliamentary time in relation to the demand from departments for new legislation.[3] For example, the Home Office, Scottish Office, Department of Environment, and Department of Health and Social Security each annually secure parliamentary time for only about one-fifth of the topics that they would wish to see the subject of new legislation. Legislation can also be a constraint because it requires ministers to be explicit about the means as well as the ends of their policies. In the words of a civil servant experienced in drafting legislation:

> Very often you don't see the pitfalls and traps until you write your instructions to parliamentary counsel. Having to be so specific, you suddenly realize you have been talking nonsense for months.[4]

Once a measure is introduced, it is subject to review through a series of procedural mechanisms that are not only time-consuming but also of dubious relevance to the impact of the law. For example, amendment procedures intended to clarify a bill in Parliament may be used by the opposition to reiterate differences about principles. Even though critics realize that

[2] See D. E. Butler and J. Freeman, *British Political Facts,* pp. 124 f; Gavin Drewry, "Reform of the Legislative Process: Some Neglected Questions," *Parliamentary Affairs,* XXV:4 (1972), pp. 300–02; and Jean Blondel, *et al.,* "Legislative Behaviour," *Government and Opposition,* V:1 (1969–70), pp. 75 ff.

[3] See Bruce Headey, *The Job of Cabinet Minister,* and Valentine Herman, "What Governments Say and What Governments Do," *Parliamentary Affairs* (forthcoming).

[4] Quoted in John Clare, "Who Makes the Decisions that Change our Environment?" *The Times,* May 9, 1972.

what they dislike will inevitably become law, they may emphasize controversy rather than seek to remove drafting weaknesses.[5]

The government enjoys substantial powers to make binding rules outside the exhausting process of parliamentary legislation. In World War II, the coalition government exercised great authority while passing fewer laws than in an average peacetime year. The government can exercise the unlimited prerogative powers of the Crown, derived ultimately from medieval concepts of royal sovereignty, in such fields as foreign affairs and defense. Many executive orders are issued by authority delegated to the government by Acts of Parliament. Formally, these executive decrees are issued as Orders in Council. Statutory Instruments provide another procedure for executive rule making outside the conventional parliamentary routine. Statutory Instruments, typically rules of relatively minor importance introduced to permit administrative flexibility, arc notified to Parliament. A Statutory Instruments Committee of the Commons scrutinizes these measures and can, if it wishes, call a rule to the attention of the Commons for possible rejection as exceeding powers authorized by Act of Parliament. If this is not done, the instrument becomes binding as law. The number cited as objectionable is usually less than ten a year, hardly 1 per cent of the annual total.[6] In case a government acts without justification under any of these broad grants of authority, as its ultimate resource it can legislate retrospectively to give *ex post facto* justification for what it has done.

At some point in the process of implementation, policy involves the discretionary use of statutory powers. This is true for matters of major import, concerning management of the economy or foreign policy, as well as for thousands of daily acts of administrative routine, concerning the grant of a disability pension, or planning permission to build an extra room on a house. While single decisions may be limited in scope, the

[5] See Gavin Drewry, "Reform of the Legislative Process."

[6] See Frank Stacey, *The Government of Modern Britain* (Oxford: Clarendon Press, 1968), p. 208.

result can be of intense significance to the individual concerned. Many decisions involving the discretionary use of statutory powers are taken by special-purpose administrative tribunals. The volume of the work of the tribunals is great in aggregate; even excluding Inland Revenue cases, tribunals hear more than 175,000 cases in a typical year. Bodies handling more than 10,000 cases annually include industrial tribunals, local valuation courts, national insurance bodies, rent tribunals, traffic commissioners, and supplementary benefit appeal tribunals.[7]

Money is a second major resource of British government. The government's revenue depends upon the total gross national product (which in Britain is large in aggregate as well as in per-capita terms), the methods it uses to secure revenue (income tax, customs and excise taxes, local rates, insurance-like contributions for welfare services, loans, etc.), and the yield from these resources. In an inflationary period income tax will be buoyant, rising with rises in money wages, but taxes on corporate profits may vary downward as well as up, as company profits fluctuate with economic conditions. New taxes can be introduced, like the 1964 Labour government's Selective Employment Tax, which was grossing almost £2,000,000 annually in revenue before it was abolished by the Conservatives, to be replaced by VAT (Value Added Tax) in 1973. Income tax accounts for about one-third of central government revenue, and customs and excise taxes – principally on oil, tobacco, and drink – account for another third. The remainder of revenue comes from a variety of sources. In local government, taxes on property account for more than one-fifth of revenue, and central government grants for more than one-quarter. Local authorities also raise money by loans and by making charges for services provided, such as council houses.[8] Tax revenues are not only a means of financing government, but also of regulating behavior. For example, high taxes on whisky are intended to limit the consumption of drink, and

[7] *Social Trends*, Vol. 3, p. 152.

[8] See *Annual Abstract of Statistics* 1972 (London: HMSO), Ch. XIII; and "Survey Shows French Pay less Tax than British," *The Times*, January 1, 1973.

high tariffs on imports to stimulate the purchase of domestic goods.

The government's share of national income can be calculated at one-third to nearly one-half of the nation's total, depending upon definitional criteria. Britain takes a relatively high proportion of its gross national product in taxes by comparison with other European nations, and even more, by comparison with the United States. While citizens complain about tax levels, they also complain about the failure of government to provide services that cost money. The ceiling on what government can raise in revenue in a given year is a variable, not a constant; it fluctuates with political circumstances and with economists' forecasts of the economic consequences of a surplus or deficit in public expenditure.

Manpower is a third resource of government. Public employment today accounts for about one-quarter of the total labor force in Britain. Of these 6,000,000 employees, more than one-third work in local government. Employees in the nationalized industries are also more numerous than those in central government. The number of people working in a given policy area does not necessarily indicate its importance: the Treasury and Cabinet Office are among the smallest government departments in Whitehall, but not among the least in significance. Numbers of employees reflect the type of service that a department is expected to provide. It requires, for example, far fewer people to formulate welfare policies than it does to sort the daily mail.[9]

Land is a fourth major resource of government. In addition to being a major land owner, the central government benefits from the traditional centralization of land ownership in the hands of the monarch and the nobility. Crown lands can be put to public use (e.g., London parks or forestry reserves) and large landed estates of nobility can be given to the National Trust for recreational purposes and to avoid death duties. Even prior to the passage of government legislation regulating land use, private owners of large estates maintained planning controls by granting restrictive leaseholds to tenants in cities.

[9] Sir Richard Clarke, *New Trends in Government*, pp. 119 ff.

Today, the government enjoys the power to regulate the use of land through planning legislation. It can also acquire land by compulsory purchase. Laws on compulsory purchase and compensation tend to favor the government as purchaser rather than the private seller. The ability of central government to allocate land has been most notably used in the creation of New Towns. Since 1945 the government has established twenty-eight New Towns on "green field" sites outside congested urban areas of Britain. By 1971 these new towns had a population of 1,100,000 people, and are planned to expand to twice this population.

Symbols can be a valuable resource of government, because they stimulate an emotional response that cannot be so readily secured by other means. Such symbols as the Queen and the Union Jack have no specific material use. They can, nonetheless, evoke positive emotional responses. It is difficult to assess the specific input of symbols, for they usually reinforce or supplement other resources of government. Symbols do not appear to be of great importance in encouraging allegiance. Symbols may be invoked when other resources are less likely to avail. For example, in 1940 Winston Churchill used patriotic symbols because at the time the government had few other resources to invoke. To note this is not to denigrate the significance of symbols in extreme situations. In two great wars of this century, hundreds of thousands of Englishmen have died for King and Country.

The resources of government can be deployed in a variety of ways, in efforts to influence conditions in society.

Figure XI.2a shows the simplest way by which government can affect social conditions: paying money benefits directly to citizens. The individuals in receipt of money benefits are, in turn, expected to spend the money to improve (or at least, not worsen) their conditions. For example, the elderly are expected to spend their pensions to maintain health, and parents are expected to spend childrens' allowances to assist in raising their family. The decision about how to spend money is left to the individual beneficiary. In the second illustration, by contrast, the government uses resources to produce services that individuals are expected to consume for their potential

FIGURE XI.2 *The Use of Government Resources to Influence Social Conditions*

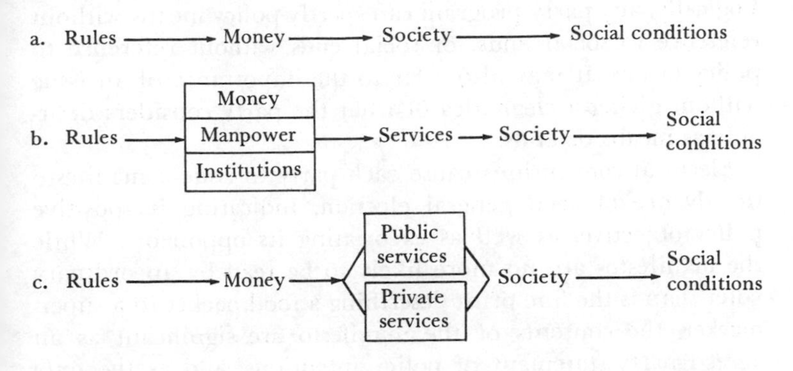

benefit. For example, schools and hospitals are not individual goods, but rather means by which individuals may gain better health and education. The third model reflects a complex situation, in which public and private agencies both affect social conditions. For example, both local authorities and private companies build houses; their joint effort is meant to provide a good standard of housing in society. Each of the three models in Figure XI.2 has one point in common. It shows the resource inputs of government as means, not ends. The desired outputs of social conditions are at several removes from these inputs. Many things can intervene between the first and the last step in the process.

THE INTENTIONS OF PARTIES

The resources of government are neutral; they can be put to many ends. In England the governing party is expected to stipulate what these ends should be. But because resources are not infinite and government is not omnipotent, a politician's choice of ends is no more than a statement of intent. Even an action that lies wholly within the scope of government, like a decision to transfer a government office from an overcrowded part of London to a region suffering unemployment, will have social consequences outside the control of government.

The translation of party policy into desired social consequences is a complex process. The political difficulties of securing agreement about statements of intent may lead partisans to regard a declaration of intentions as their final output. Logically, any party program can specify policy means without reference to social ends, or social ends without reference to policy means. It may also refer to the importance of an issue without giving a clear idea of what the party considers desirable as means or ends.

Electoral conventions cause each party to issue a manifesto in advance of each general election, indicating its positive policy objective, as well as excoriating its opponents. While the manifestos are no more likely to be read by an ordinary voter than is the fine print describing a food packet in a supermarket, the contents of the manifesto are significant as an agreed party statement of policy intentions, and as the *only* comprehensive policy document issued collectively on behalf of the party. The 1964 Labour manifesto merits careful attention, because the party had thirteen years in opposition to prepare plans to advance its aims. The Conservative manifesto of 1970, prepared in six years in opposition, reflected an effort to advance the party beyond the work of the Conservatives in office, 1951–64.[10]

By starting with the list of political issues reviewed in Table IX.2 (p. 304), one can note to what extent these concerns are included in the manifesto, the clarity of statements of intent, and the relation between statements of intent and actions in office.

The analysis displayed in Table XI.1 shows first of all that both parties carry out many intentions stated in their party manifestos. The Conservative record is particularly striking; within two and a half years of taking office, the party had taken affirmative action concerning nine of the eighteen topics under review. By contrast, in six years of office, Labour had positively carried out four pledges; a fifth, a major pensions act, was pending in Parliament when the 1970 election was announced. The Conservative government is also noteworthy in that it has reversed its policies on four issues whereas the Labour govern-

[10] For texts, see F. W. S. Craig, *British General Election Manifestos 1918–1966* (Chichester: Political Reference Publications, 1970).

TABLE XI.1 *Party Manifestos and Government Actions*

	Labour government 1964–70	*Conservative government 1970–73*[a]
Pledge fulfilled:	Secondary schools Nationalization Income tax changes Race relations Pensions	Industrial relations act Common Market Secondary education Housing Agriculture Income tax changes Welfare eligibility Commercial radio Pensions
Uncertain/ ambiguous:	Agriculture Foreign policy	Political demonstrations Rhodesian independence Foreign policy
No pledge:	Industrial relations law Government spending Hanging Abortion Commercial radio	Hanging Abortion
Action opposite of pledge:	Common Market Housing Free Health Service	Nationalization Abolished Stormont Government Number of colored immigrants Government spending
Not an issue 1964:	Northern Ireland Political demonstrations Rhodesian independence	

[a]Conservative entries are classified as of October, 1973. Classification based upon the 1964 Labour manifesto, and 1970 Conservative manifesto.

ment reversed itself on three. But Labour had fewer explicit commitments for the subjects under review. The Conservative manifesto had specific policy pledges concerning sixteen of the eighteen issue areas selected; hanging and abortion, the two issues without pledges, are traditionally not treated as partisan issues. The review indicates that most major concerns of government can be anticipated in advance of an election; only three problems confronting Labour in office were not an issue before the 1964 election.

The major statutes of the British welfare state vary enormously in the clarity with which their intent is stated, and there is no legal requirement that an Act of Parliament carry any statement of intent. For example, the last major franchise reform, the Representation of the People Act of 1949, has no preamble stating its objectives; it simply lists alterations in rules regulating the conduct of elections. The repeal of an existing statute may also be carried without a stated objective. The act to end capital punishment was not intended to encourage murder, but simply to stop a form of punishment that was against the conscience of most MPs. Objectives may be stated in very vague and general terms; the landmark 1944 Education Act was intended "to promote the education of the people of England and Wales." Often legislation specifies clearly the new institutions and procedures to be established but leaves vague their intended impact on society. The National Health Service Act, 1946, is distinctive in stating clear though general goals – to secure improvement in physical and mental health by the prevention, diagnosis, and treatment of illness – and specifying administrative means to these ends. The Coal Industry Nationalization Act, 1946, states intentions clearly: to get coal from the mines, to secure efficient development of the industry, and to sell coal "at such prices as may seem to the directors best calculated to further the public interest in all respects."[11] The statement of multiple objectives risks conflict between objectives, as the history of the nationalized coal industry illustrates.

In some models of governing, government spending is treated as the output resulting from the impact of political and social demands upon government. But in an analysis of social consequences, money must be considered a policy input, along with legislation and personnel. Whether spending produces a desired effect and whether an increase in desired consequences is proportionate to increased spending are contingent results, not certain outcomes. For example, one cannot say that the country that spends the most money will inevitably win a war, or that the more money that is spent on an ill-

[11] For introductions to a variety of statutes, including those cited here, see G. Le May, *British Government, 1914–1953*.

conceived policy, the better its impact will be. Moreover, many measures of significance do not necessarily cause substantial changes in public expenditure; the comprehensive schools policy is intended to reorganize the use of existing resources. Expenditure can change with no substantive change in policy, if levels of social demand rise and must be met. For example, if elderly people live longer, the cost of public pensions rises in aggregate, although individual pensions do not change.

The concentration of executive and legislative authority in the Cabinet and the concentration of budgeting powers in the Treasury give the governors of Britain the opportunity to review public spending annually and to make adjustments in spending patterns. These changes provide some evidence of policy priorities. Since the introduction of the annual Public Expenditure Survey in the mid-1960s, requiring each government department to forecast its spending requirements five years ahead, the government of the day has increased its ability to indicate what it would like to spend more money on in the not too distant future. While changes in expenditure levels may reflect changes in levels of demand, for instance, if more young people should gain qualifications for university entrance, the decision to persist in meeting established commitments to individuals in the face of rising aggregate costs is itself a statement about priorities.

The Treasury classifies the expenditure of central government under six major headings; these in turn are divided into twenty-five subheadings, including categories to allow for short-term fiscal adjustments. The groupings are in order of total expenditure: social services, environmental services, defense and external relations, commerce and industry, debt interest, nationalized industries, and miscellaneous services (Table XI.2). Social services take more than two-fifths of total expenditure, and housing, roads, and other environmental services one-sixth. This shows the extent to which public expenditure is intended to assist the individual and collective welfare of Englishmen. Aid to commerce and industry, especially the nationalized industries, may be considered a collective service to society, providing the basis for jobs and, through economic growth, greater resources for public expenditure. The two other major spending programs – defense and payment of

TABLE XI.2 *The Public Expenditure Priorities of the Wilson Government (in percentages)*

	Millions of £ spent, 1967–68[a]	*(1) Achieved annual increase, 1964–69*	*(2) Difference from average*	*(3) Intended annual rise, 1969–72*	*(4) Difference from average*	*Change (3 – 1)*
Defence, foreign affairs	2,977	-0.7	-6.6	-2.6	-5.6	-1.9
Commerce and industry	1,318	9.0	3.1	4.2	1.2	-4.8
Environmental services	3,172	4.7	-1.2	4.7	1.7	0.0
Social Services	7,028	6.0	0.1	4.4	1.4	-1.6
Financial, other services	822	7.1	1.2	5.2	2.2	-1.9
Nationalized industries	1,783	2.4	-3.5	-1.7	-4.7	-4.1
Debt interest	1,936	7.0	1.1	-0.4	-3.4	-7.4
Total £s; average, cols.(1) and (3)	£19,036	5.9		3.0		

Source: *Public Expenditure 1968–69 to 1973–74* (London: HMSO, Cmnd. 4234, 1968), Tables 1.1, 1.3.
[a]All £ figures in constant 1969–1970 out-turn prices.

interest on the debt – are not welfare measures, but rather intended to prevent worse befalling society.

Annual alterations in public expenditure are of limited size, and often indicate considerations that affect the means rather than the ends of government. For example, in fiscal 1972–73, public expenditure was estimated to rise from the previous year by a net total of £1,227,000,000. Of this total, one-fifth arose from changes in estimates of costs and another fifth resulted from economic measures intended to influence the national economy. Only 15 per cent of the change concerned spending on social services, and another 23 per cent, spending on environmental and related services.[12]

Small annual changes in public policies can have substantial significance. The changes occurring in 1972–73 were less than 5 per cent of all public expenditures, but the total change was almost equal to total annual public spending on housing. Because increases and cuts in public spending are not spread evenly across all policy areas, their potential impact is magnified. In the course of five years, the effects of annual increases can accumulate and compound.

The spending record of the Labour government shows that priorities were not what a reader of the party's 1964 manifesto would have expected or what the Labour Cabinet wished to sustain in the early 1970s. Excluding relatively small sums spent on financial administration, the two spending categories that rose most rapidly were grants to commerce and industry and interest on the debt (Table XI.2). Neither of these activities directly affects social conditions; they could only be indirectly significant. Both concern aid to capitalist enterprises; concurrently, subsidies and capital expenditure of nationalized industries were cut. Spending on social services was at the average for the whole of government, but environmental services were below average, notwithstanding the importance given housing prior to Labour's election in 1964. Only in defense expenditure did the Labour government achieve a stated aim, cutting expenditure there.

When the Labour Cabinet in autumn, 1969, prepared its

12 See Cmnd. 5178 (HMSO, 1972), Tables 1.3, 2A.

future expenditure plans, it showed policy intentions differing substantially from its immediate achievements. First, the government projected an increase in public expenditure of 3.0 per cent per annum, a rate almost one-half of the rate of increase for its first five years in office. This decision reflected political judgments about the best way to manage the economy. Within this lower rate of expenditure increase, Labour showed major shifts in relative priorities. While each expenditure heading might have suffered, on average, a 2.9 per cent fall in its rate of growth, the Labour government showed that it wished to give first priority to environmental services, by making no cut at all in its rising expenditure pattern. It also scheduled social service expenditure to be cut less than average, and to continue growing at an above-average rate. The chief cuts were to be imposed upon debt interest and subsidies to commerce and industry, policies that had consumed the most rapidly rising amounts of money previously. The ability of the Labour government to achieve these priorities, where it had previously fallen short, cannot be evaluated; the return of a Conservative government in 1970 brought new men to government.

Like any new government, the Conservative administration of Edward Heath inherited many long-established policy commitments. Moreover, it took office after the budget for the forthcoming year had already been prepared. In the course of seeking to impose its own priorities upon public policy through public expenditure, it faced many short-term economic and political problems. By the time it issued its public expenditure plans in December, 1972, it had sufficient experience of office to recognize many constraints upon change, while it also had many incentives to impose its expenditure priorities upon government.

The Conservative government declared its intention of increasing public expenditure by 2.5 per cent per annum from fiscal 1972–73 to 1976–77. While the sum sounds small proportionately, in absolute terms it represents an increase of £3,655,-000,000 in constant-money value. The budget total is the sum of seven cuts and twelve increases in expenditure (Table XI.3). Among the increases, nine are above average and three below.

TABLE XI.3 *Changing Public Expenditure by Function, Plans for 1972–73 to 1976–77*

Programs	*Expenditures 1972–73 (millions of £)*[a]	*Estimated % of average rise to 1976–77*[b]	*Estimated change (millions of £)*
Other military defence	61	12.6	37
Law and order	847	6.2	232
Roads	1,013	5.5	243
Arts	41	5.1	9
Education & libraries	3,569	5.0	762
Health & personal social services	2,917	4.8	608
Nationalized industries capital expenditure	1,811	4.8	3.7
Overseas aid	275	4.2	49
Miscellaneous local services	1,257	3.7	199
Defence Budget	3,003	2.4	301
Social security	5,050	1.3	275
Northern Ireland	711	0.1	4
Financial admin., common & miscellaneous services	873	0.0	-2
Research councils, etc.	141	-0.7	-4
Debt interest	2,350	-1.4	-75
Housing	1,415	-3.2	-174
Public transport	287	-4.6	-49
Agriculture, fish, forestry	582	-4.7	-103
Trade, industry & employment	1,670	-5.5	-600
EEC and other overseas services	205	c	157
Contingency, shortfall, price adjustments	-194	–	–
Total expenditures	£27,884		

Source: Cmnd. 5178 (HMSO, 1972), Table 1, et al.
[a]All costs in constant £.
[b]Average of the average rises for 1976–77 is 2.5%.
[c]Not calculable because of the effect of Britain joining EEC during the period.

The inspection of percentage rates of change can be misleading, however, insofar as they do not take account of the size of the expenditure base that is changing. For example, the highest percentage increase, "other military defense," rises only

£37 million in absolute terms. By contrast, the below-average increase in defense spending costs an extra £301 million. Because some of the programs with high proportionate increases in expenditure – e.g. roads, education, health, and nationalized industries – were already big spenders in 1972, the overall average growth in public spending could only be kept at 2.5 per cent by proposing substantial cuts in housing, trade, industry, and agriculture.

The intentions of the party in office – whether expressed in money terms or in more or less precise sentences in a manifesto – are one important element in a dynamic model of policy-making, but not the only element. Politicians become experienced in explaining to their partisan followers why all of their intentions cannot be realized as quickly as they had hoped. If their explanations are not sufficiently acceptable, the electorate reserves the right to put the governing party out, in the hope that the opposition will be better able to achieve commonly valued goals, or offer a better package of alternative intentions.

TO WHAT EFFECT?

Evaluating the impact of public policy is a matter that concerns politicians as much as it does social scientists. If a govment cannot achieve its intentions, this tells us something about the limits of its power. If it does not know whether it has achieved its intentions, this tells us even more.

The relatively sophisticated machinery developed for evaluating current and future levels of public expenditure has not been matched by equally sophisticated techniques for evaluating the consequences of public expenditure. According to the Treasury, public policies "are measured in terms of their inputs – numbers of staff employed, goods and services purchased, and so on . . . because of the difficulty of measuring the output of the services." When evaluating the *social* consequences of current programs, the Treasury has relied "mainly on the feel of departments, rather than on an objective system of information." By contrast, in evaluating the *economic* consequences of social policies, the Treasury has developed an elaborate methodology showing the economic impact of activities that formally have noneconomic objectives, such as children's allowances or pensions for the elderly.[13]

In the wake of American experience with PPBS (Planning-Programing-Budgeting Systems), the Treasury began to experiment with evaluation research.[14] The result was the establishment of PAR (Program Analysis and Review) under the Heath government. PAR is intended to ask a few fundamental questions about continuing activities of government: What is the object of this program? Should the government be seeking to do this? What are the effects of the existing means to these ends? Can the same resources be employed more efficiently? Could the same end be achieved more efficiently by alternative means? The questions are common sense, yet the answers are by no means easily ascertained, whether one relies on impressionistic feelings or operations-research techniques. No quantitative analysis can be undertaken until objectives are defined in quantitatively measurable terms.[15] This can most easily be done if policy inputs (e.g., spending money) are substituted for social outputs (e.g., building a better community). The novelty and difficulty of PAR work, plus the fact that it must be applied to specific programs rather than broad departmental concerns, have made work proceed slowly since 1970. Because the analysis evaluates the work of identifiable civil servants and ministers, reports are not intended for publication, thus shielding the department concerned with the evaluation from criticism.[16]

To review the impact of government in any particular area

[13] See Her Majesty's Treasury, *Public Expenditure White Papers: Handbook on Methodology* (London: HMSO, 1972), pp. 23; and Eighth Report from the Expenditure Committee, Session 1971–72, *Relationship of Expenditure to Needs* (London: HMSO, 1972), pp. 80 ff.

[14] For examples see S. R. Parker *et al., Effects of the Redundancy Payments Act* (London: HMSO, 1971); and W. B. Reddaway, *Effects of the Selective Employment Tax:* First Report (London: HMSO, 1970).

[15] For difficulties in doing this, see *Report of the Review Committee on Overseas Representation* (London: HMSO, P. P. XLIV, 1968–69), Annexes D, J.

[16] See, e.g., Peter Jay, "PESC, PAR and Politics," *The Times,* January 31, 1972; Sir Richard Clarke, *New Trends in Government,* pp. 42 ff; and Hugh Heclo and Aaron Wildavsky, *The Private Government of Public Money.*

of society, one must attempt to answer a series of questions: What is the intention of government? What actions does the government take? What social conditions are found? What link, if any, is there between government actions and social conditions? One cannot assume that whatever happens in society is the consequence of government action or that actions inevitably have desired (or any) consequences. To array together data about government actions and social conditions is not to argue that correlation proves causation. Many things outside the control of government can alter social conditions, and some policies are intended to prevent conditions from getting worse, rather than to produce positive improvements. The policy areas chosen for review here are topics that constantly recur as major headings in party manifestos, parliamentary debate, public expenditure white papers, and government statistical reports. By reviewing activities since 1951, one can begin to appreciate the dynamic properties of policy, as well as of society. During this period, England experienced the rise of affluence and the first problems of "postindustrial" societies. Given the inadequacy of published information about the impact of specific policies, one may give a little attention to many topics. Incidentally, this illustrates the extent to which the impact of government is not constant from policy area to policy area, but is itself a variable. While no one would claim that individual welfare is solely determined by public policy, the intentions and expenditure of the contemporary British welfare state give a high priority to individual welfare at every stage of the life cycle from birth to old age.

Health. Since World War II, successive governments have declared a positive intention to maintain and improve health conditions. The means to this end include preventive health services, such as prenatal clinics, free milk and vitamins for infants, as well as medical and hospital services virtually free of charge. Spending on health services totals approximately 10 per cent of all public expenditure, and tends to rise. Both parties agree on health objectives, even though they occasionally disagree about the means of policy.

One standard measure of health, the infant mortality rate, has moved substantially downward through the century. The death rate for infant males below the age of one has fallen from 80 per thousand infants in 1931, to 36 in 1951, to 20 in 1971.[17] In the same period, life expectancy rose from 58.4 years for males at birth to 68.5 years in 1969. A similar rise occurred for women, reaching 74.7 years in 1969. Both trends are consistent with the intention of policy makers. Changes in the health of the adult population are not so easily evaluated. The average number of days per year in which workers are certified as ill has risen from 12.8 days in 1953–54 to 16.7 days in 1968–69. In part, this increase reflects changes in the labor force. In addition, higher rates of sickness benefit appear to have encouraged some workers to stay home from work, when previously they would not have done so. A government report characterizes this as "a general increase in the proper use of the national insurance scheme."[18]

Family Size. No British government has had a comprehensive family policy. The Labour government introduced a scheme for family allowances in 1946; this provides weekly cash benefits to parents with two or more children. In 1970, the grant was paid to more than 4,000,000 families. Under the National Health Service, family-planning clinics have increased from 91 in 1950 to 1,039 in 1971. The Abortion Act, 1968, and the Divorce Reform Act of 1968 each have implications for family size.

Birth rates have not altered in response to family allowances. The effective birth rate rose in the 1950s, then fell in the 1960s. The fall may reflect the substantial increase in the number of women attending family-planning clinics, amounting to 735,000 in 1971. The most apparent consequences of changes in family policy are registered in abortion and divorce rates. In 1967, the last full year prior to the Abortion Act, approximately 10,000 abortions were legally performed. The total rose to 133,000 in 1971, most of which could not have been carried out legally prior to the Act. Similarly, the liberalization of

[17] All figures in the subsequent discussion are taken from *Social Trends*, Vol. 3, unless citations appear to other publications.

[18] See F. E. Whitehead, "Trends in Certificated Sickness Absence," *Social Trends*, Vol. 2, pp. 20 f.

divorce laws increased divorces from 2.1 per thousand married people in 1966 to 4.6 per thousand in 1970.

Education. The minimum age for leaving school was raised from fourteen to fifteen in 1944, and to sixteen in 1972. Expenditure on education has risen dramatically in absolute terms and as a proportion of the budget and gross national product, even after allowance is made for the rising numbers of children of school age. The government has sought to encourage more young people to stay at school beyond the minimum age for leaving, so that they could gain a higher educational qualification. The comprehensive schools policy has also been intended to raise educational achievement.

Because school attendance is compulsory, changing the minimum age for leaving has a virtually certain effect. The proportion of young people staying at school voluntarily has increased too. The number and proportion of young people leaving secondary school with good examination results have risen, as have the numbers taking university degrees. Because young people are only a small proportion of the total adult population of England, these changes initially appear of limited significance; their importance is cumulative. It could be argued that government policy is not the cause of more young people's gaining more education, but rather a consequence; governments have expanded educational facilities in response to pressures of student demand. Nonetheless, it is a necessary condition of an increase in university graduates that the government finance the extra university places. Little evidence is yet at hand to assess the effects of the move to comprehensive secondary schools.[19]

Housing. Because of a housing shortage that resulted from bombing in World War II and an inheritance of nineteenth-century houses of low standard, every British government since the war has accepted the need for more new housing, although there have been differences about means to this end and about paying for it.

New housing policies rapidly resulted in changing condi-

[19] See Alan Little, Christine Mabey and Jennifer Russell, "Do Small Classes Help a Pupil?" *New Society*, October 21, 1971.

tions for which government itself was immediately responsible. In 1947, council houses constituted one-twelth of less than 12 million houses in England; by 1966, they constituted one-quarter of a much-increased national stock of houses. In nineteen years council houses had more than quadrupled. The government-sponsored slum clearance program has caused the proportion of families in England living in houses lacking hot water, a fixed bath, and an indoor toilet to drop from almost half in 1951 to one-quarter in the late 1960s.[20] The number living in overcrowded conditions has declined by more than half in the period. This reflects the actions of private builders (often assisted by indirect government subsidies) as well as council house building. In the 1950s and 1960s government targets for new housing were reached, though in the latter instance, not sustained because of economic difficulties.

Employment and Earnings. Since 1944, successive British governments have sought to maintain full employment. Governments have sought to maintain earnings and, since the late 1950s, to assure regularly rising real earnings through continuing economic growth. The governing parties have differed on matters of degree; no party has challenged the desirability of full employment and rising earnings.

Successive governments have kept unemployment rates low for nearly all the postwar period. In 1951 the monthly average rate was 1.2 per cent, in 1961 1.5 per cent, and the same in 1966. The level of unemployment remained low while the labor force grew in size from 22,610,000 in 1951 to 24,857,000 in 1966. In the late 1960s, however, the annual unemployment rate increased, averaging 2.4 per cent in the period from 1967 to 1970, and reaching 3.6 per cent in 1971. This highest figure reflected a conscious government decision to allow unemployment to rise in order to reduce inflationary pressures in the economy.

Earnings of adult male manual workers, the largest group in the labor force, rose by 85 per cent from 1951 to 1961, more than double the increase in the index of retail prices. In the 1961–70 period money earnings doubled, while prices rose by

20 See Constance Rollett, "Housing," p. 306.

half. Because real wages were higher in 1961 than in 1951, the absolute value of the rise in earnings in the 1960s was even higher. In the same period, however, the numbers of the working poor below the official poverty line rose from an estimated 370,000 persons in 1960, less than 1 per cent of the population, to an estimated 2 per cent of the population in 1970.[21]

Leisure. No British government has ever had a comprehensive policy for leisure. To do so might suggest that the whole of a man's life was subject to government regulation. Governments have given greater priority to employment, education, health, and housing policies. In the 1960s, both Labour and Conservative governments began to designate ministers with responsibility for sport and recreation, parks, sports fields, beaches, and similar public facilities. Government decisions on television, cinema taxes, and public holidays also affect how people spend their leisure time.

The extent of leisure is limited by the amount of time spent in work and sleep. The leisure time of male workers has increased slightly in two decades. A 44-hour week, normal in 1951, was replaced by a 40-hour week in the early 1960s; the average hours worked per week was 47.8 in 1951 and 44.7 in 1971. The amount of weekly leisure that a working man enjoys is a function of the amount of overtime worked; the 1971 figure showed a decline in hours worked because economic difficulties limited overtime that year. Leisure has increased through longer holidays with pay. In 1951, 3 per cent of the work force had more than two weeks holiday with pay, but by 1971, 92 per cent were entitled to more than two weeks holiday per year. These changes in the allocation of time between work and leisure result from union-management bargaining.

The Condition of the Elderly. Public care for elderly people dates back to medieval charitable foundations. Today govern-

[21] See Peter Townsend, "A Million More in Poverty since 1966," *The Times,* March 10, 1971.

ment makes provision for the elderly in many different ways: pension payments, flats built especially for the elderly, and health services, home helps, and domiciliary care. Yet whatever provision is made, public officials know that with elderly people, the final result will be ill health and death. The chief government provision is a weekly pension; the parties disagree about how it should be financed, but all political groups recognize its political importance.[22]

The life expectancy of the elderly has risen very slowly in the postwar period, as a persisting consequence of the living conditions experienced by today's elderly during the first four decades of the century. The money value of pensions has risen steadily; it is not limited by prior contributions. In part the increase has followed rising living standards and in part it has been the consequence of inflation. In 1951, a pension was 21.7 per cent of the net average earnings, and in 1968, 26.6 per cent of a much higher level of earnings.[23]

Many of the policies of British government do not concern individual benefits, but collective goods such as military defense, land-use planning, or national economic conditions. Policies concerning collective goods affect people without exclusion, even though their consequences may not be equally desirable for everyone.

Defense and Diplomacy. Since the conclusion of World War II, British governments have undergone a fundamental reorientation in foreign policy. As the costs of being a major world power have escalated, England has declined to a second-rank status, relinquishing claims to influence events by military force or through diplomacy sanctioned by force and massive economic influence. The demission of authority occurred in stages, commencing in 1946, when America was called upon to maintain a balance of power in Greece and Turkey against the Soviet Union, with England accepting a role as a loyal but

22 See Hugh Heclo, "Pensions Politics," *New Society*, September 22, 1971.
23 See Brian Abel-Smith, "Public Expenditure on the Social Services," *Social Trends*, Vol. 1, p. 19.

limited partner. It continued through the conversion of the Empire into the Commonwealth. Entry to the European Common Market in 1973 is meant to provide a positive alternative, making England coequal in a group that can collectively be a significant diplomatic, economic, and military power.

The consequences of this shift in political status can be readily measured in some areas. For example, the proportion of public expenditure devoted to defense and external relations has declined from 24 per cent in 1951 to 18 per cent in 1961 to 13 per cent in 1971. The number of men in the armed services has declined from 827,000 in 1951, when conscription still prevailed, to 368,000 in 1971. In the postwar period, the British Army has fought in only two military conflicts outside the territory of Empire and Commonwealth: the Korean War and the abortive invasion of the Suez Canal. Involvement in Northern Ireland, an integral part of the United Kingdom, has been the British Army's third bloodiest "war" since 1945. A total of 231 men were killed in the first four years of the Army's active presence, a figure exceeded only by casualties in Korea and in Malaya.

Domestic Order. All political parties favor public order; although there are differences between Conservative and Labour MPs on some aspects of crime and punishment, both parties have hesitated to make these differences electoral issues. Public policy has been reformist by reducing the number of antisocial acts classified as crimes, and liberal in substituting fines or short sentences for long-term imprisonment as the usual punishment for many offenses. The total number of police man-hours worked in proportion to the population has remained more or less constant throughout the century.

The level of reported indictable crime has risen from 616,000 incidents in 1951 to 1,858,000 in 1971; the increase is substantial even after allowance is made for changes in the age structure of the population and the greater opportunity to commit such crimes as car theft. The overwhelming proportion of these crimes are theft, burglary, and robbery. The number of murder and manslaughter cases has remained below 500 per annum throughout the two decades; the number of indictable assaults and sexual offenses has increased. In the face of a rising crime rate, the police have managed to retain a constant level of effectiveness, as measured by the ability to clear up cases; the proportion of indictable offenses cleared by the police was 47.1 per cent in 1951 and 45.4 per cent in 1971. The rate of offenses cleared up has been consistently high for crimes against the person, and much lower for crimes against property.[24]

Environmental Planning. The concentration of land ownership in small numbers of families resulted in much private planning of land use before the existence of the welfare state. The Town and Country Planning Act of 1947 greatly extended the planning controls of local authorities, and the review powers of central government. In addition to protecting amenities and land use within urban areas, planning controls have been used by both parties to influence regional developments by a combination of physical constraints and economic incentives. The policies of planning have been adopted with the intent of maintaining full employment in populous areas suffering from industrial decline and of preventing overcrowding in London and the densely populated Southeast of England.

The effects of positive planning measures can be seen most clearly in the environmental field. The level of smoke emission has dropped by two-thirds from 1951 to 1970 in consequence of legislation, and the proportion of river-miles classified as grossly polluted has decreased from 6 per cent to 4 per cent from 1958 to 1970. The road-building program has resulted in safer roads; the numbers of persons killed and seriously injured have increased by three-quarters, while motor-vehicle mileage has increased by three and three-quarters from 1951 to 1971. The number of acres of land classified as "green belt," and thus not available for building around major urban centers has risen to more than 3,500,000 acres by 1972.

In the same period, regional population distribution has

24 See Nigel Walker, "Crime and Penal Measures," in A. H. Halsey, editor, *Trends in British Society since 1900,* pp. 534 ff.

remained relatively constant within England. London and the Southeast had 30.2 per cent of the United Kingdom population in 1951 and 31.1 per cent in 1971. At the same time the North, one of the smallest regions and most affected by persisting unemployment, has had its share of population drop by 0.3 per cent, while showing a slight increase in absolute numbers. The proportional distribution of population has changed very little within English regions in this century, although the effects of absolute population change can produce dispersion problems in an era when housing densities are far lower (another act of government policy) than in 1901. The disparity in the proportions of unemployed between northern and southern England has also declined since 1951, although at times this has been because of a rise in unemployment in the South.

Macroeconomic Policies. The government has sought to manage the economy since World War II. Management of the economy involves a complex set of activities. Two objectives have been of persisting importance throughout the postwar period: economic growth and price stability. The desire to stimulate growth arose first from the need to repair the damages of war and, from the late 1950s, to provide higher living standards and greater resources to finance government policies. Price stability is important not only for domestic considerations, but also because the international exchange value of the pound is particularly sensitive to short-term speculative movements of currency in reaction to inflationary trends. As the flight of funds from London to harder-currency countries could literally bankrupt the Bank of England in a matter of days, this pressure cannot be ignored.

Britain's position as a leading industrial nation has never been based upon a high annual rate of growth, but on the advantage of having a low but steady rate of growth compound for more than a century and one-half.[25] In every decade of the nineteenth century, the average per-annum growth was below

[25] See Phyllis Deane and W. A. Cole, *British Economic Growth, 1688–1959* (Cambridge: University Press, 2nd edition, 1967), Table 73.

2.0 per cent per capita. In the 1948–60 period, the British rate was 2.3 per cent per annum, higher than the United States, but not high by international standards. In the 1960–70 period, when government sought to achieve economic growth at the rate of 4 per cent per annum, the average annual change was 2.9 per cent, a figure lower than the United States (4.0 per cent) and lower than all of the eight countries now joined with Britain in the European Common Market. In reflecting upon the experience of the period, the government's economic adviser, Sir Alec Cairncross, said, "I believe that the direct influence of governments on economic growth is relatively modest and that the common belief to the contrary in this country has been actually pernicious, tempting governments into policies which have had the very reverse effects for which they were designed."[26]

In postwar years (i.e., since 1945) the government's efforts to achieve price stability and maintain the purchasing power of the pound have faltered, both domestically and internationally. The cost of living index rose by 41 per cent from 1951 to 1961. By 1968 prices had risen by 81 per cent in comparison with 1951 – and were still rising. The increase in prices was associated with a decline in the value of the pound. It had an exchange rate of $4.20 until the 1949 devaluation to $2.80; it went to $2.40 in 1967 and was allowed to float to lower levels in 1972. In addition, the use of the bank rate to regulate credit has resulted in an unstable but generally rising rate of interest for persons wishing to borrow money, whether it is for a home purchase or for long-term investment by industry or government.

The impact of government policy is greatest in fields in which responsibility for a collective decision is centralized in its hands, such as levying taxes, or in which it enjoys compulsory powers, like fixing the minimum age for leaving school. This does not mean that government is the only influence upon what happens, but that only the government can decide how conflicting considerations will affect the laws of the land. In

26 *Essays in Economic Management* (London: Allen & Unwin, 1971), p. 21.

many fields, the impact of government policy is substantial, but it cannot claim sole responsibility for changing social conditions. For example, the police have been able to clear up a constant proportion of crime but have not been able to prevent the number of crimes from rising. Police officers would say that the rise in crime is a consequence of social change or of other government policies, whereas the rise in numbers of criminals apprehended reflects the impact of police policy. In some cases, government is more certain that a policy will have an impact than what the impact will be. For example, entry to the European Common Market was intended to have major and multiple consequences. But no government could hope to anticipate all of these consequences, nor could proponents and critics of the Common Market agree about its likely impact. In some areas of life, the impact of government is limited by choice. For example, no British government has promulgated a population policy. In the words of one Cabinet minister, "It would mean a policeman in every bedroom." [27]

It is of little use to evaluate the actions of British government simply in terms of its ability or inability to achieve stated objectives, because "all other conditions" do not remain equal. The world will never hold still; an important part of any government is reacting to information about changes in its environment. One need hardly be surprised if governments fail to reach objectives that are very difficult or simply impossible. In some cases, efforts to carry out a policy may lead to the adoption of means that its original proponents consider undesirable. For example, a campaign to improve the living conditions of gypsies may result in applying coercion to gypsies to make them abandon itinerant caravans and settle in council houses.

It could be argued that the foregoing review (and the works cited therein) do not provide conclusive evidence of the causal significance (or insignificance) of major social policies of British government. The criticism is not only valid but also im-

[27] Reginald Maudling, quoted in David Wood, "Birth of a Population Policy," *The Times,* March 8, 1971.

portant in its implications. To say that social scientists cannot demonstrate the impact of government policies not only shows their limits but also shows the limits of men who act in government, for British government has undertaken little research about the impact of its policies. To say that governors may be unaware of the effects of their policies is not to say that the myriad actions of government are without consequences. The effects of government cannot be hidden from those who experience their impact directly. Busy public officials, greatly burdened with the problems of making and administering policies within the institutions of government, may reckon that the most they can do is carry out the intentions of policy makers. Once they have done this, it is the role of those most directly affected to make what they can of the consequences.

TO WHAT GOOD?

Any attempt to analyze the impact of government on society is likely to start or end as an attempt to evaluate "the good society." The foregoing discussion surveys data relevant to current political controversies, but it does not make assumptions about what constitutes good conditions in society. There can be virtual unanimity within a society about the desired directions of policy. For example, nearly everyone would favor the elimination of infant mortality or illness among people of working age. But this is not to say that everyone would agree about the level of infant mortality or sickness that is good enough in an imperfect world. Some differences reflect conflicts in priorities: Should housing, pensions, or education benefit more from the allocation of society's limited resources? For family planning, theologians and ecologists will disagree about the direction in which public policy ought to point. By definition any social condition that is the subject of political discussion will reveal conflicting opinions about the rate, form, and direction of social change. Political parties provide the most general definition of the aims of government, even though general aspirations are often not linked to particular policy prescriptions.

In a literal sense, Conservatives might be considered to oppose all changes in society, or to prefer the *status quo ante*. In practice, there has been no politically effective group within the Conservative Party since 1945 successfully advocating reactionary policies. Members of the Monday Club and, as an individual, Enoch Powell, from time to time advocate repealing welfare state measures passed by Conservative as well as Labour governments – but with little effect. Within an industrial society and a welfare state, it is difficult to advocate reverting to a preautomotive, nineteenth-century economy. Conservatives dissatisfied with the status quo argue for a "post-welfare state" society.[28]

Within the Conservative Party, there are differences about the extent to which change should be anticipated or accepted only as a last resort. As an implicit premise of many policies, Conservatives expect that the relationships of individuals within society should be altered little. Conservatives are more concerned with society as a whole and less with altering relationships between groups within society. Concern with collective goods is shown by the importance the Conservatives have traditionally given foreign affairs as a "national" good. It is also reflected in the assumption that the benefits of economic growth can be shared by everyone in proportion to their established stake in society. Rising incomes need not change income inequalities, if all incomes rise proportionately.

The Conservative bias toward maintaining existing social relationships shows very clearly in the party's welfare policies. To use the language of Fabian Socialists of another era, the party favors a national minimum for all, provided by the state if necessary. This principle justifies acceptance of welfare programs in such fields as health, education, housing, and pensions. But it also encourages individuals to make provision for their own welfare, above and beyond the national minimum provided all citizens. This can be done through tax allowances and other policies encouraging homeownership, private pensions schemes, the payment of private school fees, and

[28] For a variety of change-oriented but laissez-faire economic views, see publications of the Institute of Economic Affairs, London.

private health insurance. Socialist critics charge that the party encourages people to make private provision for their own welfare by keeping state benefits low. Conservatives reply that only by providing many benefits selectively to those most in need will there be sufficient public resources to meet the many claims for welfare that the modern society makes upon government.[29]

Within the labor movement, there are differences about priorities for the good society. These differences on priorities reflect differences in philosophy.[30] As Aneurin Bevan once said, "The language of priorities is the religion of Socialism." Those who enunciate different priorities adhere to conflicting versions of a Socialist faith. The difficulties of the 1964–70 Labour government highlighted these differences. Revisionist Socialists have argued that the best way to improve the social conditions of the English people is by a rapidly rising rate of economic growth. Many policies can be viewed in terms of their likely contribution to growth. This can provide the resources to increase the quality and range of public provision for social betterment. In distributing benefits, a Labour government should favor poorer members of the community and ask those who benefit most in absolute terms to contribute most to rising government expenditure. The principle of redistribution is already institutionalized in the progressive income tax. Because greater public spending is meant to be financed by growth, there is no necessity to take anything away from any section of society, rich, poor, or of average income. In 1964 Harold Wilson campaigned with the claim that Socialist planning itself provided the best basis for economic growth. The record of his government has been variously interpreted as casting doubt upon the efficacy of Socialism, Wilson's status as a Socialist, or both.

An alternative Socialist vision emphasizes equality. While

[29] The pamphlets of the Bow Group and its quarterly, *Crossbow*, contain a variety of articles and Conservative points of view.

[30] Publications of the Fabian Society present a variety of Socialist viewpoints. See also the periodicals *Socialist Commentary*, London, and *Tribune*, London.

equality of opportunity is not distinctly Socialist, equality of achievement is. Equality of opportunity is likely to lead to inequality of achievement, insofar as natural abilities are randomly (that is, not evenly) distributed within the population, and the motivation to make use of opportunities is affected by family and other circumstances outside the influence of government policy. In pursuit of equality of achievement, government may be urged to discriminate positively on behalf of those least likely to succeed in conditions of equality of opportunity. For example, state nursery schools may be provided for children living in slum areas before they are made available to children living in pleasant middle-class suburbs.

Equality is not an individual benefit, like a minimum wage. Instead, it is a collective good, reflecting the relationship of one citizen to another. From this perspective, raising the standards of the lowly is but one part of the task of governing; "preventing the more prosperous sections from benefiting disproportionately from increases in public expenditure" is another.[31] In principle, egalitarian objectives could be achieved without any economic growth, by taxation and other policies forcing the redistribution of the existing sum of national income. For its part, growth may not encourage egalitarianism, for a 10 per cent increase in earnings for a man making £40 a week is £4, whereas it is worth £8 to a man making £80 a week. The Labour Party has always been more concerned with equality of status than with equality of income; many Socialists argue that equality of status is both more important and more readily achieved than income equality. The comprehensive-schools policy is a characteristic Labour means of encouraging equality of status.

The Labour government's record from 1964 to 1970 showed the difficulties of achieving greater well-being through economic growth, as well as the difficulties of achieving greater equality by redistributive social policies. Problems showed up not only in the slight change in income differentials between manual and nonmanual workers during this period, but also

[31] Peter Townsend and Nicholas Bosanquet, editors, *Labour and Inequality,* p. 8.

in the insistence of one part of the labor movement, the trade unions, upon maintaining income inequality as between groups of manual workers.[32]

Debates about the particularities of welfare policy should not obscure the fundamental importance of differing criteria of choice. Whatever the circumstances, a proponent of proportional change will always prefer a policy that least disturbs relationships among individuals in society. An egalitarian will regard as good changes in the distribution as well as in the sum total of benefits. Though differences in values are absolute, in specific political situations most politicians are concerned with degrees of difference. Few Conservatives would claim that their party could govern without causing some changes in English society. Likewise, few Socialists would expect the next Labour government so to transform society that one-half the work force would no longer have less than the median income, and the other half more.

Since debates between political theorists concern the conditions of ordinary people as well as intellectuals, it is relevant to examine how ordinary people evaluate the society in which they live. Measuring levels of social satisfaction is difficult, because of differences between individual criteria and differences in the intensity with which people hold their views.

The survey evidence reviewed in Chapter IV showed that in the most fundamental matters of political legitimacy – support for authority and compliance with its laws – Englishmen give allegiance to their regime. But it would be misleading to infer from this that people are necessarily satisfied with everything that government does, just as it would be misleading to infer political disaffection from dissatisfaction with social conditions. Englishmen may write angry letters to the newspaper or demonstrate against housing conditions, but they do not react rebelliously like their neighbors in Northern Ireland.

Popular satisfaction or dissatisfaction with a wide variety of

[32] Cf. Wilfred Beckerman, editor, *The Labour Government's Economic Record, 1964–1970;* Peter Townsend and Nicholas Bosanquet, editors, *Labor and Inequality;* and, for a long-term historical analysis, see Guy Routh, *Occupation and Pay in Great Britain, 1906–60* (Cambridge: University Press, 1965).

TABLE XI.4 *Social Satisfaction by Class, 1973 (in percentages)*

Satisfied with	Total		Satisfied	
	Satisfied	Dis-satisfied	Middle class	Working class
The work you do	71	14	80	65
The leisure you have	71	26	71	71
Your housing	71	26	80	65
Your standard of living	64	33	77	56
Childrens' education	54	20	59	52
Your family income	49	47	59	42
The future facing your family	47	34	55	43
Britain's world position	27	64	30	26
Honesty and behavior of people in this country today	21	69	23	19

Source: Unpublished figures from a Gallup Poll survey, February 1973.

social conditions was the focus of a Gallup Poll survey in February, 1973. The survey was well timed to record dissatisfaction, for it occurred when voters were responding negatively to both parties at by-elections. It also came after a decade of media discussion of the question: "What's wrong with Britain?"

The replies show a high level of satisfaction with many features of life in England today, including many conditions for which government accepts responsibility. An absolute majority express satisfaction with five of the nine conditions surveyed: work, leisure, housing, standards of living, and education. A plurality are satisfied with their income and future prospects (Table XI.4). On only two points are a majority dissatisfied. Dissatisfaction with England's place in the world is understandable, given the decline of the country's great power status. What is especially noteworthy is that most Englishmen show the highest level of dissatisfaction with their fellow citizens, regretting the standards of honesty and behavior in the country today.[33]

When levels of satisfaction are examined separately by class,

[33] The attitudes expressed have been stable at least since 1970. See Gallup Poll, *Political Index,* No. 151 (February 1973), p. 39.

middle-class people consistently show a slightly higher average level of satisfaction. The average difference between the level of satisfaction of middle- and working-class people is 11 per cent. It is greatest for those areas of life most closely related to occupation: standards of living, family income, housing, and job satisfaction. Because the differences are limited in size, there is no basis for depicting the middle-class respondent as satisfied and the working-class respondent as dissatisfied. Englishmen in each class are satisfied with a majority of conditions in their society today. They also agree about what they don't like; both rank as their chief dislike the behavior of their fellow citizens.

When the same Gallup respondents are asked whether "people like yourself have enough say" in major institutions of contemporary society, a different picture emerges (Table XI.5). At no point does a majority express satisfaction with its voice in society. A total of 23 per cent said they thought people like

TABLE XI.5 *Social Influence by Class, 1973 (in percentages)*

Do people like yourself have enough say in:	*Total*		*Proportion saying yes*	
	Yes	*No*	*Middle class*	*Working class*
Services in shops	44	46	49	41
The education of their children	41	40	45	38
Working conditions	30	48	37	25
How newspapers present news	26	58	28	25
Policies of employers	25	52	33	20
Television programs of BBC	25	66	28	23
Policies of trade unions	22	59	22	22
Television programs of ITV	24	65	26	23
How local authorities handle things	24	68	29	21
How the government runs the country	23	71	29	18
How banks and building societies operate	21	51	27	18
Services of the nationalized industries	17	73	19	16

Source: Unpublished figures from a Gallup Poll survey, February 1973.

themselves had enough say in the way the government runs the country, but 71 per cent believe the opposite. The dissatisfied include a majority of supporters of the governing Conservative party, as well as a majority of opposition supporters.

Middle-class and working-class Englishmen agree about their lack of influence. In none of the replies to twelve questions did a majority in either class consider that people like themselves had enough say in what was done. While working-class people are consistently less likely to see themselves able to influence major social institutions, the differences between them and middle-class people are consistently small. The average is 7 per cent, less than the differences found between classes in reply to questions about satisfaction with life.[34]

The dissatisfactions that Englishmen express today do *not* arise from material concerns. The majority of Englishmen show a high degree of satisfaction with many basic conditions of life. Even if one cannot state precisely the impact of public policies on employment, housing, and standards of living, the governors of England's mixed-economy welfare state can claim, with an expectation of popular agreement, that their efforts have had a positive effect upon popular well-being.

What Englishmen are dissatisfied about today is a perceived lack of individual influence upon the major collective institutions of contemporary society. This dissatisfaction is "political" in the board sense of the term. It is not a negative judgement about what major social institutions do; instead, it is a negative judgment about how these institutions are controlled. To suggest that large organizations are a concomitant of large-scale industrial society, and inevitably have a degree of oligarchy, may be empirically accurate. But it does not answer the normative complaint that this ought not to be the case.

While the dissatisfactions expressed are political, it does not follow that Englishmen wish the government to intervene to increase popular influence upon extragovernmental institutions in society. There can be little popular expectation of government's providing a remedy, when 71 per cent think that

[34] Dissatisfaction is not dependent upon party control of government; similar responses were obtained in a survey reported in *Ibid.*, June, 1969, p. 37.

people like themselves do not have enough influence upon the way central government runs the country, 68 per cent see themselves with insufficient influence upon local government, and 73 per cent see themselves without enough influence upon the conduct of nationalized industries. The countervailing power of trade unions and large financial institutions is not seen as adequate to promote popular influence, for a majority of Englishmen think that people like themselves do not have enough influence upon these central economic institutions. For the same reason, an increase in the flow of information through the mass media also appears insufficient.

The problem facing both governors and governed is how to combine the advantages of centralized authority – in economic and social institutions, as well as in the highly centralized government of Britain – with popular demands for greater influence.[35] Because a sense of little influence is found among young and old, middle-class and working-class, men and women, and Conservative as well as Labour voters, there can be no certainty about the direction of the impact upon society of new procedures intended to increase popular influence. While increasing participation is often considered radical, the preferences of the populace – especially on humanitarian issues – are not what is conventionally termed liberal or radical in England. (See Table IX.2, p. 304).

[35] Cf. Samuel Brittan, *Capitalism and the Permissive Society* (London: Macmillan, 1973); John Gyford and Stephen Haseler, *Social Democracy: Beyond Revisionism;* and contributions by Jo Grimond, Geraint Parry, and Anthony Barker to "Community Politics: a Discussion," in *Government and Opposition,* VII:2 (1972).

CHAPTER XII

A Changing England?

It is needful to keep the ancient show while we secretly interpolate the new reality.

ANY SPECULATION about a changing England is conditioned by what is expected to alter when politics changes.[1] Focusing upon institutions might lead one to argue that there has been no "fundamental" change in England since the Glorious Revolution of 1688, or even since the Norman Conquest. An electoral focus might suggest that every election that results in a change in the governing party inaugurates a "new" politics. In this chapter, three topics particularly merit attention: institutions, policies, and political values. Changes in one dimension of politics do not necessarily require changes in another. For example, England could turn from a monarchy into a republic with little alteration in public policies. Similarly, the persistence of an institution in name does not mean that nothing of consequence has altered. For example, Parliament today is far different from what it was a century ago, and the consequences of nationalizing an industry today are different from what was perceived twenty-five years ago.

Policy changes can be grouped into three categories: nominal, ordinal, and continuous. The biggest changes are nom-

[1] For a general discussion of the topic, see Richard Rose, *People in Politics,* Ch. 8.

inal, a change in kind. For example, the reaction against immigrants represents a new way of thinking about British citizens in terms of color not class. Some changes occur at precise points in time: the signature of a treaty or the enactment of an Act of Parliament. But often changes that cumulatively result in discontinuity – for example, Labour replacing the Liberals as the alternative governing party – take decades to accomplish.

Many changes of great political importance reflect changes best measured in orders of magnitude. For example, British government had been providing some health services prior to the passage of the National Health Service Act in 1946. But the service thereby established was different in scale from what went before. The increasing value that British governments have placed upon economic growth since the early 1960s does not mean that previous governments were uninterested in expanding national wealth. It reflects a big shift in the relative priorities of British government, as between economic growth with its attendant frictions and troubles, and economic stability with its attendant constraints.

The everyday issues of politics often concern small increments of change across a long continuum of choice. Typically, welfare policies involve changing the money value of a benefit by 5 or 10 per cent. Changes in the rate of economic growth are measured in tenths of 1 per cent. Small changes along a continuum provide the best opportunity for compromise; for instance, in a debate about whether pensions should be increased 5 per cent or 10 per cent, an increase of 7½ per cent is a readily available alternative.

Some political changes have a special significance, because they are irreversible. For instance, once a government has declared war, in a literal sense it can never go back to exactly what it was before. Politics in England at the end of World War I was different from that at the outbreak of that war; the same thing happened after World War II. Many policies are virtually irreversible, because of the strength of cultural values. For example, it would be legally possible to take away the vote from women or persons below a given income. But no party hoping for political success would conceivably advocate this. Similarly, it would be legally possible to deport all non-white English residents. But practical as well as moral objections make it very unlikely that England will return to the status of an all-white society.

By contrast, some political changes are cyclical, like the movement of the Conservative and Labour parties in and out of office. There is no pendulum-like regularity to their movements, but there is a pattern of ups and downs in the fortunes of the two parties since 1945. In economics, governments since the war have moved back and forth between policies giving priority to economic growth, and those giving priority to a favorable balance of payments and price stability. The inflation-deflation cycle is aptly known as a "stop-go" policy. Within the lifetime of a single Parliament, the relationships between the Cabinet and its supporters are likely to fluctuate too, according to the government's successes and failures. In each instance, the existence of a pair of alternatives – to return to a previous position, or to maintain the current position – offers harassed policy makers a choice that ceases to exist, once irreversible decisions have been made. It may also signify that the net result of many changes back and forth will cancel out, as wages and prices overtake each other in a spiral of competition, or as floating voters first give the Conservatives, then Labour their favor.

CONSTRAINTS UPON CHANGE

Few political changes take place with the quickness with which a Prime Minister can be changed by a general election. Yet this event, occurring hours after the result is conceded, does not alter everything about the control of government. It takes several days for a Cabinet to be formed, months for ministers to become familiar with their new departments and substantially longer for them to leave an imprint upon that work. Once new men enter office, they may find themselves more changed than the government, for constraints upon policy do not disappear with a new Cabinet.

Parliament, Cabinet, and the civil service are shaped by laws, customs, and conventions, these can only gradually be altered. Even a revolution would not result in a new statute book overnight. At most, it would only repudiate an existing regime. Unwritten customs and conventions embodied in cultural and role expectations are further constraining influences. Laws, if necessary, can be rewritten in a day; the customs and conventions of government cannot be changed in a day, because they are embedded in the minds of men. Politicians and partisans share cultural beliefs that make many political changes literally unthinkable.

When slogans of change are on many lips, "sitting tight" is a posture that speaks louder than words. This is best illustrated by proposals to reform the civil service. The appointment of the Fulton Committee in 1966 to examine the structure, recruitment, and management of the civil service reflected a widely felt desire – within and outside Whitehall – for changes in an institution that had last been the subject of major structural reform in the nineteenth century. Yet the desire for change did not mean a wholesale rejection of existing methods of public administration. First, there was a conscious desire to maintain positively valued features of the civil service, such as its reputation for financial probity and nonpartisanship. Second, there was a desire to minimize the effect of disruptions upon the clients of the civil service. Routine and precedent provide predictable and economical ways of dispatching its great volume of detailed work. Third, the hundreds of thousands of civil servants with permanent pensionable positions could not be fired or moved about at will, without violating contractual obligations. Fourth, the civil servants placed in charge of change themselves reflect outlooks developed in their previous work in the civil service. The first Permanent Secretary of the "reforming" Civil Service Department, Sir William Armstrong, had already been in Whitehall for thirty years, and had started learning his job in the very different climate of Whitehall between the wars. The first individuals recruited to the "reformed" administrative ranks in 1971 are, by the normal process of seniority, likely to reach very senior posts in government only after the year 2000.

What applies to the civil service also applies to other aspects of the executive branch of government. The device of a

Prime Minister and Cabinet is an eighteenth-century "innovation," and ministerial responsibility a nineteenth-century doctrine. The consequences of such institutions and conventions have changed substantially through time; their continued existence inhibits change. The idea that Cabinet ministers should answer to the House of Commons greatly restricts the range of persons who can be asked to direct the actions of the governing party. Local government can be altered without any cumbersome procedure of constitutional amendment; only an Act of Parliament is required. In 1945, Winston Churchill's government established a commission to review a major part of the subject. Commissions continued to sit and report for more than two decades. The "reformed" local government will not be instituted throughout England until 1974. Changes in the House of Lords move at a similarly slow tempo. The future of the House of Lords has been debated ever since its powers to obstruct legislation were greatly curbed in 1911. The hereditary basis of the Lords remains unaltered. Changes in the House of Commons have been more numerous but not so great as to destroy continuity with the past. Sir T. Erskine May's guide, *The Law, Privileges, Proceedings and Usage of Parliament,* first published in 1844, remains, in its suitably amended 18th edition, the standard work on the Commons. The most visible changes, for instance, the frequent alteration of the names of Whitehall departments, do not alter activities or personnel, but reshuffle units among departments and ministers, or simply alter the department's letterhead.

The conditions of society at a given point in time constitute additional constraints upon change. However great the intended change, policy makers must start from what is already there. The governors of England may long for the freedom from international economic and diplomatic commitments that small but prosperous neutral countries enjoy. Economists struggling with the problems of "remodernizing" the world's first industrial nation may long for the advantages of developing new industries without the incubus of declining ones. Ecologists may contrast unfavorably the density of population in England with the dispersion of population in Canada or

Sweden. In the foreseeable future, at least, these ideas must be classified as wishful thinking. There is no escaping the immediate fact: England is a large, old industrial society, greatly involved in affairs outside its boundaries.

In time, almost anything can be changed. The island of Britain may even be joined to the Continent of Europe by a bridge, tunnel, or a land passage. Other things that once seemed more farfetched may occur even sooner. The longer the time taken to alter conditions of English life through political action, the greater the delay in realizing benefits. To politicians concerned with immediate events, this may be argument against action. To those concerned with future generations, it may be an argument for beginning work today, so that at least posterity may enjoy the benefits.

The time required for government policy to have an impact varies from issue area to issue area. To think of issues in terms of time required for change might put them in the following order:

Immediately changeable. Many features of the economy for which the government is responsible can (or must) be altered quickly. This is most notably true of the bank rate and other determinants of the exchange value of the pound. If not forestalled, a run on the pound can literally bankrupt the Bank of England in a matter of days.

Changeable in a few months. The public esteem of political leaders and parties can rise or fall significantly in a few months. These fluctuations, reflecting very crude political judgments, occur at a much faster rate than parties, institutions, or the basic personalities of politicians change. The 1970 British general election provided an especially vivid demonstration of this. In January, the Labour Party trailed the Conservatives substantially in all five opinion polls, only to be ahead in all the polls in May, and on the losing side when the election result was declared in mid-June.[2]

Changeable in up to five years. An Act of Parliament

[2] See Richard Rose, editor, *The Polls and the 1970 Election* (Glasgow: Strathclyde Survey Research Centre Occasional Paper No. 7, 1970).

normally takes several years from the point at which a minister decides that a bill should be prepared to formal enactment. Consultations must be undertaken with affected pressure groups, with the administrators responsible for the bill, and with lawyers concerned with the language of the statute. The Cabinet must give the measure priority in the queue for legislation, and Parliament will require several months to discuss and propose amendments. Once the bill is enacted, administrators require time to implement the new measure, and the public must become accustomed to it. Because a government need not call a general election more than once every five years, there is time for a newly elected governing party to establish a substantial legislative record. But if it does not commence this work within eighteen months of its election, it is unlikely to have time to see its measures through before once again risking its future with the electorate.

Changeable in a decade. Many major activities of government require substantial time to plan and implement, as well as time to secure formal authorization by Cabinet. A particularly long time is required for major capital investment programs for such things as school buildings, hospitals, or roads. For example, to help meet the rising demand for university education, six new universities were founded in England between 1961 and 1965. Because each literally commenced on a "green field" site, growth came slowly. By 1971, the largest had 3,500 students and the smallest 2,100. These universities were smaller than the institutions antedating them. It was the expansion of established institutions, rather than the creation of new universities, that accommodated the bulk of the rising student population in England in the first decade of great university expansion.

Changeable in a generation or more. Any proposal to alter society by altering education can require a generation to take effect, as the first cohort of beneficiaries moves from nursery schools to adult life. Life-expectancy rates cannot show the full effect of the National Health Service until well after the year 2000, when for the first time the whole population will consist of persons who have had its benefits all their lives. Inasmuch as many individuals maintain lifelong party loyalties, their deaths and the maturing of a new generation are required to alter partisan dispositions of a substantial proportion of society.

The extent to which governments see themselves constrained may be indicated by examining public-expenditure forecasts. The Labour government of Harold Wilson entered office with a series of commitments to increase public expenditure greatly. In 1969 it estimated that it could raise the level of public expenditure by 37 per cent, measured in constant prices, from fiscal 1964–65 to 1970–71. The following year the Conservatives entered office with the intention of strictly regulating the level of public expenditure. In 1972 the Conservative government forecast that instead of remaining constant, public expenditure would rise by 17 per cent from 1971–72 to 1976–77.[3] The Labour government found that it faced a ceiling upon what it could spend, because of limits of resources. The Conservative government found that demand pressures required it to increase public spending, even though it would have preferred not to do this. The 20 per cent gap between the Labour and Conservative estimates of increased expenditure indicates approximately the extent to which governments consider they have room for maneuver, within overriding political constraints.

Present initiation of change can become a constraint upon future choice. For example, the dedication of a large land area to a new airport will prevent the land around it from being used for housing or recreation in the future. A decision to build new houses will not only change the nation's present housing stock but also, once the houses are built, constrain the future housing stock. Council flats normally require sixty years of useful life before the initial investment can be justified by the Treasury. This means that even if a change in government policy, architectural design, or social evaluation makes a particular form of building, such as high-rise flats, undesirable ten years after they are built, tenants are likely to remain in them for another half-century. New hospitals,

[3] See Cmnd. 4234 (HMSO, 1969); and Cmnd. 5178 (HMSO, 1972).

schools, and roads also become a part of the nation's accumulated future stock of social capital. Constraints upon change can thus provide a floor as well as a ceiling for social conditions a decade hence.

PRESSURES FOR CHANGE

The first problem of any government is not how to change policies, but how to meet existing commitments. As commitments become difficult to meet in a given policy area, the argument for changing policy gains in strength. Whatever the government does, the consequences of policy will not remain constant, because of alterations in the environment that the government seeks to influence. The forces for change differ greatly in strength, speed, direction, and, not least, in predictability.

Demographic change is the most inevitable force altering society, and among the hardest for a government to control by legislation. An increase of 10 per cent in the population means that the economy must expand by 10 per cent in order to keep constant the gross national product per capita. Problems increase disproportionately, if population growth occurs among children and the elderly; the dependent portions of the population place pressures upon schools, hospitals, and geriatric services. Table XII.1 illustrates the importance of both absolute and relative changes in population. Between 1931 and 1941, the population of the United Kingdom increased by 2.2 million people, but the number of children fell by a million, thus reducing the need for educational services. In the following three decades, the number of children increased by one-third from the 1941 level; an extra 3.4 million children require schools, and the proportion of youthful dependents in society has risen too. In the past forty years, both the absolute number and the proportion of pensionable people have almost doubled. In consequence, the proportion of people of working age in the population has fallen by one-tenth even though their absolute number has increased.

Population trends create pressures to provide more of the same public services (expanding universities in the 1960s) or more of different services (expanding nonuniversity forms of

TABLE XII.1 *The Changing Age Structure of the United Kingdom, 1931–2001*

Year	*School age 0–14*		*Working age 15–64*[a]		*Pension age 65 plus*[a]		*Total (Millions of people)*
	Millions of people	%	*Millions of people*	%	*Millions of people*	%	
1931	11.1	24.3	30.5	66.1	4.4	9.6	46.0
1941	10.1	21.0	32.5	67.2	5.7	11.8	48.2
1951	11.4	22.5	32.3	63.9	6.9	13.6	50.6
1961	12.3	23.3	33.0	62.1	7.7	14.6	53.0
1971	13.5	24.2	33.3	59.8	8.9	16.0	55.7
1981 (projection)	13.5	23.2	34.6	60.0	9.6	16.8	57.7
2001 (projection)	15.2	23.5	38.5	61.5	9.5	15.0	63.1

Source: *Social Trends*, Vol. 3, p. 59.
[a]For women, pension age begins at 60.

further education in the 1970s). Doing nothing in response to population change also has consequences. If demand rises more quickly than supply, the scarcity value of higher education or a bed in a home for the elderly will increase. The population forecasts for 1981 indicate that demands for government services will level off from children of primary school age, but the demands of the elderly will rise, though less steeply than in the decade 1961–1971.

The forecast population rise from 1971 to the year 2001 is 13.3 per cent, a lesser rate of growth than in the preceding thirty years. This news, while welcomed by planners concerned with pressures on national resources, is no more than a provisional estimate.[4] It is the lowest of a range of possibilities, from 63.1 million to 74.6 million Britons by the year 2000. The accuracy of the forecast depends upon the time period chosen. The further into the future one looks, the greater the allowance that must be made for error. For example, about four-fifths of England's 1981 population was already born at the time the 1971 projections were made, but only about half of the population that will be here at the turn of the next century is yet born.

Changes in population occur, even when aggregate numbers remain constant; each decade, millions of elderly Englishmen die, and millions of children become adult citizens. At the 1970 general election, the median voter had been born about 1925. The passing of the elderly steadily and inexorably removes those who have firsthand experience of England's role as a world power prior to World War I. The entry of new cohorts of young people to the ranks of adult citizens increases the proportion who have no personal experience of the general strike, the interwar depression, World War II, or any period when affluence was not the expectation of most people in society.

Family, older friends, and established adult institutions of society constitute important pressures for continuity in the

[4] See Jean Thompson, "The Growth of Population to the End of the Century," *Social Trends,* Vol. 1 (1970); cf. Colin Stewart, "The Hazards of Population Forecasts," *New Society,* September 23, 1971.

attitudes of different generations of Englishmen. The age profile of English society shows that young people cannot dominate it by their numbers. Young adults, like the elderly, are one among many minorities. Unlike the elderly, young people are not likely to have adopted political attitudes based upon experience or had time for experience to confirm their views. Hence, they are potentially changeable, even volatile. But young people may change their attitudes, as they experience marriage, raising a family, and other problems of subsequent stages in the life cycle.

Of immediate political relevance is the existence or extent of a "generation gap" in politics, that is, a difference in the political outlooks of the young, as against the middle-aged and elderly voters. The greater preference of young people for the Labour party and of the elderly for the Conservatives cannot be taken as proof of major differences in outlook, because partisans can disagree among themselves about policies. A better measure of the potential generation gap is provided by comparing differences in the political attitudes of age groups with differences in the attitudes of Conservative and Labour supporters. If generation differences have become a major basis for political disputes, then age differences in political attitudes should be greater than party differences.

The attitudes of young and old Englishmen can be compared on ten issues for which data have already been presented about partisan outlooks (Table XII.2). Party differences are greater on five issues, and age differences greater on another five issues. Party differences are much stronger than age differences on two major economic issues: steel nationalization and entry to the Common Market. Young and old people differ most notably on two issues concerning life style rather than economic matters: abortion and commercial "pop" radio. It is particularly noteworthy that party differences are stronger than age differences on comprehensive schools, a question on which young people might be expected to have a particularly distinctive outlook. Party differences have been stronger than age differences for many years. When Butler and Stokes asked a national sample their views about six economic and welfare issues in 1964, party differences were greater than age on five

TABLE XII.2 *Policy Preferences by Age and Party (in percentages)*[a]

Policy preferred	Age			Party			Most significant difference
	Young	Old	Difference	Con.	Lab.	Difference	
Steel nationalization	25	18	7	4	46	42	Party 35
Common Market	44	34	10	60	24	36	Party 26
Comprehensive schools	57	30	27	32	61	29	Party 2
Internment in Ulster	61	46	15	67	45	22	Party 7
Colored immigrants going	54	70	16	67	56	11	Age 5
Britain remaining world power	31	43	12	45	35	10	Age 2
Hanging to punish murder	81	88	7	89	80	9	Party 2
More controls of political demonstrations	77	88	11	85	81	4	Age 7
1967 Abortion Act	58	30	28	48	47	1	Age 27
Commercial radio	57	17	40	41	40	1	Age 39

Sources: As cited in Table IX.2, this book.
[a]Young category usually includes ages 21–35; old, 65 plus.

of the six issues: nationalization, trade-union power, strikes, the power of big business, and pensions and social services. Because the attitudes of middle-aged Englishmen, the median group in the adult population, consistently fall between the young and the old, the "destabilizing" effect of age differences is further diminished. Only if the axis of political debate turned to divide voters along life style rather than welfare and economic issues might politics become a contest between generations, rather than parties.[5]

Economic activities constitute another inexorable pressure for political change. Even nil economic growth means change, because economics is about the continuing transformation of resources into goods. The importance of international trade to England makes it particularly sensitive to changes in world markets. Some major export industries have declined greatly in this century. For example, in 1913 Britain exported 73 million tons of coal and in 1971, 2.6 million tons. Similarly, the export of printed cotton goods declined from 1,230 million square yards in 1913 to 416 million in 1935, and 57 million in 1971. Some industries, such as shipbuilding, have experienced enormous short-term fluctuations in their trade. Concurrently, new industries have developed as prominent export earners. For example, in 1913 Britain exported 7,500 automobiles; in 1935, 43,900; and in 1971, 721,000. In 1954 the *Annual Abstract of Statistics* did not give any entry for exports of man-made fibers; in 1960, 49 million pounds were exported, rising to 212 million by 1971.[6] Changes in the terms of trade can have great political impact, even though the volume of exports and imports remains constant. If the cost of imports falls relative to the price of exports, this strengthens the exchange value of the pound and benefits the economy generally. If the price of imports rises relative to the price of exports, this has an adverse effect on government

5 See Philip Abrams and Alan Little, "The Young Voter in British Politics," in Richard Rose, editor, *Studies in British Politics;* and Ronald Inglehart, "The Silent Revolution in Europe", *American Political Science Review,* LXV:4 (1971).

6 Data from the chapter on External Trade in relevant volumes of the *Annual Abstract of Statistics.*

economic policy. The influences determining the terms of trade are largely outside the control of British government, and can alter greatly on short notice.

Within the domestic economy, movements in wages and prices have strong "destabilizing" effects upon government economic policy. Reciprocally, government policy may reduce or accelerate these movements. For example, the index of weekly wage earnings for industrial workers stood at 100 in 1930 and 196 at the end of the war in 1945. It has continued to rise since. By 1968 earnings in current money values were eight times the level of 1930, and double that of 1955. Prices too have risen, but not so greatly. The cost-of-living index has moved from 100 in 1930 to 236 in 1955, and 356 in 1968.[7] The limited success of Conservative and Labour governments in efforts to stop the upward wage-price spiral emphasize the extent to which governments react to rather than determine economic changes.

The entry of Britain to the European Common Market is an extreme example of a political action intended to force economic and social change; in turn, this is likely to have a political feedback, affecting both the conduct of government and the actions of parties and voters. The expected consequences of British entry are multiple. Proponents and opponents of the Common Market disagree about whether they will cause a change for the better or for the worse. Skeptics wonder whether any external economic union can alter the fundamental problems facing British government today.

The biggest potential political change is also the most remote: the merger of British sovereignty in a supranational European institution. Federalists are the first to assert that the institutions of the contemporary European Common Market are far from the federalist ideal. England is not alone among Community members in its wish to preserve sovereign powers, while concurrently enjoying advantages from pooling resources and responsibilities for limited political purposes. The immediate political consequence of British entry to the

[7] For details, see A. H. Halsey, editor, *Trends in British Society since 1900,* pp. 121–22.

Common Market is that many home civil servants, long accustomed to think only of the domestic implications of their policies, will have to begin to "think European" that is, consider to what extent national policies harmonize within the Common Market. Whitehall officials directly involved in Common Market negotiations with representatives of eight other sovereign nations will have to accept that there is more than one locus for decision making affecting politics in England. Striking a bargain with the French and Germans on farm-price supports is different from striking a bargain with the National Farmers' Union. Short of withdrawing from the Common Market, British government will not be able to pass an Act of Parliament overriding Common Market regulations that are valid under Britain's treaty of accession. English judges may be asked to undertake a task that they have heretofore avoided: determining the validity of an Act of Parliament. As long as the law of the Community primarily concerns commercial matters, the supremacy of Community law will be of restricted popular significance; potentially, it is of considerable import.[8]

COPING WITH CHANGE

The inevitability of change does not necessarily make it easy to cope with. *After* the event, many decisions look easy or obvious. But politics concerns actions taken in times of uncertainty. In retrospect, it may appear inevitable that Britain would have to devalue the pound in the face of economic difficulties of the 1960s. Yet arguments among economists, among administrators, and between and within parties carried on for years. Immediately after the election of a Labour government in October, 1964, Harold Wilson decreed that it was "impossible" to consider devaluation. In the event, the only thing that proved impossible was maintaining the estab-

[8] See, e.g., Sir Leslie Scarman, "Law and Administration" and Sir Christopher Soames, "Whitehall into Europe," both in *Public Administration,* L (Autumn 1972); *First Report from the Select Committee on European Community Secondary Legislation* (London: HMSO, 1973); and Helen Wallace, *The EEC: Parliaments in Community Decision-Making* (London: Chatham House: PEP European Series No. 21, 1973).

lished exchange rate. Even when devaluation was forced, the rate at which the pound was pegged to the dollar was a matter of choice.

Introducing political change is costly in terms of time, money, and, not least, political controversy. Therefore, every British government must allow many policies to carry on unexamined, in order to have time to concentrate upon a few initiatives of its own and react to events that require immediate response. The Fulton Report aptly describes how Whitehall copes with policies on a routine basis:

> The operation of existing policies and the detailed preparation of legislation with the associated negotiations and discussions frequently crowd out demands that appear less immediate. Civil servants, particularly members of the Administrative Class, have to spend a great deal of their time preparing explanatory briefs, answers to parliamentary questions, and ministers' cases. Generally this work involves the assembly of information to explain to others (civil servants, outside bodies and so on) the policies of the department, how they are operating and how they apply in particular cases. Almost invariably, there are urgent deadlines to be met in this kind of work. In this press of daily business, long-term policy planning and research tend to take second place.[9]

Even when the intention of the government is no more than maintaining the status quo, say, existing levels of economic growth and unemployment, governors find that they must run hard to remain in the same place. One reason for this is that these conditions can change without any conscious government intent, as an indirect consequence of other policies. Another reason is that delays in the flow of information to government may cause administrators to persist in policies long after they have ceased to have their desired effect. A former government economic adviser, describing the problem of monitoring routine policies, has said "the hardest thing to forecast is where you are now." [10]

[9] The Fulton Committee, Vol. 1, p. 57.

[10] Lord Roberthall, quoted in Sir Alec Cairncross, *Essays in Economic Management*, p. 129.

The ability of British government to act and act successfully in response to unexpected change is best shown by government in wartime. Both World Wars I and II imposed many burdens upon a Whitehall machine unprepared for a long war. Both wars also involved the mobilization of civilians as an important part of the war effort. State intervention undertaken in wartime had important carry-over effects in the peace years that followed. Wartime brought new institutions, such as the Cabinet Secretariat and Central Statistical Office, as well as expanding greatly the services of the welfare state. But wartime government provides ambiguous tribute to the coping strategies of peacetime governors. Wars were not won by continuing peacetime methods, but rather by introducing institutions and personnel that had not been (or could not be) introduced in peacetime. In World War II, for example, three of the most important members of Cabinet – Ernest Bevin, Lord Beaverbrook, and Sir John Anderson – were, respectively, a trade-union leader, a press lord and a senior civil servant. None would have found himself in Cabinet but for the war. The same is true of the Prime Minister, Winston Churchill.

No peacetime political event can create a crisis of the intensity, scope, and duration of war. Many so-called crises in domestic politics are extremely trying while they last, but very short-lived in their consequences. Few people today refer to the Profumo scandal of 1963 or the Bank Rate Tribunal of 1957, even though each at the time received great political attention. When important issues arise unexpectedly and require urgent actions of enduring significance, government must act without plans, in circumstances that do not allow much time for thought about long-term consequences. For example, the British government decision to put troops in the field in Northern Ireland in August, 1969, was taken under the immediate pressure of riots; there was no plan for how the troops would get out. Four years and eight hundred deaths later, the government still had troops in Ulster – and it was still looking for a viable plan of action.

One way in which a government can respond to demands for action is by delay. Refusal to perceive demands is the simplest form of delay. Alternatively, a government can appoint a committee to investigate the situation; this will buy time for contemplating policy alternatives, and allow the government to see whether it is compelled to act at all.[11] For example, in response to Nationalist by-election successes in Labour strongholds in Scotland and Wales, on October 30th, 1968, Mr. Harold Wilson announced the establishment of a Commission on the Constitution to investigate "what changes may be needed in the central institutions of government in relation to the several countries, nations and regions of the United Kingdom." The Commission reported five years later.

In a limited number of policy areas, the implications of long-term demographic and social changes are clear sufficiently far in advance to plan alternative ways of coping with future events so as to avoid decision making by crisis. Since the beginning of the 1960s, higher education policy has reflected a high degree of planning, and self-conscious government choice between priorities. This is true not only of the 1963 proposals of the Robbins Committee to expand greatly the universities, but also of the 1972 Conservative government decision to expand considerably the nonuniversity section of higher education. In both instances, the trends in youthful demand for university places could be estimated three to five years in advance by analyzing numbers in secondary schools, numbers passing examinations required for university entrance, and applications for university places. As costs mounted, both the unit costs and aggregate costs of different forms of higher education have been estimated with growing attention to detail.[12]

The introduction of decimal coinage provides another example of a policy based upon planning, albeit in a different tempo. The abandonment of the nondecimal pounds-shillings-pence system of coinage was first debated in Parliament in 1816. At that time, the Napoleonic wars had created a shortage of metal coins in England, but made the introduction of

[11] See A. P. Herbert, *Anything But Action?* (London: Institute of Economic Affairs, 1960).

[12] See Richard Layard, John King and Claus Moser, *The Impact of Robbins* (Harmondsworth: Penguin, 1969); and *Education: A Framework for Expansion* (London: HMSO, Cmnd. 5174, 1972).

an alien (i.e., decimal) form of coinage suspect. Two decades later, Charles Babbage, a Cambridge professor and pioneer of ideas basic to modern computing, offered a detailed scheme for converting the existing currency into decimal coinage. In 1855, a government report recognized the advantages of decimal coinage. The government did not respond positively until 106 years later, when it established a committee to review the subject once again. In 1971, 155 years after the topic was first raised in Parliament, England adopted a system of decimal currency along the lines recommended by early nineteenth-century reformers.[13]

In economic policy, the government regularly monitors indicators of the state of the nation in order to arrest or reverse changes that threaten to "disequilibriate" the desired balance of government policies. For example, monthly unemployment figures, adjusted to make allowance for seasonal variations, are publicly scrutinized to see whether the government has done "too much" or "not enough" to restrain cost-push inflation related to employment levels. Similarly, monthly balance-of-payments figures are regularly scrutinized to see what government actions are necessary to prevent a drop in the exchange value of the pound or, alternatively, what surplus is available to permit reflation of the economy and a fall in unemployment rates – until the balance of payments has moved from being too much in credit to too much in deficit.

The government of the day hopes to make its short-term adjustments in the economy consistent with medium-term plans stated in its annual public expenditure forecast. Both Conservative and Labour governments have found great difficulty in doing this. After five years in office, Mr. Wilson's government announced plans for a steady growth in public expenditure averaging 3.0 per cent for the next three years. It did this after accumulating a record of increasing public expenditure in the years from 1964 at rates of 3.8, 6.7, 6.6, 9.0, and 1.6 per cent.

Only the last and lowest figure was consistent with the

[13] See A. A. F. Timms, "Hundred Year Delay in Completing the Change to Decimals," *The Times*, February 12, 1971.

economy's growth rate.[14] The Heath administration entered office in 1970 with a similar intention of keeping the increase in public expenditure steady. In its first three forecasts, it estimated the five-year increase in expenditure at 2.2 per cent, 2.7 per cent, and 2.5 per cent. The rate was lower than that proposed by the Labour government, consistent with a different set of Conservative priorities for public and private expenditure. But the five-year forward forecasts are belied by the figures for current rates of government spending. The figure for the actual amount the government is spending in the year it issues the forecast has steadily risen, from a rate of 2.6 per cent in 1970–71 to 3.9 per cent the following year and 6.2 per cent in 1972–73. In order to keep the five-year average steady, the government keeps reducing its estimate of what it hopes to spend in the fifth and most distant year of its forecast.[15]

In reaction against the difficulties of planning, both theorists and practitioners have noted advantages in taking decisions on a short-term ad hoc basis, in a manner usually described as "muddling through." In this model, a politician is expected to take an immediate decision in the light of immediate consequences, without regard to long-term implications. For example, in preparing the historic National Insurance Act of 1911, David Lloyd George took a crucial decision about the financial basis of welfare payments at the top of the stairs while going to dress for dinner. "I am inclined after all to be virtuous," he said, selecting the alternative considered more respectable according to the conventional wisdom of the day. His civil service advisor wrote: "We were embarking upon an unknown sea. No one could say what would happen with universal compulsory insurance, and everyone held different views." [16]

[14] See Cmnd. 4234 (HMSO, 1969), p. 8. All calculations in constant prices.

[15] See Cmnd. 4578 (HMSO, 1971), p. 6; Cmnd. 4829 (HMSO, 1971), p. 11; Cmnd. 5178 (HMSO, 1972), p. 9.

[16] W. J. Braithwaite, *Lloyd George's Ambulance Wagon* (London: Methuen, 1957), p. 127. For the subsequent evolution, see Hugh Heclo, *Modern Social Politics in Britain and Sweden* (New Haven: Yale, 1974).

The concept of muddling through is ambiguous; everything depends upon whether one emphasizes the muddle or "winning through."[17] It is more appropriate for efforts to cope with emergencies when imponderables are numerous and decisive; it is least suited for coping with political problems involving long-term large-scale capital investments, like building roads or universities. The evaluation placed upon this tactic will differ according to the perspective of persons involved. Those who are caught in the muddle are likely to be less satisfied than those who view the problem in a broader analytical framework. Cumulatively, muddling through can lead policy makers to hit upon an acceptable and durable decision by a process of trial and error. Alternatively, a decade of trying first one policy, then another, can result in "muddling around in circles."

"NOW AND IN ENGLAND"

The most important of all political changes – alterations in the values and beliefs of the political culture – are the most difficult to measure or anticipate. They cannot be extrapolated like a line on the graph, nor can they be predicted with the actuarial certainty with which one can forecast primary school population from a knowledge of the number of infants under the age of five. Yet once the meaning of politics alters, then much else changes in consequence. For example, the altered evaluation of the role of government in nineteenth-century England prepared the way for the development of the twentieth-century mixed-economy welfare state.

Every political culture reflects a mix of political outlooks. The ability of Conservatives to invoke preindustrial values to justify its contemporary welfare policies is a reminder that past and present values can both point in the same direction. A decade hence, as a decade ago, England will still be a society with a distinctively "mixed" political culture. The

[17] For contrasting emphases, see David Braybrooke and C. E. Lindblom, *A Strategy of Decision* (New York: Free Press, 1963); and Richard Rose, "Models of Governing;" and "Coping with Urban Change," in Richard Rose, editor, *The Management of Urban Change in Britain and Germany* (Beverly Hills: Sage Publications, 1974).

question thus arises: How, if at all, are the contents of this mixture changing? The first edition of this book, written in the early 1960s, discussed a variety of cultural norms important in English politics.[18] Attention was also given to subcultural differences between Conservatives, Socialists, and Liberals. Rewriting this book a decade after allows one to reexamine basic political values from the perspective of the 1970s.

Many basic features of the political culture have not changed. Englishmen still agree upon the value of liberty and the choice of government through ballots cast by universal suffrage. They continue to trust the good will and *bona fides* of their governors and the civil servants who do most of the day-to-day work of government. The growing attention to the personalities of politicians and "inside-dopester" reporting substitutes for, rather than supplants, the older conventions of privacy. There is a continuing positive belief that groups affected by government policy have a right to be consulted before government acts. The private corridors of Whitehall, rather than the public stage of Parliament, continue to be the chief scene of consultation. All parties to government also continue to endorse evolutionary rather than revolutionary change.

Many political symbols continue to unite Englishmen in positive emotional responses. The monarchy is subject to criticism from time to time, and the Duke of Edinburgh has been heard to complain about the cost of running Buckingham Palace. Reactions show a calm acceptance of the monarchy — even at a time when many other traditional institutions are subject to criticism. The response of Englishmen to symbols of nationality is positive, and unself-conscious. In the lengthy debate about British entry to the Common Market, opponents emphasized differences between European and English customs. Proponents do not claim that entry would make English people less distinctive; England's contribution to the European Community is said to lie in the very distinctiveness of its virtues.

[18] The argument is summarized in a table at page 56 of the original American edition.

In some instances, the persistence of outlooks maintains subcultural differences. In the 1970s, as in the 1960s, there is a substantial difference between attitudes of Conservatives and Socialists toward collective vs private provision of welfare services and collective vs market mechanisms to plan the economy. The experience of both the Wilson and Heath governments has, however, emphasized similarities in actions, if not in cultural beliefs. The Labour government of Harold Wilson abandoned its commitment to economic planning midway through its term of office, and the Conservatives within two years of taking office in 1970 were engaged in massive intervention in the economy. There still remain different expectations of government action. Socialists see fewer limits on the scope of government action than do Conservatives; they also expect more beneficial results to follow from government action. Liberals of all parties remain the chief proponents of noninterventionist policies in moral questions. The symbol of "Socialism" remains emotionally divisive. "The Red Flag" brings some politicians singing to their feet, while others grimace or sit still.

Traditional symbols have declined in their emotional power. Younger Englishmen do not know from firsthand experience the older "Land of hope and glory" or the wartime England of "Their finest hour." The government's acceptance of England's declining world influence has accentuated this change. Continuing national economic difficulties have made it clear to younger and older Englishmen that "Things ain't what they used to be." The declining regard for tradition is also illustrated by a lower confidence among MPs in the traditional institutions of Parliament. The change has occurred among all political groups; thus, it has not intensified differences within the English political culture. At one period in the 1960s, "modernization" was a popular slogan, until confidence was lost in the ability of modernizers to overcome the constraints of the past and present.

Changing cultural values can lead to greater agreement among Englishmen, when a change represents one group "catching up" with the ideas of others. What was once new is then assimilated into the conventional wisdom. In the past decade, Conservatives have given less weight to values and beliefs rooted in the past. In part, this reflects the change of generations. Harold Macmillan, the Conservative Prime Minister in 1960, was born in 1894, and Edward Heath, Prime Minister in 1970, was born in 1916. Deference to politicians on grounds of birth or gentlemanly upbringing does not appear as important in the England of the 1970s as in the England of 1960s. Edward Heath, like Harold Wilson, owes his present-day success to winning a scholarship to Oxford.

Many of the economic problems of the 1960s and 1970s arise from a changing attitude toward change itself. The older Conservative emphasis upon maintaining the status quo and minimizing government activity has been set aside. Voters as well as politicians now reject a static view of the economy. In the 1950s it was still possible to regard economic change as a temporary phenomenon. After decades of depression and a decade of wartime and postwar austerity, many Englishmen had little sense of mass affluence, even as a goal. In the 1960s the idea of a rising standard of living began to be taken for granted by large masses of Englishmen. Concurrently, politicians in both parties began to emphasize economic growth. They did so because increasing prosperity was considered electorally popular, and necessary to meet a rising demand for public services. Today, all political leaders are firmly committed to a dynamic rather than a static model of English society – even though no government has yet found a means to reconcile rapid economic change with existing resource constraints and other valued goals.

The authority of leadership has been eroded in extrapolitical spheres of English life. University heads, ecclesiastics, executives in the mass media, employers, and trade-union leaders find that their directives no longer receive the compliance that was once readily given. In politics, the central institutions of the regime still retain the allegiance of subjects. The contrast between Westminster and Paris during the events of May, 1968, is as striking as that between Westminster and Washington during a major demonstration. The authority of the regime has only been challenged directly at the point at which economic and political values meet: industrial relations. Union members have upon occasion defied the law as substantively "unjust," even though undoubtedly a lawful Act of Parliament. Trade unionists claim that the new consideration is not their refusal to comply with authority, but rather Conservative disrespect for cultural norms inhibiting legislation. The Conservative government, has avoided describing this challenge to one law as a challenge to the diffuse authority of government. To see what happens when such a challenge does arise, a government at Westminster need only look to the Northern Ireland portion of its domain. Occasionally, an Army officer has been heard to speak of Belfast as a "warm-up" for troubles within other parts of the United Kingdom, but there is no significant group of Englishmen to support a terrorist campaign in London like that in Belfast.

Cultural changes in the past decade have intensified two differences within English society. Entry to the European Common Market has emphasized traditional differences about England's place in the world. "Little Englanders" are against any connection with continental or extracontinental nations. Conservatives with ties to the old (and white) dominions as well as Socialist proponents of a multiracial Commonwealth have argued for political and economic alternatives to the Common Market. Differences of opinion exist within as well as between the parties. The main spokesmen for the two parties have debated England's place less in terms of principles and more as a question of what constitutes "good" terms for entering the Common Market.

Domestically, differing views of equality have become more intense than a decade ago. Conservatives have never regarded equality as an object of government policy. Older Conservatives have taken for granted traditional differences of esteem and wealth. Younger Conservatives have defined equality in terms of equality of opportunity: It is a means to a more efficient and equitable society. Inequality of rewards is accepted as a natural consequence of equality of opportunity; greater rewards are expected to go to those with more ability, more willingness to work, or more luck. Socialists have emphasized equality of esteem as their ideal; they have also favored narrowing income differentials, even if it is not practicable to abolish them. Socialists take the result of Conservative values, inequality of rewards, as their starting point. They argue that this prevents equal opportunity, for a child born into the home of wealthy and successful parents will have a better chance for success than a child born into a conventional working-class home. The conflict not only exists in the abstract, but also in relation to many concrete issues of politics, ranging from the retention of hereditary honors and fee-paying secondary schools to the settlement of wage disputes by government arbitration. Successive governments have failed to establish a national wages policy because there is no agreement within society about what constitutes a "fair" wage.[19] The past decades have seen an intensification in the desire of both Labour and Conservative governments for a wages policy and in trade union resistance to it.

A decade of political events has maintained a "mixed" culture, but one in which the mix is not quite the same as before. Areas of agreement remain substantial, and some changes have increased agreement between adherents of differing political outlooks. Politics has not ceased to be full of controversy; if the controversy is mostly about the policies of government, and rarely about its claim to authority.

Any attempt to spell out the dimensions of future change must emphasize a few general criteria. A traditionally minded Englishman might emphasize the value of conserving achievements from the past, not least maintaining a form of government with fully legitimate authority. Socialists might be less concerned with forms of government and more concerned with the achievements of government, especially the redistribution of wealth, status, and political power. Economists might declare that all talk of desired change is meaningless, unless the governors assure to society the resources required to maintain existing material standards or reach those to which they aspire. Humanitarians might argue that the next major de-

[19] See John Goldthorpe, "Social Inequality and Social Integration in Modern Britain."

velopment in English society should relieve the handicapped rather than the productive groups in society. Libertarians might argue for the removal of more and more government constraints upon behavior. Yet radicals might argue that the government should intervene actively in social relations to manufacture a strong sense of community among its citizens.

In the troubled days of the 1930s, R. H. Tawney, a leading Socialist theorist noted that reflecting upon alternative futures is "uncongenial to the bustling people who describe themselves as practical, because they take things as they are." He proceeded to tell his fellow Englishmen:

> The practical thing for a traveller who is uncertain of his path is not to proceed with the utmost rapidity in the wrong direction: it is to consider how to find the right one. And the practical thing for a nation which has stumbled upon one of the turning points of history is to consider whether what it has done hitherto is wise, and if it is not wise to alter it.[20]

Michael Oakeshott, a prominent Conservative philosopher, viewed the failure of grand designs to bring about a new order in Europe from the perspective of 1951. He wrote, in an equally apposite but opposite way:

> In political activity, then, men sail a boundless and bottomless sea; there is neither harbour for shelter nor floor for anchorage, neither starting-place nor appointed destination. The enterprise is to keep afloat on an even keel; the sea is both friend and enemy; and the seamanship consists in using the resources of a traditional manner of behavior in order to make a friend of every inimical occasion.[21]

A global judgment upon politics in England must include two contrasting points. First, the major problems of public policy that have faced England in this century have usually not been handled promptly. In peacetime, particularly, government has been slow to take action, and often prefers inaction to decision. But viewed in comparison with more than

[20] R. H. Tawney, *The Acquisitive Society* (London: Bell, 1921), p. 2.
[21] Michael Oakeshott, *Political Education,* p. 22.

one hundred countries in the United Nations, England is outstanding for its durable representative institutions, and the allegiance that its citizens give to political authority. This achievement is rightfully a cause for pride. The more uncertain the events that the future may bring, the more useful and valuable are political resources derived from a successful past.

Appendixes

A. PRIME MINISTERS AND GOVERNMENTS

The following is a list of the Prime Ministers of Great Britain since the beginning of the century. The name of the party or parties included in the parliamentary majority is given in parentheses; the chief party is italicized.

1895–1902	The third Marquess of Salisbury (*Conservative*)
1902–1905	A. J. Balfour (*Conservative*)
1906–1908	H. Campbell-Bannerman (*Liberal*)
1908–1916	H. H. Asquith (*Liberal;* then *Liberal* & Irish Nationalist; in wartime, *Liberal,* Conservative, & Labour coalition)
1916–1922	David Lloyd George (Wartime *Coalition* until 1918, then Coalition Liberal and *Conservative*)
1922–1923	A. Bonar Law (*Conservative*)
1923	Stanley Baldwin (*Conservative*)
1924	J. Ramsay MacDonald (*Labour* & Liberal)
1924–1929	Stanley Baldwin (*Conservative*)
1929–1931	J. Ramsay MacDonald (*Labour* & Liberal)
1931–1935	J. Ramsay MacDonald (National Labour, *Conservative* & National Liberal)
1935–1937	Stanley Baldwin (*Conservative*)
1937–1940	Neville Chamberlain (*Conservative*)
1940–1945	Winston Churchill (Coalition of *Conservative,* Labour & Liberal)

1945–1951	Clement Attlee (*Labour*)
1951–1955	Winston Churchill (*Conservative*)
1955–1956	Anthony Eden (*Conservative*)
1957–1963	Harold Macmillan (*Conservative*)
1963–1964	Sir Alec Douglas-Home (*Conservative*)
1964–1970	Harold Wilson (*Labour*)
1970–	Edward Heath (*Conservative*)

B. NOTES ON FURTHER READING

The footnotes of this book are intended to provide bibliographical guidance to students wishing to read more about the subject, as well as giving credit to sources of information and ideas. The footnotes are not intended to provide a comprehensive list of publications, but to give interested readers a start. A lengthy bibliography of books can be found in John Palmer, *Government and Parliament in Britain* (London: Hansard Society, 1964 edition). Lengthy bibliographies of journal articles can be found at the end of two readers edited by Richard Rose, *Studies in British Politics* (New York: St. Martins, 1969 edition) and *Policy-Making in Britain* (New York: Free Press, 1969). The selections in these readers complement the contents of this book.

There is no such thing as a good short history of modern England. Any standard encyclopedia will provide a brief outline guide. Biographical data concerning politicians of the past can be found in the *Dictionary of National Biography; Who's Who* provides factual details about contemporary politicians. The best single reference volume for twentieth-century politics is D. E. Butler and J. Freeman, *British Political Facts, 1900–1967*. Anthony Sampson's *The New Anatomy of Britain* is the third edition of an informative journalistic guide to the major personalities and institutions of contemporary society.

A student of contemporary politics will find *Whitaker's Almanack,* an annual publication, a useful compendium of political, economic, and social information. *Social Trends,* an annual volume prepared by the Central Statistical Office, collates a large quantity of useful official data, and gives bibliographical guidance to further sources. *Britain: an Official Handbook* provides prose descriptions of many features of

English life in a manner intended to be clear to foreign students. *The General Household Survey: An Introduction* (London: HMSO, 1973) provides detailed analysis of social conditions measured by survey data.

Contemporary political discussion can easily be sampled by reading the daily and weekly press. *The Times* and *The Guardian* (formerly the *Manchester Guardian*) provide the most thorough daily news coverage. Three weekly periodicals – the *Economist,* the *New Statesman* and the *Spectator* – offer political commentary from three distinctive points of view. *New Society* contains comment and reports about a wide variety of topics; it reports the problems of the welfare state, as well as reviewing promptly major government reports.

The chief academic journals concerned with British politics are *Political Studies, Parliamentary Affairs, Public Administration, Public Law,* and *Political Quarterly.* Journals carry reviews providing up-to-date information about newly published books in the field.

Index

320.441
R72 Cop 1

JN231 .R67 1974
Rose, Richard, 1933-
Politics in England; an interpretation.

SEP 22 2006

JAN 17 1980